Psychoanalysis

Unveiling the Past
Discovering the New

Psychoanalysis

Unveiling the Past
Discovering the New

———◆———

SELECTED PAPERS OF
JOHN S. KAFKA, M.S., M.D.

IPBOOKS.net
International Psychoanalytic Books

Psychoanalysis: Unveiling the Past, Discovering the New
Copyright © 2016 by John S. Kafka, M.S., M.D.

International Psychoanalytic Books (IPBooks),
30-27 33rd Street, Astoria, NY 11102
Online at: www.IPBooks.net

Cover painting: *Transitions*, by John S. Kafka, Mixed media on paper.

Interior book design by Maureen Cutajar
www.gopublished.com

ISBN: 978-0-9980833-1-5

Library of Congress Control Number: 2016955101

Contents

PART TWO:
SELECTED WRITINGS:
THEORY, TECHNIQUE, AND PSYCHOPATHOLOGY

PSYCHOSES, SCHIZOPHRENIA

TIME AND MEMORY

SOCIETY, TRAUMA, HOLOCAUST

Foreword

When I start writing or publishing a project, I frequently have dreams that relate to these projects. As I prepare this book of my selected writings. I just had a dream in which I was a stowaway on an ocean liner. My associations to this dream led me to the fact that I had twice escaped the fate of being killed in the Holocaust. I was an Austrian Jew who was in a boarding school in France when the Germans marched into Austria in the 1938 "Anschluss." If I had not left France for the United States just before the German army occupied France, I would have been handed over to the Germans and would have perished in the Holocaust.

My stowaway dream is related to my personal story that will be described later. As an escapee from the Holocaust, who several times had to adjust to very different cultures, I never felt fully grounded in any of them. I was always perceived as a bit of an outsider and I never stopped fully experiencing myself as a stowaway. And stowaways should not call attention to themselves.

I realize, as I prepare this book, that this stowaway background feeling may have contributed to my not emphasizing sufficiently the centrality and importance of some ideas in my work, especially ideas that are far removed from "common sense" and therefore would brand me as an outsider, a stowaway.

Although these ideas and their *relevance* to applied psychoanalysis, psychoanalytic theory and practice are addressed and discussed in different sections of the book, I want to introduce and name them in this foreword to emphasize their unity and internal coherence.

Of particular clinical importance is the notion of my term, "The Atmospheric Object." To introduce the topic here, Freud thought that psychoanalytic treatment of psychotics was not possible because they could not form a transference to a person, an "object." Decades of clinical work with schizophrenic patients has taught me that a constellation of characteristics forms a kind of "atmospheric" object that can be clinically useful. Still related to the topic of psychic object formation to psychic reality is the notion that *objects* are based on patterns of spatial and temporal "subjective equivalences." (Klüver, 1933)

Most distant from *common sense* comprehension is the notion that "time is mind," (Kafka, 1989, pp. 51-78) ultimately based on the recognition that there is no psychic reality if there is not at least a minimum of short-term memory. "Time is Mind and Mind is Time" (my phrase) goes beyond Loewald's "Time ... the inner *fibre* of what we call psychical" (Loewald, 1962, p. 268) that still holds on to a "thingness," (my phrase), a concrete object of the temporal.

Immediately following this foreword, an autobiography begins, a chapter published in *Psychoanalyse in Selbstdarstellung (Psychoanalysis in Self Representations*, Volume III, which was written at the request of Ludger M. Hermanns. This version of the German translation was co-edited by Professor Lou Rose for the *American Imago* and my *Selected Writings*. This first English translation will be published in the *American Imago 73(#4): 385-415, 2016.]*

After the Table of Contents, my out-of-print 1989 book *Multiple Realities in Clinical Practice*, begins with an updated introduction that takes into account theoretical and scientific advances, the original introduction which is a guide to the reader as well as the core of my clinical and theoretical work, and chapters from the book.

Papers following the 1989 book *Multiple Realities in Clinical Practice* are grouped into general themes.

Theory, Technique, and Psychopathology: "On the Occasion of Freud's

150th Birthday. On different 'False Memories' From Screen Memories to *Déjà vu*" (chapter 8); "The Analyst's Autonomy: Individuation and Flexibility of Technique" (chapter 9); "Challenge and confirmation in ritual action" (chapter 10); "How Do We Change?" (Chapter 11); "Ambiguity for individuation—A critique and reformulation of double-bind theory" (chapter 12).

Psychosis, Schizophrenia: "Chestnut Lodge and the Psychoanalytic Approach to Psychosis" (chapter 13); "The Romantic and Classic Visions In the Therapy of Psychosis: A Personal Perspective and an Evolving Theory of Schizophrenia" (chapter 14); "On the Question of Insight In Psychosis" (chapter 15); "The Dream in Schizophrenia" (chapter 16).

Time and Memory: "Psychoanalysis and the Temporal Trace" (chapter 17); "Consciousness and the Shadow of Time" (chapter 18).

Society, Trauma, Holocaust: "Psychoanalysis and Democracy" (chapter 19); "The Traumatized Individual in the Traumatized Society: Treatment, Memory, and Memorials" (chapter 20).

It is difficult to select a few articles from a much larger bibliography which is listed in the appendix. In this age of the "cloud," much of my work is accessible. I conclude this volume, however, with the paradoxical end note about the never-ending clinical psychoanalytic process and psychoanalytic thought and a paper about the relevance of psychoanalysis to modernity.

References

Kafka, J. S. (1989). Déjà Vu, Drugs, Synesthesia, and the Mind-time Synthesis. *Multiple Realities in Clinical Practice.* New Haven and London: Yale University Press, pp. 51-78.

Kafka, J. S. (1995). "Worlds In Between—Multiple Realities in my Life and Psychoanalytic Thinking." Chapter in *Psychoanalyse in Selbstdarstellung (Psychoanalysis in Self Representations,* Volume III, pp. 141-187. Editor: Ludger M. Hermanns. Publisher: Edition Diskord Tübingen.

Klüver, H. (1933). *Behavior Mechanisms in Monkeys.* Chicago: University of Chicago Press.

Loewald, H.W. (1960). On the therapeutic action of psychoanalysis. *International Journal of Psycho-analysis* 41:16-33.

---•◦•---

The 1989 original version of *Multiple Realities in Clinical Practice* was published by Yale University Press, New Haven. The copyright is now owned by John S. Kafka. The Library of Congress information in the 1989 original versions follows:

Library of Congress Cataloging-in-Publication Data
Kafka, John S., 1921-
Multiple realities in clinical practice / John S. Kafka.
       p. cm.
Bibliography: p. Includes index.
ISBN O-300-04350-3 (alk. paper)
I. Psychoanalysis. 2. Reality. I. Title.
       (DNLM: I. Psychoanalytic Therapy. WM 460.6 K II m]
       RC506.K33 1989
       616.89' 17—dc I9
DNLM/DLC
for Library of Congress 88-38238

[This is a chapter (translated from the German) in *Psychoanalyse in Selbstdarstellung (Psychoanalysis in Self Representations*, Volume III, pp 141-187. Editor: Ludger M. Hermanns. Publisher: Edition Diskord Tübingen, 1995. The contributors were asked to relate their life-histories to the development of their psychoanalytic theories and to their evolving clinical styles. This version of the translation co-edited by Professor Lou Rose for *AMERICAN IMAGO* and my *SELECTED WRITINGS]*
This version of the German translation was co-edited by Professor Lou Rose for the *American Imago* and my *Selected Writings*. This first English translation will be published in the American Imago 73(#4):385-415, 2016

Worlds In-Between: Multiple Realities in My Life and Psychoanalytic Thinking

John S. Kafka

I. Language and *Selbstdarstellung*

Although I have not lived in a German-speaking area since I was thirteen years old—the age I was sent to boarding school in France—I think it is appropriate to describe the following reflections with a German word: "*Selbstdarstellung*," or self-representation. Geographically, Linz, Austria, remained my home, and Austria remained where I spent practically all my school vacations, until the country was annexed by Nazi Germany in 1938. Psychologically, the German language played and still plays a singular role in my inner life, a role that is, at the outset, important to highlight—more important than explaining, for instance, that my father and his brother inherited from their grandfather a business that went by the name of *LUSKA* (*LU*dwig und *S*igmund *KA*fka), *K. & K.* (Purveyor to the *I*mperial and *R*oyal Court), and that the company specialized in brandies, canned foods, vinegar, mustard, and pickles. But it is also true to say that the German language did not develop in me. It got stuck. As a result, I do not quite take for granted the meaning of German words, and I must attune my listening carefully. Such microscopic dissection of words occurs far less frequently to those who speak, and have always spoken, German as a matter of routine. A *Selbstdarstellung*—which differs from the story of a life, or from an autobiography proper—describes this peculiar situation: the author occupies a place away from one's self, over there, a place from which one looks back at oneself. The meaning of self-representation, in this case, corresponds to the distance from language itself. One becomes an observer.

And now as soon as I think it and mouth it, this word "observer"— *Beobachter*—falls apart. I remain fully aware of this fact, and this pronounced awareness shows me how much my life and my self-representation are linked to Nazi history. For when I think of the word *Beobachter*, I immediately think also of the *Völkischer Beobachter*, or *People's Observer*, the name of the major Nazi daily that frequently had horrible caricatures of Jews on the front page.

As I grew up and attended school, language then broke down, became stuck, but so did another part of my life. My father died from a heart attack when I was six years old. For many years, I had dreams in which his all-white figure came from the bathroom to the bedroom. In the first of my two analyses with Edoardo Weiss in Chicago (1946-1949 and 1953-1954) unfinished mourning became a prominent theme, and later, when I participated in a central European psychoanalytic conference in Bad Ischl, where the dialect is similar to the one in Linz, my father, about whom I had not dreamt for many years, reappeared in my dreams almost nightly. He spoke to me in the only language, with the only intonation, that he had used with me. Maybe these two aspects of the emigrant's fate deserve more consideration in the literature: deracination contributes to unfinished mourning. In my life, these two elements—Nazi history with all its direct and indirect effects and the early death of my father—conjoined to resurface in me again and again.

II. Memory and Nachträglichkeit

My mother was born in St. Gallen in Switzerland. Her father came from Lengnau, one of the two Swiss communities in which Jews had been allowed to live for hundreds of years. She was twice married to Austrians, and twice widowed, the first time when she was twenty-three and the mother of a daughter barely two years old. About five or six years later, she married my father, Egon Kafka. Eight years after their marriage, he rushed home from a business trip to arrive before Yom Kippur and after the festive evening meal on the way to the synagogue he suffered a fatal heart attack. Later I was told that my nine-year older half-sister and I had been sent ahead so as not to arrive late to temple. That evening I was taken to the house of my aunt Lilli (my father's sister) and her husband, my uncle Edda, who now became my guardian. Uncle Edda was Dr. Eduard Bloch, who held the title of *Ober-Medizinalrat*, literally "Superior Medical Councilor." Austria loved titles, and still does. During Adolf Hitler's youth, Eduard Bloch had been the Hitler family's physician.

As I remember it now, I stayed about two weeks in the Bloch household. I had the feeling that something terrible had happened, that someone had probably died, but I thought the deceased was my paternal grandmother. I still remember in which room, on which couch, and under which picture my sister, dressed in black, came to me and told me that my father had died. I was inconsolable.

Today I have the feeling that I was coming closer to my father during the months before his death. I specifically remember the following. In the late afternoons my family held a daily ritual that had been initiated by my grandmother. Rudolf (my father's older brother), my father with his wife and children, my aunt Lilli, and sometimes, I think, also uncle Edda came together for tea, conversation, and family counsel. During one such *Jause*, someone told a joke. Everybody laughed. I wanted to know what was so funny but was told I was too young to understand. After I protested loudly, my father took me on his lap and explained something to me. I do not know anymore what he explained, but I remember my feeling of triumph that I *could* understand it after all. This specific positive memory of my father, who had died so early, became important during my first analysis. Now, as I write about it, I ask myself, what this could have to do with my quite ferocious determination never to let go of what I do not understand and my intense desire to be recognized for my ability eventually to comprehend it. Even as a child, I was told that I ruminated too much, and I am still a ruminant. I think I am especially aware of unfinished tasks. It is perhaps a variation of the theme of the outsider, and a bridge, I believe, to my interest in psychoanalysis, to the style of my psychoanalytic work, to my interest in communicating with psychotic people, and my tenacious persistence in trying to understand them.

It is also a sign in my self-representation of what Freud called *Nachträglichkeit*, badly translated in the *Standard Edition* of his works as "deferred action," when "retroactive attribution of meaning," as suggested by Helmut Thomä, might be better. The theme of *Nachträglichkeit* has always interested me, and although experimental psychological work has shed additional light on aspects of it, I have continually returned to the theme, especially in recent years. Of particular interest to me are the effects of *Nachträglichkeit* on our experience of time. We know that new information changes the past—Freud already showed that. But the phenomenon of *Nachträglichkeit* is a two-way street, one in which we encounter the traffic—the never ending two-way traffic—in which the different influences of varying resolutions of the past exert their effects on the perceived present and the projected future, and continue to shape ever different presents and futures. The very structure of temporal experience thus evolves through *Nachträglichkeit*: we deal with ever changing perceptions, perspectives, and psychic realities, and in the process, we structure a new past. And the psychic presence of that other past leads to a different view of the present, to different expectations of our future, and to different efforts to forge that future. Thus even a modestly honest self-representation by a self-observing analyst is a tiring task, a demanding affair. The realization of a connection between my contact with my father shortly before his death and the quality of how I understand and relate to the world—and the internal consequences of acquiring this new piece of awareness—offers only small sample of the work of *Nachträglichkeit* generated by the process of *Selbstdarstellung*.

When I began to write this *Selbstdarstellung*, I had an examination dream. The major problem I encountered in the dream was: *all available papers were already covered with sheets of writing*. Reflecting on the dream, I then had the thought: *I have already lived through all of that*. I now had doubts. Did I really want to re-experience what I had *lived* through by once again working on and through it all? No wonder that I, or anyone, begin the task with ambivalence. But I have also presented myself as a ruminant, as someone who keeps digging around in himself. Should this somewhat self-caricatured portrait not remain in my finished *Selbstdarstellung*? We do know something about the meaning of caricature and self-caricature. In part, it is an outsider's challenge to the others, to the insiders, not to take *themselves* too seriously.

III. Ambiguities

The Linz Kafkas were assimilated, not especially religious, but still active in the small Jewish community. We had one of the few kosher households in Linz and my mother's maternal grandmother was the daughter of a rabbi. In fact, I still possess a booklet from 1913 about Jewish cultural activities in the local B'nai B'rith Lodge. It includes not only serious but also humorous essays, one of which described how my uncle Rudolf, the author of philosophical essays and a book of poetry, might attempt to sell *LUSKA* wares to Tagore, the Indian philosopher.

My mother was a "beauty." Not only did I find her such: others often spoke to me about my beautiful mother. She was tall and blond and, at some point, I must have learned that these characteristics defined a certain ideal. She particularly admired my tall, blond friend Hildebrandt. His looks came much closer than my own to my mother's view of a handsome boy. I remember her warnings to avoid making certain grimaces: they could accentuate certain undesirable facial features (the Kafka grandmother had too big a mouth, some Kafkas had too wide a nose). I examined myself carefully in the mirror. It was Hildebrandt who later told me his father had forbidden him to play with me because he was Aryan and I was not.

I have specific memories of *when* I thought my looks changed. I experienced sharp breaks in my appearance, especially one such break when, from one day to the next, I felt that I would no longer have to fear that this or that physical characteristic would be unacceptable. There exists, I think, a connection between one's experience of sudden changes, of discontinuities, and my later psychoanalytic idea that breaking points in one's physical and psychological self-picture can be modified in psychoanalysis. A less disruptive sense of one's own development, a sense of continuity, can be a major gain of psychoanalytic treatment. My mother's comments about my sweating also added to my fears. I particularly remember one of her comments that girls do not like to dance with boys who have sweaty hands. Fortunately, Grete Pollack, a girl of my age and my neighbor—we practically grew up together—did not react to me as my mother had predicted. Grete lost her parents in the Holocaust, but she was saved in a children's transport.

My mother was also very tender and affectionate, full of energy and the joy of life. She liked to travel. People, landscapes, and good food enchanted her, and it was important for her that she enchanted other people. Her "presence" was impressive. I remember, for example, that a few years after our emigration we had arranged to meet in the lobby of the Waldorf-Astoria in New York. I was in the American army and had a furlough. My mother lived in a one-room apartment but loved the atmosphere of beautiful hotel lobbies. We decided to go to the theater. I inquired at the ticket desk in the lobby whether we could still get tickets to a particular show and was asked if I lived in the hotel. When I said no, I was told that only hotel guests could get tickets there. When I brought my mother the bad news, she only said "ridiculous," walked with her usual, royal posture to the desk and was instantly taken care of.

Below I will write of her tenacity, the fighting ability that came to light especially at the time of our emigration, but here I will mention that I always had the feeling that my mother admired strong, challenging men who eventually showed themselves to be too brutal or who took advantage of her. A "dear man" who would do everything for her would be seen as a weak one. She even said of some good-hearted, weak people: "There is *nothing* to him, nothing in his back nor his front." My mother contributed in this way to my later interest in the toleration of ambiguity, a quality that I needed. I studied this issue intensively and found that it was not the ambiguous communication—the double bind—but rather an intolerance of ambiguity itself that was pathogenic. My mother, somehow, actually felt quite happy when I escaped her double-binding instructions to me. I found out later that, in her early years, she had needed to develop her own ways to escape from her own mother's binding techniques.

IV. Perspective and Subjectivity

In his hours of leisure my father played piano and harmonium. I remember his relaxed and beautiful playing, and I was told how nicely he improvised. Yet, he also carried more of the burden of the daily business than his brother Rudolf. My mother spoke of his older brother—a friend of the prominent, "bohemian" Viennese essayist Peter Altenberg—in a somewhat derogatory manner as "a beautiful spirit," an aesthete. I have a 1901 book of poems, *Of the Eternal Dream*, written by Rudolf Kafka, and a long, earlier essay, "*Weltanschauung und Perspektive*" ("*Worldview and Perspective*"), that he wrote as a young man and that was published in 1897 in the humanistic journal *Die Gesellschaft*. In that essay he developed the idea that the use of three-dimensional perspective in art had to do with the recognition of the *subjective moment*, specifically the recognition that everyone possessed a different subjective moment. The painter who applied three-dimensional perspective implicitly acknowledged that persons far away occupied the centers of *their* own worlds. Rudolf Kafka does not use the phrase, but in effect he argues that the development of three-dimensional perspective implies a *diminution in narcissism*. I am intrigued by the fact that long before I had read Rudolf's essay, when I was a teaching assistant in a Rorschach course, I wrote an unpublished paper about the perspective response on the Rorschach test. There I developed some ideas that were quite similar to those of uncle Rudolf.

Much has been written about my legal guardian, uncle Edda. The Jewish family doctor of the Hitler family, Eduard Bloch diagnosed the breast cancer of Hitler's mother and he was the man Hitler called a "noble Jew." It is sad that some people took seriously what I consider a caricature of psychoanalysis, a cocktail-party version of psychoanalytic psychohistory, which explained Hitler's gratefulness "psychoanalytically" as unconscious hatred. My uncle showed me two postcards that Hitler sent him from Vienna, one of them signed with "your ever grateful Adolf Hitler." The search for any possible explanation for Hitler's fanatic obsession to murder Jews, however, is understandable because it is difficult to accept the fact that even until now there *is* no convincing explanation. Here I do not want to go further into the details of this story, but my efforts to show that we are dealing with a caricature of psychoanalytic psychohistory has cost me much energy over the years.

Uncle Edda never quite became a real father figure for me. He was goodhearted and friendly and he had very pronounced ideas about the importance for me of a classic, humanistic education. Maybe he was, or I perceived him as, too good-hearted *generally*—he had the reputation of being a "poor peoples' doctor"—to be close to *me* especially.

More important in my life than uncle Edda and uncle Rudolf were their wives, aunt Lilli and aunt Irma. Their culture was brought nearer to me than that of the uncles. Aunt Lilli exuded a soft and careful atmosphere: I remember her very serious piano playing and her endless cracking of nuts during table conversations. Aunt Irma, who had no children, was very motherly to me. I felt very close to her, and my mother may have seen her as a rival. I played a great deal in her big, beautiful garden. She taught me everything about nature, animals, plants, and the beauty of the body. She was not the "beautiful Mrs. Kafka," but she had a nice voice and she sang in Vienna in a choir directed by Bruno Walter. She also was a follower of anthroposophy.

A few years before the *Anschluss*, after Rudolf's death, aunt Irma moved to Vienna. I had been told that she had to report to the police for a document check. Friends warned her about deportation, but apparently she said that she could not believe such horror stories and still went to the police. In 1999, with the help of the Austrian historian Brigitte Hamann, I found out that aunt Irma in fact succeeded in getting to Prague. From there, under the name of Irma Kafkova, she was deported to Theresienstadt and later transported to and killed in Auschwitz.

V. Schooling

Years earlier, shortly after my father's death, during Christmas vacation in the first grade we visited a sister of my mother, who was married in Innsbruck. A ski teacher there had been a former mountain troop officer in Tirol and in the course of his career had broken most of his limbs. But they had healed and he inspired me. He showed loving understanding for me. I do not know if my mother or my aunt had told him that I had lost my father shortly before. With his combination of tender understanding and male skiing teacher wisdom, he became an ideal figure for me. My love for skiing was born there but later it became especially important for me to ski at least as well and, if possible, better than my Nazi classmates.

My half-sister married young to a man sixteen years older than she. Her husband also took a somewhat fatherly interest in me, and it was he who explained to me the facts of life. But when I was sent to Montbéliard for boarding school, my contact with this newly found father figure was weakened, despite my spending vacations in Austria.

I remember that I was rather unhappy when I was thirteen and fourteen. I thought about the meaning of life, philosophized, and even became religious for a short time. For a couple of months, I followed the ritual of putting on *tfillin* and said morning prayers, but neither morning prayers nor *tfillin* lasted long. In Austria, I had already lived through the beginnings of the Nazi era. For a time, I was the only Jew in my class, and in early adolescence I moved from assimilation to a Jewish nationalism. First, I was in "Blue-White," a Zionist youth movement similar to the *Wandervögel*, but then changed to Jabotinsky's youth group, the Betar. I thought the group's tougher stance was needed to present a harder position in the face of the Nazis around me. In the Betar, they taught us some Jiu Jitsu for self-defense.

Why was I sent to school abroad? Two of my mother's sisters had married Alsatians. One of my uncles—Siegfried, a successful businessman and industrialist in Strasbourg—regarded Austria's future pessimistically, and even though my mother did not share his pessimism, he exerted a strong influence on her. She told me, and probably had convinced herself, that it would only help if I learned French—maybe I could use it some day in the diplomatic service. I do not know whose fantasy that was.

My recent past in Austria may have contributed to my general unhappiness, but in any case I hated many things in the boarding school. Out of self-defense, and because my language was ridiculed by some classmates, I learned French well—and in a hurry. I became obsessed with the idea: *because I speak German, I should try to travel to Germany and attempt to assassinate Hitler. Since I do not do it, I must be a coward.* After the second year in the boarding school, I threatened my mother with suicide if I had to go back there. As a result, my mother rented us a small house in Nancy. I left the boarding school and became a student in the *Lycée Henri Poincaré.*

During the school year, my mother spent longer and longer times in our little house in Nancy. But she also traveled, and was often in Austria to visit family and friends. Because I was happy to have escaped the boarding school and because my life was filled with interesting schoolwork and good friends, I tolerated my mother's many absences quite well. In memory of this time, my half-sister, who died in 1998, referred to me as "the prisoner of Montbéliard."

I became a very good student. I had teachers—graduates of the *École Normale Superieure*—who inspired me, especially in French and philosophy. My greatest pride was that, even though French was not my mother tongue, I was nominated to represent my school in the *Concours Génèral de France* in French and philosophy. I had also a few very important girlfriends. "*Je me sentais bien dans ma peau.*" I felt good in my skin.

My uncle Siegfried's business partner had succeeded in getting two of his nephews out of Germany and enrolling them in the same boarding school to which I had been sent. Still another of his German-born nephews, Henri Bloch—who had come to Nancy with his widowed mother—was already an academic star in the university there. Six to nine years older than I, Henri became important for my further development, defending me against family pressure—especially coming from my uncle Siegfried—to choose a commercial career. My actual contact with Henri

Bloch and his mother was limited but they were a safety net for me. Later, Henri again played an important role in my life: he was at the University of Chicago during my time there. Eventually he took an important position with the United Nations and became a successful financier. He was often held up to me as a shining example, not so much because of his success but because he cared so well for his widowed mother. Very tied to her, he married late, and I gradually came to think that Henri actually demonstrated to me how important it was to keep *some* distance from a widowed mother.

VI. In Exile

The *Anschluss* occurred shortly before I was to take my exam, the *Baccalauréat, 2ème partie.* No need to describe the fears for our family's fate in Austria. Only later did we find out what happened to whom. Some fates remain unknown to this day. My mother succeeded, with the help of relatives and friends, to get a French visa for my half-sister, her husband, and her child. Since Linz had a special meaning for Hitler, it had to become the first "Jew-free" city. My half-sister and her family lived with my aunt in Innsbruck until they traveled to France in August 1938.

In 1939 our situation in Nancy became especially delicate. The police told us that the situation was unclear: Austria did not exist anymore and we were in danger of internment as "enemy Germans." We were advised to travel from the border region to the center of France as soon as possible. My mother was on vacation in Vichy with her sister and uncle Siegfried. My brother-in-law had never driven a car but he learned in a few days. We bought an old car, took along everything we could, bound mattresses onto the roof and followed the refugee trek going south. We moved slowly since there were also horses on the road and the nails from the hooves caused many flat tires. I do not remember exactly whether the journey from Nancy to Vichy took three or four days. We were not allowed to turn on any lights and we spent the nights on the side of the road. I prepared for the second part of my exam and studied in the car whenever possible. The University of Nancy had relocated to Clermont-Ferrand, and my exam was to take place there shortly.

That summer of 1939 we remained only a few days in Vichy. The nights we all spent in the hotel with my uncle, my aunt, and my mother. Because French authorities were rounding up and interning Austrian and German Jews as "enemy aliens," we did not write our names in the hotel's register. A year earlier Uncle Siegfried had rented apartments in Brive-la-Gaillarde in the south and now the family headed there by car.

I still remember the great contrast between the fears of war in the northeast—in Nancy many sand bags were placed in front of store windows—and the relaxed, joyous atmosphere of the south. We arrived on a feast day, a *kermesse*, and the war, Hitler, and the German border seemed very far from the people there and for a short moment even from us. We settled down in Brive, where there soon gathered a small group of Austrian and German Jewish refugees. I prepared for the *Baccalauréat, 2ème partie*, in philosophy that I had to take at the end of the summer in Clermond-Ferrand. Even though I had been selected to represent my school at the *Concours Génèral de France*, I had failed the *Baccalauréat* philosophy exam in Nancy earlier that spring. Why? One of my teachers told me that my paper had been too complicated (on occasion I get similar feedback about my papers today). But I think my failure had more to do with the fact that I was very busy and very involved with a girl. In any case, political fears were not the reason. Despite the flight from Nancy to the south of France, I passed the exam in Clermont-Ferrand "with distinction."

In Brive-la-Gaillarde, I discovered that a small, private Catholic secondary school was looking for a German teacher. I went to see Father Renaud, principal of the École Bossuet. Yes, he could use me even though I was merely one year older than my oldest students. The other teachers were not only Christians but also Catholic priests, and he said it would be better not to tell the students that I was a Jew. When I asked Father Renaud what I should do when I was expected to say a prayer at the beginning of every class, he responded that he would introduce me as one who was used to saying his prayers in German. And what, I asked, should I do about crossing myself? He thought and said smiling: "*Pourquoi ne pas faire l'étoile de David? Personne ne le remarquera.*" Why not make a Star of David? Nobody will notice.

During the summer of 1939, French officials had decided that German and Austrian refugees had to report weekly to the police. Soon the men, but also the women, were being interned in camps. My brother-in-law had to go to Angoulème. (He was eventually released (and did, as I will describe below, emigrate under complicated circumstances). At the French internment camps in Angoulème and in the more infamous Gurs, Jewish internees were ultimately handed over to the Germans and killed in the concentration camps. Father Renaud spoke about my situation to the father of one my students—a former minister in the French government—and thanks to their influence I was allowed to continue to report weekly to the police instead of being interned. At the same time, I enrolled at the university in Bordeaux. My subject was philology, and once or twice every week I went there for seminars, using a special travel permit from the police. One day, however, Father Renaud said that he thought he could not protect me for very much longer. As an enemy alien, I could not enter the French army and soon would have only a choice between the foreign legion and internment.

My uncle Siegfried—the butcher's son who became an industrialist— was a man of clear vision who thought independently. He had advised my family to send me to school outside of Austria, but he did not believe that the Maginot Line would save France. He asked his son-in-law—a reserve officer in the French army on a short furlough to visit family in Brive—for information concerning the production of French weaponry. After this visit, at the beginning of 1940, he urged my mother to get American visas for herself as a Swiss and for me as a minor. We accelerated those efforts. Siegfried's distant relative—an industrialist in Chicago—gave us the necessary affidavit, and in March 1940 we were able to travel to America on the Swiss immigration quota. We left France on the next-to-last passenger ship, *De Grasse*. Later I heard that Father Renaud suffered a heart attack on the day France capitulated.

VII. Splits and Adjustments

My mother and I brought one thousand dollars in gold coins to the U.S. When we were asked for personal belongings at the arrival in New York, we showed the coins, which were immediately taken away and replaced by paper money. It was, at that time, not allowed to own gold in the U.S. The gold coins would have had much more value than the paper money, but we did not know that. The arrival in the New World was such a tremendous experience that it overshadowed everything.

In France, on the way from Brive-la-Gaillarde to Le Havre, we had spent a night in darkened Paris. The difference between Paris in the dark and the life and lights of New York, the difference between the fear of internment and the experience of freedom of movement with its casually friendly aspects and the "nobody-gives-a-damn about what you do" atmosphere—as I experienced it—had an almost manic effect on me. In some refugee families, the contrast between explosions of a greedy hunger for life in some family members and depressive self-seclusion and rejection of anything new in others produced severe tensions and difficulties. I saw such a contrast in my half-sister's family. She reacted with a new hunger for living, while my brother-in-law, who would lose his mother and seven sisters in the Holocaust, wanted to remain mostly alone, secluded in a darkened room. Such a situation imposed heavy consequences for children at that time, but one can also observe this impact of the Holocaust and refugee experience in the next and further generations. Early marriage, problematic partner choices, and a second fleeing from a home that could not dissipate the heavy atmosphere all emerged as possible consequences.

After a few days in New York, we rode by train to Chicago. The relatives of my Alsatian uncle met us with a chauffeur in a large car and drove us to an apartment they had found for us. It was very close to their luxurious apartment on the shore of Lake Michigan, but our apartment—expensive for us at forty dollars per month—was directly on the Illinois Central line. The constant noise, day and night, was deafening.

On the first afternoon in Chicago—I think it was a Saturday—our relatives invited us to their home. In the evening, the son, a couple years older than I, wanted to show me the Chicago nightlife. We went to several bars, where he showed me the dice games one plays with bar girls that specialized in this activity. He lent me a dollar. Apparently, I had beginner's luck and won a couple of times. He paid for the drinks with the money I had won.

The relatives had a position for me in their factory. Monday morning, the son (he had the title of vice-president) picked me up by car and drove me along Lake Shore and Michigan Avenue, through the north and west and on to the poor areas in the industrial zone. The contrasts were overwhelming. In the factory (the second largest mattress factory in the U.S.) my relative brought me to his big office, asked for the manager of the maintenance crew, and introduced me to this German-American who had apparently been informed about me. He in turn brought me to the personnel office, gave me my gear, introduced me to my colleagues, and showed me my work for the next few weeks, namely, to paint the toilets in the factory. To my surprise (a very European surprise), I found out that the brother of the factory owner also worked on the maintenance crew. My wage was thirty cents per hour (then the legal minimum wage), twelve dollars per week less Social Security. I still have the original of my first Social Security card. After those first days in Chicago, I hardly saw my relatives any more. The trip from our home to the factory took one and a half hours using the Illinois Central train and then the elevated. After a couple of weeks, I was rather summarily fired from my job. It was never clear why, but I think it had something to do with my not understanding that one had to "keep smiling and move faster" when a supervisor came by. I did not fit into the team.

With the help of a Jewish organization, I got a second job: assistant to the maintenance man in a summer camp for girls outside the city. Pay was one dollar per day, with free food and lodging.

That summer France fell. I fearfully followed the news on my boss's car radio. My mother contacted the lawyer who had sent us our visa affidavit in France. He knew a senator (or perhaps it was Everett Dirksen, then still a congressman) who helped us obtain a visa for my half-sister and her family. Clergy did not—or at least did not then—fall under the regular quota system, and although he was never active, my brother-in-law's studies in his youth justified the statement that he could qualify as a rabbi. Furthermore, the *grand rabin de France* had given him the necessary papers documenting his qualifications. That fact saved the lives of the family; otherwise the waiting time for a visa would have been too long. Through aggressive personal lobbying, indirect contact with a senator, and vital help from the lawyer, my mother then was able to secure American visas for my half-sister, brother-in-law, and their child. They tried to leave on the day the Germans occupied France, but the Spanish border was closed and they became literally trapped between countries. Somehow they got back into France and from there onto a small boat to North Africa where they were interned near Casablanca. From Africa, they were able to travel on an overcrowded ship to America. My half-sister's youngest daughter was born two weeks after their arrival in New York.

By the end of the summer, my work in the vacation camp for girls had turned out less than successful. I had repaired roofs. Everything seemed to be in order, as for a while it refused to rain. But then, it rained! I did, however, become a good linoleum layer and was asked to repair a boat: it sank the very same day in the luckily not very dangerous lake. Once again, I was fired.

I looked for work in Chicago and answered various newspaper ads that sounded about like this: "Looking for intelligent young man able to adjust. No special skills needs. Will be trained by us." In hindsight it is amusing what strange people I met in their strange offices in the sky-scrapers of Chicago. But because money was very short, I did not always find it funny at the time. Once I had the opportunity to be trained as a Jiu Jitsu instructor—but without pay until I found students. A Christian association thought I would be potentially very useful to promote un-derstanding between Jews and Christians. I was supposed to collect money from Jewish business people and explain the tasks of the associa-tion. I could keep 25% of the money and I rapidly understood that the rest belonged to the people in the association who really did nothing besides print a few brochures. These people explained to me—rather shamelessly I thought—that my pay would be pretty good. I collected all the information about the outfit and informed the Jewish organization, B'nai B'rith, about the fraud.

Our relatives' lawyer helped me to get a new position in the mattress factory, this time in the shipping department. He also thought that I should become a secretary. (At the time, male secretaries were in de-mand for certain jobs.) He helped me to enroll in evening courses in business English, typing, and shorthand. The work in the shipping department was not easy and it was badly paid but I was found to be satisfactory. I worked there almost half a year, until I found something better.

At least I thought it would be. But the information that one got from other refugees and Jewish organizations was not always correct. In any case, my new position in a lampshade factory with Hamilton Industries was difficult. The packers were paid by the piece and therefore moved with tremendous speed. I prepared cartons for different combinations of lampshades and was always driven to work at maximum speed, but I was *not* paid per piece. After I was promoted to packer and earned more, I found out that if one works faster the pay per piece was reduced so that one had to work increasingly faster. I felt like Charlie Chaplin in *Modern Times*. Efforts to found a union were without success during my time. My English became better and I acquired some office skills so that other work opportunities opened up to me, if only modest and badly paid ones. For a time, I worked at the Illinois Central Railroad where I supervised the work of several women who manually transferred pension information from a formerly independent railroad pension system to the general social security system—one of the most monotonous jobs I ever experienced. I also worked on the translation of a technical booklet about Jeep maintenance from English to French. It must have been part of the preparation for the invasion of North Africa. I remember a poem on the first page. The title was "Ode to a Blitz-Buggy." My translation was "Ode à une boghie de blitz."

My mother cooked for fancy parties and gave language lessons to children. When she cooked, I sometimes came late at night to help with the dishes. I also went from drugstore to drugstore to collect orange peels (then orange juice was always freshly squeezed), which my mother candied. I sold the candy from door to door. Once when I carried a big load of orange rind on the Illinois Central from downtown to our apartment, my triple paper bag broke and I was left standing with some embarrassment in the middle of hundreds of wet orange peels.

Having earned the equivalent of two years of college credit for my French *Baccalauréat*, I took evening courses in junior college until I received a half scholarship to Chicago's Central YMCA College—now Roosevelt University—where I prepared for the B.A. degree. I thought that Industrial Psychology offered the best compromise between my interests and my realistic job opportunities, although it was the courses in Abnormal Psychology that attracted me. At that time, German and Austrian refugees more or less in my age group formed an informal club and had social contact. We all worked very hard, most of us studied, and although several of my friends eventually had impressive professional successes, we held badly paid, menial jobs. In Waukegan I found a somewhat better paying job in the shipping department of a small paint factory where I had to find the best and cheapest shipping routes for its products. Waukegan was a distant suburb and I could read and study on the train. But soon I found what I thought an even better position as a "purchasing agent" in a small laboratory supply house in Chicago. I liked the title, until I realized what was really expected of me: I was supposed to study the new price control regulations and find legal ways for getting around them. There was a maximum price, for example, for a gallon of carbon tetrachloride. When I told the owner that there was no way around the regulation, he observed that there was evidently no maximum price for carbon tetrachloride in smaller containers. Thus carbon tetrachloride from our company became only available in ¾-gallon containers.

I had met socially a buyer for a large chemical factory and asked my boss whether I would get a commission if I could make a sale. Yes, I was told. I arranged the deal, but never saw a penny. The reason was that "salesmen get commissions and, after all, my title was purchasing agent." This experience did not inspire me to pursue a career as a businessman.

VIII. Psychology and the Army

I succeeded in getting a psychology internship for a few months beginning in 1944 in the Chicago State Hospital, a huge institution. Tracy Kendler, a highly intelligent, young psychologist, impressed me greatly. Although I had already seen a few psychotic patients in courses on abnormal psychology, it was in the State Hospital that I had my first more intensive contact with psychotic and other seriously disturbed patients. There I also saw that even a highly intelligent clinical psychologist had, and seemed destined always to have, a lower position than some of the much less sophisticated psychiatrists. That insight influenced my choice of profession later on. I did not want to be an underling. The development of the occupation of clinical psychologist was still in the early stages.

I finished my evening school in psychology and obtained my B.A. diploma, but I was in the American army before the graduation ceremony. After initial military classification interviews, a small group of us were separated from the crowd of future infantry soldiers. We speculated about what we might have in common. There were many who had worked for the postal service, others had managed small businesses, and there was an anthropology student who had already done some teaching. After we completed the basic military training, we were placed in general service units that dealt either with military mail or personnel matters.

After six weeks of pretty hard infantry training, I was trained as a separation counselor. In this position, one interviews soldiers before they leave the army and fills out documents that should help the veterans to get positions in the civilian world. We had to show how this or that skill they had learned in the military was useful in specific civilian occupations. We were supposed to be helpful in their return to civilian life. Theoretically, this sounded worthwhile and interesting, but because one had so little time for any one soldier, the whole thing became nothing more than a formality. I found the work boring. I wrote a letter to Colonel Ebaugh, the psychiatric consultant for the 8th Service Command, in which I told my life story, recounted my education, and was anything but modest in the description of what I had learned in the psychiatric hospital. In his written answer to me, he said I could have been court-martialed for contacting him outside the chain of command. But he was glad I had written and I should soon hear about another assignment. This was a course at the Institute for the Crippled and Disabled in New York, the institution in which most modern rehabilitation techniques were developed. One of my teachers there was Gustav Bychowski, a Polish psychoanalyst who had emigrated to New York. I still remember his lecture about dreams of patients who had amputations and phantom limbs. Unfortunately, I could not use much of what I learned there in my actual army assignment.

Even though officially I became a rehabilitation counselor and worked in a military hospital in El Paso, Texas, I did not do much more than interview wounded and psychiatrically disturbed soldiers after their hospital stay and before their discharge from the army. I filled out their documents. Among the patients were severely wounded, plastic surgery patients and some interesting psychiatric cases, but my contact with them was short. When I asked one psychiatric patient—whose diagnosis was psychoneurosis mixed type (the diagnosis most often made by doctors whose psychiatric military training took only six weeks)—whether he were nervous, he responded: "Nervous? Hell no, I'm pregnant."

The most dangerous events during my military career were a couple of Sunday afternoon trips with some army friends to a Mexican border town. One or two soldiers did not return from there when they went into an off-limits area. When I had a few days' furlough, I traveled a little deeper into Mexico and was surprised that so close to our world there were still Indians who came from the mountains to the cities without shoes and only clad in loincloths. I was in El Paso when the war ended in Europe and the news of Hiroshima reached us. German rocket engineers and technicians worked in a camp close to the hospital. Since I spoke German and had a little psychology training, I was given the task to test a German rocket technician who behaved strangely but could not be easily understood or diagnosed by the psychiatrists. Because this task freed me from my generally boring work, I did not stop this man when he continued for three days to see more and more things in the Rorschach cards. The content of his responses was not bizarre until he finally told me that a particular color was that of a stone that he would personally find on Mars and use to cure cancer. This technician, who had been a rocket fanatic since his early adolescence, was repatriated to Germany.

During my army time, my mother moved from Chicago, where she had started a "fur flower" business, to New York, a better place for such a fashion invention. She did not make those fur flowers herself. She collected remnants from furriers. She designed the fur flowers and hired other refugees, mainly women, who made the flowers by hand. My mother was a good saleswoman and soon counted the best department stores among her customers. *Women's Wear Daily*, the most important fashion newspaper, published an article about the Paris Fleur Company and about her. She was described as descending from generations of flower makers. Even though she became relatively successful, she could never allow herself to live in a bigger apartment than her one and one-half room efficiency in New York. She emphasized to me that she never made it to a real bedroom in America.

After my discharge from the army in May 1944, I applied for a position in the first Veterans Administration clinical psychology-training program at the University of Chicago, where Carl Rogers, in his modest, non-directive style, reigned as king. I remembered the situation of the psychologists in the psychiatric state hospital and decided to take up medicine.

Because I was a veteran, the government paid for my medical studies and bare living expenses for four academic years. The psychology studies in Chicago would begin in the fall, but Cornell University had an intensive summer class in chemistry, the equivalent (in credits) to a year of course-work. Since I was missing the necessary preparatory medical courses, I took it. How I envied a girl who I got to know that summer at Cornell who took the following subjects: landscape watercolor painting, horseback riding, and the history of film! Painting and drawing had been important to me since my childhood. I thought about using my veteran study money to attend the *École des Beaux Arts* in Paris. But instead...

IX. The Case for the Single Case

In Chicago I worked hard. The pioneering Veterans Administration program in clinical psychology consisted of academic courses at the university and practical work in the outpatient clinic or hospital. In the clinic, I worked under the psychologist Hedda Bolgar who came from Vienna. Later I became her university teaching assistant in projective techniques (mainly Rorschach). Later, I also had contact with Beck, whose sophisticated psychoanalytic understanding of Rorschach was truly impressive. But first I worked at the clinic, took the psychology courses, became a teaching assistant, and at the same time took premedical courses that I found very difficult.

I also started my own psychoanalysis with Edoardo Weiss, the founder of the Italian Psychoanalytic Society, who had emigrated from Italy to Chicago. I knew that he personally had a positive attitude toward lay analysis and that fact, among others, made me choose him (I had my doubts that I could get into medical school.) Weiss also allowed me to pay part of the fee later. My motivation and energy were greater than I can imagine today: pre-medical courses, psychology courses, work in the clinic, a teaching assistantship, my own analysis (four times a week), some art classes, and a very important girlfriend!

My supervisors in the Veterans Administration Clinic were good to me and helped me in various ways. Grete Bass, a psychiatrist born in Vienna, worked there. Her husband, the sculptor Egon Weiner, taught at the Art Institute of Chicago and agreed to criticize my drawings. With a sharp and never failing eye that could distinguish the genuine from the merely effective, he influenced me greatly. During some hours in the clinic, when not much was going on, I was allowed to correct papers that had to do, for example, with my teaching job. And as soon as Bolgar and the Chief of the Clinic thought that my analysis might both do me some good and also help in my work, they gave me time off for my analytic hours as well.

The prerequisites for admission to various medical schools differed in only minor respects and I knew I had to apply to many universities to have a chance at all. Because so many veterans wanted to study medicine and now had the necessary money, there were as many as fifty applicants for every place in some medical schools. Some schools required a course in physical chemistry. The level of this course at the University of Chicago was so high that I was not sure that I could pass it at all, even if I were to do nothing else that semester. I had even less chance to pass it with the high grade necessary for admission to medical school. I took this particular course in another school. These were complicated years!

In psychology, Heinrich Kluever, a professor at the University of Chicago, deeply impressed me. He passionately pursued ideas and findings relevant to his field of interest even if he had to move far from his original academic area and learn entirely new disciplines. This German-born Gestalt psychologist developed a revolutionary new dye that permitted simultaneous microscopic examination of the nucleus and axon. He made major contributions to the understanding of temporal lobe functions, he discovered the so-called "Kluever-Bucy Syndrome," and he studied the effects of mescaline. Most important for me was Kluever's focus on the individual case, the "exception." His concept of "subjectively equivalent stimuli" influenced me greatly.

Despite the presence of Carl Rogers, the statisticians were then the real academic elite in the Department of Psychology at the University of Chicago. Ward C. Halsted developed neuropsychological tests, but he was more closely connected with the medical faculty. Ralph Reitan, who worked on his dissertation under Halsted and later became prominent in neuropsychology, was in the Veterans Administration Clinical Psychology training program. Kluever's ideas were the foundation of much of Halsted's work but, in my opinion, Halsted never gave him the credit he deserved, and generally the students in clinical psychological training had hardly any contact with him.

Every year Kluever held a seminar titled "The Case for the Single Case." His audiences consisted mostly of psychology students who concentrated on statistics. Kluever showed them that most scientific breakthroughs came about when a researcher stubbornly studied the individual case or exception. I do not know if the phrase "rage to understand" fits Kluever, but without any conventional, professor-like showmanship he conveyed his intensity for understanding and his passion to explain, and his respect for the exception contributed to my working on some individual cases for decades without becoming defensive about it.

Kluever based his concept of subjectively equivalent stimuli in experimentation, in which he showed that *different* stimuli were experienced *as if* they were identical. A few experiments of my own and many of my clinical and theoretical works are connected with his idea that objectively different but subjectively equivalent stimuli form the building blocks of our psychic realities. Specifically, I have applied the idea to the experience of time: not only can one experience differing stimuli as identical and identical stimuli as different, but one can also experience objectively differing *time* intervals as subjectively equivalent and objectively identical intervals as subjectively different (longer or shorter). Affects and transferences always play a role and influence the structuring and restructuring of these *cognitive* developments.

In *Multiple Realities in Clinical Practice* I summarized what these ideas contributed to the understanding of our psychic life, from the normal to the psychotic. I had developed the hypothesis that schizophrenic thought disorders were characterized not by a radically different logic but rather by different *objects* dealt with according to the usual logic. But how were such different, personal and idiosyncratic, not common sense objects formed? My hypothesis, schematically, began with the recognition that some perceptual processes are carried to completion while others are interrupted. I theorized that subjective equivalences of the products of both completed and interrupted perceptions led to idiosyncratic objects, while usual objects derived from normal, more or less finished, uninterrupted perceptual processes. Dynamic or biological factors could explain the disruption of these perceptual processes. In any case, the possibility that one can come to understanding idiosyncratic objects is greater than the possibility that one can come to understand a totally different logic. In other words, through intensive work with an individual patient, his or her personal objects can become comprehensible.

X. Clinical Psychology

Even though I applied to many medical schools, I was not accepted in the first year. I had written my Master's thesis (about time perception) under William Neff (mainly known for his works about auditory localization). He introduced me to his friend Harlow Ades, who was a neuroanatomist and professor of anatomy at the Emory Medical School in Atlanta. My peculiar preparation and my background interested Ades; he supported my application and introduced me to Carl Whitaker, professor of psychiatry in Atlanta. I had finished my courses, which led to my Ph.D. in psychology, and I had passed my "prelims," but I had not yet written my doctoral thesis when I was accepted into medical school and moved to Atlanta. A great barrier was overcome, but it interrupted much in my life, including important relationships. My personal psychoanalysis with Weiss also suffered a break.

At that time, there were no African American students at Emory University. The hospital was segregated, with separate sections for white and black patients. In the black hospital, anesthesia was not given for simple births, but in my junior year I delivered more than fifty African American babies. Generally, medical students had to have experience with black patients before they were allowed to perform the same procedures on whites. I later observed that we were permitted to work fairly independently with black patients, and as a result we had more practical experience than many other students who received their medical training in northern states.

Despite a few good friends and girlfriends, I never quite lost my feeling as an outsider in the South. During the summer months, I usually returned to Chicago. I received a small grant from Emory Medical School to study the EEG in hypnosis at the Institute for Juvenile Research at the University of Illinois, and I took or audited courses at the University of Chicago. There I met my wife, who received her Ph.D. in physiology from Chicago and later became a neuroscientist. We were already married during my last year at Emory, where she was able to take a research job at the medical school.

Because my GI bill money was coming to an end, I took an on-call job in a private hospital in Atlanta for one year. I started IVs and inserted urinary catheters during the night. After medical school, however, I returned to Chicago on a rotating internship at Michael Reese Hospital and continued my analysis with Edoardo Weiss. In Chicago, a program had been put in place combining psychiatric residency—either at Michael Reese, the University of Chicago, or the University of Illinois—with formal psychoanalytic training. Candidates could be accepted to both the residency and the psychoanalytic institute. The selection process included a group-stress interview. I was not aware that the one to which I was invited would also be a planned stress interview.

It was known that the very influential Roy Grinker, Sr. was generally opposed to Michael Reese interns continuing their residencies in the same hospital. Furthermore, considerable tensions existed between Weiss and

Grinker. A dozen people sat around a large table for my interview, which Grinker began with the exclamation: "Tell us something about yourself!" I hardly had said two sentences—something like "I was born in Linz, Austria, and my father was…"—when he interrupted me: "Are you not a little bit too defensive?" I had just started to answer when he interrupted me again: "Do you feel threatened by my question?" In an obvious, or so I thought, ironical tone, I replied: "No, of course not." Later I found out that my response had been interpreted as my not being in touch with my feelings. Because I was a psychologist and had been an assistant for a Rorschach course, a psychologist on the committee asked me what I had thought in the past of my own Rorschach responses. I thought I handled myself rather well during the interview, despite obvious attempts to shake me up. I was not, however, accepted to the program, and that was hard for me.

I had also applied for a Yale residency, but because Yale was perhaps the best place—or at least one of the two or three best places—in the country, I had been holding out very little hope of being admitted there. Yet, two weeks later, I received the acceptance letter. Of course, that meant that I had to interrupt my analysis with Weiss.

I could write extensively about my three years at Yale. Fritz Redlich was chair. I had a great deal of contact with Theodore Lidz, Steven Fleck, and Eugene Brody. For a short time, I went into therapy with Jules Coleman, who was also an inspiring teacher. Seminars led by Lawrence Kubie and especially by Hans Loewald were high points of my experience. After my residency, I was lucky to have continuing contact with Loewald until his death in 1993.

I had heard Frieda Fromm-Reichmann lecture on several occasions and after my Yale residency I decided to apply for a position at Chestnut Lodge Hospital. I had two interviews with her, the second taking several hours. After, she sent me to Edith Weigert, who asked me among other things why I wanted to work with psychotic patients; non-psychotic patients, she said, would be hard enough. I also met with Otto Will and Harold Searles. In the summer of 1957, the year I began to work at Chestnut Lodge, I received a public health scholarship as part of my salary. Fromm-Reichmann, however, died shortly before my arrival.

I was accepted as a candidate at the Washington Psychoanalytic Institute and began my training analysis with Winifred Whitman. This took four years in addition to my three years with Weiss. (Ping Nie Pao, with whom I became good friends, arrived about a year after I started to work at Chestnut Lodge and was also in analysis with Whitman.) At the Lodge, Will and Searles counted among the supervisors who were most important for me. Will supervised me for two to three years and Searles for seven years on different cases. Although significantly influenced by their ideas and techniques, I was able to establish some distance from both and to develop my own theories, technique, and style. Among my psychoanalytic supervisors, however, I must make special mention of Robert Cohen, who was clinical director of the National Institute of Mental Health. The clarity with which he crystallized central themes from a series of analytic sessions had a lasting effect on my work and on me.

I stayed at Chestnut Lodge for ten years. After six months to a year there I had been allowed to take private patients, and in my last two, I developed together with social workers a program that made it possible to bring patients' family members from outside the city (sometimes even outside the country) to the Lodge for a few days. On such occasions, family members had intensive contact with some staff members; I have written about the latent family based on this experience.

My work at Chestnut Lodge and the National Institute of Mental Health, first in the Family Development Section of the Child Research Branch, later in the Schizophrenia Research Branch, complemented each other and led to several publications. The double-bind theory—the hypothesis that paradoxical communications play a central role in the etiology of schizophrenia—was of enormous interest to me. But my work at the Lodge and later as research consultant in the Family Development Section (Wells Goodrich had invited me to work there) led me to formulate a critique of the theory. As mentioned above, I found that intolerance of ambiguity rather than paradoxical or double-bind communication acted as pathogenic factors.

Much of my research had to do with psychosis, mainly schizophrenia, but papers about self-mutilation and about non-traditional marriages (the latter written in cooperation with Robert Ryder) also dated from this period. My thinking about schizophrenic thought disturbances and about the atmospheric, idiosyncratic objects of schizo-phrenic patients developed very slowly and led not only to other theoretical questions on the subject of psychosis, but also to thoughts about the problem of consciousness. The relevance of that problem to the schizophrenic's world later gelled for me, as did the significance of work with psychotic patients for understanding otherwise particularly puzzling neurotic problems, for example, animate and inanimate differentiation in different levels of severity of psychopathology.

As I built a general psychoanalytic practice, and as I became more active as a teacher and training and supervising analyst at the Washington Psychoanalytic Institute, I also began to teach and supervise psychiatric residents, including, sometimes, medical students at the George Washington University School of Medicine. I continued for many years to work with one or two psychotic patients. When a split threatened the Washington Psychoanalytic Institute, I became more involved with the organizational aspects of psychoanalysis. As I saw the situation, one group of senior analysts and their followers perceived themselves to be the personifications of a purer psychoanalytic truth than the rest of us. They attempted to form another institute, a parallel institute, but in my opinion they also strove to destroy the existing one. The motto, "I am purer than you," evoked in me the association: "I am Aryan and you are not." Because the organizers of the potential new institute made such a small group, one of the organizers asked for special help at a meeting of the Board of Professional Standards of the American Psychoanalytic Association. I did something atypical for me. I was not a member of the Board. I was just sitting in the audience, but I stood up and asked to speak. I said the situation reminded me of the story of a young man who had killed his parents and then asked the judge for leniency because he was an orphan. When a few of the "splitting" teachers threatened the functioning of the institute by suddenly refusing to teach, I became Chair of the Curriculum Committee to help get control of the situation and to reorganize the faculty. That was the beginning of my institutional engagement, my later work on committees, and eventually my services as President of our Psychoanalytic Society and as Chair of the Education Committee.

XI. Language and Immigration

The fact that emigration forced me to learn foreign languages, together with the interests and ambitions connected with my refugee past, ultimately played a part in my becoming involved in the institutional side of the International Psychoanalytical Association. I was among those who were excited about the rebirth of a psychoanalytic movement in Eastern Europe and I took an active part in this development.

Many years ago, in 1976, Helmut Thomä invited me to come to Germany as a visiting professor. Since then, I had been a regular visitor and participant in scientific and social events, especially the so-called psychoanalytic "Vital Pleasures" ski seminars organized by colleagues from Ulm (we also had one German-American "Vital Pleasures in the Rockies" seminar). Contact with Thomä and his family, with Horst Kächele and his family, and with many other friends continued to develop. During one of these seminars, I met Helga Breuninger. (She had a ski pole that was also a flute. She stood over Thomä and played it when he had fallen in deep powder and was digging himself out. An unforgettable picture!) Breuninger organized a series of seminars about the current consequences of Nazism. My participation in some of these colloquia led to my cooperation with Werner Bohleber.

I could write about much else in this *Selbstdarstellung*: personal losses and grief, the joys and anxieties connected with a growing family, the personal and professional achievements of my wife and children. Because of Marian Kafka's neuroscientific studies of the rhythmicity of neuroreceptor activity, there are some points of contact between her and my work. I could write about doubts and hesitation, paths taken and avoided, and about many ideas, projects, and feelings that preoccupy me now. Many, but not all, of them are still connected with psychoanalysis.

But a *Selbstdarstellung*, a self-representation, is meant as an introduction of oneself, a first contact. Therefore, I will close with a hello rather than a good-bye, and with a reflection on the possibilities of writing self-representations in the present.

I have thought that the *Selbstdarstellung* of a refugee, an emigrant, should be written in several languages. Could that not be the beginning of an entire literary genre? Today, when more people than ever move from one country to another—because they want to or because they have to in these new times of mass migration—could not the effort to use a mixture of languages lead to a desired "ethnic dirtying?" Let us create an "in-between" language of the migrant masses! That *interlingua* project would fit well with Derrida's idea to publish not only final texts but also drafts of sentences and still partially readable erasures—those first efforts at putting things into words.

In *Multiple Realities in Clinical Practice* I developed the idea that every perception, every psychological event, recapitulates its ontogeny. When language—or more exactly, a set of languages—enters the picture, then the recapitulation provides a language journey. But the situation is even more complicated and interesting than can be explained by a simple chronological sequence of a series of migrations. Refugees and exiles think of different topics in correspondingly different languages. I went with my mother to the market and, until a short time ago, maybe even today, I knew the names of vegetables better in German than in any other language. I still count mostly in German, think of literature more in French, and practice business, medicine, and psychoanalysis in English. Some languages seem to fit with— seem to *love*—some themes, domains, and ideas more than others. And all these facts influence the language in which I think first.

Why not, then, confront ethnic cleansing with ethnic dirtying in, for example, a German-Turkish in-between language newspaper! Such a journal would resemble my mother's letters, in which the proportion of different languages changed as she crossed national borders. In-between languages would also suit psychoanalytic reports on work with multilingual patients, especially when the analyst is also multilingual. Here I was lucky with my first analyst, Edoardo Weiss. I could communicate to him in German when I thought that a German word fit best with what I felt.

In this connection, I want to recall a multilingual patient of mine. French was one of his languages and he usually made his self-observational remarks in that language. But sometimes, when he caught himself using empty words defensively, he also turned to French, saying simply: "*Je suis en train de meubler le silence.*"

I am in the process of furnishing the silence.

Part One

Multiple Realities
in Clinical Practice

Published in 1989
Yale University Press, New Haven and London
Copyright owner: John S. Kafka

Update to the Introduction to

Multiple Realities in Clinical Practice

What do I want to add, change, or emphasize in this short additional introduction to *Multiple Realities in Clinical Practice*? The clinical material and most of the psychoanalytic theoretical considerations, remain pertinent. In general, there remains a good fit between the hypotheses about the importance of the temporal organization of the brain, in the original English publication, and the direction in which neurobiology has since moved adding rich specific data. A section in chapter one of the 1989 book has the title "Psychoanalytic Restructuring of Past Experience." At that time, I was not using the term *Nachtraeglichkeit* or *aprés coup* that are in common usage now in the psychoanalytic literature dealing with the retroactive attribution of meaning. As a matter of fact, I was focusing on the retro-active or retrospective change in the sense of duration of a past event. The usual psychoanalytic discussions of *aprés coup* do NOT deal with this retrospective evolution on which I focus. On the other hand, I do not deal explicitly with *Nachtraeglichkeit* in the original English version of the book. I refer the reader to my other selected writing for different discussions of *aprés coup*, especially the chapter "Psychoanalysis and the Temporal Trace." There, I refer to recent neuro-scientific work about the movement of cerebral activation from mid-brain to frontal cortex corresponding to the change from immediate recall to psychologically elaborated subsequent memory.

Since the publication of my 1989 book, *Multiple Realities in Clinical Practice*, there has been a large body of work in neuro-psychoanalysis that is relevant to and resonates with my observations, ideas, and hypotheses described in my book and in my papers. Mark Solms' clinical research with brain damaged patients is a case in point. My description of "atmospheric object" corresponds closely to his description of a patient with Korsakoff's syndrome " ... he is trying to find a certain thing, but what he finds instead is a whole lot of things around it that are *symbolically connected*, one might say, in the broadest sense, to the topic that he is actually looking for." (Solms, 2015, p. 84) While Solms describes a patient with a specific diagnosis, I hypothesize on the basis of clinical findings and neuro-biological understanding that "atmospheric" objects are omnipresent in our mental life.

The book focuses on the theme that the analyst's effort to comprehend the analysand's psychic realities is central in clinical work. In the sense that epistemology is a "branch of philosophy that investigates the origin, nature, methods and limits of human knowledge," (The Random House College Dictionary; Revised Edition 1980, p. 445), psychoanalysis takes place in a laboratory of epistemology in which the analysand's knowledge and understanding of his reality is investigated. Beyond readily seen clinical uses, however, observations in the psychoanalytic laboratory extend and blend with other philosophical and scientific research that may at first glance seem far removed from clinical work. In *Multiple Realities in Clinical Practice*, I describe a patient who was convinced that the earth was shrinking when she walked faster and arrived at her destination sooner than usual. This is an example of a resonance between data observed in the clinical laboratory and the space/time relationship studied by physicists, logicians, and mathematicians. Because such resonances have been neglected, I want to focus on it in this introduction. We still tend to think of *reality testing* and *common sense* as more closely connected than they are. Einstein's equation involving time and space is far removed from *common sense*, but has considerable tangible effects on our *reality*. The functioning of nuclear reactors involve Einstein's equations and produce electricity.

In the psychoanalytic laboratory of epistemology, constant objects emerge when different patterns of stimulation are experienced as subjectively equivalent. In general psychology, *object permanence* refers to observations such as that a table seen from different angles is still the same table. In psychoanalysis, *object constancy* is achieved when the young child recognizes that the same mother can be frustrating or gratifying. The objects of our psychic reality are subjectively equivalent patterns. Subjective equivalences also determine our sense of elapsed time. This is especially striking in psychoanalysis. The fixed outer temporal frame of the session contrasts with the situation within the frame, in which the fluctuating experience of intense wish or fear distorts clock time. Identical intervals can be experienced as different from each other, and different clock-time intervals can be experienced as subjectively equivalent. Psychic reality in the psychoanalytic laboratory is a pattern of temporally moving subjective equivalences. Mental processes of constructing and deconstructing equivalences create time that, independent of such mental processes, does not exist. This leads me, in the last pages of the chapter, "Déjà Vu, Drugs, Synesthesia" to the radical statement that *mind is time.* It is difficult to imagine any conclusion more distant from common sense. I am not only using the occasion of *Multiple Realities in Clinical Practice*'s re-publication as part of my *Selected Papers* to call attention to the function of psychoanalysis as a laboratory of epistemology, but also, and foremost, to the possibility of reaching by its use conclusions such as *time is mind*, conclusions that are pertinent to human experience and congruent with modern physics, mathematics, and formal logic.[1]

---

[1] This re-publication of *Multiple Realities in Clinical Practice* occurs after Gödel's work, that led him to the conclusion that "time does not exist," has received much attention even in the popular scientific media. Gödel, a mathematician and logician, was apparently the only person at Princeton that Einstein considered his equal. To quote Jim Holt, "Einstein had shown that the flow of time depended on motion and gravity, and that the division of events into 'past' and 'future' ... was relative ... Gödel ... believed that time „ as intuitively understood, did not exist *at all*. Gödel found ... the possibility of a hitherto unimaginable kind of universe ... The equations of general relativity can be solved in a variety of ways ... Gödel came up with a solution to the equations of Einstein's general theory, a solution in which the universe was not expanding, as in the "Big Bang" model, but rotating. Gödel showed that the geometry of a rotating universe mixes time and space. By completing a sufficiently long round trip ... a resident of Gödel's universe could travel back to any point in his own past ... (Some) physicists marveled that time travel ... was apparently consistent with the laws of physics." (Holt, 2005. p. 81)

References

Holt, J. (2005). "TIME BANDITS What were Einstein and Gödel talking about." *The New Yorker*, Feb 28, 2005, pp. 80-85.

Solms, M. (2015). *The Feeling Brain, Selected Papers on Neuropsychoanalysis*. Karnac.

Definition: "Epistemology." *The Random House College Dictionary, Revised Edition*. 1980. p. 445.

Since astronomers' calculations of the time span of the original Big Bang continue to become ever more infinitesimally small, the idea has been advanced that there *was* no such event but that the Big Bang is always *now*, an idea strangely consistent with the conclusion that time as a reality separate from mental process does not exist.

In addition to Jim Holt's article, "TIME BANDITS What were Einstein and Gödel talking about," *The New Yorker*, Feb 28, 2005, pages 80-85. And, for instance, Rebecca Goldstein's book, *Incompleteness: The Proof and Paradox of Kurt Gödel*, (Atlas/Norton), and Palle Yourgrau's book, *A World Without Time: The Forgotten Legacy of Gödel and Einstein*, (Perseus).

Introduction

Multiple Realities in Clinical Practice

The conviction that we all share a commonsense reality is the basis of ordinary daily communication. Although we are aware of the fluidity of our perceptions, we operate in our daily lives with confidence that we can agree on certain self-evident structural stabilities in our physical world. This physical world provides the base of our commonsense psychological realities; it is the medium in which our communications and the expression of our needs and wants take place. We have confidence that we can return from our dreams and our flights of fancy to the common ground of commonsense reality. We cannot take this ability for granted in some of our patients, however, and we may describe the degree to which their *reality-testing* capacity is or is not intact. Our patients alert us to the mechanisms by which reality or realities are constructed and evaluated, the *sense* of reality strengthened and weakened. We encounter the phenomenon of *derealization* with its uncanny affective component of being *not of this world*, the affect of dread.

The processes that lead to our shared commonsense reality, processes that include socialization, are absorbing and complex. As we study them, however, and look more closely at the development of our knowledge of the world, at epistemology, it dawns on us that this admittedly essential common ground of our common-sense reality may be narrower than we had thought. Only a subtle and highly differentiated

7

spoken or unspoken language can do justice to our rich personal realities, whereas an analogy can perhaps be made between the essential, but limited, ground covered by commonsense reality and the world that can be described in Pidgin English.

Most of us are aware at times of discrepancies between our own reality perceptions and those of others. Such discrepancies sometimes do, but often do not, present a problem for us. Patients, however, even those whose reality testing is not in question, bring to our consulting rooms the problematic aspects of such discrepancies. It is not sufficient for them to share with others the common ground pf commonsense reality. They have a need to include in the realities in which they move and function some terrain extending beyond these narrow limits. Whether they know it or not, they seek a therapist with a wider stance, one who conveys a feeling that he or she is ready to encompass, potentially at least, a wider and widening reality, even if its eventual forms and dimensions are yet uncertain. A significant portion of the psychoanalyst's work reaches beyond *understanding* (providing a common base and platform that *stands under* the currently shared realities) to *comprehending, encompassing*, and *widening* his reality perceptions. If the psychoanalyst implicitly conveys to the patient the readiness to expand his own reality perceptions, the patient will sense that he may not be alone in both his current and his developing worlds. This book, therefore, is about the expanding framework for *comprehension*, the inclusion of different organizations of reality, organizations that have their own developmental patterns and rhythms.

As a therapy, psychoanalysis differs from other approaches by aiming not only at change or elimination of symptoms but at changes that are organically related to the individual's comprehension—whether or not such comprehension finds a pathway to conscious verbal expression—of the origin and function of symptoms, defenses, character structures, and ways of perceiving the world. This book is thus also about the process of psychological change, and that signifies a change in the perception of what things mean. Our realities on close examination are precisely that: *what things mean.*

Although psychoanalysis has always been concerned with psychic reality, most clinical psychoanalysts, on the one hand, justifiably distrust armchair philosophizing, especially of the vaguely existential kind, and, on the other hand, are often not in touch with some relevant experimental work on perception and cognition. Yet it is precisely clinical work that constantly brings one in contact with questions about the nature of knowledge, questions of how convictions, with their cognitive and affective charges, are formed and changed. Unless his philosophobia causes him to slam the door shut a priori, the clinician must confront some epistemological issues. Thus, finally, this book considers some of these clinically based questions about the nature of knowledge.

I will write about my understanding and treatment of neurotic and psychotic patients, about a clinician's perspective on some broad epistemological questions, and about the contributions, in turn, of epistemological insights to clinical issues. The constant interplay between clinical and theoretical work sometimes gives the analytic office its most peculiar stamp, that of a laboratory of philosophy. Some organizing themes have emerged in the course of this work, hypotheses about how multiple-reality organizations evolve through affectively determined perceptual processes and how temporal phenomena occupy a central place in our efforts to understand mind.

A major aspect of the psychoanalyst's training consists in uncovering the roots of his or her own ways of perceiving and relating to the world and the origin and context of personal values. Such self-knowledge plays a major role in the formation of the analyst's attitude of not imposing perceptions and values on the analysand, to avoid "contamination" and to facilitate the blossoming of genuine autonomy. The reader of an analyst's writings, however, may be helped in the understanding and critical evaluation of the ideas put forward by knowing something about the author. After all, the major themes that characterize the writings of a psychoanalyst are rooted in his life and work experience, and their development can best be understood in the context of his scientific autobiography.

In one sense, the multiple-reality theme entered my life quite early. The tirst thirteen years in Austria, the next six in France, and the years since then in the United States confronted me with different cultural realities, which, to a significant degree, I had to make my own. The tempo of these different settings impressed me forcefully. I have vivid memories of the heavy um-pah rhythm of a Tyrolean band that was playing at a railway station when I left Austria and of the almost frantic tempo of a quick-stepping "Chasseurs Alpins" band that marched past the railway station at my first stop in France. My focus on tempo and time had early roots, and a teacher in France who presented Henri Bergson's work beautifully and enthusiastically helped my ideational elaboration of vaguely felt preoccupations. To the necessity of dealing with different ethnic realities and tempos was added the necessity of living, and making a living, at very different socioeconomic levels—as a student in Europe, a laborer in my first years in the United States, and then as a student again, moving from the humanities to psychology, to medicine, to psychiatry and psychoanalysis. All this further prepared the ground for my preoccupation with multiple realities.

Although I did not initially plan specifically to investigate an area labeled "multiple realities," the theme emerged in various guises as I moved on my personal voyage from one phase of my life to another. As a student, as a psychoanalyst, as a research psychiatrist, and as a person with the usual human curiosity, I found that the limited areas on which my attention was customarily focused began to coalesce into broader formulations. Throughout, an openness to philosophical and epistemological thinking shaped the context of my developing perspective.

The work of Heinrich Klüver, one of my teachers at the University of Chicago, seemed to deal directly with the rigorous study of multiple psychological realities. His approach, to which I shall return on several occasions in the body of this book, involved the study of sets of different physical stimuli that the organism treats as subjectively equivalent. His work can inform and enrich even a clinical understanding of the concept of object constancy.

It is, of course, the psychotic patient who most strikingly lives in a different reality. The description of the consulting room as a laboratory of philosophy is particularly apt here. Epistemology changes from an abstract discipline to one of literally vital importance for the psychiatrist who refuses to accept the idea that psychotics "do not make sense." The awareness of different reality organizations is the essential tool of the therapist treating psychotic patients. Although these problems forced themselves on me first in my work with such patients, I later learned how much the awareness of different reality organizations is also a useful—in my view, essential—instrument in the treatment of nonpsychotic patients. I have become increasingly convinced that in most instances in which psychoanalysis is carried to an appropriate depth, the changes in subjective reality are such that issues of reality perception are pertinent. In this book I will elaborate on the theme that a simple-minded distinction between cognitive and affective functions is erroneous. I will describe how I have come to view cognitive and perceptual processes as in their very essence affectively informed and determined.

Psychoanalysis was not the first therapy with which I became acquainted. Carl Rogers was among my early teachers; despite my appreciation of the man and the useful components of his approach to therapy, its inherent limitations made me look elsewhere, and my search led me to psychoanalytic training. I have often been struck by the degree of disappointment shown by some colleagues whose only therapeutic training was in psychoanalysis when they discovered flaws or limitations in psychoanalytic theory or technique. It was relatively easy for me to take these limitations for granted since I could contrast the richness offered within the psychoanalytic framework with approaches I had previously encountered. I found room here for the progressive development of my ideas concerning multiple realities and their application to the study of family structure and the treatment of neurotic patients—those with character disorders or borderline personality structure—and, within limits that will be spelled out, psychotic patients.

Symptom-oriented treatment facilities are currently fashionable, at least in the United States. There are, for example, separate anxiety clinics, depression clinics, phobia clinics. The interest in psychotherapeutic approaches to the psychoses is at a low ebb, although some lip service is given to the need for psychotherapeutic work in conjunction with psychopharmacological treatment. Nevertheless, increasing numbers of investigators and clinicians have a sophisticated nonreductionistic approach to what is essentially the mind-body problem as it is encountered in our field. An argument could perhaps be made that the rapid progress in the biology of the central nervous system has so far led to more understanding of the biological events "connected" to "normal" psychological processes—perception, affect, and thought—than to the biology of psychopathology. Increasing understanding of the enormous plasticity of the central nervous system makes plausible the idea that specific stresses during specific developmental phases can lead to biologically definable changes. And not only may questions of etiology be clarified but the effective range and limitations of psychotherapeutic interventions may be better defined. The study of mechanisms of memory may be particularly pertinent here (Squire, 1986). In any case, it is my belief that most clinicians operate nowadays with some rudimentary formulations about "biology."

Thoughts about the biology of perception form a background for some of my formulations, and I will attempt to make them explicit. My tentative model of the schizophrenic disorders, for instance, specifies an area in which biological explanations may be pertinent. My focus in this context is not on the philosophical mind-body problem as such but on the conscious model that informs the clinician's operations and may also determine research strategies at a time when one is forced to operate with an admittedly incomplete model. The broadly conceived model of schizophrenic disorders that will be presented gives a prominent place to perceptual processes and to questions of sensory compartmentalization versus synesthetic phenomena. For such a model, biological research dealing with neurotransmitters and receptors involved in localization and spread of nervous impulses is pertinent. This may be the case even if the broader model utilizes concepts such as "conflict," "impulse," and "drive."

A preoccupation with the question of what size organism is the most appropriate unit of study characterizes my work and represents a theme with multiple roots and multiple ramifications. On the more clinical level, questions of preference for therapeutic-focus on the individual, the family, or the group are related to more theoretical questions about the optimal size of the psychobiological unit to be studied. There may not, however, be an absolute correspondence between the most informative unit size for purposes of the theoretical study of specific questions and the optimal unit size for therapeutic application. For me, the interest in the question of appropriate unit size has coexisted with and informed my therapeutic focus on the individual. It may even have strengthened this focus. The gradual sharpening of my idea that temporal rather than spatial dimensions are the more promising topics of study in our field may have played a part here. In retrospect, it is conceivable that the possibilities of optimal temporal, rhythmic resonance between individual therapist and individual patient may have influenced my decision to focus on one-to-one therapeutic and psychoanalytic work, although I have worked with couples, families, and groups and occasionally still do so.

Spatial models of mental structures, it seems to me, carry more danger of reification, and thus I have been increasingly concerned with the possibilities of expressing ideas in temporal terms, with issues of appropriate temporal units and problems of temporal expansion and contraction in psychic life. My preoccupation with time has alternated between two polarities, although I have attempted to construct a connecting bridge. One polarity is clinical, phenomenological, and experimental; the other—although I have reservations about the use of the term here—is more "philosophical." Connected with the first polarity is a focus on temporal aspects of perceptual processes—the notion that each perceptual act recapitulates the ontogeny of perception. This idea, which has clinical and experimental underpinnings and also significant diagnostic and therapeutic implications, will be developed in the body of the book. Let us note, however, that if the infant's early perceptual discriminations involve the distinction between what is inside and outside his body (in other words, the establishment of the size of the organism), the distinctions between animate and inanimate objects and between characteristics that ultimately lead to the differentiation of the spatial and temporal dimensions, then these distinctions, rapidly recapitulated in each adult perceptual act, represent the axes along which realities are organized.

Because of the complexities of the idea of perceptual recapitulation, unfamiliarity with the notion that the history of the development of perception is unrolled in each perceptual act, I would like to introduce here the more familiar description of another recapitulative experience. It is said that individuals confronting sudden mortal danger often experience a rapid rerun of their whole previous life. This recapitulation of the "perception" of one's life, described as conveying a sense of completeness and including a reexperience of emotional change and evolution, is highly condensed and packaged into an unbelievably short time span. I believe that traumatic conditions are not essential for this phenomenon to occur and that even in ordinary circumstances each perception involves a recapitulation of its development. The affective and therefore the transferential history are also packaged in this recapitulation. The preconscious richness of our affectively informed contact with ourselves and with the world depends on and derives from the overtones of recapitulation and condensation, the constant rapid replay of our cognitive and emotional histories. What distinguishes individuals facing mortal danger is that they are conscious of such recapitulation. The experience of time at such a juncture will also be a topic of major interest.

My overarching concern with time is not limited to such issues as the recapitulation of ontogeny, the development of perception in each perceptual act. Although I do not start with an explicit philosophical position (or philosophy of science), the more "philosophical" polarity of my preoccupation with time rather than space is related to the Zeitgeist derived from modern physics. Psychoanalysts, I believe, have timidly neglected the insight of modern physics that, in order to understand certain phenomena, one must understand the relationships among matter, time, and energy rather than merely the commonsense meanings of these terms. Such an insight may be pertinent to our field. Biology, too, emphasizes systems of energy rather than commonsense matter—for example, in discussions by molecular biologists of the nature of cell membranes. I will examine models of the nervous system based on temporal rather than spatial characteristics. I will argue that the focus on time permits a new perspective on the mind-body problem and perhaps makes less shocking Hans Loewald's radical statement that "time is the fiber of mind." Focus on temporal structure, as I hope to demonstrate, has immediate and practical effects on clinical work. The issue of the size of the organism seems to be anchored in a reified spatial dimension, but even a cursory examination of that question dispels the idea; the individual who sees himself as part of a group at that moment changes his temporal perspective, since the unit that contributes to his "reality" may well extend beyond his individual life span. The moments of maternal-infant fusion are perhaps the most obvious examples of temporally different reality.

Order and structure are topics in which clinical and philosophical preoccupations meet. In clinical psychoanalysis we encounter the word *structure* in the context of "structural change." The study of change in psychoanalysis and an examination of the concept of structure in this context have led me to another facet of the multiple-reality theme. A retrospective view of cases in which significant change, perhaps structural change, occurred led to the discovery that such cases were characterized by a change from animate to inanimate features of "objects" encountered in the analytic work. This observation in turn led to the following question: can the analysand's experience of objects changing, on a symbolic level, from animate to inanimate and vice versa—a change in the relationship to objects—be connected to the perceptual discrimination between the animate and the inanimate, and even to the infant's development of this differentiation? It would indeed be intriguing if a connection could be established between "structural" change in the psychoanalytic sense—the shift from "insight" to "active" change—and the early distinction between the animate and inanimate worlds. The possible pertinence here of the work of the physicist Ilya Prigogine on structural changes will be discussed. There is also much current interest in "state-specific" learning, a topic akin to Paul Federn's separate "ego states." I will explore the possibility that these different ego states may be characterized by the different animate or inanimate structures. I will propose that the "entitlement" of certain narcissistic patients is related to their lack of differentiation of the animate and inanimate.

The ability to treat the same object as both animate and inanimate is often discussed in a developmental framework and related to Winnicott's work on transitional objects. My emphasis on the creative and therapeutic uses of a multiple reality that encompasses the realities of the same object as both animate and inanimate and my critique and reformulation of double-bind theory have considerable affinity with Winnicott's work. My thesis is that intolerance of ambiguity (including the ambiguity concerning the animate and inanimate nature of objects) rather than paradoxical communication tends to be pathogenic. Compared to the relative stability of the inanimate world—it is fixed in place, *in space*— the movement of animate beings—the ability to change position and attitude from moment to moment—emphasizes its *temporal* characteristics. My own extension or elaboration of the transitional realm between the animate and inanimate worlds introduces the notion of the transitional between the spatial (or "material") and the temporal—an idea that bears some relationship to Gilbert Rose's extension of the transitional experience to the "transitional process" (1980). In discussing transitional experience I will also take into account that the animate being has temporal intentionality—orientation toward the future. One may speak of an animate directionality, but even the animate being may experience the past as being fixed, as being experientially unchanging and therefore quasi-spatial, less temporal. Experientially the past may be associated with deanimated "deposits" until the latter are revitalized, reanimated because their meaning—brought into new contexts because of life events or by psychoanalytic reactivation—*changes,* that is, enters the explicitly temporal dimension. The role of rituals in either enlivening or deadening the past will also be examined.

Awareness of the processes by which each patient forms both the more ephemeral and the more lasting aspects of his or her realities fosters in the therapist a profound respect for the validity of the individual's universe. This added respect colors the atmosphere of the consulting room and underlines the analyst's nonjudgmental stance, which is a major component of the psychoanalyst's training. The arguments that a value-free position is unreachable in practice have led some clinicians to downplay the importance of efforts to approximate it. In one sense, however, psychoanalysis cannot escape the issue of morality. Psychoanalysts are determinists: antecedents determine behavior and psychoanalytic theories are invoked in the courtroom when attempts are made to connect the criminal's upbringing with his crime. At first glance, moral issues, "free" will, and (psychic) determinism seem to have nothing to do with the perception of the size of the organism. On second look, the very courtroom argument hinges on the question of whether the appropriate unit size is the larger or the smaller one, the family or the individual. In general, the behavior of an organism may be "determined" if this organism belongs to a larger one—or to an organism whose duration, whose life span, is longer than that of its component parts. The behavior may be seen as "free" if the organism is separate and apparently "independent." An observer will come to different conclusions when studying an individual ant within or without the context of its colony. In clinical work perceptions of the size of the organism fluctuate—individual or family, for instance—and we will explore the connections between organisms' size and free will. Such issues are pertinent for an understanding of the development of a sense of autonomy in psychoanalytic treatment.

My ideas about ambiguity continued to develop when I introduced Gödel's concepts in my critique of double-bind theory (Kafka, 1971b). At that time the idea of outside-inside ambiguity, which is essentially another way to talk about the uncertainty of the absolute size of an organism, began to take increasingly formal shape for me. These ideas probably seemed more esoteric prior to Hofstadter's popularization of Gödel (Hofstadter, 1979), but even now they are somewhat distant from the clinician's everyday concerns. Yet I believe that a clinical approach that reaches far enough must deal with the organization of the individual's realities, and some propositions dealing with the nature of our realities are formal—that is, they lie in the field of formal logic. The difficulties lie with the clinician's prejudice regarding a humanistic/scientific or philosophical/scientific dichotomy. Perhaps it is derived in part from a commonsense but antiquated mind/body dichotomy.

The development of the ideas outlined in this introduction thus involved, and continues to involve, movement from clinical practice and observation to theoretical elaboration, return to clinical work equipped with new theoretical formulations, and then further engagement in theory building—an ongoing process consisting of slow swings and rapid oscillations. This description essentially describes clinical work itself, as I understand it, and even the more theoretical formulations represent one set of traces left by such psychoanalytic or psychoanalytically informed endeavors. The back-and-forth nature of such traces to some extent limits the sequential orderliness of their presentation, and some repetition is unavoidable. I believe, however, that what is repeated in an ever-widening context becomes altered by that very process.

In what follows I will first speak of time, timing, and temporal perspective, with an emphasis on the clinical situation. Chapter 2 focuses on multiple realities in thought and object formation. In chapter 3, I will return to time and mind, after having found more solid footing in the theory developed in chapter 2. I will also in this chapter describe the development of some of my ideas during research with LSD and Sernyl in the 1960s, a time when interest in those drugs was at its height, both because of widespread experimentation with consciousness-expanding substances and because of their possible significance as keys to a better understanding of hallucinatory behavior during psychosis.

In chapter 4, the multiple-reality formulations are applied to issues of diagnosis and treatment. I will here consider the counter-transference elements embodied in the establishment of diagnostic categories and the idea that animate-inanimate confusion is limited to specific areas of conflict in some diagnostic categories and not in others. The chapter includes clinical data illustrating a connection between therapeutic structural change and alteration in the animate-inanimate discrimination dichotomy.

The focus of chapter 5 is on schizophrenia and schizophrenic thought disorder, subjects par excellence for the investigator of multiple realities. The chapter includes an excursion into the assessment of the dreams of schizophrenics—work I did some years ago in response to an invitation. At that time I recognized the fit of the paradoxical topic of the dreaming schizophrenic with my central interests: how do those whose waking reality sometimes seems so dreamlike dream?

Chapter 6 explores the widening applications of the multiple-reality approach—for example, to the study of rituals, family dynamics, and group behavior. The concluding chapter examines the compatibility of the multiple-reality emphasis with psychoanalytic theory and clinical practice and sketches the prospects that may lie ahead.

The close connection between clinical and theoretical thinking enriches a psychoanalyst's daily work. Such mutual reinforcement is the most powerful antagonist of possible burnout, and since the affect-cognition dichotomy is an artificial one, a technique well founded in theory is the basis of a genuinely humanistic therapeutic approach. For this to be so, however, there must be a personal and critical engagement with theory, an integration of theory with the broadest personal vistas. It is my hope that the presentation of my integrative efforts will contribute to the reader's individual integrative work.

For the reader who is familiar with the original version of *Multiple Realities* or the new reader who is particularly interested in specific topics, the original introduction offers a concise guide.

Chapter 1

Time, Timing, and Temporal Perspective

A hospitalized patient, Ms. R., once informed me that the earth was shrinking between the central unit of the hospital complex and the recreation building. After several days and repeated observations I realized that she was walking much faster than usual. The visibility, the touchability, of objects in space gives the spatial dimension a concreteness that the temporal dimension lacks. Somehow, for most of us, time seems to shrink and expand more easily than space. Time more easily seems and is described as shorter or longer than space even though we have to use these spatial words to describe the temporal interval. Extreme expansion of time—or the contraction of the history of a *lifetime* to fit the experienced expanding moment—may be described in retrospect by the individual who has faced mortal danger. Clearly, the priority of a spatial over a temporal reality anchor did not exist for my patient whose earth was shrinking, nor for other patients with whom I have worked. Gradually, in my efforts to understand the workings of mind, the construction of different realities, time has also assumed a position of priority.

In a psychiatric context the most common reference to the topic of time occurs in the mental-status examination. The patient is or is not oriented in time. Every clinician has encountered patients whose time sense is profoundly disorganized but who have learned how to *pass* mental-status examinations by a variety of techniques, such as looking at the date in a newspaper or asking other patients. Clinicians have also learned techniques to counteract such cheating. The question of the connection between temporal information and meaningful temporal experience surfaces immediately. The limitations of a future-oriented temporal perspective in depressed patients are perhaps the next most common psychiatric references to the topic of time. Analytic contributions, despite some increase in recent years, have been relatively scarce.

The first psychoanalytic panel on *The Experience of Time*, in which I was a participant, was held at a meeting of the American Psychoanalytic Association in New York in 1971. Introducing the panel, Hans Loewald pointed out that Freud experienced frustration in his attempts to deal with the concept of time but that in psychoanalysis as a treatment procedure, as a research method, and as a body of theory, concepts and phenomena related to time are essential. Loewald reminded us just how essential they are:

Memory, forgetting, regression, repetition, anticipation, presentation, representation, the influence on the present of the past in terms of thought, feeling, and behavior; delay of gratification, sleep-wakefulness rhythms, variations and abnormalities in the sense of elapsed time; the so-called timelessness of the id; values, standards, ideals as future-oriented categories; concepts such as object constancy and self identity—all these are central in our work. Add to this the consideration of time in the psychoanalytic process, such as schedules and the ending of hours. Furthermore, psychoanalysis is unthinkable without the theory of evolution and ontogenesis of mental development. . . . Fixation, delays, detours, arrests, and developmental spurts are major factors in shaping mental life and its disturbances. Emotional reworking of developmental factors in the present leads to more harmonious, less disturbed integration of personality and thus, to some degree, to mastery over the shape of the present and of the future . . . .

How is time—objectively measured by clocks as duration— subjectively experienced? What distortions of objective world-time do we observe; how can we understand and explain them? Phenomena such as *déjà vu*, screen memories, amnesias, contractions of time in dreams and fantasies, fall under the rubric of time experience and its variations. . . . Symbolic meanings of time play a role in mental life; how do such meanings intermesh with the development of the concept of time as duration and succession of events in physical time-space? What determines the rise of this time concept in secondary-process ideation? . . . Time can be seen in terms of reciprocal relations of past, present, and future as active modes of psychic life. In our psychoanalytic work, we discover the interaction and relation between these three temporal modes of psychic activity in the play of transference, in the impact on the present of conscious and unconscious remembering and anticipating. (Reported in Kafka, 1972, pp. 650-51)

Initially I will discuss four time-related clinical topics, some briefly and some more extensively: (1) gross temporal disorientation, (2) interpersonal timing, (3) psychoanalytic restructuring of past experience, and (4) temporal perspective.

Gross Temporal Disorientation

Gross temporal disorientation is widely recognized and discussed in the psychiatric literature. We are all sufficiently familiar with some degree of disorientation in our lives that we can appreciate some aspects of massive disorientation. Although we maintain some temporal orientation in ordinary sleep, the time lost under anesthesia has a more disorienting effect. Boring's courageous early research on temporal orientation perhaps deserves special mention (Boring, 1933). He awakened farmers in a quiet rural area and asked them what time it was. Then he identified himself as a researcher and inquired what cues they had used to make the temporal judgments. The sensation of fullness in the bladder was one of the major cues. Thus Boring learned that *coming to one's senses*, as the term applies to time sense (temporal orientation), involves taking an inventory in which the assessment of bodily pressures, needs, and appetites apparently plays a prominent role.

That most of us seldom have to live with temporal diurnal disorientation is attested to by the fact that we are usually successful in setting our internal alarm. In the evening we decide when we wish to wake up and are often able to do so without the help of clocks. Similarly, if at times we feel much older or younger than we are, we *know* that we feel older or younger. Contrast this with certain disoriented patients, who have to live like actors in that they never know which parts of their lives they will have to incorporate into the roles they are asked to play. They resemble Billy Pilgrim, the central character in Kurt Vonnegut's novel *Slaughterhouse-Five* (1969).

> Listen: Billy Pilgrim has come unstuck in time. Billy has gone to sleep a senile widower and awakened on his wedding day. He has walked through a door in 1955 and come out another one in 1941. He has gone back through that door to find himself in 1963. He has seen his birth and death many times, he says, and pays random visits to all the events in between. He says. Billy is spastic in time, has no control over where he is going next, and the trips aren't necessarily fun. He is in a constant state of stage fright, he says, because he never knows what part of his life he is going to have to act in next. (p. 20)

The term *actor* is particularly apt, since some patients learn to act quite well. Many learn to act as though they were much less confused than they actually are. The intermittent moments of knowledge about their confusion lead to skillful defensive maneuvers. The only way they can be one up on the psychiatrist is to take advantage of the fact that sometimes they know better than he when they are *off*. I am getting ahead of my story, however, a story connected with the theory that the movements in and out of psychosis are much more rapid than is generally believed. But let us now move from psychotic disorientation to a brief look at nonpsychotic daily life.

Interpersonal Timing

In the give-and-take of ordinary conversations, the timing of speech and gestures is determined in part by the speaker's assessment of the characteristics of the listener and by a complex network of mutual expectations. The better I know my friend, the more accurately I can assess his mood, his interest in a topic, his appreciation of the levels to which I carry the consideration of the topic, and the many other factors that codetermine not only what I communicate but also the rate and changes of rate of my communications. Feedback—verbal and nonverbal—constantly influences this rate. Certain patterns of unpredictability can have disorienting effects (Kafka, 1957b), and the analyst's silence and his unpredictable breaking of the silence can contribute to the mild disorientation in which temporal restructuring occurs.

Psychoanalytic Restructuring of Past Experience

The fact that the psychoanalyst observes the restructuring of past experience in the present deserves to be in the center of the picture. The analyst is interested in the effects of such restructuring on the experience of time and on temporal perspective and, conversely, in the effects of changes in time experience and perspective on the nature of such reorganization. Some experimental evidence bears on this clinical subject.

In a complex study, Ornstein (1969) demonstrated the retroactive effects of new information on judgment of past duration. His approach can be schematically indicated as follows: Subjects in one experimental group learned a series of apparently random numbers and then were asked how long it took them to learn the series. Subjects in another group learned the same series and then were given a code that transformed what was apparently a random series into an ordered one before being asked how long it took them to learn the series. The subjects who were given the code and whose actual learning period was the same estimated the learning period as shorter than did the subjects who were not given the information that would have permitted them to reorganize—re-code—their experience retrospectively. It is well established that ordered numbers are learned more rapidly than random ones. Subjects given the code that transformed the apparently random series into an ordered one after learning them estimated their learning period as though they had known the ordering code at the time of learning. New information had indeed had a retroactive effect on judgment of past duration.

In an experiment some years ago (Kafka, 1957a), I studied how some persons approached the task of judging the duration of a series of intervals during which they were left—with different sets of instructions—in a darkened room with an autokinetic light. These periods were interspersed with rest intervals in a completely dark room, the duration of which they were also asked to estimate retrospectively. The responses of the experimental subjects were tape-recorded. Typically a particular interval for instance, the second time I was in the dark room—was estimated first and then served as an anchor, as a reference unit, to which the others were compared as being, for instance, a little longer or only about half as long or shorter by a third. The choice of reference intervals seemed to be related to clinically discernible moods and affects since depressively tinged affect seemed to be associated with the choice of dark reference units. This tentative finding would have to be confirmed by a predictive study. In any event, the patterns of time judgments did suggest that some overestimators who used *dark* reference intervals made larger corrections in arriving at estimates of *light* intervals. What does this mean? The individual makes an effort to judge the intervals correctly. He or she selects a *dark* interval as reference unit presumably because of the belief that this interval can be judged more correctly than the others. *Dark* intervals are often overestimated, and this is the case for this individual. By making a larger correction in arriving at estimates of *light* intervals, the experimental subject acts as if he or she knew that the *dark* interval had been overestimated, apparently using self-observation operating below awareness since the conscious decision to select the *dark* reference interval was based on the belief that it could be judged most accurately. The effort to reconcile contrasting and differentially grained experiences of duration can be studied in clinical work as well as in such a setting. (I use the term *grain* as in photographic film—the varying sizes of *now* perhaps representing temporal distance between moments of self-awareness.)

The time-related aspects of the psychoanalytic situation include the following:

1. The patient's analytic hour, his extended time-out (from work, usual activity, usual style of behavior and communicating), is the analyst's extended and relatively usual time-in.

2. The analyst, more than the patient, assumes that contiguity of communication (and of experience) has *possible* meaning implications transcending contiguity as such.

3. The analyst, more than the patient, assumes that the temporal distance of communication (and of experience) does not eliminate the possibility of *meaningful* connection and may even be a *defense* against such connection.

4. The analyst may thus be said to be both a condenser and a dilator of time.

5. Sequence may be translated in the context of clarifications and interpretations as having specific meaning as such. Sequential dream *phrases*, for instance, may be translated into prepositional clauses: dream scene A followed by dream scene B may be interpreted as "*if* A, then B."

6. The analyst, a condenser and dilator of time who attaches unusual meanings to sequences and pays strict attention to the beginning and ending of sessions, yet seems also to live in a different temporal world which he treats *loosely*, may for all these reasons be seen by the patient as dealing with time in a most peculiar way.

7. The patient who finds that some of these peculiar dilating and contracting ways of looking at time are productive and meaningful in furthering insight may—by identification, by other mechanisms, or by cognitive processes—learn to utilize them in looking at his own temporal experience.

8. The stage may thus be set for reorganization or, in the language of experimentalists, for recoding of time experience.

Despite the use of the word *coding*, however, the following brief clinical illustration deals with *time feeling* rather than with even a subjective *time image*—in analogy to the distinction between Federn's "bodily ego feeling" (1952) and Schilder's "body image" (1950). The analyst's sensitivity to the patient's changing experiences of duration can facilitate clinical work because of the intimate connection of subjective time experience and affective life.

Mr. Brown, a professional man who had been raised by adoptive parents, lived alternately with his mistress and his wife during the course of his analysis. In one analytic session, when he had been living for a prolonged period with his wife, he spoke of his feeling of progress in his analytic work but also spoke at length of his difficulty in *seeing himself* during his most recent prolonged period with his mistress, which had terminated almost two years previously. After the analyst commented that he had seemed more different from hour to hour during that period than he did now, the patient gradually began to describe his feeling that periods spent with his mistress had a different time texture from periods spent with his wife and children. Although his description of people, situations, and feelings was complex, his focus was on the struggle to re-experience and reintegrate his time-out, his discontinuity of experience, his effort to *see* himself both in more constant times and in saccadic periods of rapid mood changes. He then talked about the eventual termination of the analysis, his anticipated joyful and nostalgic feelings. This was followed by talk of his plans to ask his adoptive parents about his biologic parents, whom he believed they knew. Historical details that he had never mentioned before about his adoptive parents began to come out, and fantasies about his biologic parents as well. He then said that there might be a connection between characteristics of his mistress and of his fantasied parents. In the next session, in the context of expressing fears about what he might discover concerning his origins and how he would react to the discoveries—and in the context of talking about plans, wishes, and fears for his future—he reported a dream of being in a corner room from which one could see in two directions.

Connecting events and feelings differently—in a sense, therefore, bringing new information to bear on episodes re-experienced during psychoanalysis—permits a reorganization and reinterpretation of time feeling. Experiments dealing with the effects of new information on time experience may be somewhat analogous to this aspect of clinical development. In a metaphorical representation of the process, I visualize a rod traversing many layers of fluid with different angles of refraction; the psychoanalytic restructuring functions as if it were stirring up and intermixing these layers. In that way, the treatment may enhance the patient's sense of continuity and facilitate the widening and future extension of temporal perspective.

Temporal Perspective

I have addressed the problem of temporal perspective in work on the clinical use of autobiographical projections into the future, or future autobiographies (Kafka and Bolgar, 1949). We modified a technique used by Israeli (1936) so as to adapt it for use as a projective technique for veterans—psychiatric patients who had previously been exposed to so much testing that diminishing returns had set in when conventional evaluative procedures were used. When it became important to evaluate the clinical status of such test-sophisticated and test-weary individuals, we asked them to make future projections, using the following instructions: *This is a day in [five years hence]. Describe the course of your day.*

After the task was completed, we asked our patients to again place themselves five years in the future and list the major events of their lives going backward from that future date. With this second step we wanted to investigate whether or not there was a continuity from imagined future through actual past in such a projected retrospective view. In my refraction metaphor, one can visualize the rod as traversing fluid layers representing future, present, and past. If the layers have fixed viscosities and are not intermixed, differential refraction will produce apparent angles in the rod, whereas a degree of mixing or amalgamation will make the rod appear straight. If affective components differentially alter *reality testing* of future projection, current experience, and memories of the past, these different *viscosities* will be revealed. The second step in the procedure thus supplemented the information obtained in the first.

Our patients were given the two instructions of the future autobiography (FA) procedure in a face-to-face situation, and there was some
pressure to respond rapidly. Under these circumstances it became clear
that at first wishes and/or fears were prominent. The shift to an assessment of what was realistically possible or likely was impossible for some,
difficult for others, and less difficult for still others; the difficulty varied
in different areas of life—for instance, in work, marriage, and parenting.
We found it convenient to use the following three points of reference:

1.   To what extent is the future structured?
2.   To what extent are reality factors taken into consideration?
3.   What is the specific content and what are the significant emphases
     and/or omissions of the FA (future autobiography)?

Light was thrown on point 1 primarily by the difficulty the subject had
in performing the tasks. The degree of difficulty was reflected by the
subject's productivity, the variety of content, comments about the task,
hesitations, blushing, perspiring, and sometimes discrepancies in content in the two forms of the FA.

Occasionally a subject finds it almost impossible even to grasp the
idea of future. One severely depressed patient misunderstood the instructions repeatedly and proceeded to write about events five years
before rather than five years hence. In general we confirmed the frequently reported observation that turning toward the future is an
especially difficult task for depressed subjects. We also noted a con-
striction of the temporal field, both future and past, in some patients
with recent traumatic experiences.

Information on point 2, the consideration of reality factors, came
mostly from the clinician's evaluation of the FA in the light of all other
information about the subject. When, for instance, an adult subject with
meager educational background and rather modest intellectual endow-
ment saw himself as studying brain surgery five years hence, we thought
we were justified in speaking of some disregard of reality factors.

The approach to the content analysis—point 3—was not essentially
different from that used in the analysis of other projective material. The

relative amounts of detail employed to describe different elements of the subject's future life were especially noteworthy. A single young woman, for example, gave a detailed description of her future son, including his behavior, his name, and his face, voice, and hair color. The only specific mention of a husband, however, occurred in the following sentence: "My husband is in the bathroom already, and now I am making breakfast, listening to my son's early morning discoveries, and seeing if he is getting dressed for nursery school."

In some FAs all people are anonymous, but in some that are rich in detail and full of real people, it is interesting to note the devices used by subjects to avoid facing those living people and some of the problems associated with them. Displacement of emphasis is perhaps the most subtle and flexible of such devices. It is as if unstructured, confused areas, holes, or blank faces were left in the otherwise well-completed structure of the individual's future. Murray (1938) has expressed well the relationship between the *enduring purpose* and the resolved conflict. The less the conflicts are resolved, the less one should expect synthesis and creative integration in future autobiographies. In any such procedure, the areas, or themas as Murray called them, that are the least integrated— that is, in which enduring purposes are relatively absent—can be expected to be related to unresolved conflicts. In our work with the FA, anxiety and evasion, but also extremely optimistic statements—especially when the subject could not justify his optimism—pointed toward such unresolved conflicts. When a subject described in his FA how good he felt (five years in the future) about one area in his life (for example, his work) without giving any details about it, invariably we found that this area represented a most severe problem at the present time.

The depressed subject mentioned above who repeatedly misunderstood the instruction finally wrote, "I feel as though everything is going fine and I have made something of my life. I like the new position." But he was unable to say what the new position would be and was only able to specify, "I would come in regular dress clothes—not working clothes—wouldn't be real tired out." He spontaneously added later, "I'm afraid that I won't be able to make a living. In five years I'll be ten times as bad as I am now."

In general our observations led us to formulate the following hypotheses:

1. The early reaction to an invitation to formulate a FA is a strongly affective one (either hope or dread).
2. The speed with which the shift to a reasonably realistic description of the future can be accomplished is a function of at least three factors: (a) the relative lack of important unresolved conflicts, (b) the effective functioning level of immediate defenses, and (c) the subject's intelligence.

Toward the end of our study we began to compare the future autobiographies of husbands and wives. Although we did not pursue this procedure systematically, it immediately became apparent that the technique could bring into sharp focus areas of conflict and areas of congruence of expectations. The technique also highlighted differences and similarities in the reality-testing functions of the two spouses.

Although this look at the marital dyad dealt specifically with future perspective, it can illuminate many other time-related matters that are also strikingly important in the psychotherapeutic or psychoanalytic dyad. Among them are the effects of transference developments on interpersonal timing and on temporal disorientation and the confusing sensations when an analytic session seems endless to the analyst and short to the patient, or vice versa. When the termination phase approaches, however, not only is the analysand in touch with his own range of available temporal graining but analyst and analysand also have a subtle mutual understanding of such graining, of the temporal perspective in which it is placed, and of how temporal perspective is reexperienced in a telescoped form in an individual hour. Jaffe (1971) has described how his patient perceived a reconstruction in a series of the analyst's interpretations—in effect, an indication that the analyst anticipated termination, for which the patient said she was not quite ready.

The individual's personal temporal graining, the patterns and textures of the grids that are available to him, organizes the flow of his experiences into object constancies in at least one sense. To the extent, therefore, that the analyst is responsive to his patient's multiple ways of graining experience of time, he is responsive to his patient's multiple realities (Kafka, 1964). Acquaintance and reacquaintance with the possibilities of shared rhythms of organizing experience contribute to the analysand's exploration and development of individual variations of common rhythms and realities. Perhaps some congruence between the analyst's and the patient's future perspectives, at least in terms of the *possibilities* of the analysand's future, is also achieved at this point.

Thus, in the study of temporal experience, the clinician and the experimenter discover that their findings are applicable to each other's world. I will develop the concept of *temporal graining of realities* at greater length after other theoretical, experimental, and clinical aspects of the encompassing concept of *multiple realities* have been examined more closely.

Chapter 2

Thinking and the Constant Objects: The Double Bind Upended

In everyday usage people tend to speak as if there were one universally recognized commonsense reality. But at the same time most of us are aware not only that different individuals have different perceptions of reality but also that our own perception of reality can change with the passage of time and in varying environments. Modern physical science has gone further in recognizing such variable perceptions and has found the idea of a commonsense reality inadequate to its tasks, as illustrated by the realities dealt with by quantum and wave theory. In the field of psychiatry and psychoanalysis, the limitations of the concept of one commonsense reality are so striking that therapists must approach the problems emerging from their encounter with multiple realities from every available direction. Although I will emphasize the practical clinical and technical applications of a concept of multiple realities, the formal logical considerations cannot be ignored.

The psychiatric patient's psychological reality at any one moment is a particular pattern of organization of stimuli, and such patterns are in constant flux. Nevertheless, psychiatrists and psychoanalysts apply a concept of reality testing in which the reality is the commonsense reality of stable objects, of objects and people with a considerable degree of rigid identity. Although this identity is a building block of common sense, psychiatrists—using their own common sense—are constantly faced with the problem of comprehending the apparent lack of a sense of rigid identity in their patients.

In approaching this problem, *comprehending*, or *encompassing*, should be differentiated from *understanding*. We may learn to understand a mathematical formula containing the negative of a square root, but most of us, most of the time, will not be able to comprehend it.[2] To comprehend, or encompass, something means that it becomes part of our experience. This means that we must feel it, but it cannot be the total of our felt experience. We must grasp it by means of something that is bigger than the object to be grasped. To comprehend, encompass, the problem of identity in psychiatry—the identity of the self, the identity of other persons, and the identity of objects—we must use a conceptual tool that is wider than the concept of identity. Even to describe the development of a reality based on some constancy, we need a concept dealing with the organization of stimuli, a concept that does not take identity for granted.

Artiss (1962, p. 140) and Arieti (1963) are among the authors who have dealt with this problem. Artiss describes how the child permits his parents to define reality for him by granting them the "naming prerogative." To present this concept, Artiss uses the device of a hypothetical argument between parent and child. The child questions the authority of the parents to give him a name. If the child refused to grant his parents the prerogative to name him John Doe, he would, for instance, be able to say, "I'm Jesus," and then the "schizophrenic analogue would have already appeared." Although designed to illustrate identity formation, Artiss's hypothetical argument between parents and child is a formal

---

[2] It is my private belief, which is not essential to the theme being developed here, that the march of science is from understanding to comprehending. This belief is related to the observation that theoretically derived mathematical formulae often soon find practical scientific applications in the world of experience. My belief may also be related to the great interest that some schizophrenic patients show in new scientific developments. For example, for some delusional patients who see themselves as observed from a distance, the invention of television has served as a kind of proof that they are not so crazy after all. I also believe that each new scientific invention may induce hope in some patients, that their "wider reality" will be less derogated.

device particularly dependent on the rigid identity of words precisely because it is an argument. In an example from my own experience, Mary, an adult patient who literally struggled with the problem of the naming prerogative, had had severe generalized dermatitis during the language-learning period, which had hampered the integration of language with body experience (this patient will be discussed in more detail later). The conceptual framework I am developing here, building on such examples, uses the fluidity of perception more than the rigid identity of the word.

Arieti, in discussing schizophrenic thought processes, quotes Von Domarus's principle, which states: "Whereas the normal person accepts identity only upon the basis of identical subjects, the schizophrenic may accept identity based on identical predicates." Arieti writes, "If ... a schizophrenic happens to think, 'The Virgin Mary was a virgin, I am a virgin,' she may conclude 'I am the Virgin Mary.' . . . For normal persons a class is a collection of objects to which a concept applies. ... In paleological thinking ... a class is a collection of objects which have a predicate or part in common" (p. 59). Arieti, however, fails to point out in this context that what is part and what is whole, what is subject and what is predicate, are not building blocks of experience but are themselves the results of experience. When a patient has experienced a *characteristic* of a person as being more fundamental, more lasting, more "identical," than the person as a whole, this characteristic acquires qualities of the *subject*, and the person, then merely a personification of the more stable idea, acquires qualities of the *predicate*.

For example, Dorothy L., a highly intelligent schizophrenic patient (also to be discussed later) who was in remission, told me that during her recent psychotic episode a nurse with a foreign accent and blonde hair had seemed to her to be the literary character Heidi. After many years of work with me, the patient was able to communicate that because she had loved the book *Heidi*. Heidi-like characteristics were much more important and more stable to her than a person's identity as a whole. She experienced neither herself nor anyone else as having any continuity of existence, any identity as a person, at that time. The idea or feeling of "Heidiness" did have some continuity. What is subject here and what is predicate? Such accounts have led me to think that a technically more useful term than "feeling of identity" is "subjective equivalence over a period of time." "Subjective equivalence" refers to Heinrich Klüver's "method of equivalent stimuli" (1933).

Klüver observed that the increasing refinement of experiments in comparative psychology led to the decreasing psychological significance of the findings. A traditional approach in comparative psychology would be to study the smallest difference between two stimuli to which an organism can respond. What is the smallest difference in grayness, for instance, that the animal can perceive? Klüver felt that the more experiments of this kind were freed from "interfering" factors, the more they approached physiological experiments, perhaps ultimately the study of the biochemistry of the end organs. When experimental refinement reduced the significance of the findings, Klüver then thought it would be more meaningful to study how *great* the difference between stimuli could be before the animal would fail to recognize similarities. Let us say, for example, that an animal is trained to jump for food and to select the square when confronted with a large black square and a small red circle, both on a white background. If we now present the animal with the same foreground figures on a blue background, will he still jump for food and select the square? Is the situation subjectively equivalent? The answer cannot be taken for granted, but if it is affirmative, we might further complicate the situation by confronting the animal with the red circle and a large black oval instead of a square. In that way we could test the range of subjectively equivalent stimuli for the animal trained originally to jump in response to a large black square on a white ground.

It can easily be seen that on the one hand this kind of experiment is related to tests of abstract reasoning, and that on the other it is related to the problem of object constancy, as the term is used in general psychology. As I shall demonstrate, it also contributes to the psychoanalytic meaning of the concept. In general psychology, object constancy refers to the phenomenon whereby a table, say, seen from different angles, with their different retinal images, remains the same table for a normal person. Subjective equivalence is thus related to the identity of the objects. The patterns of subjective equivalence for any person are, of course, largely determined by emotional and motivational factors. It is thus conceptually possible that at a particular time I will see my neighbor as more subjectively equivalent to my current self-perception than my own memory of how I was yesterday. In such a situation, one can talk of identity fusion with the neighbor. For anyone working with psychotic patients, these are not far-fetched conceptualizations. In the context of these considerations, a feeling of identity can be described in terms of the experience of subjective equivalence of ego states over a period of time. (I am here referring to ego states as though we were dealing with particulate units, in a sense "quanta," and not, in this context, as transitional "wave" phenomena.) The concept of subjective equivalence is not foreign to the usual frame of reference in dynamic psychiatry. For example, the coalescence of "the good mother" and "the bad mother" into "mother" might be regarded as the establishment of a subjective equivalence. The concept can also be applied to the idea of "transference."

To summarize thus far: commonsense reality and commonsense logic, which have limits in everyday life and are inadequate in physical science, are even more inadequate in psychiatry. Commonsense logic is based on the principle of identity. We cannot "comprehend" the concept of the feeling of identity using a conceptual tool smaller than, not encompassing, what is to be "grasped." Psychological reality for a person at any one time is a pattern of organization of stimuli and can be described in terms of a pattern of subjective equivalences. The advantages of this descriptive concept are twofold. First, subjective equivalence is an operational concept that permits a bridge from psychiatry to other behavioral sciences. It leaves room for information obtained by the usual psychodynamic approaches—such as the fusion of "good" and "bad" mother into "mother." But the pattern of equivalences can be studied in terms of many theoretical approaches, such as imprinting, conditioning, the views of Piaget. and so forth. Second, the concept has a wide scope of applicability, ranging from problems of abstract thinking to those of subjective identity and object constancy. It thus allows a rational approach to the paradoxical thoughts and contradictory perceptions that are demonstrated with clinical examples).

Although no one pattern of subjective equivalences is in and of itself any more valid, true, or real than any other pattern (just as Euclidean geometry is no more valid than any other geometry), the parents of the nonpsychotic child have succeeded in giving more weight to one pattern of subjective equivalences than to the multiplicity of other possible patterns. A solid anchor in one reality coexisting with an ability to encompass many realities, even paradoxical patterns of subjective equivalences, could be described in terms of the ability to "regress in the service of the ego."[3]

Let us now consider the implications for work in psychiatry of such a relativistic view of psychological reality. Much attention has been paid to the psychiatrist's culturally determined value system and the effects of his value orientation on his work. The values generally considered are in the traditional area of ethics; routine value judgment in favor of "commonsense-identity logic" is not made explicit. But patients are as sensitive to value judgments concerning formal aspects of their thought as they arc to derogatory value judgments concerning their feelings and aspirations. As I indicated, specific technical applications of the concepts refer to the place of paradox in psychotherapy and therapeutic management. The recognition that some significant therapeutic steps involve, in *retrospect*, a paradox should not be mistaken for advocacy of contrived irrationality. I might here compare the therapist in the treatment situation to the chief of a clan or a head of state. Just as a clan chief or national leader often holds his position because more realities are acceptable to him than to those he leads, the therapist can be of help to the patient because of his wider perspective on possible realities.

The idea of wider reality is implicitly present in the classical psychoanalytic attitude of free-floating attention. The history of psychotherapeutic approaches to psychotic patients shares an evolution from a narrower to a

---

[3] It could also be discussed in terms of the child's acceptance of contradiction, as opposed to his malignant vulnerability to a double-hind situation, in which he reacts to contradictory injunctions by denying their existence. I believe that this denial of contradiction changes the mere expression of ambivalence into a true double bind. I shall say more about this later.

wider stance. Paul Federn advocated different therapists for the same patient in the regressed and compensated phases of his illness (1952). My conversations with several clinicians who have worked with Frieda Fromm-Reichmann revealed that her interest in id contacts between therapist and psychotic patient changed to an emphasis on ego contacts, contact with the intact or mature areas. More recent developments in psychoanalytically oriented treatment centers, conceptualized only in retrospect, show a gradual diminution of such "either-or" attitudes. The therapist who may have joined the patient in deeply regressive material in one hour may the same day participate with the same patient in a matter-of-fact discussion about the work program in an all-hospital meeting. In a dynamically oriented hospital, a therapist may even see a patient in a wet-sheet pack on one day and invite him to a meal outside the hospital the next day. The therapist's ability to reject stereotyped notions about incongruity may be a potent therapeutic factor.

The following are examples of shifts in experienced reality—examples of apparently paradoxical situations, collected in work with hospitalized patients.

A woman who had made considerable social improvement requested a change to outpatient status. The request was refused because the social improvement was interpreted as a calculated facade and because such a move might be utilized as a distancing maneuver. The patient pointed out that her ability to *calculate* her behavior was, after her wildly psychotic period, a sign of improvement that should lead to outpatient status. The therapist recognized the existence of a paradox but did not change his position. The same patient soon thereafter made a perceptive report to the administrator about happenings on the ward during the weekend. Upon hearing the report, a nurse said to the administrator, "Why don't you make her a staff member?" The administrator thought the suggestion had merit, and the possibility was seriously considered that a patient for whom outpatient status had just been refused should be paid to work as an aide in the *patient* work program. This represents, I believe, a true shift in reality. At the moment when the administrator agreed to give the patient a job as an aide, he perceived her, and she perceived herself, in a different "reality." The patient's experience should not be confused with Alexander's "corrective emotional experience," which is based on conscious role playing. The notions developed here may be useful in conceptualizing the multiplicity of roles in any hospital program in which patients not only help other patients but may even assume positions of responsibility for each other (Kafka, 1964).

In another example of the retrospective shift, Mary had for years used self-mutilation as a blackmail technique. After one of several symptom-free periods, she requested outpatient status because, she said, continued living with disturbed patients might lead to recurrence of her symptom. The therapist supported the patient's request, but the administrator said, "No, it's the same old blackmail." The reality, however, had changed: the therapist, who recognized the patient's new self-perception, no longer saw such a request as blackmail.

The last example supplies a developmental analogy: when a mother permits her baby to take the first step, she does not "overcome her fear," she does not "accept the possibility" of the baby's fall. Rather, for a moment the reality for mother and baby must be that he is not going to fall, a wider reality that to the bystander looks like a delusion or a *folie à deux*. We are here, I believe, dealing with the primary paradox of individuation, the symbiosis that permits the child to step away from its mother, when love and mutual acceptance of separateness become subjectively equivalent.

Multiple Reality and Double-Bind Theory

Being anchored in one reality while retaining the ability to encompass many reality organizations is obviously related to the problems of interest to double-bind theorists. In contrast to such theorists, who have argued that exposures to multiple and contradictory injunctions or realities tend to be pathogenic, I have been impressed by the positive, "healthy" aspects of the ability to tolerate different reality organizations. Nevertheless, double-bind theory seemed a promising approach to difficult problems. In 1964 I was consultant to a project at the National Institute of Mental Health in which characteristics of newlywed or about to-be-wed couples were being studied. The study was *prospective* in that it assessed the potential influence of characteristics of the couples on such future traits of their children as psychological health and the nature of pathology. Before beginning the study, we asked ourselves what characteristics of the prospective parents should be investigated in a project designed to circumvent the usual vicissitudes of retrospective genetic reconstructions. We concluded that a hypothesis and research design based on *formal* characteristics of communication patterns would be easier to manage than a hypothesis deriving from the infinite number of possible kinds of content. Double-bind theory offered such a formal hypothesis and seemed to deserve closer scrutiny.

The paradoxical communication that is a primary element of double-bind theory is related to the more general topic of ambiguity. A number of separate clinical and theoretical projects can be profitably considered under the heading of ambiguity, especially its positive aspects—that is, the significance of the hunger for and tolerance of ambiguity. The formal definition of ambiguity can help us understand its implications and the nature of paradoxical communication. Although in everyday language, information is often said to be ambiguous when it is conflictual, in the language of formal logic, information is ambiguous only when the conflicting data are of different "logical types"—that is, are on different levels of abstraction. Formally, ambiguity is an abbreviation of the expression "ambiguity of types" or—more completely—"ambiguity of logical types." A *paradoxical* communication can always be shown to consist of conflicting data that are on different levels of abstraction. Although psychologically we associate ambiguity with uncertainty more than with paradox, ambiguous and paradoxical communications are logically synonymous.

The aspects of double-bind theory that have been best developed formally emphasize that *overexposure* to paradoxical communication is pathogenic or, more specifically, schizophreno-genic. Since my own clinical observation suggested that the unavoidable exposure to ambiguous situations in daily life was less tolerable, more "dissociative," and more "uncanny" for those who had early *underexposure* to paradoxical communications, I found myself in apparent opposition to the main tenet of double-bind theory. Furthermore, underexposure of the offspring to ambiguity during crucial developmental phases seemed related to parental fear of paradox. Although double-bind theorists also refer to "therapeutic double binds," those are *formally* similar to the pathogenic variety. They are described as occurring in a more benevolent interpersonal atmosphere, but their formal similarity creates conceptual difficulties that constitute an obstacle to the research application of the theory.

If it had indeed been possible to identify pathogenic double-bind communications on the basis of formal characteristics alone, it would have been relatively easy to locate young parents who have a tendency to communicate in this fashion, and their offspring could have been contrasted later with those of parents not prone to issue such double-bind messages. Difficulties encountered in other objective studies using the double-bind concept have been reviewed by Olson (1969). Our own difficulties in identifying "pathogenic double-binders" were related to (1) the problem of discriminating between benevolent, "therapeutic" binds and pathogenic binds, (2) the ubiquity of paradox (for instance, wives asking husbands to be spontaneously more affectionate [Ryder 1970]), (3) the observation that in human communication the level of abstraction is in constant flux, and (4) the finding that shifts in levels of abstraction could probably not be differentiated from shifts in role relationship. Double-bind theory thus was not directly useful for the intended research design. Nevertheless, the analysis of the difficulties and a critical examination of the theory contributed to a reformulation of ideas concerning paradoxical parental communication.

Critical Evaluation of Double-Bind Theory

Double-bind theory states that a history of exposure to inescapable communication traps is schizophrenogenic, and it attempts to explain the patient's feeling of being trapped, an experience to which the therapist has easy empathic access. Bateson et al. (1956) give recognizable examples, such as that of a young man who had fairly well recovered from an acute schizophrenic episode and was visited in the hospital by his mother. Glad to see her, he impulsively put his arm around her shoulders, but she stiffened. When he withdrew his arm, she asked,

"Don't you love me any more?" In response he blushed, at which point she told him not to be so easily embarrassed and afraid of his feelings. The patient had received the messages that he must and that he must not show his affection to his mother in order to keep his ties with her. Impressed by and sensitized to such impossible, no-win situations, the clinician seems to encounter them everywhere. The father of Susan, a schizophrenic girl, for instance, had made major changes in his career as a clergyman in order to pay for her treatment in a private hospital. Despite a recent heart attack, he had left his pulpit and had become a hard-driving, nationally prominent lecturer and author. During a visit to the hospital he explained both to his daughter and to the staff that he owed his newfound energy, the renewal in his life, to the financial needs of her expensive hospitalization. One could say, on the basis of these data, that the patient was caught in a double bind. If she made successful efforts to recover rapidly, she might deprive her father of the reported source of renewal in his life. If she failed to improve sufficiently to be discharged from the hospital, the associated financial need might impose a "killing" work load on father. On the face of it, she was in a no-win situation.

A similar trap apparently characterized the following case. Bernard, the musically talented son of a conductor, had received communications from his family throughout his early life to the effect that the only truly valuable lifetime activity was to be a musician. At the same time he had been told again and again about tragedies associated with sons of musicians who had attempted to follow in their fathers' footsteps. He was told that in such a situation, the competitive effort was destructive not only to the son but also to the family name, to the father's name. Despite his fervently expressed wish for musical training, it was withheld from him in the musically saturated household. At the age of six or seven, he developed a peculiar mannerism of running to his father, making a "staccato" contact, briefly throwing his arms around him, and then running away from him as fast as he could. Prominent features of the clinical picture were extreme vacillation from notions of grandeur to feelings of abject worthlessness, a fractionation of self-representation, and a general ideational lack of continuity.

I will later amplify this and other case material, but for now these examples show that the "damned if you do, damned if you don't" situation described by double-bind theory offers a seductively elegant and immediately plausible framework in which to place clinical observations. As an example of a therapeutic double bind, Bateson et al. cited an episode from a case treated by Frieda Fromm-Reichmann (later fictionalized in *I Never Promised You a Rose Garden* by "Hannah Green"). At one point the patient informed the therapist of her delusional god. The therapist responded that she did not believe in this god and then instructed the patient to ask her delusional god for permission to work in therapy with the doctor. The therapist thus had her patient in a therapeutic double bind. If the patient was made to doubt the existence of her god, then she would be agreeing with Fromm-Reichmann and admitting her attachment to therapy. If she insisted that the god was real and asked his permission to work in therapy, then she would be implying that Fromm-Reichmann was "more powerful" than he—again admitting her involvement with the therapist.

Like the pathogenic double bind, the therapeutic one is formed by conflicting information involving a shift in the level of abstraction. As I indicated above, the similarity of the formally defined features of therapeutic and pathogenic binds greatly complicates attempts to identify them differentially for research purposes in the study of actual communication sequences. This is especially true *if one conceives of and looks for paradoxes that may "promote individuation"*—and in this sense could perhaps be called therapeutic—*in nontherapy situations.* Bateson and his coworkers, however, focus on the role they ascribe to the double bind in the etiology of schizophrenia when they indicate the necessary ingredients for a double-bind situation: (1) two or more persons, (2) repeated experience, (3) a primary negative injunction, (4) a secondary injunction conflicting with the first at a more abstract level and, like the first, enforced by punishment or signals that threaten survival, and (5) a tertiary negative injunction prohibiting the victim from escaping from the field.

What most specifically, pointedly, and interestingly distinguishes this from other conflict theories is the focus on the shift in the level of abstraction. Such qualitatively different conflicts are paradoxes. How does a paradox, a term synonymous with "ambiguity of type," differ from a contradiction? Watzlawick et al. (1967) illustrate a contradiction by a stop sign to which is nailed another sign reading "no stopping at any time." In this *contradictory* situation one has the *choice* of obeying one or the other of the two injunctions. Correspondingly, if a father tells his son not to tattletale and also asks him how his younger sister got into trouble, the father is making *contradictory* requests. Presumably, the son can *choose* which injunction to obey. The role relationship between father and son in the context of the "no tattletale" injunction, however, is different from their role relationship in the context of the request for information about the sister. The latter request may carry the implication "Son, in this particular situation, you are seen as more like an adult, like me, and you should help me protect and educate a child." Questions of such possible shifts in levels of abstraction raise doubts about the existence of "pure" contradictions in ordinary communication. This is another factor complicating the identification of paradoxes, as opposed to contradictions, when communication sequences are analyzed for research purposes.

Watzlawick et al. formally illustrate a paradox by a photograph of an overpass spanning a roadbed. On the overpass is a sign saying, "Ignore this sign." This sign, presumably a practical joke, is formally not contradictory, but it creates a true paradox through its self-reflexivity. In order to ignore it, one must notice it. But the very act of noticing it disobeys the injunction itself. Therefore, the sign can be obeyed only through disobedience. The nature of such paradoxes was studied by Whitehead and Russell (1910). Russell's theory of types observes that paradoxes involve different levels of abstraction that are not immediately apparent. The "Ignore this sign" paradox, for instance, contains such a hidden shift since the *word* "sign" and the *material sign* on which the word is written involve different levels of abstraction. Whitehead and Russell would say that in the preceding sentence I have made explicit the hidden shift in "logical types"—I have communicated about the paradoxical communication; that is, I have "metacommunicated" and have thus *escaped* the paradox. This aspect of a formal logical approach to paradoxes is relevant to double-bind theory, which postulates that someone who is inundated by paradoxical parental communications, coupled with taboos against "metacommunicating," is at greater risk for schizophrenia. Another aspect of Whitehead and Russell's work is even more congruent with the reformulation I am proposing, as I shall demonstrate.

Reformulation of Ideas on Parental Paradoxical Communication: Formal Basis

My reformulation focuses on the effects of relative parental *avoidance* of expression of paradox and of poor parental tolerance of ambiguity. These effects are experiences of *dissonance* for the developing offspring, who inevitably is confronted by other experiential data that are ambiguous and full of paradox and that somehow have to be included in his "reality." In contrast, parental *tolerance* of the irreconcilable paradoxes that the child must encounter in his educational and playful exploration of his expanding world help him to cope with those paradoxes. The parents' casual reactions to phenomena that everyone is compelled both to notice and not to notice can help with the child's gradual integration of parental realities and his own evolving formulations of realities. Such integration also helps the child relate to his parents as positive objects, in the psychoanalytic sense of the word, at the same time that it makes possible a necessary degree of accommodation to the paradoxical systems that are to represent reality.

Although this thesis is primarily derived from and will be supported by clinical observations, the following brief additional excursion into modern formal logic reveals forcefully a congruent theme.

Bateson et al. focused on Russell's techniques for *escaping* paradoxes, but Whitehead and Russell recommend the use of their escape technique only *after* one has been caught in a trap. They specifically warn, however, against too much caution about avoiding traps. They point out that reasoning would have to come to a standstill if rigorous attempts were made to avoid the *possibility* of paradox even in the most formal logical chain. Specifically, they talk of the *necessity* of ambiguity of types in order to make a chain of reasoning apply to any of an infinite number of cases, which would not be possible if one were to avoid using typically ambiguous words and symbols. Thus, even the classical syllogism contains some "ambiguity of types." For example, let us consider the syllogism "All men are mortal. Socrates is a man. Therefore, Socrates is mortal." Not quite so, Russell would say: we do not know that Socrates is mortal until he is dead.

In arguing for the necessity for ambiguity, Whitehead and Russell do not present formal proofs. Kurt Gödel (1931), however, has gone beyond them by proving *formally* the necessary incompleteness of a finite system. What Gödel formally proved is that "if arithmetic is consistent, its consistency cannot be established by metamathematical reasoning that can be represented within the formalism of arithmetic." (Nagel and Newman, 1958, p. 7)

Nagel and Newman, who have made Gödel's work accessible to the nonmathematician, point out that his argument does not eliminate the possibility of strictly finitistic proofs that cannot be represented within arithmetic (p. 98). But no one today appears to have a clear idea of what a finitistic proof that is not capable of formulation within arithmetic would be like. What is significant about Gödel's work in connection with my proposed reformulation is his demonstration that one has to jump to ever more inclusive levels of abstraction even in formal logical procedures in order to avoid triviality. He thus offers formal support to Whitehead and Russell's more impressionistic warning *not* to avoid the possibility of paradoxes. This is congruent with a clinically based reformulation emphasizing the psychological necessity of appropriate exposure to ambiguity. Gödel's demonstration may also facilitate a sharpening of conceptual focus in this reformulation: the developing individual, who must operate in an *open* system, experiences dissonance for which he has not been prepared when his parents operate and communicate as though a *closed* system were the only one in existence.

While self-consistency in a closed system is associated with triviality in modern logic, analogous reduction to one level of abstraction, in operational terms, is unthinkable in living systems, especially in human experience and communication. The study of our very perceptual process bolsters the idea I presented in the introduction—that with each perception we pass rapidly through various stages and levels of organization. I will later discuss in some detail the tachistoscopic presentation of Rorschach cards (Stein, 1949), which shows that in reacting to such a display we recapitulate our perceptual history. For now, I want to underline that the briefest tachistoscopic exposures result in the most "concrete" responses, resembling those of a child, and longer exposures involve higher levels of abstraction, adult responses.

Thus, as I hinted earlier, a rigorous distinction between contradiction, which involves one level of abstraction, and paradox, which involves more than one level, cannot meaningfully be applied to ordinary human interchanges. A conversation, words spoken and heard, any living communication, can be placed in more than one level of abstraction. Strictly speaking, *any* contradiction is a paradox, but what creates a sharp paradoxical experience—as with the "ignore this sign" sign—is the degree of un-preparedness for the nature of the shift in the levels of abstraction involved.[4]

Psychological "reality" depends on our abstracting level of the moment. Earlier in this chapter, I referred to Klüver's (1933, 1936) study of how great the differences between stimuli can be before a subject fails to recognize similarities. His method determines the limits of *the levels of abstraction* within which there is still *subjective equivalence.* I emphasized that such patterns of subjective equivalence—the patterns of organization, of abstraction—are the very building blocks of our realities, of our patterns of object constancy, as the term is used in both experimental psychological *and* psychoanalytic literature. If one individual's "reality possibilities" are thus tied to the range of his levels of abstraction, his communication to another depends on some degree of correspondence between his and the other's range

---

[4] Certain transitional periods, such as courtship and early marriage. involve considerable shifts—for which one may be poorly prepared—in role relationships and in the levels of abstraction that have to be bridged. If the magnitude of the shifts makes it necessary, semi-ritualized intervention of third parties permits bride and groom to have a discontinuity of experience before they are presented with a "new reality." Some social factors that help bridge experiences of discontinuity have been considered in "Separating and Joining Influences in Courtship and Early Marriage" (Ryder et al., 1971). In a later chapter the place of rituals in shifts in role and in levels of abstraction, and the connection between these shifts, will be more fully explored.

of levels of abstraction. In chapter One, I discussed the timing in ordinary conversation. It is our judgment of the level of abstraction to which any partner in a conversation will carry our words that largely influences this timing (Kafka, 1957b). Searles' (1965) clinical descriptions of disorienting, "crazy"-making patterns of communication imply veritable acrobatics in shifts of levels of abstraction.

We are prepared for some of the distances that can exist between levels of abstraction but not for others. The differences between these kinds of distances are *objectively quantitative*, but they lead to experiences that differ in *subjectively qualitative* ways. Psychologically, shifts in abstraction level for which we are prepared are associated with experiences we may continue to call contradictions; shifts for which we are not prepared are associated with experiences we may continue to call paradoxes. The former are related to *ambivalence* and the latter to a somewhat *uncanny* feeling, a mild form of which we experience when we think of ourselves as trapped (when in a mood in which we cannot quite laugh it off), as by the "ignore this sign" sign.

My use of the terms *ambiguity* and *paradox* in further clinical discussions will reflect these considerations. Mary, the self-mutilator, for instance, who cuts herself to find out whether or not she is alive, is trying to escape from *ambiguity* and not from a simple contradiction, since the distance between the levels of abstraction involved in experiencing "aliveness" and "deadness" is not one for which she is at that moment prepared. I will explore the ambiguity of aliveness and deadness, and its connection to the animate and the inanimate, more thoroughly later.

Reformulation: Clinical Basis

My interest in paradoxical communications and the observation that they were ubiquitous ultimately led me to question their schizophrenogenic role, even in the light of qualifications specified by double-bind theory for their pathogenicity (Kafka, 1971b). In a later chapter, I will deal more systematically with schizophrenic thought disorder, but some comments on related factors are appropriate in the present context.

As I mentioned earlier, on closer analysis of double-bind data, I gained the impression, in opposition to the theory, that there might be a relative *paucity* of ambiguous expression in some families of schizophrenic patients. Ringuette and Kennedy (196b) found that a group of double-bind experts—that is, individuals who had been involved in the development and formulation of the double-bind concept—had a poor interjudge reliability in identifying double binds in letters written by mothers of schizophrenic patients. In my experience, when clinicians tend to agree on the existence of a double bind, they are referring to situations in which patients, and more typically parents of patients, have made striking and bizarre defensive maneuvers when confronted with the paradoxes they had expressed. Compared to random clinical material, the paradoxes themselves are often not particularly unusual; it is the response to confrontation that forces the issue into the therapist's awareness. The letters in the Ringuette and Kennedy study do not permit the clinician to observe such responses to confrontation with paradoxes.

In the example, cited earlier, of the clergyman who communicated to his hospitalized daughter, Susan, and to the staff that her expensive hospitalization was forcing him to adopt a "never more happy" life-style and a pace that was also "killing him," the paradox itself was not so unusual. But the response to confrontation with the paradox—which involved the issue of the clergyman's life or death on one level of abstraction and the quality of his life on another level—was notable. In a late afternoon interview, the family consultant at the hospital made an initial attempt to play back to the father the no-win situation in which his communication was apparently placing his daughter. An appointment was made to explore the matter further the next morning. When the family consultant arrived for the interview, he was given a message saying that the father had unexpectedly had to join his other daughter, who lived in another city, because she had telephoned him about a sudden disturbed and involved relationship with her psychiatrist. Shortly thereafter the family transferred the patient to another hospital, and the father never responded to the family consultant's efforts to communicate with him.

Sometimes intolerance of ambiguity is revealed by the rigidity, tending to the bizarre, with which family myths are maintained. In the earlier example of Bernard, the symphony conductor's son, intensive analytic work with the patient for a decade, plus direct contact with members of his family when the patient was hospitalized, revealed to the therapist the rigidity of several family myths and the extent to which the father was seen as a frozen mythical figure. At first the paradox arising from this situation seemed impressive, for on the one hand the family assigned the only and ultimate value to the grandeur and untouchability of the paternal figure, and on the other hand they reinforced the taboo against emulating it. This paradox is not so unusual, however, if we consider it against the background of the patriarchal culture from which the family came. Attempts by the therapist to discuss with the patient's mother the no-win situation in which her son was placed met with blank stares and total incomprehension. Such a possibility was simply not in the accepted script. When the therapist then tried to approach the matter indirectly, by discussing the lives of various family members, he repeatedly encountered the style of defending the untouchability of the myth, as illustrated by the following example.

The patient's mother was describing how her now-deceased husband had been determined to pursue his own inspired musical career despite the tremendous pressure placed on him by his own family to follow a technical career. With great emphasis, she said that on the same day on which he was supposed to register for a technical course in his hometown he went instead to register at the musical conservatory in the city of X. The therapist, indicating that the clarification of minor matters can sometimes be of importance in connection with therapy, asked if it was possible that he registered a few days later, since the city of X is a great distance from the hometown. "No," she said, again emphatically, "he took a plane so he could do it the same day." Although this supposed event occurred long before the era of commercial aviation, the "same day" of registration was part of the literal and verbatim untouchable family myth and could therefore not be tampered with even if the recital of surrounding circumstances had to be distorted. For that family, mythical structures could not be approached with the playful ambiguity to which they are particularly vulnerable. Herein lies the connecting link between the life-and-death seriousness of the defense of the family myth and the problem of tolerance of ambiguity. The child prepared to deal only with rigid myths is poorly prepared to deal with living beings and live experiences.

In a sense, the timeless rigidity of such a defensively perpetuated mythical being or object is the opposite of the fluidity of play, of the toy, of the transitional object (Smith, 1983; Winnicott, 1958). A lack of preparation for the necessary integration of ambiguous experience was also the common element in the following two cases, which will be reported in more detail in a later chapter. The *uncanniness* that characterized the experiences of a self-mutilator, Mary, and of Anna, a patient who had many déjà vu sensations, could be traced to paradoxical experiences for which they were especially ill prepared.

The term *uncanny* (Freud, 1919) is an appropriate descriptive word for the feelings that Mary conveyed about her state just prior to cutting. Her sense of uncanniness was related to contrasting convictions, both equally strong, that she must somehow be alive but that at the same time she did not feel alive. Cutting was an escape from this intolerable burden of ambiguity.

I have now come to see that she used her own body as a transitional object—transitional in this case between animate and inanimate—and that this was a special case of an attempt to work on what Winnicott calls the "perpetual human task of keeping inner and outer reality separate yet interrelated." Winnicott's development of the theme that a "neutral area of experience which will not be challenged" is important during specific development phases—he says the pattern of transitional phenomena begins to show at somewhere between four and twelve months (p. 232)—is congruent with the theme being developed here. Experience that will "not be challenged," which seems to me to correspond to the tolerance of ambiguity, permits the gradual formation of an attitudinal "membrane" which is egosyntonic to the extent that it has not been prematurely and externally imposed but has been individually established through much active exploratory crossing and recrossing of cultural border territory that is poorly or ambiguously defined. In my work with Mary, I experienced some sadistic feelings that I believe were at times an escape for me from *my* uncanny experiences, which were triggered by my contact with her. These uncanny experiences were related,

I believe, to the patient's "undigested," dissociated transitional states involving the animate versus "inanimate" nature of her own body, to which I shall return later.

Anna, the patient who reported many déjà vu experiences and who came to psychoanalysis in connection with hysterical fugue states, experienced minor repetitions of such states during her sessions. The consistent association of synesthetic and déjà vu phenomena in her case (which will be described later in some detail) led me to develop (Kafka, 1966) the following formulation in an attempt to explain this connection. As a schematic introduction to the idea, imagine that a particular wave pattern on an oscilloscope represents visual, auditory, or tactile stimuli. A responding organism or electronic scanning machine is then asked if this is a familiar *visual* pattern. Obviously, if the response is to the *pattern*, whatever the sensory modality involved, the likelihood that it will be familiar is much increased. That is, a déjà vu or related sensation will be aroused if the pattern of the visual stimulation evokes a corresponding echo in *any* other sensory compartment, be it auditory, tactile, or the like. In other words, if a certain pattern of stimulation, let us say a visual pattern, occurs at a time when the sensory compartments are particularly interwoven, particularly blended, the chances that the pattern will arouse a feeling of familiarity are multiplied.

Schachtel (1947) has eloquently developed the theme that infantile amnesia is related *not* to the content of early infantile experiences but to the fact that the schemata of experience are different from the adult ones. Synesthesia is more characteristic of early experiences, and sensory compartmentalization is more characteristic of later ones. In chapter 3 I will report detailed clinical evidence that the patient who had many déjà vu sensations had experienced premature demands for task-oriented behavior involving sensory compartmentalization at times when playful, "dreamy" synesthetic experience was wished for and would have been more appropriate. I came to conceptualize some of her difficulties as related to insufficient opportunity to cross and recross without challenge the transitional area between synesthesia and sensory compartmentalization.

The experience of uncanniness, of weirdness, of something unearthly or supernatural, is produced when our experience cannot be dismissed—

when it carries conviction, but does not make sense. Two contradictory experiences, both convincing and thus affectively charged, result in the sensation of uncanniness. The uncanny affect of the déjà vu experience ("I just caught myself experiencing something as familiar which I know is not familiar") has a similarity to the slightly uncanny affect one experiences after having been trapped by reading the sign "Ignore this sign." If feelings of uncanniness are understood as occurring when typically ambiguous experiences of about equally convincing strength are present simultaneously, we can see that this condition is met in the déjà vu experience. One doubts one's senses, one has trouble with one's "me-ness." I no longer believe that synesthesia is necessarily involved in déjà vu experiences, but I still believe that some ambiguity—be it sensory blending versus sensory compartmentalization, animate versus inanimate, linear versus nonlinear systems of "causality," or some other source—may be particularly strange and unacceptable to individuals of whom well-compartmentalized behavior was demanded at a time when parents usually fulfill this function and permit the child to indulge without danger in the richness of blending and other ambiguous experiences.

As I shall elaborate later, for the self-mutilator and for the patient with fugue states and déjà vu experiences, therapy involved processes of reacceptance of, or perhaps acceptance of, or more specifically a *learning to be less unfamiliar with*, feelings of estrangement from their usual way of experiencing the world. The fear component of the experience of awe which accompanies the simultaneous sense of familiarity and unfamiliarity is diminished. The uncanny comes to contain less dread. In my work with hospitalized patients (Kafka and McDonald, 1965; Kafka, 1966), the risk that the patient will be removed from treatment by a parent highly intolerant of ambiguity has led me to work with families in ways that combine necessary myth breaking with precautionary measures. These techniques include contact with a large number of family members and the selective joint interviewing of individuals who have avoided being alone with each other (see chapter 6). If, for instance, it is observed that whenever a joint interview of daughter and father is scheduled, one or the other becomes sick, has a pressing business appointment, or finds some other means to cancel the scheduled session, a special effort is made to understand and overcome this avoidance. Such specific resistance often is the door behind which a family myth is hidden.

Comment

Formal and clinical considerations of two kinds of conflicting communication—contradictions, which *theoretically* involve one level of abstraction, and paradoxes or ambiguities, which involve more than one level—have led me to the belief that human experience and interaction always involve more than one level of abstraction. *Subjectively*, people tend to react to conflicting material that involves distances in levels of abstraction for which they are prepared by seeing it as contradictory and associating it with feelings of ambivalence, particularly when the contradictory pulls are of approximately equal strength. Conflicting material involving distances in levels of abstraction for which people are prepared are seen as paradoxical or ambiguous and are associated with experiences of dissonance, of uncanniness, various degrees of loss of feelings of "me-ness," or depersonalization—particularly when the conflicting data are of approximately equal strength (as in déjà vu).

All human living involves considerable paradoxical experience and struggle with paradoxical systems that represent reality (from mild déjà vu sensations to wave versus particle theory). More centrally, individuation without alienation involves the development of personal "realities" that incorporate paradoxical discontinuities from maternal or parental realities. In the reformulation that I am emphasizing here, parental tolerance of ambiguity—communicated in a style, to a degree, and with timing appropriate for the developmental level of the child—is conceptualized as necessary for the offspring's individuation and for the prevention of "pathologic" degrees of "splitting," alienation, and dissonance. Such a beneficial, nonpathogenic tolerance must be embedded in a communication system in which an anchoring in a reality common to parent, child, and culture has been achieved—an overlap in the child's, the family's, and the larger society's "subjective equivalences" or in their levels of abstraction.

Such formulations relating to the positive aspects of ambiguity have implications for research and therapeutic conceptualizations. As I described earlier, our attempts to identify parents or parents-to-be who were pathogenic double-binders were not successful—probably in part because of the difficulties inherent in double-bind theory. In a related area of investigation, Ryder and Goodrich (Ryder, 1966, 1968, 1969; Ryder and Goodrich, 1966; Goodrich and Boomer, 1963) generated interaction test data concerning the modes of behavior of couples confronted with irreconcilable information. Spouses were given a "color-matching test," with instructions implying that the experimenter was interested in visual functions. Sitting opposite each other, the spouses faced panels containing individually numbered fields of color. The husband's panel was not visible to the wife and hers was not visible to him. Presumably the panels were identical, and, indeed, when both were asked, for instance, to name the color associated with the number 4, both said "dark purple." From time to time, however, the experimental subjects encountered a situation in which the number and the color on the two panels did not match. Subjects in these experiments may decide, for instance, that their spouses or the experimenters are tricking them, they may doubt their own functioning, they may to varying degrees leave the question open, and they may or may not communicate about their doubts or tentative conclusions. In terms of the formulations advanced here, I would hypothesize that couples and/or individuals whose task performance deteriorates when they are confronted with irreconcilable data *and* who do not metacommunicate about the paradoxical situation in which they find themselves might be expected to deal poorly with their individuating offspring if the children confront them with reality experiences paradoxical to their own. The merits of any such prediction concerning parental help or interference with individuation, of course, hinge on the extent to which performance in a laboratory task with one's spouse is predictive of naturalistic behavior with one's child. Attempts to rate ambiguity tolerance in interview material are still crude but may be of some limited use. Some adaptations of Berlyne's (1966) experimental techniques to determine the optimum ambiguity range—optimum for the maintenance of interest—might also be useful in identifying parents with wide and narrow optimum ranges (Hohage and Kuebler, 1985).

In the framework of the reformulation being proposed here, the therapeutic double bind is conceptualized more parsimoniously than in the original theory, as a kind of replacement in therapy of what was missing during crucial developmental phases—that is, adequate exposure to paradoxes that prepare the person for life as a separate and unique individual, paradoxes that I see as an essential component of the very process of individuation. This therapeutic application of ambiguity does not imply any planned or calculated use of paradox or irrationality. Rather, it refers to handling of the ambiguities that naturally emerge in the flow and counterflow of transference and countertransference in the relationship by the use of communications and metacommunications that are appropriate to the mixture of developmental levels characterizing both the patient and the therapist.

The temporal dimension of multiple-reality organizations is not specifically addressed by double-bind theorists and did not play a part in my critique and reformulation of the hypothesis. Gradually, however, obvious temporal reference in the very notion of object *constancy* led me to a synthetic view of the themes of multiple realities and time, which are discussed in the next chapter.

Chapter 3

Déjà Vu, Drugs, Synesthesia, and the Mind-Time Synthesis

In a psychiatric context, the ancient philosophical problem of the nature of reality tends to lose much of its abstract quality and to gain a personal poignancy, because estrangement—alienation from reality—may mean tragic personal isolation. The central importance of time will emerge as we continue to examine, from clinical, experimental, and theoretical perspectives, the phenomena related to estrangement from consensually validated reality.

In the previous chapter, I discussed Klüver's (1936) use of the concept of subjectively equivalent stimuli in studying the building blocks of psychological reality. I will continue to relate some of his formulations to clinical data and to psychoanalytic concepts by elaborating their relevance not only to an understanding of object constancy (Kafka, 1964) but to the related issues of ambiguity, paradox, and time.

Although Freud dealt with issues of misperception of reality, especially misperception of the difference between male and female genitalia, for him there was basically one (commonsense) reality, which is or is not perceived correctly. Hartmann (1939) deals with some aspects of the relativity of reality, but for him this relativity is circumscribed—he still finds a fairly solid foothold in an "average expectable environment." Such stability, even though limited, becomes acutely problematic for such authors as Loewald, Wallerstein, Novey, and Lichtenstein. They differ in their emphases on developmental, social, or psychic structural issues and in the degree to which they see the social and intrapsychic structural-reality problems as separate or related. But they share such concerns as the collapse of ideas about commonsense reality, the crisis in consensual validation, and the waning of agreement on the average expectable environment. Novey (1955) goes so far as to emphasize the fundamental similarity between "normal" ordered reality systems and delusional systems.

Lichtenstein traces "the transformation of 'reality' since Freud" (1974, p. 353) and illustrates with case material the "changing function of the id" (p. 358) and of the superego that results from a radical alteration of reality perception. With reference to the id, Lichtenstein says, "To use the sexual experience in the service of a desperate effort at affirmation of the reality of the self and the other ... is a shift in the function of psychic structures" (p. 360). With reference to the superego, he describes a patient who was not schizophrenic but who, after some experimenting with psychedelic drugs, began to feel that there were really no objects, that everything was force—energy that flowed through what was living and what was not living, in unbroken waves or vibrations. She began to read articles on modern physics in *Scientific American*, which bore out her feeling that there was no such thing as objectivity or mechanistic laws, and that the ordinary reality of everyday life represented only one limited dimension of what was real. She was, however, unable to bridge the inner gap between a reality perception that, as she said, absorbed her into an inner space and the competitive world around her. She felt temporarily at peace when she could be in touch with nature, but she yearned for a shared life with others, emotional contact, and meaningful communication, and this, more and more, evaded her (p. 363).

Keeping Lichtenstein's description in mind, let us return to the notion of object constancy and its connection to subjective equivalence. As I commented in chapter 2, in psychoanalysis, object constancy usually refers to the coalescence of partially conflicting images—for example, the bringing together of the images of the gratifying "good" mother and the frustrating "bad" mother into one internal representation of a mother figure. Anna Freud, in an address at the International Psychoanalytic

Congress in Vienna in 1971, spoke of the ability to maintain object constancy as the ability to continue to love the frustrating object.

Before proceeding, 1 wish to point out that Klüver's "subjective equivalence" can be used not only in reference to object constancy—that is, to the identity of objects—but also in reference to time. Many of the clinical and experimental data on time discussed in chapter One are elaborations of the everyday observation that time passes faster on some occasions and more slowly on others. This must mean that *objectively different* time spans can be *subjectively equivalent*.

For Lichtenstein's patient, there were "really no objects" since no one pattern of subjective equivalence was consistently dominant. She was *aware* of a kind of floating energy or force flowing in waves through both inanimate and animate objects and creating, in rapid succession, different patterns of subjective equivalence. This description is congruent with clinical distinctions (Kafka, 1964) between subject and object, between self and non-self, which may disappear or recede into the background because of the subjective equivalence of some fragmentary self-representations with fragmentary mental representations of others. I have encountered analogous issues in investigations of psychotic phenomena and psychedelic drug experiences (Kafka, 1964; Kafka and Gaarder, 1964). In Lichtenstein's patient such blurring of borders apparently made communication difficult with those around her, who perceived the world differently—that is, in terms of more stable, more lastingly differentiated objects.

Other influences on the formation of a system of subjective equivalences are motivational factors—the drive organization and its current state of activation. The organization of patterns of subjective equivalence is obviously related in some way to the nature of early object relations. In addition, for the development of stable patterns of object constancy in the psychoanalytic sense, relatively stable patterns of object constancy in the "perceptual" sense are almost certainly necessary. The two meanings of the term have overlapping elements arising out of the same matrix. The study of drugs that profoundly affect perceptual processes has yielded some particularly pertinent data. My own participation in studies of two substances with very different effects, LSD and Serynl, has provided me with useful illustrative material.

Illustrations from the Study of LSD

If perceptual processes are closely linked to object constancy, the distinction between compartmentalization and synesthetic perception becomes of great interest. Synesthesia, as I have noted, means the blending of sensory modalities—for example, the mental linking of colors with music or other sounds.

Before LSD became a street drug, I took part in an organized research program on psychedelic substances with several psychoanalyst colleagues who worked with psychotic patients. We took LSD on Sunday, saw patients on Monday, and studied some effects of the LSD experience on the therapeutic work. I want to emphasize that research with the substances we used was authorized at that time and that we did not see patients while acutely under the influence of the drug. We specifically wanted to investigate if the memory of an experience with a drug thought to mimic psychotic experience would facilitate our understanding of and therapeutic work with psychotic patients.

Some of my fellow therapists felt that the LSD experience had no effect on their therapeutic work, and we all recognized that a multiplicity of factors, including the social setting, can influence an LSD experience, which can range from ecstatic delight to profound terror. Nevertheless, we felt that some generalizations could be attempted since some similar formal characteristics of the experience had been described by many LSD subjects. They felt in tune with each other, although the experiences were intensely personal and were reported as such. The awareness of a common chord—an awareness that was a necessary consequence of the multidimensionality of the LSD experience—seemed to be the formal characteristic about which generalization was most justified.

An extensive literature already existed on LSD-25 and related drugs, but there were not many recent psychodynamic studies of those substances. A comprehensive review of the literature published by Linger (1963) revealed that differences between the drug-induced state and naturally occurring psychopathologic conditions had been stressed (Hochetal, 1958). But LSD-induced ego states (Savage, 1955) *congruent* with some aspects of naturally occurring psychopathology had also been described and called to the attention of psychotherapists. Investigators of LSD action expressed the opinion (Abramson, 1959) that anyone who attempted to use LSD as a therapeutic tool should himself have experienced the effects of the drug. In our search of the literature, however, we had not found studies dealing specifically with the effects of the psychotherapist's LSD or other psychotomimetic experience on his subsequent therapeutic work.

Direct observations were made on five psychotherapists who took doses of 75 to 250 micrograms of LSD-25 after appropriate medical screening. Two of the psychotherapists took LSD-25 on two occasions, and three took it once. Although larger dosages were generally associated with more intense effects, in our limited experience neither repetition nor dosage variation systematically altered the pattern of the drug experience or the pattern of its effect on subsequent therapeutic work. Complete medical facilities, an observing physician and nurse, and tape recordings of the drug sessions were provided. Some psychotherapy sessions following the therapist's LSD experiences were tape-recorded, as were a series of clinical discussions among the five experimental subjects. In addition, they discussed their experiences with eight other psychotherapists who had had LSD experiences elsewhere. In preparing the study for publication, we attempted to present a distillate of trends in our own observations and in those of others (Kafka and Gaarder, 1964).

We described two classes of effects on the therapist's work. The first concerned the more immediate, more spontaneous, less thought-through effects—perhaps those which the therapist himself might notice with some surprise. The second class comprised theorizing stimulated by the more spontaneous LSD effects.

Although the richness of the experience makes one uncomfortable with any summarizing statements, we did attempt some generalizations about the phenomenology of LSD. Much of it can be described in terms of a collapse of the categories of formal logic. Under LSD the subject experiences himself as A and B at the same time—for example, as a self-observer in a drug experiment and simultaneously as a line in a musical structure. The multiple layers of experience, the multiple levels of meaning, all seem to him to be equally valid, even though the subject is aware that only one of the levels of meaning is accepted as the appropriate one by his colleagues who are not under the influence of the drug.

To what extent can LSD produce schizphrenialike states? One therapist under LSD said, "I know this is such-and-such a place and such-and-such a date, but all this doesn't have the significance you ascribe to it." Somewhat similar comments are occasionally made by schizophrenic patients when they show clinical improvement. Peter, about whom I will say more in chapter 5, could differentiate the hallucinated voices of father and God, but found the distinction of no significance to him. Furthermore some regressed schizophrenic patients behave appropriately in such situations as a fire in the hospital unit. This may illustrate both their access to information and the selectivity of their responses to stimuli and situations that also "make a difference" in their framework. In a high percentage of cases (but not in all of them), observers can correctly distinguish tape-recorded LSD interviews from similar interviews with schizophrenic patients (Abramson, 1959). Investigating the characteristics of the exceptions—the patients who cannot be distinguished from the LSD subjects—might yield enlightening results.

To return now to the main theme here—the effects of the LSD experience on the therapists' work with patients—first, the multidimensionality of their LSD experiences diminished the "either-or" type of questions that several therapists asked of their patients. In trying to describe the multidimensionality of the LSD world, we found it useful to use an extended concept of synesthesia, which goes beyond the usual sensory synesthesia of seeing, hearing, tactile sense, kinesthesia, and temperature sense to include mood, emotion, space, and time. In a world in which the distinction between subject and object has disappeared, the feeling of one's body is in constant flux—for example, one may feel a surface becoming an S-shaped line as in a surrealist movie, and a line coming toward one splitting up into time. One may feel primary energy before it has taken on the form of any specific sensory modality.

After experiencing this "multidimensionality in all directions," this collapse of logical categories, one therapist felt that he could understand why patients, particularly psychotic patients, had previously reacted to either-or questions as though they were somewhat insulting and inappropriate. For example, while working with a delusional, hallucinated psychotic patient whose gestures and words had often indicated that people were putting thoughts into her head or taking them out, he had often found himself curious about specific aspects of this experience: did her skull seem to soften? did the hand reach in? and so on. It did not occur to the therapist to pursue this kind of questioning with every delusional and hallucinated patient, but it had in this case because of her specific intonations and gestures. After he had taken LSD, however, his curiosity about how the patient experienced the putting in and taking out of thoughts seemed an idiotic preoccupation. Acknowledging that to the patient led to a widening of the field of therapeutic communication.

The therapist's experience of simultaneous multiplicity of meaning and particularly of synesthesia in the extended sense also led to another LSD-connected development in therapy with the same patient. An endless and exasperating repetitiveness characterized some of her psychotherapy hours. At one point she explained that she repeated what she said (which was usually requests) and did not respond to answers, questions, or discussions in order not to lose the trend of her thought and also not to lose herself, not to lose her identity, not to lose her goals. Weeks after this explanation, the patient exhibited a curious pattern of behavior. When she complained that she was being mauled and manhandled by the ward personnel, the staff pointed out that she had initiated a pattern of planting herself in front of doors or in passageways, always "in the way" of someone. The therapist's LSD experience of "verbal-postural synesthesia" helped him equate this behavior with her repetitive verbal behavior. He told her that apparently one meaning of her behavior was a physical statement of "I am here—this is me, this is me," and so forth. The patient seemed pleased and complimented him by saying, "This is a very beautiful ashtray—did you make it?"

For some of the therapists in our experiment, several facets of the LSD experience contributed to a greater tolerance for silence in the hours. One was the feeling of the inappropriateness of many either-or questions. Possibly, also, a blurring of the distinction between animate and inanimate objects during phases of the LSD experience was a factor. For one therapist, some voices, for instance, seemed to be mechanical and dead, whereas certain objects—like the bedstead that he was gripping while affected by LSD—were experienced as full of living energy. The "physiognomy" of furniture, a pattern in the rug, and the like provided such an overwhelmingly rich experience that after having taken LSD, and particularly in the presence of a patient who seemed to respond to the physiognomy of objects, he was more willing to join the patient in silent experience of the environment. One patient repeatedly asked him to come to her room so that she could "explain things" to him but would invariably fall silent when he complied. His LSD experience of the richness of the physiognomy of objects made this behavior seem less bizarre, since he could assume that she was silently asking him to share such richness.

An increase of confidence in the accuracy of social perceptions during the LSD experience, and for at least some time thereafter, could also contribute to the acceptance of silence. In at least one instance such confidence even contributed to the therapist's issuing a sharply worded request to the patient to be silent. The day after he had taken LSD, while working with a neurotic patient, he felt much more certain than on other occasions that the patient, although mouthing many words, was not "communicating meaningfully." Somewhat to his own surprise, he heard himself telling the patient emphatically to be quiet when he really had nothing to say. The startled patient responded with a four-letter word, became silent for almost twenty minutes, and then started to communicate more thoughtfully and meaningfully.

Because of an LSD experience of panic about the disintegrative threat, one therapist became freer in having vigorous physical contact with some psychotic patients when they were struggling against impending loss of contact. He became very skeptical about notions that the psychotic patient is easily threatened by the therapist, since in his recent LSD experience he had recognized that the terror of losing contact is immeasurably greater than the fear of hostile contact. In addition to using more physical contact with psychotic patients, he made more liberal use of wet-sheet packs as an "orienting" restraint during therapy hours.

Some of the therapists noted that when they were under the influence of the drug, the pattern of their whole experiential world could be shattered by a sudden noise, such as a sneeze. This led them to become more alert to a patient's behavioral changes following the occurrence of a sudden stimulus. That a sudden kaleidoscopic shift from one world into another is a recurrent event for some psychotic patients is a hypothesis for which there is much clinical evidence. It is our impression that the kaleidoscopic changes of the LSD experience and of some schizophrenic conditions are phenomenologically similar. After our LSD experience, we felt that some schizophrenic patients sensed that their therapists had to some extent "been there" and could recognize an altered, easily shattered world, and that this widened the area of communication.

Like our specific changes in clinical technique following the LSD experience, our related *theorizing* about therapeutic concepts was rooted in the multi-dimensionality of the LSD experience. Although it was described in many different ways, the richness of meaning of all events, perceptions, and experiences was generally commented upon by subjects taking LSD.

Because at times the LSD richness may have a driving quality—"I can't keep up with it"—one of the theories we formulated hypothesizes that hebephrenic silliness is an understandable escape from meaning. The conviction that meaning itself, in its formal characteristics, can be threatening may well influence therapeutic work with hebephrenic patients. Before taking LSD one therapist felt that he might have been much too concerned with content in treating a hebephrenic patient, overcautiously staying with the patient in the area judged to be less anxiety-producing than most others, the area where the patient could communicate with "silliness." After the specific recognition that *formal* qualities of meaning can be threatening, the therapist was more likely to experience the patient's acceptance of meaning as a monumental vote of confidence in the relationship as it existed at that moment. Had not the patient, out of despair or trust or both, accepted the therapist's kind of meaning as his own, when previously an overwhelming number of kinds of meaning had been equally valid for him? With greater ease and with less caution concerning the *content* of the communication, the therapist could then exploit the temporary acceptance of meaning—of secondary process, one might say—by the patient.

Another theoretical notion that can affect therapeutic work is related to the fluctuations experienced by the LSD subject, in and out of various levels of loss of ego control and reality contact. The LSD experience reinforced our familiar preoccupation with the question of whether or not a patient, especially a psychotic patient, is in voluntary control of a particular symptom. One of the therapists who took LSD felt at times that there was only one point in which he was one up on the colleague and the nurse who were with him during the experiment—namely, that he knew better than they did when he was more or less "gone." He was very reluctant to give up this secret. Some time after his LSD experience, when he was in doubt about the voluntary components of psychotic symptoms in a patient, he expressed his doubts to the patient but now also put into words his recognition of the patient's need to be ahead of him, to be one up in this respect. His expressed acceptance of the patient's need for this secret apparently produced a twinkle of recognition in the patient and maintained some continuity of communication at a time in therapy when communication was extremely tenuous.

Although our work with psychotics provided us with the most explicit examples of effects of the LSD experience on our therapy techniques, we also felt that the experience had considerable, less explicit effect on our work with nonpsychotic patients. For example, observations of our own post-LSD dreams led us to pay more attention to what we called the dimension of "abstract expressionism" in dreams reported by neurotic patients, by which we mean the degree of feeling and rich emotional meaning carried by an abstract and formal pattern (Kafka and Gaarder, 1964).

After the LSD experience one therapist had dreams unusual for him in their formal characteristics. He dreamed, for instance, about "an almost but not completely smooth, progressing line, with one of the small wiggles in it representing the Nazi period and six million Jews killed." Upon awakening he felt that he had dreamed and experienced the "expanse of history." Gradually, after the LSD experience, the formal characteristics of his dreams returned to their more usual pattern.

We speculate that perhaps a greater emotional meaning invested in abstract pattern in dreams of our patients corresponded to what would be described in Rorschach terminology as a more dilated *Erlebnistyp*— that is, an increase in kinesthetic and color-determined responses. We further conjectured that more feeling associated with abstract patterns in dreams of neurotic patients might correspond to a loosening of defensive structures. After our LSD experience, we paid more attention to these possible meanings of the dimension of abstract expressionism in patients' dreams.

In generalizing about the effects of our LSD experience on our therapeutic work, we were aware that much of what we had described was in tune with the Zeitgeist of phenomenologic and existential awareness in psychiatry and was not necessarily and exclusively related to psychotomimetic drugs. Nevertheless, we believed that our attempt to study such effects had enriched our knowledge of therapy, therapists, and psychopathology as well as the phenomenology of drugs. Some of the effects may have been simply the result of a new and dramatic experience, whether traumatic or pleasurable, or of the therapist's greater insight into previously less exposed areas of his functioning; some may have been related to the confrontation with techniques for holding onto reality and consequent diminution of anxiety; and some may have resulted from the sharing with our patients of a world in which the selective filtering that we call secondary-process functioning operated less than in most other situations. In our study we did not consider some broader questions concerning therapeutic uses of psychotomimetic substances— for example, the usefulness to patients in psychotherapy of taking these substances; the possibility of therapist and patient simultaneously taking the drugs; or the effects of a drugged therapist, with or without a co-therapist, seeing the patient. Investigation of these broader issues would involve the question of whether these techniques permit exploration beyond the secondary process while at the same time permitting self-observation, communication, and integration.

To summarize our LSD study, undertaken at a time when LSD was more widely legally approved as a research tool and was not yet a street drug, we distinguished the following immediate effects of the therapist's

LSD experience and a few later, more theoretical ones. The collapse of logical categories, the multidimensionality of the experience, blurring of the borders between animate and inanimate objects, the importance of the physiognomy of objects, and increased confidence in social perception were believed to be among the factors leading to diminution of either-or questions. Increased attention to the physiognomy of objects and greater sensitivity to communication through posture or actual position in space led to an extension of nonverbal communication and therefore to greater tolerance for silence. More theoretical notions included the idea that hebephrenic silliness may be an attempt to escape the threat of the richness and multiplicity of meaning and the idea that some patients may need to obscure the degree to which they fluctuate in and out of psychosis in order to be secretly one up on nonpsychotic persons, who have the advantage of a stable reference structure.

Illustrations from the Study of Sernyl

In another part of our study of the effects of therapists' drug experience on their understanding of and therapeutic work with patients, Dr. Kenneth Gaarder took the drug Sernyl (I-[I-phenylcyclohexyl] piperidine HCL) by intravenous injection; I served as the principal observer of his reactions. Sernyl's chemical structure, neurophysiological mechanisms, and psychological effects are completely different from those of the LSD-mescaline-psilocybin group of drugs.[5] When Gaarder reported on the work in a Chestnut Lodge symposium in the fall of 1963 (Gaarder and Kafka, 1963), we had no idea that the study would be among the last authorized human experiments with this dangerous substance, now better known as PCP. In our unpublished report, from which I will quote extensively, we were attempting to serve two functions. First, we wanted to contribute to general knowledge about an important new mode of

---

[5] For recent studies ot PCP and mental processes, see Murk S. Senders, John F. W. Keana, and Eckard Weber, "Phencyclidine and Psychotomimetic Sigma Opiates: Recent Insights into Their Biochemical and Physiological Sites of Action," *Trends in Neuro-Science* 10(1987): 263-302; It (1988): 37-40.

producing psychotomimetic effects. Second, we wished to report a finding about the phenomenology of the Sernyl experience that had not been previously observed.

In describing Gaarder's reactions, we made certain assumptions: that both schizophrenics and psychotomimetic drug subjects undergo a *multiplicity* of experiences in which there are profound alterations of the ego; that these can be described as a series of "ego states," which are often strikingly different from one another; that within each state there is a particular organization of the cathectic forces of the ego, differing from that of other states in the quality and quantity invested in the various agencies of the ego; that there are transitional stages in which the ego and its energies are involved in change from one state to another; and that the study of psychotomimetic states, transitions between states, and the intervention by which these states and transitions may be altered can be a means to further understanding of ego states and transitions between them in general.

In the meager psychiatric literature concerning Sernyl, it is usually described as having the unique property of selectively inhibiting the function of the sensory system. Thus, its main effect is to produce the equivalent of sensory deprivation rapidly, without the need for isolation apparatuses. All sense modalities are inhibited without primary toxic effects on consciousness, thinking, or motor activity. With increasing dosage of Sernyl, there is a gradual loss of peripheral sensations—pain, the sense of position, and so on—and of such senses as vision and hearing. Largely on the basis of clinical neurological examination of subjects, investigators have deduced that the site of action of Sernyl is the primary sensory center of the body, the thalamus, although the midbrain and sensory cortex are also implicated (Meyer et al., 1959; Luby et al., 1959). Authors differ in their interpretation of the relative importance of Sernyl's effects on internal versus external sensations. Those who have studied the drug as an anesthetic agent for surgery have no question about its capacity to diminish external perception (Meyer et al., 1959). Those who have studied it in combination with sensory deprivation by apparatus stress the loss of internal perception (Luby et al., 1959; Pollard et al., 1960) because a person who has taken Sernyl experiences fewer symptoms and less distress when isolated than when in an unrestricted environment.

As with sensory deprivation, important effects on thought processes and motor behavior occur secondarily until with high doses the subject is in a catatonic trance. Other major effects observed at various doses are the feeling that one's body parts do not belong to oneself; a subjective feeling of being dead; the inability to conceptualize and carry on complex conversations; and loss of the sense of the presence of the unvisualized visual environment and also of tunnel vision, so that existing visual space is a small circle in front of the subject. Sernyl proved unsatisfactory as a surgical anesthetic because these effects complicated the postoperative course with transient psychotic episodes. Sernyl has also been observed to produce acute discomfort and agitation in chronic schizophrenic patients. It has been tolerated better by children and older people than by young adults (Meyer et al., 1959; Luby et al., 1959; Pollard et al., 1960).

In summary, Sernyl makes it possible to study the interrelationships of enteroception, exteroception, body image, thought processes, motor activity, and reality constructs as they combine dynamically to create the living ego. Studying Sernyl became particularly important in exploring schizophrenia in the light of Gaarder's hypothesis that schizophrenic thought disorder is the result of sensory deprivation to which the patient has contributed by interpersonal and intrapsychic mechanisms (Gaarder, 1963).

Our observations were confined to a single subject (Gaarder) who took a relatively small dose (3.3 mgm intravenous [0.05 mgm/kg body weight]) just once. Gaarder was well acquainted with the literature about Sernyl but had not seen the drug in use. The effects began within ten minutes after the injection of the drug and were over within forty-live minutes. They were followed by several hours of a hangover type of hypersensitivity to noise.

In the following excerpts from the tape recording of my exchanges with Gaarder at the height of the experience, note the dullness, the thinking difficulty, the bewilderment about existential questions, and the lack of interpersonal sensitivity revealed in his responses.

KG: . . . something is going on here and uh—uh—I'm alive—and uh—

I'm doing something for some reason, and I don't know what it is I'm doing and uh—what's happening to me now—and words are things like that what is happening?—what is to say what is happening? is a word—and people talk—and what is talking?—and uh—I don't know what's going on. . . .

KG: . . . I'm a person in a—there's a time-place continuum—and uh— something is going on here—what it's all about I don't know and who I am and where and how and all that kind of thing and I'm in an office—and an office is a thing which people sit in because they want to talk to one another and Sigmund—Sigmund Freud—I haven't thought about Sigmund Freud for a while—Sigmund Freud is a man who figured out something—oh—uh—I don't know. What's a psy- chiatrist? It's very [laughs]—it's a very interesting experience. I'm experiencing something and I don't know what's going on, and I don't know what saying what's going on is saying. . . .

KG: . . . uh—am I alive? Or—what's alive?

JK: You're alive—whatever it is.

KG: What is it?

JK: Hell—you take this drug so you can tell us! You took a drug.

KG: Who ? Me? [Laughs]

JK: You.

KG: When?

JK: How long ago do you think you took it?

KG: Let's see—let's see—I took a drug in—oh—about fifteen minutes ago, I guess—didn't I?

JK: How did you figure out the time?

KG: Have I been talking quite a bit?

JK: Mmm-hmm.

KG: Good! Well—whatever else happens at least I'll know what I said— but who am I?—what am I doing? I mean why am I—uh—what's going on?

RM [technician]: I'm going to take your blood pressure, Ken.

JK: Would it make you feel better if I tell you what's going on? Do you want to know?

KG: Yeah.

JK: You took Sernyl—that's a drug you're interested in—you're a psychiatrist, and you took this Sernyl to see how it makes you feel, and you're under the influence of that drug right now.

In the literature on Sernyl, the subject is usually described as being strongly aware of a strikingly altered body image, characterized by feelings of floating away from one's own body or of being dead and being a corpse, with a profound subjective awareness of this as *bodily experience* (Bakker and Amini, 1961). It is of interest that Gaarder did not have such an experience. Although he was aware of the possibility of its occurrence from his previous reading, he was to a high degree set in an intellectual, conceptualizing mode as he underwent the experience. Aware of the apathy of subjects described in the literature, he was determined to keep talking about what was happening so that the tape recording of his experience would have sufficient material on it. In addition, the self-imposed structure and activity of language may have had an important effect in limiting the extent of his disorientation. Whatever the reason, he did not experience loss of body image but instead wondered intellectually if he were alive or not; he was unaware of his body in the way a person is when intensely involved in other spheres.

Gaarder's salient experience, both at the time he took the drug (as tape recorded) and retrospectively, was a profound change in thinking in which there was a loss of the meaning of logical categories and of the experience of causal relationships. He retained all the essential "facts" about himself and his situation at the moment—time, place, person, role, and a memory of having seen several patients and a supervisor that morning—but he was unable to establish relationships between these facts and was bewildered about them. Just as others who are described in the Sernyl literature profoundly believed that their body-image experiences were real, to the same degree Gaarder reported feeling profound bewilderment about the questions he posed. Perhaps he kept repeating the questions as a means of maintaining contact.

Because Gaarder had also taken LSD, he was able to contrast the experiences. He felt that in both there was a loss of the relatively restricted and narrowly channeled logical connections that characterize the more usual, "normal" modes of thinking. However, whereas LSD enabled him to see the richness and multiplicity of diverse meanings of relationships between things and was a "creative" experience, taking Sernyl resulted in a loss of meanings of relationships between things and was a bewildering experience.

The general lack of richness of the Sernyl experience was manifested in three other areas. The first was the subject's feeling that *he did not care much about the interaction with his observers* and was not terribly affected by the subtleties of what they did and said; in order for them to have a very striking effect on him they had to put their message across very forcefully. The psychological heaviness, the lack of subtle modulation of thought and feeling, was strikingly contagious to the observer, who felt that dull repetition of orienting statements was useful to the subject, perhaps especially so if accompanied by some physical contact. This was in striking contrast to the LSD experience, in which the observer was easily caught up in a kind of intricate psychological dance of thought and feeling. For the subject also this contrasted with his LSD experience, in which he felt much too much in tune with the observers and too subject to a snowballing effect of their mutual interaction into, for example, a paranoid or an intensely sentimental interchange.

The second area of impoverishment was the *inability of the subject*, as noted by the observer, *to identify* with anyone who was not like himself. Thus, in a psychological test involving inspection of photographs of people, the subject could accept and consider only those who were closely like himself—that is, young men. Even there, his associations were sparse, but pictures of children, young women, and older people were totally rejected. This contrasts sharply with the *widening* of associations that we and others noted with LSD and that has been observed with similar drugs.

The third area of impoverishment was *visual perception*. In retrospect, the subject had the conviction that his perception had been subtly altered to a restricted mode that might best be characterized as similar to a cartoon style, as in "Little Orphan Annie." Its characteristics are a stiltedness and plainness of what is perceived—flat, simple, homogeneous areas, sharp, straight margins, and a lack of fineness of detail and texture.

Finally, for several hours after the acute effects of the drug had worn off, Gaarder felt withdrawn and apathetic and experienced a hangover, as is reported in the literature. In so doing, he felt he gained some insight into the physiological nature of hangovers in general. His mild headache seemed to get worse if noises increased or if someone attempted to talk with him. He began to understand a hangover as an acute hypersensitivity to stimuli, so that headache and a wish to withdraw were the primary reactions to relative overstimulation. This is comparable to the observations of Gottlieb's group (Luby et al., 1959) that a person taking Sernyl feels relative tranquility in isolation and irritability in an unrestricted environment.

In summary, we observed that the Sernyl experience differed from the LSD experience in the following ways: instead of marked body-image distortions, there was body-image amnesia; interpersonal sensitivity seemed to diminish; the capacity to identify also seemed to attenuate; the mode of perception seemed to change into one lacking richness of detail; and the hangover following Sernyl seemed to be based on hypersensitivity to stimuli.

After our Sernyl experience, we reported hopefully that psychotomimetic drugs might have a great practical use in creating a specific chemical stress that forces a shift of ego cathexis. They could provide a situation in which the subject and the therapist-observer could deduce which interactions enhance ego control and adaptive mastery and which interactions thwart it. In other words, they offered the potential of a laboratory for the experimental study of the psychotherapy of the psychoses. National recognition of the dangers of such substances, however, soon ended such experimental work.

Our excursion into drug experiences illustrates rather dramatically different possibilities of organizing reality. Particularly striking is the contrast between the expansion into multi-dimensionality provided by LSD and the narrowing that resulted from Sernyl. A vivid example is the loss of meaning apparent in the verbatim conversation recorded when the subject was under the influence of Sernyl. We observed that a fractionation of temporal experience, the loss of continuity connected to the dramatic diminution of short-term memory, washes out meaning. An individual with temporal disorientation—for example, Kurt Vonnegut's Billy Pilgrim, to whom I referred earlier—may be in "a constant state of stage fright . . . because he never knows what part of his life he is going to have to act in next," but at least he can still act. The loss of meaning connected with the fracture of extremely short time frames, the loss of meaning of what is perceived, makes acting impossible.

The study of psychedelic drug experiences and psychoanalytic clinical material suggested to me a hypothesis linking synesthetic phenomena to a temporal phenomenon, the déjà vu or, more generally, the "déjà " experience introduced in the previous chapter.

Clinical Use of Synesthesia

As in the discussion of LSD, I will be using an extended concept of synesthesia, including not only the blending of sensory compartments—vision, hearing, and so forth—but mood, emotion, space, and time as well. I will illustrate the state by describing in greater detail a patient mentioned briefly in chapter 2.

Anna was an attractive woman in her early thirties, a wife and mother of superior intelligence and advanced academic education. The symptom leading to her referral for psychoanalysis was a fugue state—the most marked of several such episodes—lasting several hours, during which she was in the recreation room of her home with her children, apparently functioning appropriately but unable to recall her actions later. The period was filled with déjà vu sensations and was experienced as uncanny and frightening. During it she experienced fragmented dream images having to do with operations and giant surgeons. Her symptoms also included phobias regarding driving a car and answering telephones and longstanding preoccupations with possibilities of disaster. The phobias had emerged gradually over a number of years but had become more pronounced during the previous three years, after her husband's brief hospitalization for an unconfirmed coronary occlusion.

In the course of psychoanalysis lasting several years, the meaning of the dreamlike images of the fugue states became understandable. The patient had grown up in a small French Canadian town in which her father's family was prominent. Her mother had been reared in an orphanage, and her background had been extremely deprived. Although the patient's father had some scientific training, he only operated a small appliance repair shop and never became financially or otherwise fully independent of his parental family. During the mother's pregnancy with the patient, her two-year-old son died of a renal disease. The patient was thus the only child of a mother who was grieving and chronically depressed. The patient herself had recurrent episodes of pyelitis with high fevers during her childhood.

The patient often experienced the home atmosphere as oppressive. Somewhat masklike smiles, parental—especially maternal—interest in what the patient called "peace-of-mind literature," and the mother's description of her own deprived childhood reinforced the patient's fear of disaster and loss, and also contributed to feelings of guilt. Premature demands were often made of her. For example, when she asked her mother what she should do about bullies who threw stones at her on the way to school, her mother answered blandly that she should search her conscience, where she would find the right thing to do. The patient had also felt reproached when "things came easy"—when, for example, she did well in her studies with little effort.

As the only surviving child, the patient could powerfully influence the mood of her parents, who were fairly isolated socially; thus she began to develop and maintain feelings of omnipotence. She saw her father, who "could make any toy with his hands," as omnipotent until her early adolescence, and her identification with him was strong in many areas. Gradually, however, the patient had recognized the extent of her father's inadequacy and dependence on his own parents. On this basis she had formed some derogatory opinions of men.

When she left home at eighteen to go to college—the same one her father had attended—she intended to be "a better man than Father" and experienced leaving home as liberation. But soon after, her father suddenly died. The patient had made light of her father's anxiety—expressed in his letters to her—about anticipated gall-bladder surgery. He died on the operating table, apparently because heart disease had been misdiagnosed as gall bladder disease. The patient developed a strong fear of her destructive powers, especially when her omnipotence functioned in the service of competition, and she began to feel that it was dangerous to be liberated from oppressive feelings, dangerous to take matters lightly, and even more dangerous not to anticipate disaster. The dreamlike fragments of the fugue state related to her father's death, the patient identifying both with the destructive surgeons and with the victim suffering retaliation for destructive wishes. The fugue episode had occurred when hostile and competitive feelings toward her husband and resentment about her feminine and maternal role were particularly marked.

As the patient's history unfolded, she was able to see connections between many previously dissociated and isolated areas. Experiencing a sense of continuity between dream material, dreamlike elements of the fugue states, and remembered events and feelings was surprising to her and offered relief.

Although the analysis, of course, involved transference distortions and their interpretation, I would like to focus on one particular aspect of this case: advance in understanding occurred during what might be described as minor repetitions of the so-called fugue states during psychoanalytic hours. In these hours, characterized by a somewhat trancelike atmosphere, references to ongoing experiences of synesthesia were prominent. A shiny object in the office, for instance, would be experienced and described as a "shrill [sounding] object." At this point the patient would report a déjà vu experience and frequently would comment about the uncanniness or awesomeness of the moment. After several minutes of "heavy" silence, an early memory of the "atmosphere"—that is, a synesthetic blending of the sounds, sights, rhythms, tastes, and smells of a certain place or time—would emerge. (The atmosphere of the father's shop was experienced with particular vividness.) A fragmented image from a fugue episode could then be traced to either a fact or a fantasy associated with the time or place characterized by the remembered "atmosphere."

In chapter 2, to clarify the association of synesthetic and déjà vu phenomena in cases of this kind, I drew a schematic analogy with a wave pattern on an oscilloscope representing visual, auditory, or tactile stimuli. I pointed out that a responding organism or electronic scanning machine can be asked if a record is a familiar *visual* pattern, but that if the response is to the *pattern*—regardless of whether the sensory modality is visual, auditory, or tactile—the likelihood that it will be familiar is much increased. In other words, if a pattern of stimulation occurs at a time when the sensory compartments are particularly interwoven or blended, the chances that the pattern will arouse a feeling of familiarity—that is, a déjà vu or related sensation—are multiplied.

Arlow (1959) reviewed much of the literature on déjà vu phenomena and made a major original contribution to the understanding of these experiences. Freud's early view, as summarized by Arlow, was that the déjà vu experience corresponded to the activation of an unconscious impression. Freud came to think, however, that an unconscious fantasy might be involved and not necessarily an unconscious impression of an actual event. Arlow also summarized later extensions of the concept by Ferenczi and Oberndorf, among others, to the effect that not only unconscious fantasies but also repressed fragments of past dreams and consciously experienced intentions that were subsequently repressed may play a part in déjà vu phenomena. Arlow stressed Oberndorf's emphasis on the reassuring quality of the déjà vu experience ("You've been through this before and will come out all right again this time") and also Marcovitz's emphasis of the déjà vu reaction as an expression of the wish to have a second chance. Arlow's original contribution was his formulation, supported by detailed psychoanalytic observations, that the déjà vu reaction contains in its *formal* structure latent elements of defensive reactions and wish-fulfillment. He treated the déjà vu experience reported to him as he would the manifest content of a dream. The person having a déjà vu experience feels that the actual, the manifest situation has occurred previously, whereas it may be that it is not the situation that is familiar but the latent meaning behind it.

Arlow criticized previous formulations for making no attempt to "account for the uncanny, disconcerting, unpleasant, anxiety-tinged affects which usually accompany this form of experience" (p. 614). He added that "the lingering sense of uneasiness or the uncanny which characterizes déjà vu appears to be in proportion to the underlying anxiety and indicates that the ego has not fully succeeded, through the various mechanisms already mentioned, in mastering this anxiety" (p. 629).

Arlow seems to relate the particular uncanny affect to the ambiguity arising from a sense that a manifest situation has occurred previously and at the same time a sense that only the latent meaning of the situation is familiar. The ambiguity here involves several levels of abstraction, since *manifest* and *latent* imply different levels of abstraction, and thus embodies the kind of paradox that I discussed in detail in chapter 2. The ambiguity and uncanniness of the déjà vu experience help establish important conceptual links between time experience (in this case an experience of temporal dislocation) and perception (in this case synesthetic perception). This is a step on the road to my formulations on the mind-time synthesis.

In his paper "Fausse Reconnaissance in Treatment," Freud says, "At the close of a treatment ... the patient may say: '*Now I feel as though I had known it all the time.*' With this the work of analysis has been completed" (1914, p. 207; Freud's italics). In the analysis of Anna, my déjà vu patient, I believe that there was rapprochement in terms of the schemata of the knowledge of childhood and the schemata of the knowledge of the adult—that is, synesthetic aspects of the childhood schemata were reactivated. The uncanny quality, experiences related to depersonalization, I see as related to premature demands for unambiguous ego functioning. I am here returning to my ideas of analysis as a process of learning to be less uncomfortable with feelings of estrangement from one's own self-experience and perception of the world, from consensually validated reality, a process that leads to tolerance or acceptance of such feelings. I want to emphasize here the word *premature*. As I will elaborate in chapter 4, perceptual processes themselves can undergo maturation, and in mature perceptual acts one can observe the recapitulation of the ontogeny of perception. Clinical data supporting my hypothesis of the pathogenicity of premature demands, including perceptual demands, will also be presented in the following chapter.

Let us now turn from a clinical preoccupation with ambiguity, paradox, and the temporal dislocation of déjà vu phenomena based on synesthetic perception to some of the theoretical themes introduced earlier. Perhaps Gödel has given us a formal logical description of the unconscious by picturing an infinitely regressing series of ambiguities of type. It is in the possibility that these ambiguities must continuously be tapped in order to promote individuation, creativity, and therapeutic work that I see a further link to a psychoanalytic consideration of the problem of the experience of time.

As indicated, the psychoanalyst's major concern with the experience of time is based on his ongoing observation of the restructuring in the present of past experiences. He is in a position to observe the effects of such restructuring on the experience of time and on temporal perspective. Related to the more general problem of paradoxical experience is the issue of integration of the discontinuous moment and the flow of continuity. This issue, which is the ego's task, can be more accurately described as the problem of toleration of qualitatively different, unreconciled paradoxical experiences.

Bonaparte (1940) refers to a communication sent to her by Freud in which he talked of analysts' "later" transformation into continuity of "successive cathexes . . . quanta issuing from the ego." Since, when psychoanalysts speak of the nature of the experience of time, the very word *later* begs the question, I believe that the problem of integration of the discontinuous moment and the flow of continuity was neither avoided nor solved by Freud. The term *quanta*, however, with its implications of the irreconcilable nature—within one closed system—of wave and particle theory, may be of special interest. Freud wrote during the period in which quantum mechanics was being formulated. Quantum mechanics was developed primarily between 1900 and 1926; Heisenberg's uncertainty principle was formulated in 1927; and at the same time physicists began to warn against irresponsible philosophizing and psychologizing based on it. I shall nevertheless attempt some psychologizing, since self-observation of psychic processes confronts us with the static-fluid connotations of the observer-observed situation and, I believe, with its paradoxical implications, related to the different levels of abstraction. An analogy is suggested between the particle and the wave, on the one hand, and the experience of the discontinuous moment and the flow of continuity, on the other. Self-observation attempts to bring together the static grasping the changing grasping the static—opposites on different levels of abstraction; these opposites can be seen as paradoxes—Gödel's infinitely regressing series of ambiguities of type, which I borrowed to serve as a formal logical description of the unconscious.

In a powerful and beautiful paper that considers the now-active presence of past and future, Loewald arrives at the concluding formulation that "psychic structures are temporal in nature" (1962, p. 268), that the very fiber of mind is time. I wonder if the temporally conceived form of the paradox of the static and the fluid is not an especially poignant statement, or perhaps the extreme formal statement, of the problem analysts meet at the limits of the study of "what we call psychical" (Loewald, p. 268). William Fry, who says, "Whenever man seeks to inspect the self, he will confront the self and discover that the self is the inspector," also states, "I have . . . discovered no technique of illustrating the *instantaneous* simultaneity created in paradox" (1968, p. 172; italics mine).

In a philosophical tour de force, which it amuses him to entitle paradoxically "A *New* Refutation of Time," Jorge Luis Borges (1964; italics mine) also brings home the extent to which we experience time as the core of the psyche. Not only does he point out how even the idealist philosophers could not follow their own logic to the invalidation of time—which Borges proceeds to do—but he also jars us with his unusual conceptual integration of an experience that seems to have at least some of the features of the déjà vu experience. "That pure representation of homogeneous objects ... is not merely identical to the one present on that corner so many years ago; it is, *without resemblances or repetitions, the very same.* ... I felt dead ... an abstract spectator ... the possessor of a reticent or absent sense of the inconceivable word eternity. . . . Time ... is a delusion" (p. 226; italics mine). Similar experiences, usually less explicitly conceptualized, are not unknown in psychoanalytic work, and when they occur, they may represent nodal points of reorganization of life perspective.

Once again, even if the term *object constancy* is restricted to a specific psychoanalytic meaning (continuing investment in an object even though that object may be a frustrating one), the concept cannot be disconnected from continuity in time. The paradox we encounter at the core of time experience—the flowing and the saccadic—is inherent in the problem of object constancy. In considering this paradox and the continuing concern with tolerance of paradoxical and *qualitatively* different experiences, we may perhaps turn with profit to the ego's more obvious task of integrating *quantitatively* different and variable experiences of duration. If we apply the subjective-equivalence concept to time itself, we recall that different clock-time intervals can be experienced as subjectively equivalent. Just as subjectively equivalent object constancies, the building blocks of psychological realities, do not correspond to "objective" constancies, so subjectively equivalent time constancies do not necessarily correspond to "objectively" equivalent *clock-time* intervals.

The concept of subjective equivalence as it applies to time adds another difficult dimension to an already difficult notion that does violence to "common sense." Reality based on subjectively equivalent objects does not take for granted a simple psychological mirroring of external reality. The basic elements of psychological reality are constructs. They are always only more or less stable constructs since the perceptual processes that play a part in "cognitive" formulations are imbedded in an affective matrix. This matrix is dependent on the activity of drives that at any one moment determine the characteristics of one's perceptual scanning. Further, such spatially conceived scanning occurs in a field in which the temporal units have no "externally" given "objective" stability, since objectively identical intervals are not necessarily "subjectively equivalent." An old and extensive literature, dating from the early period of experimental psychology, deals with the search for an irreducible "now," a temporal unit that is the smallest human "present." (In these experiments, "now" is the smallest interval that is neither overestimated nor underestimated.) Whether or not the psychological "packages" of now that I am proposing are the smallest, the irreducible ones, the organization of subjective time depends on complex ongoing equivalence operations, affectively influenced and corrected and modified by fluid adjustments dependent on evaluation of new data and constantly restructured memories.

To restate my difficult proposition: In examining the paradoxical aspects of temporal structure, one can see that embedded in the temporal framework—the temporal mesh—are subjective equivalence patterns. In terms of both the psychoanalytic and the general psychological meaning of object constancy—the idea of an *enduring* object—the object seems to emerge and disappear as the time span and time patterns change; the object varies its guise ambiguously as it moves between paradoxical roles, recurrently producing subjectively equivalent stimuli, the building blocks of both momentary and more lasting realities. Conversely, our needs and drives largely determine on which characteristics of the stimulus field we focus in order to form our subjective equivalences. In changing stimulus fields the time span necessary to locate characteristics that lend themselves to perceptions congruent with the current active drive state must itself continually expand and contract. Our drive states thus determine the subjectively equivalent time spans that anchor our temporal world.

Consider in this context the proposition that each perceptual act recapitulates the history of our perceptual development, a hypothesis supported by recent findings (see chapter 5). Our "realities" then depend on an enormously complex time grid of perception. First, I visualize different sizes of "holes in the grid"—the psychological "nows" determined by the drive states; then, it seems to me, the momentarily active, developmental progression or regression adds different "shapes" or, better, different "textural qualities" to the mesh. Different meshes, to carry the analogy further, permit the passage of different ego states in which object representations have different qualities—-as was the case for my patient with the fugue states and the déjà vu experiences. The degree to which synesthetic or sense-compartmentalized perceptual processes characterize each moment is one of the elements in constant flux. The nature of temporal graining—that is, the patterns and textures of the available grids—contributes to the organization of the flow of experience into object constancies. Some drug-induced ego states permit the exploration of extremes of perceptual widening or contraction, perhaps quantitatively but not quantitatively different from what we psychoanalysts encounter in the study of "normal" perception and in clinical work. In one sense our world has been destabilized, but not so in another sense since we have defined some dimensions of the expansions and contractions of this world.

Beyond the clinical enrichment inherent in the analyst's responsiveness to the patient's multiple and paradoxical realities, the study of time leads us to reach hesitantly for the limits of understanding. The basic relationship expounded here is congruent not only with Loewald's statement, "Psychic structures are temporal in nature" (1962, p. 264), but even the conclusion, mind is time.

Chapter 4

How Do We Change?
Diagnostics, Treatments, and "Animation"

I t is my intention here to apply the notions of multiple-reality organizations to diagnostic and therapeutic thinking. No systematic survey of current, past, and evolving diagnostic fashions is intended, nor will I attempt a systematic presentation of analytic and therapeutic techniques related to a diagnostic scheme. The wish to establish diagnostic categories that are at least relatively uncontaminated by theoretical preconceptions has led some psychiatrists to formulate diagnostic categories linked relatively closely to observable behaviors (as in the American Psychiatric Association's *DSM-III*, 1980). One area in which behaviors can be observed, however, is the response to various therapeutic interventions, which are of course based on different theoretical models. Diagnostic thinking and therapeutic thinking are intertwined, and both are involved with the pendulum swings between theory building and observation. The ease of or resistance against shifting between different internal reality organizations does have its countertransference dimension, which manifests itself in variations of the therapist's sense of effort and fluctuations in his fatigue. Diagnostic labels are not independent of counter-transference. It is therefore appropriate that diagnostic and therapeutic considerations are intertwined in the case material presented below.

For me, the pendulum swings between clinical observation and theory building have led not only to a focus on time in the organization of multiple realities but also to a focus on the boundary between and the differentia-tion of the animate and inanimate in the construction of psychic realities. The animate-inanimate issue emerged when, after several decades of psy-choanalytic practice, I looked for common elements in the patients who seemed to have "changed the most" during—and in my opinion because of—psychoanalytic treatment. Although I tried to free myself temporarily from theoretical preoccupations in the search for a central theme, one theoretical question arose immediately: If we select from our case material the analysands who have "changed the most," are we speaking of those who have experienced "structural" change? What do we understand by this term, and is there a connection between structural alteration and the step from insight to "active" or behavioral change?

Even in a psychoanalytic context, the term *structure* is used in differ-ent ways, but here I wish to focus on its meaning in the framework of structural theory—the change, for instance, from a harsh to a more be-nign superego, or more generally changes within the structures of the mental apparatus or in the relationship between the "structures" of ego, superego, and id.

Loewald discusses structural change in psychoanalytic treatment in the following terms: "If structural change in the patient's personality means anything, it must mean that we assume that ego-development is resumed in the therapeutic process in psychoanalysis" (1960, p. 16). For Loewald the analyst is a *new* object in the patient's life. He thinks of the analyst as a sculptor, but I would emphasize that the sculptor's vision of the finished statue must be influenced by the characteristics of the mar-ble. He frees the form that he sees as kept captive by the stone. Since, as I have spelled out in previous chapters, spatial analogies carry with them dangers of reification, I prefer time-based analogies and would thus pre-fer the analogy of the creation of a symphony to that of a sculpture. David Rapaport's notion (1960) that structure and function differ only in their respective rates of change is pertinent here.

Loewald's emphasis on a cooperative venture leading to the formation of a *new* structure does offer a framework for clinically derived data about the patients who have "changed the most," and his formulation of struc-tural change remains applicable: "The interpretation takes with the patient the step towards true regression, as against the neurotic compromise formation, thus clarifying for the patient his true regression-level which has been . . . made unrecognizable by . . . defensive . . . structures. . . . by this very step it mediates to the patient the higher integrative level to be reached." The possibility for freer interplay between the unconscious and preconscious systems is thus created by the interpretation. The analytic process then consists of certain integrative experiences between patient and analyst as the foundation for the internalized version of such experiences: reorganization of ego, "structural change" (1960, p. 25).

Rangell (1981) has tried to understand psychoanalytically the difference between patients whose response to insight is "So what?" or "I see this, but what shall I do now?" (p. 131) and those who move autonomously from insight to the initiation of change. Rangell refers to Waelder's statement that analysis offers patients "a possibility of working out a viable, non-neurotic, solution" (p. 135), but the limits of current formulations of the difference between those who act and those who only understand are illustrated by Rangell's need to include unspecified constitutional factors in the formation of more or less action-prone "executive egos."

Although infant observation yields data on variables that could be thought of as constitutional precursors of such characteristics, my observations of adult patients have led me to additional ideas about the more or less "action-prone" features of analysands' "executive egos." I refer to the marked differences between individuals whose behavior does or does not illustrate their experience of themselves as originating centers of autonomous action, either generally or in specific conflictual situations. I tend to think of patients as having undergone "structural changes" to the extent to which changes in the quantities and loci of self-experiences of possible autonomous action have occurred. Those in whom such changes have taken place may or may not *choose* to make certain changes in their lives, but any lack of action is for them deliberate and not the result of inhibition. Discussions with colleagues have revealed that when they think of patients who have experienced "structural change" their clinical understanding of the term approximates mine.

A retrospective view of cases in which significant change, perhaps structural change, had occurred led me to the observation that they were characterized by a change in focus from animate to inanimate features of "objects" encountered in the analytic work. This observation would be banal if it were simply a description, in slightly different words, of dead issues becoming live issues and vice versa. The form in which certain life-or-death issues were encountered in some of these analyses—specifically, brief but important *perceptions* of animate objects as inanimate—suggested the possibility that aspects of the experience might hark back to the infant's dawning awareness of the differentiation of the inanimate and animate worlds. In other words, the question arose of whether the analysand's experiences of objects changing, on a symbolic level, from animate to inanimate and vice versa—a change in the *relationship to objects*—might be connected to the perceptual discrimination between the animate and the inanimate, and even to the infant's development of this differentiation. If, indeed, the readiness for such shifts in cathexis to *symbolic* representations of the animate and inanimate depends on the individual's history of *perceptual* experiences (even if the perceptual animate-inanimate switch is clear and explicit only in some cases), awareness of such a relationship could lead to a better understanding of the development of action-prone executive egos.

In musing further about animate-inanimate discrimination as an early developmental task, I conceived of it as probably intimately connected to but not identical with the inner-outer discrimination. It is a discrimination necessary for action: the animate reacts. Nevertheless, this early discrimination is, paradoxically, not a very firm one. Does our anxiety about dying spur us to animate the universe as we do, so that we perceive living clouds and the embracing rays of the sun? At any rate, interweaving with temporal and other ambiguities, the animate-inanimate problem endures, finding expression in subtle and usually unnoticed ways that may be ego-syntonic additions to defensive maneuvers against death. In listening to their patients, analysts may unconsciously compensate for animate-inanimate slips just as they often do for other kinds of slips until they train themselves to special alertness.

Once I became aware of the possible significance of changes in animate-inanimate discrimination in clinical material, my own defensive not-hearing—my compensating for patients' slips indicating their confusion between the animate and inanimate realms—diminished. I discovered how prevalent such confusion was in the productions of many of my patients. Different features of change in the animate-inanimate discrimination characterized different patient groups, however. These variations were diagnostically important and were related to the severity of the pathology. Changes in animate-inanimate discrimination occur in, and can direct the analyst to, *discrete* conflict areas in neurotic patients. A structural alteration in this discriminatory function has occurred in these patients, and psychoanalytic work can bring about a corrective structural change. Derivatives of *widespread* confusion of the animate and inanimate realms run through most of the clinical work with borderline and narcissistic patients. This pervasiveness, I believe, accounts for some of the difficulties of obtaining structural change in such patients. In psychotic patients, animate-inanimate confusion is *massive and pervasive.* The manifestations of the problem in these patients can be subtle, however, because this confusion is so intertwined with other boundary problems. With the usual reservations about the unavoidable oversimplifications and incompleteness of summaries of the work of many years, I will now turn to clinical material, going from less to more severe psychopathology.

Clinical Illustrations

Mrs. A, forty years old, married since her early twenties, and mother of four boys, had been greatly concerned about her husband's health. Her anxiety was apparently somewhat contagious both to Mr. A and to some of his physicians: Mr. A was hospitalized twice for diagnostic workups, but they resulted in a clean bill of health. In addition, marital dissatisfaction of recent origin had led Mr. and Mrs. A to seek couple therapy at her initiative. Apparently she had been finding him much more aggressive and sarcastic than previously, and he had been experiencing her as more anxious, provocative, and critical. When the mutual accusatory pattern did not yield to treatment and the marital tension continued to increase, the therapist recommended individual treatment for both. According to Mrs. A, her husband had become vehemently opposed to the idea of any treatment for anybody, but by this time her growing depression and interpersonal difficulties with her sons and many of her friends led her to seek more consultations. Eventually she decided to enter psychoanalysis, during which the following story emerged.

Mrs. A was the youngest of a large number of children, all girls. When she was between four and five years old, a brother was born, but he died at the age of two. Mrs. A became an attractive adolescent and young woman; she had many boyfriends, whom she usually brought home to meet her family. The young man who later became her husband was studying the same narrow sub-specialty of the technical field in which her father worked. Of all the young men she brought home, he was the only one with whom her father had lengthy conversations and developed a genuine relationship—a relationship that continued to flourish after the marriage. Mr. A's career prospered, and the couple's four sons developed well. For many years Mrs. A seemed to experience no dissatisfaction with her life—or at least she gave no *signs* of dissatisfaction.

Her concern for her husband's health and the complaints and symptoms that led to couple therapy and then to her entering analysis occurred a few months after her father's death. This information, I might add, was somewhat slow in emerging because of a sequence of "errors" made by Mrs. A in giving and elaborating on her history. Eventually, however, she described how one morning, not long after her father's death, she had looked critically at her sleeping husband, had experienced him briefly as a stranger, and then had the thought, "What am I doing—being married to *that*?" She later elaborated that, for a brief moment, she had experienced him as dead—"like a piece of wood."

It will come as no surprise to a psychoanalyst reading this story that the following understanding emerged from psychoanalytic work: Mrs. A had had death wishes for her younger male sibling, who had been greatly desired by the family, especially her father. The inevitable psychoanalytic formulation involved her guilt feelings connected to her brother's death, the replacement or restitution motive in her marital choice, the centrality in her emotional life of her relationship to her father, for whom she also produced and raised her four sons, and finally the collapse of the essential meaning of her life with her father's death. The problems that had brought Mrs. A to therapy reflected the degree of resistance and the complexity of the maneuvers she had employed to avoid facing her emotional bankruptcy after her father died. When her husband was no longer serving a bridging function to her father, she began to recognize, at some level, that he was an inappropriate mate, a genuinely poor choice. Eventually she divorced her husband and relatively late in life resumed her education so that she was able to embark on a professional career. The points I wish to develop, however, could be made if the patient had instead discovered that the marriage was more meaningful than ever to her, that she was married to a man with whom she could have a loving relationship now that he no longer had to serve such a concrete bridging function.

Schematically presented, the transference-related *action* in the analysis began to surface around a remark indicating that the patient was hiding the time of her analytic session from her husband. Why? He was a violent man who didn't want her to be in analysis, but she had already told him that she was seeing a psychoanalyst. What would be the effect of his knowing the particular days and times of the sessions? Well, he might just kill her—or, (variations on the theme were rapidly played out over several sessions), he might kill the analyst. It became clear that by informing him of the analysis and making a point of being secretive about the days and hours, she was being very provocative. Exploration of the theme of provocation of violence (she might have to kill him in self-defense or in defending the analyst—from an attack on him that she would have provoked) led through dreams and associations to her death wishes directed primarily against her husband and the analyst (in various transferentially determined roles); finally, after corrections and amplification of the history she had previously given, the trail led to affectively charged memories of her brother's death and to the formulation given above.

Affectively charged recall, in a treatment in which a transference neurosis had developed, and insight—in this case leading to specific action—are the concepts used in a psychoanalytic description of change. Had there been structural change? A great part of Mrs. A's life had been organized around her guilt connected to her brother's death. One could say that her psychic reality was that she *had* killed him, a psychic reality reactivated in the heat of the transference and manifesting itself in the various "who would kill whom" scenarios related to her provocative behavior. One could also say that in a sense life had played a cruel joke on Mrs. A. She had unconsciously organized a good portion of her life as if she *had* killed her brother, and psychoanalysis had helped her to change from, escape from, the role of victim by illuminating the "adult" reality that she had *not* killed her brother. Perhaps one could say that she learned in analysis just how much she had wanted to kill her brother, in the context of her de-repressing various aspects of her wishes, including sexual ones, for her father. I believe that she learned something about the intensity of her death wish on different developmental levels, and that such learning in turn involved contact with different levels of the development of perception.

Once again the notion that each perceptual act recapitulates the ontogeny of perception is pertinent to a psychoanalytic understanding of object constancy. Such a recapitulation would bring the individual again and again into brief contact with the earliest perceptual processes, and there are indications that the discrimination between the animate and the inanimate is precisely one such process. Some years ago, for instance, Margaret Mahler (personal communication, 1973) called my attention to Stirnimann's 1947 finding that the normal infant's differential grasp shows the ability to discriminate in the first hours of life between a proferred finger, a gloved finger, a glove without a finger, and a stick.

Although insufficient and oversimplified, it is accurate to say that Mrs. A discovered in a situation laden with transference affect that wish and deed were not identical, a differentiation that was not solidly established at the time of her brother's death. Greenspan (1982) has shown that during psychoanalytic treatment different levels of learning are integrated. He speaks of somatic learning, of consequence learning, and of representational-structural learning. Different levels of learning involve different levels of perceptual development—that is, a close connection exists between perceptual recapitulation and the integration of different levels of learning. When Mrs. A admitted to consciousness the thought, "What am I doing—being married to *that?*" the literal meaning was important. *That* was not human. *That* was not animate. *That* was a thing. The frenetic activity that followed, the hypochondriasis *for* her husband, represented efforts to breathe some life into the scene.

The change in Mrs. A's life is easily visible because she *acted*—after acquiring insight—to alter her situation. Despite its importance in the background and its possible emergence at nodal points of change, material related to the animate-inanimate differentiation may not be noticed at all or may not demand focused attention in the analysis of neurotic patients with a *relatively* uncomplicated developmental history of this differentiation. As Loewald (1960, p. 25) puts it, "The analyst in his interpretations reorganizes, reintegrates unconscious material for himself as well as for the patient." I believe that the analyst's ability to be in touch to some extent with the patient's "de-animation" is therapeutically useful in general. Mrs. A, however, like many other patients without major ego deficits, was spurred into action in treatment and then in life not only through a transferentially activated confrontation with her destructive wishes but also through a regressive brief encounter with the uncanny breakdown of the inanimate-animate boundary—when her husband had been transformed into "that." Inasmuch as Mr. A, in a deep sense, had been a quasi-inert instrument of contact with her father, who was the real object of her live cathexis, the experience of her husband as "that" was of course accurate.

The domain of the ambiguity between the animate and the inanimate is the area of the uncanny, which during analytic treatment is briefly encountered by some patients (such as Mrs. A) but which is an area of recurrent or prolonged immersion for other patients. The following example also illustrates a significant encounter with the animate-inanimate boundary in treatment.

In one session, a brilliant and highly creative young scientist was discussing his doubts about whether or not to marry his girlfriend, the possibility that she might be pregnant, and related issues that could justify a considerable degree of emotional turmoil. Yet his agitation and at times his bewilderment in the session seemed disconnected from the content.

The analyst commented on that impression and inquired about other areas in the patient's life. In response, the patient was flooded with tears and suddenly recalled a dream. He was flying over a beautiful city, which he described in exquisite detail. When he flew lower and lower over the city and searched for signs of life, however, he discovered that it was absolutely dead—no bustling activities downtown, no children in the schoolyards, no life in the residential areas.

The patient's associations led to his work. In a creative storm—working night and day—he had just solved a fundamental problem, a problem that had been recognized for over a hundred years, about which many books had been written, and about which there had been many lively controversies. He had found a simple and elegant solution to the old problem—he could fly over the city now—but the intense life around a basic scientific question, an area of research and agitation in which he had been a major participant, had come to an abrupt end. The problem was dead. The significance of the patient's achievement (and "achieving," incidentally, also means killing) was soon widely recognized and led to a meteoric rise in his career. His colleagues also commented that his writing style at this point changed radically. Although working in a rigorous and highly abstract scientific field, he was often complimented thereafter about the change from the dry style customary in his field to a remarkably readable, animated style, which conveyed with simple elegance the growth and unfolding of his thought.

Throughout the patient's childhood and youth, his father had engaged him in fierce chess battles, whose competitiveness was closely connected to the patient's subsequent scientific intensity. Rich analytic material illustrated how his scientific breakthrough was related to oedipal issues and his ability to deal with an oedipal victory. This explanatory interpretation, however, does not detract from the significance for him, at the moment of profound change, of contact with the *uncanny* boundary of the lifeless, perhaps with the structural difference of the animate and inanimate.

Freud discusses such an encounter primarily in his cultural and anthropological works, although these interests are, of course, not segregated for him from clinical concerns. The topic is a central one in his paper "The 'Uncanny' " (1919), but in *Totem and Taboo* (1913) he had already touched on the connection of the uncanny experience with the animate-inanimate boundary: "We appear to attribute an 'uncanny' quality to impressions that seek to confirm the omnipotence of thoughts and the animistic mode of thinking in general, after we have reached a stage at which, in our *judgment*, we have abandoned such beliefs" (Standard Edition, 13:86).

In my psychoanalytic work with Anna, the hysterical patient discussed in chapters 2 and 3 whose presenting difficulties included fugue states and who had many déjà vu experiences during analytic sessions, I noticed a pseudoanimism, a peculiar aliveness of objects in the analyst's office, which characterized these states. The episodes proved to be defensive against the reliving of a particularly unexpected encounter with death in a situation when she had made light of potential danger. Here, the animate-inanimate issue was important in work with a neurotic, basically hysterical patient, and the prevalence of synesthetic and déjà vu phenomena seemed to contribute to the (pseudo)-animism. I will return later to the association between synesthesia, déjà vu experiences, uncanniness, and a fluid animate-inanimate boundary.

The animate-inanimate problem appears perhaps most frequently and typically in analysis and psychoanalytic psychotherapy in the work with patients with pronounced narcissistic traits. Because my ideas about the importance of the problem also have more direct consequences for therapeutic technique with such patients, I will emphasize technical considerations in illustrating the animate-inanimate issue in narcissistic patients.

A young divorcée started her Monday morning hour with a barrage of complaints centering on her inability to cope with a baby who cried at all hours of the night and a boyfriend in whom she was more interested than he was in her. In her account there was no differentiation in the tone she used to describe things that *happened* to her and things she *did*. She continued to complain about her own bad driving, her overeating, and her wish to kill her baby. The whole picture was presented as an attack on the analyst, who she said had not helped her with any of her problems. She continued, "It is not safe for me to drive. I have had some vague thoughts of killing myself, and the car seems to agree with me. Wouldn't start."

Some clinicians refer to the behavior features in this brief sketch as "entitlement"—a person's failure to differentiate between events that result from volitional action (consciously or unconsciously volitional) and external events, those that are not immediately related to identifiable intentionality. The analyst's problem in such situations concerns the ego syntonicity for the patient of such lack of differentiation—that is, the analyst must explore why it seems so natural to the patient not to differentiate between such complaints as eating too much, a car that won't start, and a thunderstorm. In his later work *Search for a Method* (1960), which has largely been ignored by psychoanalysts, Jean-Paul Sartre emphasized the distinction between *praxis* (actions resulting from intentionality) and *process* (processes related to inert matter). I believe that if therapeutic efforts with patients such as the one I am describing are successful, an important area of change is the patient's ability to differentiate between the results of praxis, on the one hand, and of inert processes or the haphazard, on the other.

A close look at the exchanges in the analytic session may illustrate a direct technical application of some of the ideas developed here. Because her car wouldn't start, my patient took a taxi. Because a friend of hers had recently been mugged, she experienced acute anxiety when the driver took her over an unfamiliar route and through a part of the city where there were few people on the street. At the time of this session, several years into the analysis, the analyst had already learned that it was unproductive for him to confront her with her propensity to treat events that she had caused in the same manner as externally caused events. Instead, the analyst asked if she had thought about the mugging while in the cab. The patient replied that she had indeed and that she had also thought about murders she had read about in the newspaper. The analyst's next intervention was based on the idea that the danger in the atmosphere, so to speak, should be addressed rather than the location of the source of the danger, because he saw the patient's difficulties as being rooted in an uncompleted differentiation of who or what can initiate action—that is, ultimately, of what is animate—from what is acted upon, the inanimate. Carefully choosing his words, the analyst said: "You have been in touch with a lot of murderous feelings since our last session. You had murderous feelings against your baby, and you had thoughts about murderous feelings directed against you." Again, what was important, I believe, was the analyst's *not* confronting the patient with the analyst's own differentiation of praxis and process, the actor and the acted upon, but rather watching carefully over the development of that differentiation in the patient. (Note also, however, the analyst's differentiation of "feelings," on the one hand, and "thoughts about feelings," on the other.) It does not advance the work if the analyst, feeling unfairly accused and held responsible for everything that goes wrong in the patient's life, responds—or, perhaps more accurately, retaliates-—with confrontation, in effect saying that the patient *should* be big enough to differentiate between what she is doing and what happens to her.

How, then, can change occur in such an analytic situation? A few months after the session described above, the patient again spoke of a series of unfortunate developments in her life. She had had a bad night. For various reasons the analyst believed that the patient was not reporting a dream. He asked, "In this terrible night, did you have any dreams?" The patient became restless and said, "Yes, but I can't remember." The restlessness continued and after a fairly long pause the patient said, "Well, there were people, and I was literally coming apart. The buttons on my blouse wouldn't stay closed." "Too many demands pulling you apart," the analyst said. "But it's not exactly like that," the patient continued. "There was something sloppy about it. Self-demeaning. I'm getting fat." Note that the patient was not attacking the analyst and did not blame him for her overeating. There were some indications of embarrassment. She used the neutral way of phrasing that had been characteristic of the analyst's way of commenting: "There was something sloppy about it." She moved to "self-demeaning," which was followed by "I'm getting fat." She was en route to the autonomous experience that she was eating too much and that she could initiate eating less. The patient proved to be en route to more autonomous experience generally.

Strachey's (1934) notions about change, identifications with the analyst, and the taking in of small doses of reality about the analyst are relevant here, along with Loewald's emphasis on the analyst's facilitating true regression and thus a new beginning, with its consequent distancing from current compromise formation. For the present purposes, however, I would like to emphasize that the analyst's technique was informed by the notion that the patient's difficulty was related to a problem in the development of perceptual differentiation. Confrontation was avoided. This made unnecessary the compromise formations that were the patient's usual response to the attacks her behavior elicited. The vicious cycle was broken. In Loewald's language, a true regression—to a state in which the animate and the inanimate were not adequately differentiated—made possible a new beginning. "Process," in Sartre's language, was gradually changed to "praxis."

Let me elaborate: the patient said she "wanted" to come to her analytic session and thought that the stalling engine was a process phenomenon, the fault of inert matter. Suppose, however, that in analysis it became clear that her neglect of her car was related to the ambivalence she harbored vis-a-vis her treatment. Then the *process* would have been changed to *praxis*. In such an analytic situation inroads on the preconscious can transform much that is "accidental" into meaningful sequence. Slips are no longer haphazard, even to the patient. I will return later to some epistemological consequences of the discovery of the uncertainty of the boundary between the meaningful and the haphazard. If we cannot trust the border anymore, is there possible meaning everywhere, or is there meaning nowhere?

Finally, I turn to case material of more severe psychopathology—to Mary, the self-mutilating borderline patient mentioned briefly in chapter 2. Such patients demonstrate in their psychopathology the pervasiveness of issues related to animate-inanimate discrimination. Mary had had a severe skin disorder during the language-learning period, and her later foremost symptomatology included repeatedly cutting her skin, when she experienced herself as inanimate, and then interfering with the wound's healing (Kafka, 1969).

Problems of limits—the limits of her body, the limits of her power, and the limits of her capacity to feel—were of major importance in Mary's analysis. Winnicott's concepts of transitional objects and transitional phenomena (1958a) provide a useful framework for the formulation of some aspects of the patient's history of object relationships. I want to develop the idea that a patient's own body can be treated by her as a transitional object and that this can be related to a history of self-injury. I will also explore some effects of this history of object relationships on the development of transference and countertransference.

When one speaks of transitional objects, the image that most easily evokes a response in the listener is Linus's security blanket in the comic strip "Peanuts." Mary illuminated for me an expanded way of thinking about possible transitional objects. One can approach this point of view by visualizing the initial frames of the films used to teach surgery to medical students. A piece of carefully cleansed skin is shown, surrounded by nonreflecting blue drapes; the location of the skin is explained in the accompanying technical commentary; and then the surgeon's gloved hand makes a rapid scalpel incision. There is a pause, which the viewer experiences as longer than it is, before blood wells up—before the viewer experiences the emotional shift from what seems inanimate surgical anatomy to confrontation with the wound. I am proposing that the self-mutilator again and again treats her own skin and body in a somewhat similar fashion, as if at some point she sees it as inanimate and transitional. In theorizing about such matters we must be careful, of course, to remain aware of the limitation of words, for we are dealing with nonverbal, largely preverbal material. Yet even catchphrases, such as "transitional object," may be useful in producing the contagious atmosphere that enables us to participate in the other person's experience.

Mary was a college student in her late teens when I started working with her. Her psychoanalytic treatment lasted almost five years, during the first two of which she was hospitalized. Her father is a dry, undemonstrative engineer, and her mother is a talkative woman with hysterical and hypochondriacal characteristics. The patient has one older brother, whose superior academic performance she envied. Her parents had been separated for several years prior to her hospitalization. A psychiatrist who had seen Mary on a less intensive basis for over a year had referred her for psychoanalysis in a hospital setting because of symptoms consisting primarily of cutting herself and interfering with wound healing. Sometimes she also swallowed pills indiscriminately, refused to take medications, or cheated in taking medications. She narcissistically considered and treated practically her whole body surface as an almost constant object of erotic fascination.

Interference with wound healing had apparently been present since childhood, probably since the age of six or eight years, but the symptoms, especially cutting, had increased in frequency since her parents' separation. Mary was scarred primarily on her arms, but her appearance was generally pasty and her demeanor listless when I started working with her.

During her first year of life Mary had been gravely ill with a generalized dermatitis diagnosed as an allergic reaction. Problems related to touching and skin sensitivity had thus been prominent since infancy. Furry pets and dolls were always common in the household, and early contacts with these objects were related to the importance of texture for Mary. Mother and daughter competed in taking care of the pets. For years prior to the parents' separation, the father had had a relationship with another woman and had totally neglected his wife sexually. Thus the mother had a strongly eroticized interest in the household pets and also in her particularly cuddly daughter, for whom the atmosphere also became diffusely eroticized. The mother instructed Mary in how to spy on the father, whose infidelity was always suspected. The father, in turn, was aware of his daughter's inquisitiveness. Mary had repetitive self-destructive thoughts and thoughts that she was in danger when she was with him—for example, it would occur to her that he wanted to push her from a bridge—and she had at least brief thoughts of how she might retaliate. Erotic feelings toward her father were thus particularly interwoven with sadomasochistic elements. The mother used a variety of conversion symptoms to force some attention from her husband and others, and she openly showed her delight when Mary similarly got her way in a situation in which that did not seem possible, such as when she somehow persuaded a bus driver to stop the bus en route so she could get a soft drink. Her feelings of omnipotence were encouraged in this and a variety of other ways. For example, from the age of fifteen on, as a volunteer in an animal care and rescue center, Mary had the power of life and death over stray animals: she could decide which were to be put to sleep and which were to be offered for adoption.

Early phases of the psychoanalytic work were often characterized by Mary's sullen, silent attitude, to which I found myself responding similarly. After two months of analysis the problem of the limits of her powers was highlighted dramatically: she developed a fulminating case of viral pneumonia which required transfer to a general hospital. She went rapidly downhill, and despite heroic measures the internist and consultant expressed the opinion that she was terminal and would not survive the next forty-eight hours. When fully conscious in the oxygen tent, she still insisted that she wanted to drink only a particular kind of fruit juice, not readily available, and refused the more common juices that were offered. At this point I told her that she was not expected to survive and that she might as well drink the available juice if she still wanted to taste any juice at all. A marked behavioral change occurred at that time. She looked frightened, talked about her fear of death, and drank the juice that was offered. This seemed to mark a clear turning point and left me with the feeling that my ability to be blunt with her had saved her life. After her recovery from pneumonia, the theme of my power over her life and death became a prominent one in analysis. Cutting of her arms and legs continued until I experienced fully my inability to save her life. She then seemed to experience more power over her own life, and self-mutilation stopped.

The unfolding of the transference provided most of the history of her development that I have described. When I sensed an unusual number of erotic and sadistic fantasies, the work of analysis identified them as representing repressed aspects of both parents' relationships with Mary, but predominantly the mother's. In discussing the analysis, I will single out for further description and theoretical consideration her experience of her own body, and my frequent echoing experience of her as not quite living matter. I will not dwell on the more routine psychoanalytic work, but there was much working through of material relating to complexities of interpersonal relationships as she eventually moved out of the hospital, became a private patient, found work, had plastic surgery to remove at least some of her many scars, and started to have increasingly frequent and meaningful dates. The intensive and complex work with Mary's family and the difficult and subtle administrative and nursing management of her hospital stay will also not be described here (but see Burnham, 1966, for a description of how she decorated almost every inch of her room with furry or other textured objects, pictures of animals, and so on).

In proceeding to a description of the heart of Mary's analysis, I return first to Winnicott:

It is generally acknowledged that a statement of human nature is inadequate when given in terms of interpersonal relationships. There is another way of describing persons . . . that suggests that of every individual who has reached to the stage of being a unit *with a limiting membrane and an outside and an inside* (italics mine] it can be said that there is an *inner* reality to that individual, an inner world which can be rich or poor or can be at peace or in a state of war.

My claim is that if there is a need for this double statement there is a need for a triple one; there is the third part of the life of a human being, a part that we cannot ignore, an intermediate area of *experiencing*, to which inner reality and external life both contribute. It is an area which is *not challenged* [italics mine], because no claim is made on its behalf except as it exists as a resting place for the individual engaged in the perpetual *human* [italics mine] task of keeping inner and outer reality separate yet, interrelated. (1958a, p. 230).

Winnicott subtitled this paper "Study of the First *Not Me* Possession," which seems to me to be pertinent to my discussion of Mary, who considered her body in precisely these terms. Early in life she had had spiked braces placed on her teeth in an unsuccessful attempt to keep her from thumb-sucking and resultant bad teeth alignment; later she was fascinated by the theme of auto-cannibalism. She had vivid fantasies about starving Arctic explorers eating parts of their own bodies to survive, and at times she actually ate small (and sometimes not so small) pieces of the flesh and skin of her own fingers.

Because of apparently life-threatening early allergic dermatitis, Mary's entire body had been swaddled and bandaged during most of her first year. As mentioned earlier, Winnicott suggests that the pattern of transitional phenomena begins to show somewhere between four and twelve months (1958a, p. 232). Particular care was given to the problem of keeping Mary from irritating her skin with her own hands. The parents also recalled the problems related to picking up and touching the baby and managed to convey a picture of what is likely to have been contact hunger and acute pain with contact.

In the course of the analysis, Mary described her sensations when she slowly and deliberately cut herself—for instance, with a razor blade or with a broken light bulb smuggled under her bed covers—while gazing lovingly at her "favorite nurse," who was "specialing" her. At first she would not feel it, but "I always stopped as soon as I did feel it," and she managed to convey the exquisite border experience of sharply "becoming alive" at that moment. This sharp sensation was then followed by the flow of blood; in her description, the blood seemed like a voluptuous bath, a sensation of pleasant warmth that spread over the hills and valleys of her body, molding its contour and sculpting its form. In speaking of her blood, Mary communicated a relationship with a transitional object—the sense that as long as one has blood, one carries within oneself a potential security blanket capable of giving warmth and comforting envelopment. Dream and fantasy material suggested that *internal* blood was probably linked to the internalized mother and that the patient felt superior to others or omnipotent because *she* could use her knowledge to make this comforting mother-blanket external. Winnicott says that the mother herself can be the transitional object ("Sometimes there is no transitional object except the mother herself"—1958a, p. 232), but he does not specifically make the point being stressed here—that part of the body (here the blood, representing the internalized mother) can be a transitional object.

Throughout a major portion of the analysis, Mary expressed concern (or threatened) that the pleasurable sensation associated with cutting would make it impossible for her to resist the temptation to scar herself, particularly her face and trunk. At times she not only felt superior to others but seemed genuinely puzzled as to how others could go through life without even occasionally indulging in the forbidden fruit of a blood bath available so readily through a "zip" in the skin. She made jokes about having zippers in the skin and reported many dreams related to shedding of skin, burned tar paper forming peeling blisters, and so on. She also reported that during her childhood in a northern city, she often had vivid fantasies during frequent snowball fights that an invisible layer around her stopped snowballs at some distance from her body. Such fantasies may have been related to her weight, which had fluctuated greatly during much of her life. She was fascinated by a magazine article describing an avant-garde artist who painted the skin of his models and then instructed them to transfer the pigment to canvas by throwing their bodies on the canvas or rolling themselves against it. For years prior to this, she herself had made designs by letting worms crawl through spilled ink onto white paper. In both techniques, the fascination lay in the use of the living body as a tool, an object transitional between living and dead matter. Worms were of particular interest to Mary for their clearly segmented structure, the fact that excretory and sexual organs were in *each* segment, and their ability to grow parts after they had been severed. (Parenthetically, one may ask if a segment of a worm is a whole or a part-object.) Perhaps it would make sense here to talk of something *transitional* between the part and the whole object.

In the countertransference, when I experienced the patient as not quite living, not quite animate, I too was relating to a transitional object. In retrospect, one of the factors that permitted me to be so blunt, or perhaps so *sharp*, with Mary when she was apparently dying of pneumonia was my experiencing her as a not-quite-living person. The degree to which one ascribes to another the quality of being alive (assuming that one considers oneself alive) depends on the ability to be empathic or to identify with the other person. With her pasty appearance and her ability to slice into her own skin without any change in facial expression, Mary seemed to treat herself as a not quite living object, or at least to consider parts of her body as something other than her own living tissue. My reaction in the face of her self-mutilations was not always "'Don't do that! Don't hurt yourself. I won't let you hurt yourself." My experience was perhaps more in line with what Winnicott has called "hate in the countertransference" (1958b); at least my subjective feelings could have been verbalized along the lines of "Go ahead, slice yourself to ribbons; let's find out if you're alive or not."

Earlier I expressed the idea that in order to permit her infant to take a first step, a mother must have the delusion that the infant will not fall, a predifferentiation delusion of unity. Work with Mary was one of the factors that have now led me to believe that another parental delusion, if you will, is necessary to permit individuation of the offspring. The delusion is that the offspring is not alive. Let me explain. It is generally believed that physicians cannot adequately treat members of their own families because they are not "objective" enough. To rephrase this: they cannot treat members of their own families sufficiently as *nonliving objects*. At crucial times, however, every parent *must* be a little bit of a doctor in treating his own offspring. A patient comes to mind, for instance, who was paralyzed in his parental function in the face of his child's slightest injury. There are some moments, borderline situations, in which not only the treatment of children's injuries but also the more general *rearing* of children demands the infliction of pain; however brief such moments may be, as parents we can handle them only if we consider the "tissue" as not quite as alive and responsive as our own.

On the descriptive level, I believe that we are on rather firm ground in applying the transitional-object concept to such a situation. This patient certainly *did* treat parts of the surface of her body as though she were dealing with not-quite-living skin, and there is much evidence to support the notion that she was much preoccupied with what was for her the very much *unfinished business* of establishing her body scheme.[6]

In applying the transitional-object concept to the *genetic* aspects of this case, to the developmental roots in the history of the patient, I feel on somewhat less firm ground. Genetically, I conceptualize the intensity of the early contact hunger, and the pain when there *was* contact, as a traumatic fixation point, an area of still strikingly "unfinished business" when analysis began, an area in which the "perpetual human task of keeping inner and outer reality separate yet interrelated" (Winnicott, 1958a, p. 230) was particularly difficult. The possibility that a dramatic

---

[6] In this context the line but important distinction between Schilder's body image (1950) and Federn's (1952) notion of a bodily ego feeling may be pertinent. This distinction refers on the one hand to the knowledge of how one's body functions as a tool, as an instrument, and on the other hand to the feeling of emotional intimacy with one's body, its being part of the "me" feeling. It is perhaps in this border area between body image and bodily ego feeling that the transitional-object concept makes the most sense.

connection probably existed in this case between the early skin disease and the later symptom may offer a lead to other such patients. Early traumatic fixation points relating particularly to the formation of the membrane of the body scheme may play a part in the developmental history of other patients with the cutting syndrome, although less dramatically. The previously developed thesis that benevolent parental communication of tolerance of ambiguity is related to the offspring's individuation without alienation would also find expression here in the ambiguity of hunger for contact and at the same time pain through contact.

Without spelling out again Winnicott's work on the formation of psychic membranes, let us focus on the membrane of particular concern here—the cutter's skin. Although sadism and masochism are usually considered two sides of the same coin, one or the other often dominates a particular clinical picture. The study of how one's own body can be a "not-me" object may illuminate the general question of the sadistic or masochistic preference. In a sense, the cutter's choice is a transitional one between the sadistic and masochistic object, his *own not-me* skin. The skin is his own—but he experiences it as *not* his own. In analysis the ebb and flow of sadomasochistic transference and countertransference may be conceptualized as related to the development and vicissitudes of the animate-inanimate differentiation, a factor contributing to the re-formation of a more integrated, more ego-syntonic body membrane and thus to the eventual elimination of the symptom.

As I have illustrated, confusion between animate and inanimate characteristics is present when major conflicts are activated in neurotic patients, and it is more pervasive in borderline and narcissistic patients. I have asserted that it is widespread in schizophrenic phenomenology and that the animate-inanimate problem seems to be near the psychotic—the autistic—core. In his work on the nonhuman environment, Searles (1960) collected much clinical material that is pertinent here. In the following chapter, I will deal specifically with schizophrenia, but in order to maintain the continuity from less severe to more severe pathology, I will offer a brief clinical illustration here.

A young man who had been hospitalized for years with flagrant schizophrenic pathology had apparently made a remarkable recovery. The degree of his insight and his descriptive abilities were considerable. In describing his emergence from psychosis, he characterized his first transitory moment of feeling normal again as "feeling that he was feeling." "Feeling that he was *not* feeling" was his characterization of his abnormal state. At such times, he felt that his surroundings—the walls, cars, rugs, and so forth—were not real, that perhaps they had been put there to fool him, to make him believe that something real *was* there. Even then he had seemed to succeed in believing in his own existence, however, in a kind of "cogito ergo sum." He existed, but there was no possibility of his having any kind of effect on what was around him. There is, he said, no possibility that what exists can have any impact on what does not exist.

I think of such a state as the absence of an *integrated* feeling of oneself as animate, and I believe that projections and projective identifications of nonexistence are involved. The patient's descriptions brought to mind science fiction stories about isolated heads or perhaps brains existing in nutrient solutions. The patient said that what saved his life ("what made me feel alive") was a psychiatric aide's saying to him, "You are somebody; you can do what you want." I do not know what factors were responsible for the patient's ability to *hear* at that particular moment, to experience himself at that particular moment as an autonomous center of action capable of "connecting" with his surroundings, of having an impact on them. When only he existed and the other existences around him were "pretend," he was not psychologically animate. Anima means breath, breathe, animate means movement—or the potential of movement—that connects; in connecting, it establishes whether the other is *inert matter* or another *animate center of autonomous action*.

Discussion

To summarize some of the ideas presented in this chapter, the following hypothesis is clinically derived and seems clinically useful. The animate and the inanimate are "representational structures" that serve as anchors in our organization of ourselves and thus as anchors in the interpersonal network that makes communication possible. Among the earliest perceptual tasks is discrimination of the fundamental structural differences between the animate and the inanimate. The individual's developmental history of perception is the foundation upon which the gradual integration of various levels of learning (somatic, consequential, and representational-structural learning in Greenspan's [1982] Piagetian schema, for instance) is based. Such integration is necessary to avoid the danger of *action* contamination of our *ideational* contact with and use of the inanimate. Regression in analysis to perceptual dedifferentiation of the animate and inanimate realms can be observed and may play an important part in structural change. Empirically, clinicians tend to speak of structural change in the analysand to the extent to which changes have occurred in the quantities and loci of self-experience as originating centers of autonomous action.

Workers in many fields, including the physicist Ilya Prigogine, are today exploring the concept of structure and fundamental differences between animate and inanimate structures. Their work is pertinent to these considerations and will be discussed at length in the final chapter.

In psychoanalytic treatment, issues related to the dedifferentiation of the animate and the inanimate typically surface in connection with specific conflicts in neurotic individuals and are more pervasive in borderline and narcissistic patients. Going somewhat beyond a summary of what I have been discussing in this chapter, *I consider it an important thesis that there is a correspondence between the dichotomies of inner-outer, temporal-spatial, and animate-inanimate (with inner corresponding to temporal and animate, and so on).* Different manifestations of these corresponding dichotomies, however, may dominate the foreground of the clinical landscape of patients with different diagnoses and those at different stages of treatment. The dichotomies occupy a central position in the psychopathology of psychosis, but the dedifferentiation of the animate and the inanimate in severely decompensated and regressed schizophrenic patients is so pervasive and so interwoven with other dedifferentiations (or "fusions") that it is sometimes difficult to demonstrate it specifically.

I would like to conclude this chapter by considering some formal aspects of the countertransference situation, effort and fatigue, and their relationship to diagnostics, therapeutics, and the particular issues I have been discussing here. My basic notion is that diagnostic categories are in some way related to the sense of effort that the therapist or analyst experiences in bringing about change in the patient, specifically change of *conviction*. The relationship between the therapist's sense of effort and the ease of change in the patient is a complex one, however, because the therapist's expectations enter the picture. For instance, an argument could be made that borderline patients are those who initially present themselves in such a way that the therapist *expects* them to act fairly "normally" and to "use insight gained" rather readily, but who subsequently behave more bizarrely and resist change more persistently than expected. In terms of the content of this chapter, they manifest more problems in the area of animate-inanimate differentiation and at the same time threaten the therapist's sense of himself as an effective, animate agent.

Also pertinent here are some observations on my fatigue and on the time of my awareness of different degrees and qualities of fatigue with various kinds of patients. These observations have had some corroboration in the experiences of colleagues. During a period when I was dividing my time between psychoanalytically based therapy with psychotic (mostly schizophrenic) and borderline patients and the psychoanalysis of neurotic patients, I found the day-to-day work more fatiguing with the neurotic patients than with the flagrantly psychotic ones. I found some reversal of this situation, however, upon returning from vacation; often, prior to meeting with a psychotic patient for the first time after a vacation, I was particularly aware of my expectation of hard work. Borderline patients tended to be on both sides of the spectrum—inducing fatigue at most times.

Later I will return to considerations of effort in a broader context, but let me note in anticipation that effort makes no sense if one does not believe that it will produce something worthwhile. Effort is thus tied to the idea of causality. If there is no causal linkage between events, they seem to occur in a haphazard fashion. The idea of the unconscious shrinks the world of the haphazard, since linkages are established or are presumed to exist where previously there seemed to be none. Perceived linkages determine our world, our psychological realities.

At the other extreme from the problem of seeing separate parts and apparent lack of continuity where actually there is unseen continuity is the problem of seeing continuity, a chain of causal connection, where actually there is *none*. An experiment by Bavelas (1970) illustrates this phenomenon. The subject of the experiment is told that there is a correct sequence of punching a group of buttons. A bell will sound, he is told, when he hits upon the correct pattern. The subject's work is rewarded with increasingly frequent bell sounds until the experiment is interrupted. When asked about the correct pattern, the subject describes it and explains which hypotheses he formed, discarded, and modified in the process of becoming totally convinced that he has discovered the right sequence. When the experimenter explains that there is no correct pattern and that the timing of the bell sounds followed a theoretical learning curve, the subject is incredulous. He gives up his conviction only after he hears another subject express a similar certainty in the correctness of a different pattern—that is, when the first subject becomes the experimenter with a second subject who is put through the same set of conditions. The sensation of effort is related to *conviction* and is connected with a representational structure of oneself as an animate center of action. In clinical work, the study of who experiences himself as making what kind of effort, and when, reveals parallels between categories of effort and patients with various degrees and kinds of pathology and sheds some light on the How of transference and countertransference and trial-identifications.

To return to my main thesis here, when there has been a wrong hookup, so to speak, when a human is experienced as inanimate, a true regression in the analysis occurs and a restructuring not only is essential but may be precipitated by the encounter. The fundamental cannibalistic anxiety of the animate-inanimate boundary—the "raw-cooked" dichotomy—is dealt with in the story of Hansel and Gretel. The witch in the story obviously cannot make the distinction between the animate and the inanimate, and paradoxically it is this nonhuman characteristic that permits Hansel and Gretel to survive. Mistaking stick for finger (unlike the normal human infant), the witch believes the children are not yet fat enough to eat. If we were to psychoanalyze the witch and make it possible for her to integrate the distinction between animate and inanimate on *all* levels of learning, she would not become a more successful witch, but her cannibalistic tendencies would undoubtedly become confined to the ideational or fantasy level. She would be much less prone to *act* like a witch and might deal with cannibalistic fantasies by reading to some children the story of Hansel and Gretel.

Chapter 5

Schizophrenia

The study of schizophrenic patients has played an important part in the formulation of many of the ideas on multiple realities that are central to this book. Once these ideas had been formulated, they were useful in the understanding and treatment of some nonpsychotic disorders as well as schizophrenia. I believe that at a time when the biological study of schizophrenia and the use of pharmacological interventions are in the ascendance, attention to psychodynamic issues of this kind is essential for a balanced approach to the disorder. Organic theories of the etiology of schizophrenia and organic treatments were on the scene long before I started working with such patients, but these early hypotheses and treatments were often disappointing, even damaging (as with frontal lobotomies). I recognize, of course, the contributions of current sophisticated biological research to the understanding and treatment of schizophrenia, and indeed, my own partial model of schizophrenic thought disorder leaves room for a plausible biological contribution. There is, however, the danger that enthusiasm for the new developments and a resultant biological reductionism may lead to the neglect of the important psychosocial observations made by those who have worked with, studied, and managed these patients for years.

For a long time, there has been a tendency among biological investigators to consider that schizophrenic patients who improved dramatically in

the course of psychotherapy with minimal or no pharmacological intervention had been misdiagnosed as schizophrenic or, more simply, had
experienced unexplained spontaneous cures. Such "exceptions" should not
be ignored. In a yearly lecture, "The Case for the Single Case," Heinrich
Klüver used to present the accumulating evidence that the detailed study
of the *exception* had led to most major scientific advances. Dynamic and
biological study of schizophrenic individuals who are the most pronounced exceptions in a population that statistically shows a correlation
between symptomatology and biological findings may help distinguish
pathogenic mechanisms from epiphenomena.

Although most experts in schizophrenia these days avoid a primitive
polarization between the dynamic and organic approaches, too often
they take refuge in a somewhat self-congratulatory claim of favoring a
"psychobiosocial" approach. In practice this approach avoids the hard
questions of the conceptual, experimental, and therapeutic bridges. In
an early investigation that began to tackle such questions, a psychoanalytic study of disorders with a known infectious etiology, paresis, yielded
interesting data (Hollos and Ferenczi, 1922). Although the infectious
etiology of the disorder was clearly established, and although formal
characteristics of the delusional systems of these syphilitic patients had
much in common (the familiar themes of delusions of grandeur or per-
secution), the content of the delusions could best be understood after a
detailed, psychoanalytically informed study of the patients' life histories
prior to the onset of the organic psychosis.

Another early study, Federn's comparison of anesthesia and normal
dreams (1952), examined the influence of pharmacological data on
dreaming and led to the understanding of dream modifications resulting
from diminished access to mobility. Authors who are currently grap-
pling with the hard conceptual issues include Steven Rose (1980), Karl
Pribram (1986), and Morton Reiser (1984), among others. As an example of useful bridging work on an experimental level, one study
demonstrated how the experimenter's *words* can influence memory
even in individuals whose memory is affected by organic factors (Squire,
1986). I refer specifically to the findings on memory because of the importance I have come to attach to the therapist's efforts to help the

schizophrenic patient integrate psychotic and nonpsychotic periods—that is, in some way to remember. In this context the old observation that there is some overlap between certain "organic" and "schizophrenic" diagnostic signs on the Rorschach test also deserves another look.

Finally, therapists who have treated the same patients dynamically prior to and during the period of modern psychopharmacology have a unique longitudinal vantage point. They have noted, for instance, that, in general, brief hospitalizations that emphasize biological treatments seem to be increasing rather than decreasing chronicity. This is only a small example of how essential it is to integrate psychoanalytic and biological modes of thinking about schizophrenia. The collaboration of dynamically (and especially psychoanalytically) trained workers with those who study and treat patients biologically can help navigate research between the shoals of biological oversimplification and psychodynamic rigidity.

Pharmacological studies are often based on large patient populations, but the merits of investigations of individual cases should not be overlooked. Long-term, detailed, intensive study and treatment of single cases permit the filtering out of conceptual and therapeutic fashions and the focusing on ideas that have stood the test of time. Single case studies, therefore, can provide promising hypotheses for formal research strategies. They can also provide some perspective on the integration of the illness into a life history and on the possible effects of therapy on the quality of life, especially during nonpsychotic periods. With these considerations in mind, I will again turn to clinical material, before dealing with more general theoretical issues.

Long-term Psychotherapy in Schizophrenia

Mrs. Dorothy L has been studied and treated psychodynamically both before and during the era of modem psychopharmacology. The emphasis on psychodynamic understanding has not precluded some use of medication, and I will discuss formulations emerging from the interaction of these approaches.

The study of Mrs. L also included two periods of double-blind pharmacological treatment on a schizophrenia research unit. After almost thirty years of work with Mrs. L, I find that certain psychoanalytic concepts and psychoanalytically informed approaches remain pertinent and useful. Some of my dynamic formulations, consistent with but not usually discussed in the analytic framework, have also emerged as important. The patient recently told me that she is thinking of writing a book to be entitled "How to Train One's Therapist." Certain emphases in my presentation are undoubtedly the result of her training activities.

Mrs. L, who is in her late fifties, is the wife of a retired executive and the mother of two children, both of whom are married, have children, and are successful in their professions. Mrs. L's father, Mr. K, was a prominent social science professor, and her mother was a rather eccentric illustrator of children's books. It is likely that Mrs. K had a disturbed period, perhaps a psychotic episode, in her late adolescence or early adult years, during which she was cared for in an attic at home. Mrs. L has a brother two years her junior and an adoptive brother seven years her junior. Both are successful in academic professions.

Dorothy L has often been told that she "tore something" in her mother when she was born. Always a tall, gawky child, she grew into a somewhat awkward adolescent, taller than most of her classmates, including boys. Her mother's lack of interest in the household, particularly anything having to do with food preparation, was striking. Meals consisted of little more than bread and water when there was no maid to prepare them. Mr. K's protectiveness of his wife went very far, and once when one of Dorothy's brothers started to complain about a particularly inadequate meal, Mr. K silently picked him up and carried him out of the room. Early pictures of Dorothy generally show a depressed expression and neglected grooming. Throughout her childhood and into adolescence, however, an aunt and a grandfather regularly took Dorothy away from her parental home, especially during the long summer months. As the only child in the alternative home, she was pampered, sometimes dressed up a bit like a doll, but always the subject of much genuine attention and affection; the household staff, which included cook, maid, and chauffeur, acquiesced to all her requests and treated her like a little princess. (There are indications that different ego-states during the course of her treatment are related to her two homes.)

Socially quite isolated in school, bossy with the brother closer in age, protective and affectionate with her younger brother, she became a hardworking and excellent student. She was consistently a teacher's pet, and her teacher's expressions of approval are important memories sustaining her at times of shattered self-esteem. Some pictures show Dorothy as an adolescent imitating elements of her father's clothing. She describes some outings with her father during which she experienced what can only be called fulfillment. She came very close to experiencing herself as his only son and sometimes also as his caretaking wife.

Dorothy had started attending college away from home during World War II but soon obeyed a call to return to the then maternal household because Mr. K had an important assignment overseas. Dorothy felt that she was summoned home to counterbalance her mother's erratic behavior, perhaps to cook for her younger siblings whenever the maid was not available. The summons home also interrupted an important romantic relationship with a fellow student. While at home, Dorothy was quite depressed; the level of her performance in some part-time courses dropped markedly, and she attempted to combat her marked isolation through brief contacts with young soldiers. She then enlisted in the women's corps of one of the armed services.

After a few months there, at the age of twenty-one, she experienced her first diagnosed schizophrenic episode. Her peers and superiors had noticed her withdrawal, neglect of her body and clothing, marked deterioration of her functioning and work, probably some delusions and paranoid ideation, and some grotesque over-conscientiousness. She precipitated her hospitalization by swallowing, in front of an officer, a medication intended for external treatment of a minor skin disorder. She was hospitalized briefly and then given a medical discharge from the service. During the next ten years, prior to my contact with her, she functioned sometimes marginally, sometimes well. She married and bore two children. She also had some psychotic episodes. Treatment modalities included psychotherapy, insulin, and electroconvulsive shock.

I have seen Dorothy L in almost continuous psychotherapy, ranging in frequency from five hours to one hour per week, for the past thirty years. During her lifetime she has been hospitalized fifteen times for a total of about nine years. No regularity or rhythmicity has been noted in the psychiatric hospitalizations. The longest period of continuous hospitalization, in the early 1960s, was four years; the shortest, one week. The total time spent in halfway houses, day hospitals, and similar arrangements is four years. She has demonstrated a wide range of schizophrenic symptomatology, including systematized paranoid features and such catatonic features as waxy flexibility, mutism, refusal to eat, and retention of urine and feces of such severity that the consulting internist feared permanent bowel damage. It must be emphasized, however, that during nonpsychotic periods the level of her intellectual and social functioning has frequently been very high. She was actively involved in the raising of her children, had a moderately busy social life, traveled abroad, studied languages and music, and was an appreciated volunteer in groups supporting artistic endeavors.

The varying lengths of hospitalization are related in part to changes in the evolving philosophy of treatment. Although I was greatly influenced by the work of Paul Federn, one of the first psychoanalysts to treat schizophrenic patients (perhaps *the* first), my approach differed significantly from his from the beginning in one respect. Federn had suggested that when in remission the patient should be treated by a therapist other than the one working with him or her during the acute phases of schizophrenia. For a variety of reasons, I wanted to explore the possibilities of bridge building between these phases by having the patient during nonpsychotic phases deal with the content brought to the surface during acute psychotic phases. This treatment approach was thought to be safer in a hospital setting, and the longest period of hospitalization was intended to serve this purpose. I have continued with the bridge-building approach, since the patient gradually became more accepting of hospitalization when it was needed. It became possible to treat her more intensively on an outpatient basis and to hospitalize her only when necessary.

Mrs. L's early admissions to hospitals could be very dramatic. She was agitated and belligerent, arrived at the hospital in an ambulance with sirens blowing, and needed to be restrained by several strong attendants. Typical of more recent hospitalizations was her hallucinating my office in her vacation home at the beginning of decompensation. At that point, she obeyed my hallucinated suggestion to check into a hospital.

Clinical observations supported by double-blind studies of Mrs. L indicate that remissions occur without the use of medication, and that remissions that perhaps occurred more quickly because of pharmacologic intervention were maintained for long periods when medication was stopped. So far, prolonged periods of medication with this patient do not seem to have been effective prophylactically. Although this does not rule out the possibility of finding a prophylactically effective medication regime, to date a limited use of medication at specific times, determined by symptomatic fluctuations and variations in her response to psychotherapeutic intervention, seems to offer more advantages in her treatment. The following medications have been used: perphenazine, amitriptyline, chlorpromazine, trifluoperazine, thioridazine, prolixin, fluphenazine, and lithium carbonate.

Some biological data will complete the background material on Dorothy L. Two brain ventricular measurements of 8.4 percent are probably within the normal range for her age group. The prostaglandin E1 (PGE1)—stimulated cyclic AMP production in the platelets of this patient—is abnormally low. Dr. M. Kafka has pointed out that this abnormality found in schizophrenic patients could conceivably be only in platelets, but is probably in the neuron as well. As the cyclic AMP probably mediates phosphorylation and activation of cellular proteins in neurons as well as platelets, a decrease in the cyclic AMP concentration intracellularly could modulate the rate and magnitude of transmission in the brain. If transmission is altered, perhaps it plays a role in the pathophysiology of schizophrenia (M. S. Kafka et al., 1980).

Although the concepts formulated about Mrs. L's condition and the therapeutic techniques used are intertwined, I will first outline the range of therapeutic techniques:

1. Carefully timed introduction of psychotic material during nonpsychotic periods.

2. Use of cold wet-sheet packs during catatonic episodes at times

when she was *not* agitated. (Crude rationale: Outer control should diminish need for inner control.) Verbal therapy was used when the patient was in the sheet pack.

3.   During nonpsychotic periods, use of a verbal therapy that at times could be described as close to classical psychoanalysis if this particular segment of treatment were seen outside the context of her overall treatment.

4.   Increasing use of interpretive, psychoanalytically based therapy during periods of transition between psychotic and nonpsychotic states. It is here that the combination of pharmacotherapy and psychotherapy can be particularly important because the transition phases may be shortened and the patient can be confronted with material she produced very recently.

The following clinical notes are from one of my therapeutic hours with the patient. They illustrate the kind of psychoanalytically based therapy that can be done with schizophrenics during phases that are transitional between overtly psychotic and nonpsychotic states.

> The patient experiences a big bowel movement as loss of her inner organs. She describes confusion between anal and vaginal orifices, feels that some skin is missing, and says she feels "something has been cut off." Direct interpretation of castration fear is made and related to her previously experienced delusional identification with men, particularly her father. I remind her of a photograph of herself in which she is wearing a tie and other male clothing.
>
> The patient asks me to hospitalize her. She tells me that previously she has denied that she is crazy, but now she knows she is. She demonstrates this by a delusional preoccupation with dirt, which characterized many of her hospitalized periods. She has to wash every few minutes; she says the insulin with which she was treated many years ago is coming out of her hair and then tells me she has relapsed because she has masturbated. It is possible for her to accept the idea that her preoccupation with dirt is connected with masturbation. She makes clear to me that her view of

the functioning society lady is incompatible with her view of herself as someone who on rare occasions masturbates. She is visibly relieved when I tell her that sometimes she asks for hospitalization because she cannot live up to the idealized society role at all times. She is incredulous when I suggest that she go to one of her volunteer functions despite the fact that she has masturbated. She asks about the "after-effects" of masturbation.

She describes a tightness in her lower abdomen which keeps her from sleeping. It becomes clear that the tightness being discussed now, when she is an outpatient, is related to the retention of feces during her previous hospitalization. It is an attempt to hold on tightly, to prevent the loss of an imaginary penis. She interprets sexual flush as a punishing change in her body. As in other sessions, we discuss bodily sensations in minute detail, and her interpretations of them. Her guilt feelings related to her having "torn something" in her mother are part of the picture.

At times it has been useful to classify and describe to Mrs. L resistances that manifest themselves in (1) her not recognizing connections (for example, masturbation and general dirt preoccupation) and (2) her insisting on false connections (for example, punishment and sexual flush).

Therapeutic work of this kind has led me to the following conceptual formulations:

1.   Reexamination of the very concept of schizophrenic thought disorder: The *constant objects* (often more "abstract," more "atmospheric," less related to individual persons) are different from those of nonschizophrenic patients. The thought operations *on* these objects are not.[7]

---

[7] Ordinary logic is used in thinking and talking about those idiosyncratic objects. "Heidi-ness," for instance, has an identity. To illustrate the point schematically, it is conceivable that the therapist would ask the patient: "Please introduce me to Heidi-ness." This would be more congruent with the patient's object world than if he were to ask her to introduce him to Heidi (see chapter 2).

2. Reformulation of double-bind theory: Parental intolerance of am-
    biguity rather than paradoxical communication is seen as a
    pathogenic factor (as elaborated in chapter 2).

3. A refinement of the concept of the therapeutic window: The pa-
    tient is seen as going in and out of psychotic states very rapidly,
    making microchanges within seconds, too rapidly for a therapeutic
    window in the usual sense. (This formulation is related to the no-
    tion of the recapitulation of the ontogeny of perception.) Therefore,
    the therapist who communicates on different levels of complexity
    at the same time is more likely to be heard by the patient.

4. An interpretation of the patient's understanding of psychotic
    symptoms: As the patient decompensates and moves toward the
    psychotic state, the *last organization* available is *oral* and often is
    clearly oral rage. I have come to understand that the patient inter-
    prets the diminution of her functioning as punishment for
    something she has done or failed to do. Since primitive oral aggres-
    sion is in the foreground, the punishment itself is perceived as oral
    aggression directed toward her. My dealing with the psychotic ma-
    terial she produces is perceived by her as an attack coming from
    me, an attack full of oral rage. My interpretation of her understand-
    ing of her own psychotic symptoms as punishment sometimes
    interrupts the vicious cycle.

In the last formulation, the central point is the patient's aversion to dealing
with psychotic material, even when there is no outright denial. It is this
aversion, I believe, that led Federn to recommend a different therapist
during the nonpsychotic states. When the same therapist remains in the
picture, however, the interpretation linking psychosis itself with attack ("It
is as if I were biting you when I don't let you off the hook and tell you that
we just can't ignore these crazy things if you want the benefits of not always living in a crazy world") helps establish the therapist in both
worlds. When this occurs at times of the patient's transition between
psychotic and nonpsychotic organizations, the link between content
(biting, for instance) and the formal characteristics of psychotic organization or disorganization can be of use in establishing some continuity.

At such periods of transition, incidentally, because of the complex mechanisms of projection and projective identification and the looseness of ego boundaries, biting or other forms of violent aggression are in the "atmosphere," and it matters little whether analyst or patient is referred to as the "biter."

If one has had the experience of working intensively for a long time and in many different ways with schizophrenic patients, some recent descriptions of psychotherapeutic approaches seem peculiarly fragmented. I do not want to minimize the relative effectiveness of such approaches, which include "supportive" and other "intensive forms of individual psychotherapy" and "psycho-educational" and other forms of family therapy (see, for instance, Gunderson and Carroll, 1983; Anderson, 1983). But it is important not to lose sight of the usefulness of the whole range of approaches that psychotherapists have employed with schizophrenic patients.

Miss R, for example, had been hospitalized in several institutions for over twenty years when I started working with her. Despite massive electroconvulsive treatment, she had remained intermittently and unpredictably violent, so that she had spent the greater part of many years in isolation rooms. I will not describe my work with this patient, which lasted well over a decade, in detail here, but I will highlight the range of techniques I used in order to provide some contrast with what I consider more "fractionated" approaches.

After prolonged observation, I arrived at the opinion that Miss R had several different psychotic organizations. I coined for myself the term *multiple psychotic personalities*, which incorporates the recognition of such varying dissociations. At times she was receptive to my calling attention to such differences in her mental organization and in her functioning. Therapeutic work around this issue led to her asking for cold wet-sheet packs when she sensed the possible eruption of violence. This development permitted a whole socializing approach. I taught her to use the telephone and to eat in restaurants, and I brought her to my home. I also met her family, making it clear that I was *not* the family's therapist and that I would feel free to tell her what I would feel free to tell her what I learned from the family but not vice versa. The meetings with the family, with or without her present, were only occasional and, of course, were in addition to the four or five weekly individual sessions with Miss R. I also went with her, her social worker, and several aides to the family's home and had meetings with all of them in this setting.

Since my purpose here is to describe the range of activities, I will not give in detail characteristics of the family structure, but will mention only a family secret that came to light—namely, the suspicion that in a previous generation, when an attempt to arrange a shot-gun wedding of an unmarried pregnant family member had failed, the reluctant groom was killed. This story, or perhaps myth, hung like a cloud over this conservative, religious, and puritanical family. If some topics have to be avoided at all costs—topics that could in some way lead to, be reminiscent of, or be associated with the theme of a secret (or myth)—the range of permitted topics can become remarkably narrow. In this case, anything having to do with sex, pregnancy, grooming, looks, fun, dancing, youth, and similar subjects was strictly taboo. Religion, with an emphasis on religious fears, was a pervasive but not much talked-about presence in the family. The permitted verbal topics did not extend much beyond work, business, and financial matters in this wealthy family. Miss R apparently referred to this focus, the specialized financial vocabulary, but also to the narrow range of topics that could be put into words when she called the family's way of speaking their "gangster language." My experiences with Miss R contributed to my expectation that etiologically oriented family studies will continue to be important in the study of the determinants of schizophrenic pathology. I look forward to the results of such studies as those of Helgard Roeder, at the Max Planck Institute in Munich, who is rigorously testing earlier family hypotheses formulated by Lidz and others, using computer-based technology (see Lidz and Fleck, 1960; Stierlin et al., 1983; in the latter volume, see particularly contributions by Wynne and the Finnish Adoptive Family Studies by Tienari et al.).

Miss R's references to "wide" and "narrow" language contributed to the development of my ideas about schizophrenic objects. These objects are atmospheric. It gradually became clear that Miss R's wide language was poetic and referred to an emotional atmosphere; sometimes it reflected

only internal states expressed metaphysically, but often it included amal-
gamated references to external conditions and internal states. "There was
an earthquake last night" referred to the patient's emotional agitation, but
also to general unrest on the ward during the preceding night. Utilitarian
language—ordering food in a restaurant or instructing a telephone opera-
tor—was narrow language, and so was her family's "gangster" language.
Miss R's *calling* it "gangster" language is, however, an example of wide language. Her reaction to family members' preoccupations, her own reaction
to what they do in the financial world, reference to the possible murder in
the family secret or myth and the associated caution, the restriction of
permissible topics—all are part of the "gangster" atmosphere. It was this
patient whom I observed walking faster than usual when she said the
earth was shrinking. I thought of Miss R and other schizophrenic patients
when I read in "The Innerworld of the Outerworld of the Innerworld"
(Handke, 1969, p. 128):

> We find ourselves in a department store:
> we want to use the escalator
> to get to the toy department
> where we want to purchase building blocks
> but since the escalator has temporarily stopped
> the immobile escalator
> on which we were walking up
> transforms itself into our breath
> which we are holding
> and the held breath
> which we now exhale
> because the escalator is suddenly moving again
> implodes into a pile of building blocks—

Wide language for Miss R also seemed to be the language of contemplation
and had a temporal meaning—contrasted with efficient, quick, and focused
communication. She agreed to use such narrow language only after repeated reassurances that she could return to the wide one and after I had
demonstrated many times that I could switch back and forth in my own

use of the two forms of communication. Usually Miss R's physical movements were slow, even, and remarkably deliberate. For years, however, there had been occasional short periods of agitation and physical aggression which gradually diminished and eventually disappeared during my years of work with her. I have sometimes considered whether her fear of being permanently shackled into a narrow world of communication and experience had contributed to her agitation. Her learning that she did not have to abandon one world to live in another may have played a part in the fading of the occasional furious agitation.[8]

Usually Miss R was far from agitated. She was unsurpassed in her skill with the most complicated jigsaw puzzles. She would sit quietly in front of the puzzle pieces, hardly moving for as long as ten or sometimes twenty minutes, and then slowly place a piece, deliberately and precisely. Even placements made early in her work on the puzzle never needed subsequent revision or correction. The deliberation shown in this task also characterized the way in which she ordinarily seemed to survey both the external world and her internal state. The wide language, as I have noted, reflected both. It was in the context of my psychoanalytically based therapeutic efforts that I came to understand something of her narrow and wide languages and of her fear that she would lose one if she used the other. This in turn permitted me to teach her to use narrow language when I went with her to restaurants and when she once again began to use the telephone. Dynamic approaches do not preclude such instructional and behavioral techniques. They give them dignity and meaning and, I believe, enhance their effectiveness. Still, it would not be difficult to find in Miss R's wide language remaining evidence of schizophrenic thought disorder. She has, however, learned the difference between wide and narrow worlds—and has apparently learned techniques

---

[8] When I discuss Miss R's possible revolt against narrowness, I should also mention the circumscribed role that had been envisaged for her since early childhood. Somehow she was the one who was expected not to get married and to become the parents' caretaker in their old age. These specific limited expectations could have contributed to the subsequent apparently bizarre disregard of her own needs and individuality. Two years older than her sister, she was kept from going to school until both sisters, dressed alike, could be driven to school together.

for protecting them both well enough to have lived for many years now—without medication—outside the hospital.

Assessing the Dreams of Schizophrenics

Although I have not thus far dealt explicitly with the "separate reality" of dreams, I hypothesize that incomplete recapitulation of the ontogeny of perception plays a part in differentiating dream objects from objects of normal working life. In dreams, as in psychosis, some perceptual processes are carried further than others. This produces the "idiosyncrasies" of dream objects. The differences between dreams and psychotic phenomena certainly deserve further study, but for now I remain in the company of those who emphasize their similarities.

If schizophrenic conditions have much in common with dreams, what thoughts and clinical data can we organize around the theme of dreams in schizophrenia? So many questions about schizophrenia and its treatment remain unanswered that I consider dealing with the clinical use of dreams with patients in this condition something of a tour de force, but some thoughts have crystallized for me. I do not *generally* consider the clinical use of dreams of central importance in therapeutic work with schizophrenic patients, but at times it may be. There are also interesting similarities and differences in ways of using dream material in the treatment of these and other patients. In a two-part article, Grotstein (1977) has elaborated such material in relation to the etiology of schizophrenia. In my own day-to-day therapeutic work, however, I have depended more on some relatively simple ideas—such as the use of dreams in the "bridging" therapeutic approach, the "evacuation" function of dreams, trauma in the life and dreams of schizophrenics, the repair of psychosis through dreams, and several other related themes. I shall briefly elaborate these various ways of making use of the dreams of schizophrenics.

It is in connection with the bridging approach in the work with schizophrenic patients that dreams have their most explicit application. Some relapses of schizophrenic patients into acute psychosis are not yet well understood, whether we try to understand them biologically, psychodynamically, or through combined approaches. Earlier in my career, I would have announced some "understandings" that I do not now claim. Over the years too many different "understandings" have been required for the same kind of relapse in the same patient. I believe, however, that the bridging therapeutic approach I mentioned earlier—having one therapist stay with the patient in times of relapse—has helped to avert further relapses in some patients, to diminish their frequency and duration in other patients, and certainly to lessen the impact of recurrences on the lives of patients and family members.

The topic of the continuity of the content of the psychosis in dream material has been developed by Douglas Noble (1951) and by Clarence G. Schulz (Schulz and Kilgalen, 1969). The latter two wrote about work with a severely disturbed schizophrenic patient who began to relate dreams after about five months of psychotherapy: "As his behavior began to improve, his psychotic thinking decreased and he began to report dreams" (p. 20). The dreams mirrored the antecedent psychotic material. It is possible that this sequence—from psychotic material to dream—is particularly clear in patients with a history of readily identifiable trauma. One aspect of the history of Schulz's patient was that his two siblings had died under tragic circumstances in separate accidents. I will return shortly to the use of dreams in the psychotherapy of schizophrenic patients with a fairly obvious traumatic history of this kind.

Another idea in the literature that has evoked an echo in my own clinical experience concerns the function of "evacuation." With reservations that will be spelled out gradually, I have found what André Green says about work with borderline patients to be applicable at times in work with schizophrenic patients:

> Dream analysis . . . is, as a rule, unproductive. . . . Dreams do not express wish-fulfillment but rather serve a function of evacuation. . . . The dream barrier is an important function of the psychic apparatus. . . . Even though the dream barrier is effective, the dream's purpose is not the working through of instinct derivatives, but rather the unburdening of the psychic apparatus from painful stimuli. . . . The dreams . . . are not characterized by condensation

but by concretization. One can also observe dream failures in these patients: wakening in order to prevent dreaming or to find themselves surrounded by a strange, disquieting atmosphere, which constitutes a transitional dream state akin to a nightmare. In more successful instances, dreams are actualizations of the self in the dream space, attempts to reformulate traumatic experiences. ... In such instances, the most significant thing in analyzing a dream is not the dream's latent content but *the dreamer's experience*. (1977, p. 38)

Whatever our eventual understanding of the etiology of various schizophrenic disorders, for immediate therapeutic and practical working purposes, I find that I function as though I believed that trauma was etiologically more important for some schizophrenic patients than for others. I think, for instance, of Eleanor M, who had her first acute episode after she had acquiesced to her mother's request that she be present in the operating room during the mother's exploratory surgery; when the mother was opened up, she was found to have a widespread malignancy. Eleanor was also the main caretaker of her dying mother, and the notion that a sedative she gave her mother killed her was at times an important element in her delusions.

Eleanor was diagnosed as schizophrenic on the basis of all the usual criteria by the staffs of several hospitals. She showed particularly flamboyant pathology; hallucinating and wildly agitated, she was denudative, smeared herself and the walls of seclusion rooms with menstrual blood, and was destructive of property and sometimes assaultive. During more than fifteen years of psychotherapeutic work with her, I found the role of dreams in her treatment an important one, as I shall describe below.

Eleanor was eventually able to leave the hospital, the frequency and severity of acute episodes diminished radically, and during the last eight years only one brief hospitalization was necessary. (Medication, on the whole, did not play a significant role in her management or treatment.) When she did not need to be hospitalized, Eleanor functioned quite well as a wife, mother, and participating member in community affairs. Her preoccupation with violence in her waking life was limited to a fascination with crime and criminals, wars, and catastrophes. Her selection of movies, television shows, and newspaper and magazine articles was almost exclusively based on such interests. Her dream life was characterized by prolonged periods during which she reported hundreds of rather repetitive dreams dealing with amputations, mutilations, and bloody scenes.

Thus, Eleanor presented contrasting pictures: she was prim and proper when not psychotic, but her dream life and psychotic periods were full of gore. Over the years of working with her, I developed a technique of using gory language in talking about her dreams and impulses ("You wanted to smash her skull and smear her brains all over the wall"). But again and again I told her my reasons for doing so, spelling out the idea that her attempts to compartmentalize such material might contribute to the psychotic episodes. In Eleanor's treatment there were long periods when the therapy resembled some of the therapeutic work done with cases of battle fatigue during and after World War II. (For example, war movies were shown to soldiers who had experienced major dissociative episodes in battle. Showings of these movies were interrupted from time to time, and when the lights went on, Red Cross girls offered tea to the soldiers.)

Despite the use of such techniques, recognition of transference elements and the genetics of the conflict had their place in Eleanor's treatment. The emphasis was, however, as André Green put it, "not [on] the dream's latent content but the dreamer's experience."

From the literature on dreams in schizophrenia and psychosis, I will cite one further notion that is in harmony with my own clinical use of dreams with these patients. In a 1953 paper, Eissler refers to a psychotic patient who in her dreams repairs the psychosis, so to speak. It is as if the dreaming ego were nonpsychotic while the waking ego was psychotic. Eissler notes that similar observations were made by Freud and mentions Freud's notion that "reality" appears like an instinct derivative in dreams of psychotics. That is, it was Freud's belief that the psychotic individual had constructed for himself a world that was so different and distinct from reality—I would say from commonsense reality—that ordinary reality broke through into dreams in the same way in which material related to "instinct" broke into dreams of the nonpsychotic individual.

Although oversimplified, these references to Eissler's and Freud's notions are related to the following clinical observations.

I accidentally discovered many years ago that when I awakened Andrew, a hospitalized schizophrenic patient with a complex paranoid delusional system, he was apparently free of delusions for five or ten minutes. I could never obtain from the patient any confirmation that he was dreaming, and any possible "repair" of the psychosis could have been the work of merely the "sleeping ego" and not necessarily of the "dreaming ego." In any case, the psychosis seemed to have been temporarily repaired during his sleep, when psychoticlike dream material occurs in the nonpsychotic individual. This repair of the psychosis was always carried over into the waking state for seven minutes (as I worked with this patient, I found it interesting to time it precisely), after which the delusions were reestablished.

Another patient, John M, had been diagnosed as schizophrenic during several prolonged hospitalizations and at one time prior to my acquaintance with him had received a series of electroconvulsive treatments. His symptoms were such that some clinicians would consider him as having a severe borderline disorder with pronounced narcissistic features. He did have frankly psychotic periods during my years of work with him, and brief hospitalizations were required, although drug abuse made it difficult to identify the precipitating factors. Dreams were important in my work with John, but my treatment of him was more consistently psychoanalytic, and my clinical use of dreams did not differ significantly from psychoanalytic dream interpretations. One feature of his dream reports, however, may relate to Eissler's observation. He often said very emphatically that his dreams now contained some "distortions." A room in which he lived or a landscape that he remembered from his childhood differed from the way it "really" was. Ordinarily, nonpsychotic dreamers consider such distortions to be part of the usual fabric of the dream. For John they were "unusual" in comparison with what he considered his *normal* dreams. During psychotic episodes, he had apparently experienced dreams in which there was much "undistorted" reality. Clinically he was able to use my observations relating to such fluctuations in his dreams in a bridging fashion. My observations served as an introduction to part of normal living—namely, normally distorted dreams. Furthermore, I learned to use the degree of distortion he reported about his dream material as an indicator of his distance from a psychotic episode, and such observations helped in his management.

As an elaborated example of this kind of reversal, one month after a psychiatric hospitalization, Dorothy L reported dreaming that her mother was dead, her father was alive, and another woman was embracing him. The patient's actual life situation at that time was that her *father* was dead and her *mother* was living. She emphasized that the scene reminded her of some Picasso paintings of his Blue Period, and further commented, "It's an interesting dream; the female figure is of undetermined age." Her sexual interest in her father had been an explicitly recognized theme in my prolonged work with her. During acute psychotic episodes she also was fused with, transformed into, or partially blended with her father. At one time, for instance, she made a point of not shaving her legs because "I have father's legs."

In addition to the patient's emphases on Picasso's Blue Period, some of her other associations involved her daughter (who liked Picasso), a period in her daughter's life when she was developing breasts, a visit to a relative who was divorcing her husband, and the patient's wish that her father had divorced her mother. In many respects these dream elements were understood by Dorothy L and were interpreted much as a neurotic patient might comprehend her own dream material after prolonged insight-oriented therapy or analysis. She explained, however, that she could have such a dream now "because last month has been going very well. My husband did not go on any trips. He cooked a lot of dinners." She then talked about her father's flirtations but discussed love very explicitly in terms of who fed whom. Mother did not feed father well; therefore, she did not love him. She made precise equations in energy terms. She could have this dream now because she had been well fed during the previous month and consequently had enough energy to work on the old problems of her father's death.

In my experience, when a schizophrenic patient can talk about the *dreamlike* atmosphere of a dream, and does not see everyday reality as the intruder in the dream, then the patient is most removed from a psychotic ego organization. In prolonged psychotherapeutic work with a schizophrenic patient such a period should not be ignored. The therapist can at such a moment deal explicitly with the apparently "neurotic" conflicts that are being presented and dealt with in the dream, but the therapist can also at such a moment introduce a discussion of the changes such material undergoes during psychotic episodes. With Dorothy L, for example, the topic of her wish to be close to her father, to be with her father, could be introduced in an effort to form a bridge between the current and the psychotic states. In the long run such an approach permits the patient to use the image of the therapist in the bridging management of her own psychosis.

On the other hand, I have also encountered in a nonpsychotic patient, Robert S, specific fear of a psychotic reaction when the vividness of the dreams was extreme—for instance, when in his dream he not only saw his own face as that of an animal but also touched his face and discovered that his skin possessed the texture of an animal's skin. Although Robert never actually was psychotic, several family members had been hospitalized with a diagnosis of schizophrenia, and his fear of psychosis was never far from the surface.

Michael, another patient—about whose schizophrenic diagnosis there was no doubt but who lived most of his life outside a hospital—made all kinds of commitments, pledged charitable contributions, and accepted invitations when he actually answered the telephone but then believed that he had dreamt the whole thing. By the time I started working with him, he had already developed a method to circumvent this problem. Since Michael did not know if he was awake or dreaming (he had multiple dreams within dreams) and since pinching himself didn't do the trick, he had learned always to ask, "What is your number? I'll call you back."

Some of the above observations tend to move away from the clinical use of dreams in the therapy of schizophrenic patients. They are nevertheless pertinent. For some patients there seem to be common elements in dreams and psychotic experience—at the very least, there are fears that certain dream characteristics herald psychotic experiences. In working therapeutically for prolonged periods with such patients, the therapist is likely to discover characteristics of dream reports that are indexes of the closeness to the surface of some psychotic phenomena. An index may be valid for only one particular patient because it depends not only on general characteristics of schizophrenic and dream processes but also on such personality variables as intelligence and intellectual style and on various characteristics of patient and therapist that determine the nature of their relationship and communication.

If one works long enough, even with deeply regressed, chronic, or deteriorated patients, one often discovers periods of relatively greater accessibility during which both content and formal elements of dream experiences can be considered collaboratively with the patient. Despite my overall recognition of the general uselessness of too much "intellect" in therapeutic endeavors, I have become less afraid of an "intellectual" approach with some patients at such junctures. It connotes a respect for formal characteristics of the patient's thought—a respect that has a therapeutic—function in itself. If one has traveled with a patient for a long time, in and out of psychosis, the intellectual approach has a different cast. The interpretation of the psychosis as an attack is a case in point. Recall Dorothy L, who sought voluntary hospitalization after she hallucinated my instructing her to do so when she was disturbed. Discussion of the form and content of dream material with the patient had been one of the tools useful in facilitating such a development—that is, previous discussion with Dorothy of the form and content of dreams enhanced her ability to observe critically some of her psychotic experiences, even with the therapist only psychologically present.

The primary-process concept is essential for an understanding of the similarities in the formation of dreams and of psychotic thought content. It can clarify for the therapist such practical problems as, for example, the equivalences and fusions of various family members in the mind of the waking schizophrenic patient (Kafka and McDonald, 1965).

Certain characteristics of the dreams of schizophrenic patients can also give the therapist information about the patient's control techniques or methods of self-management. Robert S—the patient with the telephone answering difficulties—often had "geological" dreams. Geology was one of his daytime interests, and the immensely long and slow time scale of geological events was a clue to his self-management style. One day I told him that I was reminded of a riddle popular in the Swiss city of Bern, whose inhabitants have a reputation for slowness. One Bern citizen asks another, "What is this?" while very slowly drawing an angular line in the air. The correct answer is "lightning." Very, very slowly the patient dared to break—or should I say melt—into a smile. After this it was possible for me to comment on certain catastrophic geological events in his dreams and to relate them in a therapeutically meaningful way to events in his life.

Rather than discuss the nature of the obsessive elements in the defensive structure of Robert S, I will focus on the relative *completeness* of his slow-motion perception and self-perception, and the relative completeness and appropriateness of his gradually developing affective responses. His perceptual acts recapitulated the development of perception rather slowly; he could understand the slow "flash." For this patient such qualities as "suspendedness" could have a defensively useful "quasi object constancy."

Considerations of this kind have a possible connection to the question of concreteness or "concretization" versus abstract qualities in the dreams of schizophrenic patients—and perhaps also in schizophrenic thinking generally. In chapter 3, writing about "abstract expressionism" in dreams, I gave an example of a dream consisting of a continuous line with small wiggles in it. To the dreamer, a therapist reporting a dream after an LSD experience, the line clearly represented the course of history, and the wiggle represented the Holocaust. I have come to believe that this kind of dream experience corresponds in large measure to the waking experience of many schizophrenic patients, for whom certain abstractions carry a bewildering but convincing richness of meaning or meanings. As I indicated earlier, I have been impressed by the contrasting concreteness and vividness—"the reality"—of some "schizophrenic" dreams (always remembering that in the most acute phases, dreams are not reported, and the question is thus irrelevant for therapeutic purposes). If abstract expressionist elements in waking experience have been recognized by the therapist, this may facilitate the patient's reporting the reversal in dream characteristics that, as I pointed out earlier, sometimes occurs at stages of considerable improvement—that is, a dream "atmosphere" becomes more common in dreams along with more "concreteness" in daily living.

In sum, despite our uncertainties in understanding schizophrenic phenomena and despite the observation that the most clearly schizophrenic patients—*when* they are most clearly schizophrenic—do not report dream material, it is apparent that dreams can be used in the treatment of schizophrenia. Recently, as a psychoanalytic consultant to a schizophrenia research unit studying various vigorous pharmacological interventions, I noted that in some patients whose condition changed and fluctuated rapidly, the reporting of dreams could occur almost immediately after emergence from the most severe disorganization. Dream material might be reported when delusions were still very active. The overlapping of acute psychotic manifestations and the reporting of dreams were greater here than I had observed in situations where no such forceful pharmacological interventions were attempted. I would, therefore, anticipate that the study and perhaps the therapeutic use of dreams in schizophrenia may become of greater interest to clinicians with a variety of theoretical orientations.

A Multiple-Reality Approach to Schizophrenic Disorders

Clinicians trying to work with schizophrenic patients face difficulties because simultaneously they know so little about schizophrenia and yet seem to know so much. Inasmuch as therapists may be dealing with a disease of meaning, schizophrenia presents itself as an ideal projective test, a picture into which they can read meaning—and we clinicians can read much that is personal to us into schizophrenic phenomenology. Because we cannot long survive, much less operate, in a vacuum of cause and effect, we constantly try to see and respond to meaning. The longer I have worked with schizophrenic patients, the more I have tended not to discount these projective potentials. To summarize, my ideas have been organized around the following points: (1) during schizophrenic episodes, the patient's important objects become idiosyncratic, specifiably different from those established during ordinary object-constancy formation; (2) the study of the ontogeny of perception offers clues concerning the formation of these idiosyncratic objects; and (3) the resulting theoretical formulations lead to therapeutic strategies based on the effort to comprehend idiosyncratic objects, to confront the patient with a multichannel approach to possible meaning and affect, and, especially, to help the patient to experience the therapist as a constant object in the patient's fluctuating object world.

Simple notions underlie every clinical experiment, and that is what therapeutic work with schizophrenic patients is today. As I indicated in describing the treatment of Dorothy L, one of my clinical experiments has been the use of cold wet-sheet packs in an unorthodox way. These are customarily used to restrain very agitated patients, but I have used them for catatonic patients who were immobile and mute. The crude formulation on which this therapeutic maneuver was based was the hypothesis that the patients were afraid that any movement would destroy the world. Perhaps if I kept them from moving, they would be able to tell me something. When such patients were kept in packs, some of them did begin to speak. But is this confirmation of the hypothesis concerning world-destruction fantasies, and is it solid confirmation that the pack's effectiveness resides in the substitution of external for internal controls?

One belief that has taken on significance for me in terms of my experience is that the very effort to see meaning can have some therapeutic effect. Although this belief, too, should be subjected to verification, some of my therapeutic strategies are based on it. For example, if a schizophrenic patient is wildly gesticulating and obviously hallucinating, it is important for me to enter the scene somehow. In one such instance, because of previous work with Peter, whom I mentioned briefly in chapter 3, I thought the hallucinations had something to do with his father. When I asked some questions about his hallucinations, the patient said, "Louder," and continued saying that until I finally shouted. At this point the patient said, with an expression of disgust, "Not you." I had succeeded in making my presence felt; he had noticed me, despite the hallucinations. Somewhat later in the session, he did respond to some of my questions. If I really wanted to know whether he was hallucinating father or God, he could give me an answer: either father or God would be correct. Although he felt it was a stupid question, he conveyed to me that someone or something in authority was communicating to him. He knew that people make a distinction between father and God, but it was not pertinent. His gesturing (he pointed to something high in the room) indicated that some high authority was communicating with him. This seemed both very abstract and very concrete to me, but I too had entered the scene. I had become a presence; my voice interfered somewhat with the authoritative voice to which he listened. Although he derogated me, I deserved an explanation.

My idea that some of the schizophrenic's objects can be "characteristics" rather than individuals, and therefore quite different from commonsense objects or the usual psychoanalytic ones, led to the notion of the "latent family" of the schizophrenic patient behind the manifest family (Kafka and McDonald, 1965). One patient conveyed that all the blue-eyed members of her family were interchangeable; in effect, they were the same—one object. In her mid-thirties, the patient had rather suddenly had a flagrant schizophrenic episode. But one day when I was walking with the patient and her husband on the hospital grounds I caught a glimpse of a different onset of the illness. With a fixed, laughing expression, the patient looked at her husband and said, "You're not my blue-eyed husband." He laughingly responded, "No, I'm not." When I asked him if she had been saying things like that for a long time, he responded, "Oh, yes. She's been joking like that since before we were married." So much for the acute psychotic episode! The techniques for obscuring psychotic phenomenology in some families (that is, the ability of some families to absorb psychosis) are remarkable.

In chapter 2, when discussing Arieti's quotation of Von Domarus's principle, I pointed out that what is subject and what is predicate are not building blocks of experience but are themselves the result of experience. When a patient has experienced a characteristic of a person as being more fundamental, more lasting, more "identical" than the person as a whole, this characteristic acquires qualities of the subject, and the person, then merely a personification of this more stable idea, acquires qualities of the predicate. Here "blue eyedness" had acquired the qualities of a subject. This phenomenon also appeared in the patient cited in chapter 2 for whom having Heidi-like characteristics was much more important and more stable than being the same person. As I commented earlier, such stability can be thought of in terms of Klüver's "subjectively equivalent stimuli."

Clinicians commonly talk about the concreteness of schizophrenic thought, but we also know that some schizophrenic patients can deal most effectively with subject matter on a very abstract level. A patient dealing with highly complex and abstract modern musical scales and notations comes to mind. One advantage of my radical formulation of the nature of the schizophrenic's objects is that it can accommodate both the very concrete and the very abstract.

Experienced clinicians make corrections when they note projective elements in their theory building. Many of us who have worked intensively for a long time with schizophrenic patients and are keenly aware of the limitations of our theoretical understanding of the disorder are constantly forced to look anew at phenomenology. In the face of clinical data, we are able to make shifts in our theoretical framework. Nevertheless, at any one point, every therapist operates with an explicit or implicit model for the disorder he treats. He may gradually formulate parts of the model with some precision but neglect or only vaguely sketch others. I would like to describe the parts of the model for which I have developed fairly precise ideas during my work with schizophrenic patients and the treatment strategies with which I think they are connected. I recognize, however, that the heuristic value of the treatment strategies is not necessarily dependent on the correctness of the proposed model.

Every dynamically oriented therapist who has written about schizophrenia—and even many who are not so oriented—has had to address the problem of boundaries between self (or self-object) and others, between inside and outside, and between objects. These issues, which at first glance are conceptualized spatially, move to the temporal dimension when we speak of the problem of object constancy. It is particularly in my work with schizophrenic patients, for whom the problem of (temporal) object constancy is so crucial, that I have experienced dissatisfaction with the reification connected with the spatial emphasis.

The central element in my formulation concerns perceptual theory, as it can and must be integrated into psychoanalytic thinking. The hypothesis that each perceptual act recapitulates the ontogeny of perception is central to ideas about schizophrenic thought disorder (Kafka, 1964, 1977). I have previously referred to Stein's experimental finding (1949) when he presented Rorschach cards tachistoscopically for only a small fraction of a second to adult subjects. When asked what they saw, some responded at first that it was only a flash. When urged to say more, subjects gave responses that resembled those of very young children. They might, for instance, say, "some red going up," the words accompanied by a gesture indicating the direction.

More recent and extensive related experimental work on perception by a group at the University of Lund (Smith and Danielsson, 1982; Westerlundh and Smith, 1983) demonstrates beautifully that psychoanalytic concepts are essential for understanding experimental findings in this area. Their meta-contrast technique involves the tachistoscopic presentation of paired stimuli: incongruent stimuli in one series, and the image of a threatening face implying danger to the image of a young person in another series. During one developmental phase, children close their own eyes when they see a threatening face. During a subsequent developmental phase, they perceive the image of the threatened young person as shutting *its* eyes. Among the defensive reactions that can be measured in this complex work are repression, isolation, projection, and discontinuity. Repression, for instance, is scored if the subject reports seeing a lifeless mask instead of a live threatening face. Short exposures in "percept-genesis" tests reflect ontogenetically early functional levels of the perceiver; reports after longer exposure reflect the subject's present functional state. The Lund workers point out how much perception has been neglected by psychoanalytic writers because of the strong and persistent influence in psychoanalysis of the concept that perception simply "mirrors" reality. They show how a psychoanalytic understanding of defensive operations in perceptual acts facilitates the understanding of their findings (see also Sandler and Rosenblatt, 1962; Sandler and Joffe, 1967).

I want to move now from ontogenetical recapitulation in perception to the related idea of object constancies derived from the subjective equivalence of stimulus patterns that are similar but not identical. For those who might charge that such a conceptualization of object constancy is too narrowly cognitive, I reemphasize that the stimuli we select from an external and internal environment that we scan continuously, the stimuli that form the bases of our constant objects, are chosen because of currently active drives, needs, emotions, and moods of varying intensity, and the compromises between conflicting drives.

When focusing on schizophrenia, one must remember that a perceptual act can be carried to relative completion, or it can be stopped or interrupted before completion. If all perceptual acts are carried to relative completion, the objects that are subjectively equivalent at the end of the perceptual acts are the constant objects, as this term is used in general psychology, and cannot be dispensed with in psychoanalysis—where, however, the memory of the absent object is often emphasized. In any case, the constant object of consensually validated reality can be a constant table or a constant person. But we may postulate that rapidly fluctuating patterns of intense drives, resulting in a predominance of partial perceptual acts or mixtures of partial and completed perceptual acts, characterize the perceptual world of the schizophrenic patient. Normal object-constancy patterns thus either are disrupted or may never be fully established; instead, idiosyncratic schizophrenic constancies, based on the common denominators of partial and relatively completed perceptual acts, may be prominent in the patient's object world.

At the very center of my model of schizophrenic disorders is my understanding that recapitulative perceptual processes link affective and cognitive development. More accurately, these ideas occupy that part of the model about which I have been able to formulate specific and detailed ideas. Such a model may seem ambitious, but it is compatible with various competing hypotheses—psychoanalytic, psychodynamic, and biological—concerning the genetics of the rapidly fluctuating patterns of intense drives. Here my model is open or incomplete.

If the more constant objects are synonymous with highly idiosyncratic categories (for example, all family members with blue eyes or with a certain style of moving; all material objects with shiny surfaces; all friendly creatures and friendly material objects), the application of conventional logical thought processes to these objects will result in a thought disorder. Communication with the schizophrenic patient would indeed be impossible if there were no connection between the logical operations of doctor and patient. The notion of similar logic applied to different constant objects offers more hope if (1) techniques have been developed to study the patient's idiosyncratic objects, and (2) the therapist uses these techniques in learning how to become a relatively constant object in the patient's world.

Schematically, my major treatment strategy is connected to my proposed model of schizophrenic perceptions and object constancies. The therapist must suspend his commonsense notion of what constant objects are for the patient. A highly idiosyncratic characteristic may determine which objects are subjectively equivalent for the patient and thus constant for him or her. Once the therapist thoroughly suspends common sense concerning the nature of the patient's constant objects, but continues to apply the usual logical processes to the manipulation of the constancies that he detects, the patient may sense the therapist's empathy and experience it as the removal of a major obstacle to communication; on occasion he or she may be eager to teach the therapist something about his object world. (Dorothy L told me that she wanted to continue working with me despite the distance she had to travel to see me because it had taken her such a long time to train me.) The combination of suspended common sense in one area and its retention in another results in the therapist's multichannel communication pattern, a peculiar mixture of individually tailored crazy and sane talk. This kind of communication has the advantage of taking into account the rapidly shifting ego organizations of the patient. These shifts are often too rapid for the therapist to follow, but the chance of being on target sometimes is increased by the diversity of the approach.

Finally and most significantly, the therapist's multichannel presence facilitates the linkage of various characteristics of the therapist with the idiosyncratic network of characteristics underlying the patient's constancy patterns, thus facilitating the establishment of the therapist as a more constant object in the patient's world. (Dorothy L's hallucination of my recommendation that she enter a hospital is a case in point.) Only the therapist who has become a relatively constant object for the patient can have therapeutic leverage.

Chapter 6

The Individual and the Group: Rituals and Families

Ritual belongs at the center of some wider applications of my notions of multiple realities because ritual is associated with change (from one reality to another) and with the maintenance of continuity in the presence of change. The anthropologist is concerned with the place of rituals in rites of passage from one stage of life to another—birth, puberty, marriage, death—with rituals marking the change of seasons, and with those having to do with certain role changes, such as the establishment of authority—for instance, a coronation. Although the anthropologist does study individuals and individual families, his concern is usually with the nature of rites of passage in wider groups, such as specific tribes.

Rituals and "ritualistic behavior" are also, of course, of interest to the psychoanalytic therapist. The first part of this chapter is a rather abstract and theoretical examination—from the multiple-reality perspective—of ritual and ritualistic behavior. The second part deals more with clinical matters.

Examined in greater detail, ritual is at the center of the wider applications of my ideas of multiple realities because it is involved in the "rites of passage" between different realities as I have conceptualized them: the interconnected dichotomies of time-space, inner-outer (the size of the organism), and animate-inanimate, and their paradoxical coexistences. Since

147

clinical practice permits a close look at and offers a special perspective on these reality organizations, a clinician who is interested in the integration of psychological, social, and cultural influences can contribute to the study of aspects of the behavior of the individual in groups, families, organizations, tribes, and ethno-national units.

Rituals and the Ritualistic

At first glance clinicians are more concerned with ritualistic behavior (it is a symptom) than with rituals, and anthropologists are more concerned with rituals proper. Both involve repetition. In a paper on repetition and the repetition compulsion, Hans Loewald (1971) makes the point that not all repetition is a manifestation of repetition compulsion. He elaborates the difference between a compelled tacit repetition and active repeating, working through what is being repeated. Loewald thus first makes a sharp distinction between two forms of repetition with which psychoanalysts are much concerned, the repetition compulsion, with the symptomatic overtones of the word *compulsion,* and "working through," with its curative connotations. In his paper "The Waning of the Oedipus Complex" (1979), he elaborates the idea that the same problematic is recurrent, not disposed of but reworked in different developmental stages and in the context of different life tasks. Here Loewald brings together again the two forms of repetition he had distinguished. The active reworking in different developmental stages and in the context of different life tasks is the working through that utilizes, is grafted onto, the compelled tacit repetition—I would say recapitulation—of the same problematic in the repetition compulsion. His distinction between and subsequent bringing together of repetition compulsion and working through are pertinent to the difference between and similarity of *ritualistic* and *ritual* because I see an analogy between his "compelled tacit repetition" and the inanimate as I have discussed it, and an analogy between his "active repeating, working through" and my "animate" center of action. From my perspective, however, an ongoing "reworking," recapitulation of perception is part of all the other processes that have to be reworked. The psychoanalytically understood dynamics of the repetition compulsion apply to the microworld of perceptual processes.

Rituals can produce a feeling of completeness—a whole act, a finished sequence, the achievement (at least for a while) of satisfaction, satiation, perhaps serenity. But sometimes, as in ritualistic behavior, they may instead generate a feeling of mechanical repetition or the absence of a meaning achieved, the sense of being enmeshed in an endless series of aborted sequences. Both kinds of the behavior, the ritual and the ritualistic, emerge from a concern with boundaries, such as those between the individual and the group, what is within and what is without, the concrete or concretized-spatial and the psychological-temporal.

Ritual and the ritualistic address these divisions—which are central to our understanding of psychological reality—not consciously, perhaps, but in a particularly focused manner. My thesis is that both ritual and the ritualistic attempt to confirm and to challenge shared, commonsense, everyday reality by formalizing and dramatizing the divisions and the passages between these reality organizations. They attempt to confirm for the individual that he has roots in all these realities and that his rootedness in the ontogenetic and perhaps phylogenetic early ones does not cut him off from the later realities, including the commonsense reality essential for the performance of most daily tasks—the consensually validated reality based on similar degrees of completion of *perceptual acts*. Note that I specified that the ritual and the ritualistic both make the *attempt* to confirm the individual's rootedness in multiple realities, but I believe that ritual is relatively successful and that the ritualistic owes its mechanistic, driven repetitiveness to the fact that it is basically a failed ritual.

The rituals with which a psychoanalyst is concerned in daily clinical work are manifestations of obsessive-compulsive urges. Although the degree of ego dystonicity of such urges and acts may vary, they are often considered symptoms by the analysand and may be the overt reason an individual seeks psychoanalytic treatment. As work with the patient proceeds, however, the psychoanalyst may soon think of many other aspects of almost any patient's behavior as ritualistic. The way he enters the consultation room, a particular way of reclining on the couch, a manner of rising with a characteristic jerking or a slow rolling motion, his greetings or avoidance of greetings—these behaviors may have a ritualistic quality in the analyst's eyes, not recognized as such by the patient but eventually of importance in understanding him and in formulating interpretations. The extent to which such rituals can be seen as related to those which the anthropologist studies depends on the conceptualization of the nature of both kinds of ritual.

The analyst may be especially aware of the ritual component of behavior within a given society, both through contact with persons whose behavior does not conform to social norms and through a growing understanding of the personal dynamics of conformity. My own concept of the nature of ritual leads me to believe that despite some surface differences, the term *ritual* signifies the same fundamental characteristics to the clinician and the anthropologist (Kafka, 1983). Both fields understand the structural role of rituals as in some way related to the attempt to maintain the psychological homeostasis necessary for the individual's functioning in a social context.

In my view, the occurrence of rituals at such times as birth, puberty, marriage, and death derives from the basic stabilizing function of ritual in situations with the potential for instilling dystonic feelings ranging from discomfort to terror. Two major characteristics of cultural rites also emerge in clinical counterparts. One is a precision of performance of the ritual act, in which the emphasis on the concreteness of the ritual object (the preserved limb of the saint, the specific location of the pilgrimage) coexists with emphasis on an abstract symbolism—the nonconcrete mental or spiritual charge with which the ritual performance or event is invested. Thus, the ritual is a condensed encounter of material and psychological extremes, the concrete and the abstract polarities. (Recall my previous discussion of the material-spatial "equivalence" and the psychological-time "equivalence.") The second characteristic is ritual confrontation of the issue of the boundary of the individual and the relationships between the individual and the other, the inside and the outside (the depth of the *individual* commitment to the *bond* to the bride or groom, to the community of the religious order).

As I discussed earlier, in biology what is considered a unit is in some sense arbitrary. For example, it is unclear whether certain marine organisms should be considered colonies of unicellular organisms or individual animals. The anthropologist encounters the boundary question in the study of the rites of passage when the individual "becomes a part" of the society. The clinician frequently comes to understand rituals as connected with the patient's struggles to define or protect his own boundaries. Victor Turner is an anthropologist whose central concern is liminality (1977) and the rituals that serve as stabilizers when the anxiety is greatest, when one has left one condition and not yet entered another—the way to the altar, fertility rites, last rites. Perhaps Turner and other anthropologists with similar interests might agree that the rituals they study concern, first, such matters as transcendence of the concrete, the material, the body, and, second, the boundary between individual and societal entities.

Developments in modern physics that have made inroads on commonsense understanding of matter, energy, and time, no doubt contributing to the Zeitgeist, play some role in contemporary explorations of perennial questions involving the linkage of the psychological and the temporal. I have emphasized how various authors who have approached this issue from very different angles have independently concluded that the study of mind and the study of time are intertwined. Hugh Longuet-Higgins (1968), a theoretician of communication and a mathematical model builder, proposes a model of the brain based on the model of the holograph, but he transforms the holograph by giving a temporal rather than a spatial meaning to the terms in the mathematical formulae describing its physics. In holography, each point in space has some information about all other points in space;[9] in the temporal analogue, each "point" in time has *some* information about every other point in time (past and future). Longuet-Higgins's treatment of the brain in temporal terms—rather than in commonsense, "material," concrete terms—perhaps brings us closest to Loewald's trenchant characterization of "time as . . . the inner fibre of what we call psychical" (1962, p. 268). Longuet-Higgins's model clarifies

---

[9] If we cut the holographic picture of a man in half, we obtain not a picture of an upper half and one of a lower half, but two pictures of the whole man, although they are not as sharp as the original picture.

our understanding of the unique qualities of the human mind and human consciousness—awareness that each moment, although different from that which went before and that which will follow, is rich with memory and with anticipation, with retrospect and with prospect. Without this richness of time the moment, the *psychological* now, loses its meaning. All "meaning" disappears if we empty "now" of memory and retrospect, of prospect and anticipation.

A whole literature deals with the pathogenic consequences that result when the *temporal* psychological event undergoes a transformation through reification, concretization, *spatialization.* Much of this literature is summarized by Joseph Gabel in *La fausse conscience: Essui sur la réification* (1962). Here he develops the theme that estrangement, common to ideology and schizophrenia, is grounded in such reification, the spatialization of the temporal. The "réification" of political ideology and of what he considers the inherent "ideological" nature of schizophrenia have this in common: ideology is fixed, lifeless, unresponsive to outer and inner life. Gabel's concept of ideology thus has a clearly negative connotation.

On the surface, but I believe only on the surface, this contrasts with Erik Erikson's initially positive reference to the ideological element, "the element providing a coherence of ideas and ideals" which "become part of formal rites" in the ontogeny of ritualization (1966, p. 617). Erikson says that only after the addition of the ideological element "can man be said to be adult in the sense that he can devote himself to ritual purposes and eventually be trusted to become the '*everyday ritualized*' in his children's life" (p. 617; italics mine). The "everyday ritualizer" is also the socializer.

Erikson starts out by studying human ritualization in contrast and in relation to animal ritualization as described by the ethologist. His positive evaluation of ritual derives from its roots in the mother-infant recognition, such as the appreciation conveyed by a greeting, which fosters a sense of self in the infant and helps maintain it in the mother. He introduces a more negative element when he discusses human ritualization as largely related to the existence of human "pseudo-species"—tribes, clans, classes—which consider all outsiders as enemies, and he foresees the possibility that humanity will succeed in diminishing its pseudo-species divisiveness. I believe that for Erikson ideology thus also implies a certain concretization. The positive aspects of Erikson's evaluation of the ideological result not so much from a view of ideology essentially different from Gabel's as from the position that at our current state of development, roots in a somewhat concretized group must to some extent coexist with individualism that would otherwise risk being autistic. Such dialectic conflicts are characteristic of all the developmental phases described by Erikson.

Here we meet again an untenable commonsense idea—we cannot take it for granted that the size of an organism is an absolute given. It is not only in marine organisms that it is fundamentally unclear whether a unit of a given size is a colony of unicellular organisms or a whole animal. Essential ambiguities for such complex animals as human beings arise from the person's functioning as an individual and at the same time as member of a dyad (mother-infant, for instance) and as member of a larger group. Since I believe that current prominent attempts in psychoanalysis to distinguish "self" from "ego" represent an effort to do away with an essential ambiguity on the intra-individual level, a discussion of them is relevant at this point.

In self psychology, which attempts to clarify issues related to the experiencing or self-representations of the image of the self, Kohut's (1971) name is currently in the foreground. Freud's ambiguous usage of "Das Ich" is often critically cited in this connection. Although the concept of self-representation is clinically useful, I believe that on a more theoretical level the ego-self differentiation can be a pseudosolution— that is, it can gloss over a problem that is more interesting if its unsolved paradoxical nature is faced squarely. In their discussion of *ego*, Laplanche and Pontalis mention the history of the usage of "Ich" in psychoanalysis and the conceptual problems involved:

> Some authors have sought, for the sake of clarity, to make a conceptual distinction between the ego as agency, as substructure of the personality, and the ego as love-object for the individual himself. . . . Hartmann, for example, has suggested a way of getting

rid of the ambiguity which arises in his view from the use of terms such as "narcissism" and "ego-cathexis" (Ich-Besetzung). ... in using the term narcissism, two different sets of opposites often seem to be fused into one. The one refers to the self (one's own person) in contradistinction to the object, the second to the ego (as a psychic system) in contradistinction to the other substructures of personality. However, the opposite of object cathexis is not ego cathexis, but cathexis of one's own person, that is, self-cathexis; in speaking of self-cathexis we do not imply whether this cathexis is situated in the id, in the ego, or in the superego. ... It therefore will be clarifying if we define narcissism as the libidinal cathexis not of the ego but of the self. (1967, p. 131)

Laplanche and Pontalis go on to say:

In our view this position builds upon a purely conceptual distinction, running ahead of a real solution to some essential problems. The danger of proposing a usage of "Ich" which is taken to be exclusively psychoanalytical by contrast with other more traditional senses is that the real contributions of the Freudian usage may be lost. For Freud *exploits* traditional usages: he opposes organism to environment, subject to object, internal to external, and so on, while continuing to employ "Ich" at these different levels. What is more, he plays on the ambiguities thus created, so that none of the connotation normally attaching to "ego" or "I" ("Ich") is forgotten. It is this complexity that is shunned by those who want a different word. (pp. 131-32)

Although there is ambiguity in the idea of self-observation, it is the concreteness and spatialization of a self-observing self that make the ambiguity so difficult and motivate those who want to eliminate it. I believe that the advantages of the Freudian ambiguity, which Laplanche and Pontalis also want to preserve, lie in its avoidance of a one-sided concretization (of "Ich"), which is essentially spatial and incompatible with my gropings for a new understanding of psychological reality—an understanding that has already achieved distance from common sense in recognizing time as the "fiber of mind," basically a mind-time equation. A self-ego dichotomy freezes the situation (and I admit that such freezing may at times have clinical value and may permit a useful "look" at some self-representations) and does not easily accommodate the previously developed notion of "animation" into a center of autonomous action.

The rituals observed by clinicians and anthropologists both have essentially a reality-anchoring function. For example, when Erikson discusses the recognition-greeting ritual of mother and infant, he emphasizes the formation of the individual's sense of his own existence and of a reality that, through generational "cog-wheeling" (Erikson using David Rapaport's phrase)—that is, the transmission of meaning and values from one generation to the next—links it to the reality of the group. This recognition-greeting ritual thus deals with the inside-outside (size of the group) dimension of the perceptual recapitulation. And once again I must summarize my central thesis: perceptual recapitulation of the ontogeny of perception is the basis for the establishment of object constancies. Scanning implies a temporal dimension, and motivational intensity (hunger, for instance) influences scanning speed. Furthermore, time experiences—time sensations and judgments—are profoundly affected by drive states and affects. Time judgments are based on *subjectively equivalent temporal intervals*, and dominant affects and moods determine the selection of the reference interval. My emphasis on the importance of the ever-contracting and ever-expanding temporal grids of psychic activity is in harmony with such authors as Gabel, who contrasts the temporal fluidity of psychological processes with "alienating," essentially nonpsychological, concretization and spatialization.

We are here again dealing with the difficult equation of the most "pure" psychological processes with temporal processes. Our practical need to deal with a concrete reality persists in reinforcing our resistance against the mind-time translation. Facing this difficulty permits us to make explicit a feature that is implicit in some of Erikson's remarks on developmental ritualization. As has been mentioned, Erikson links a necessary ritualization (to avoid autism) that is part of generational cog-wheeling to the development of a feeling of belonging to groups, clans, and other human pseudo-species. In Gabel's terms, the operational concreteness implied by Erikson's pseudo-species would be seen as psychologically "false" in a very specific sense, for Gabel considers projection of "bad aspects of myself" feelings as spatialization of the psychological (temporal). I will show below that when Erikson relates ritual to the basic individual-group dichotomy, the structure of this dichotomy is similar to that of the psychological-concrete (temporal-spatial) dichotomy as discussed by Gabel.

If the ritual's concern with the individual-group boundary also means a concern with the boundary of the psychological (temporal) and concretized (spatial), questions of ambiguity on one border correspond to the same questions on the other. Erikson discusses ambiguity as it relates to ritualization, to self and other, to individual and group. In summarizing basic elements of ritualization (starting with the greeting-recognition of mother and infant) he says:

> Its mutuality is based on the *reciprocal* needs of two quite *unequal* organisms and minds; yet, it unites them in *practical reality* as well as in *symbolic actuality*. It is a highly *personal* matter, and is yet *group-bound*; by the same token it heightens a sense both of *belongingness* and of personal *distinctiveness*. It is *playful*, and yet *formalized*, and this in *details* as well as in the whole *procedure*. Becoming *familiar* through repetition, it yet renews the *surprise* of recognition which provides a catharsis of affects. And while the ethologists will tell us that ritualization in the animal world must, above all, provide an *unambiguous* set of signals so as to avoid fatal misunderstanding, we suspect that in man, the *overcoming of ambivalence* is an important aim of such ritualization. (1966, p. 605; Erikson's italics)

Before examining some problems in Erikson's text, let us take a closer look at the juxtaposed topics of ambiguity and ambivalence. Since ambivalence refers to good and bad feelings toward the same object, it takes for granted an antecedent degree of object constancy, a certain solidity (concreteness) of the borders of the self, a solidity of the boundary between inside and outside. The formal logical structure of ambiguity, as discussed in chapter 2, is pertinent here, as is the finding, on a more clinical level, that parental fear of ambiguity may be a pathogenic element leading the offspring to experience estrangement and alienation when confronted with the ineluctable ambiguities and paradoxes of life.

With those points in mind, let us return to Erikson's emphasis on the relationship, in ritualization in animals and man, between the need for an *unambiguous* set of signals and the *overcoming of ambivalence*. Recall that in order to tolerate the infant's first step, the mother must for the briefest moment have the delusion that the infant will not fall. This delusion occurs at a moment of psychological lack of separation of the two individuals involved. In a sense, it is the mother's ability to laugh at herself and her delusion when the fall occurs but has no serious injurious consequences that permits the infant's further development. I would now add that it is this delusion that permits the mother, for a moment, to give an unambiguous set of signals that the first step should be attempted. The signal is unambiguous at the moment when the definition of the individual is ambiguous, when the boundaries between mother and infant are blurred. (It should also be noted here that psychoanalytic theory offers a conceptual bridge between ambivalence and the ambiguity about what unit is in the mother-infant dyad. Since the infant equates good with the satisfaction of his needs and bad with the lack of satisfaction—that is, with *need*, something he cannot himself satisfy—the differentiation of inner and outer in a sense corresponds to the birth of good and bad.) It is the phase-appropriate degree of ease with which the mother can cross the fusion-differentiation (from her infant) barrier that indeed forms the foundation of what Erikson calls "*the overcoming of ambivalence*," which is "an important aim of . . . ritualization."

While "the overcoming of ambivalence" is a term that succeeds in conveying a readiness to act, it is somewhat misleading. Ambivalence is not "overcome," it is tolerated. The distinction is important because "overcoming" sets up false expectations. Erikson himself writes:

What we love or admire is also threatening, awe becomes awful-
ness.... Therefore, ritualized affirmation, at first playfully
improvised, becomes indispensable as a periodical experience
and must find new forms in the context of new development ac-
tualities. Its perversion or absence, in turn, leaves a sense of dread
or impoverishment. ... the earliest affirmation soon becomes reaf-
firmation in the face of the fact that the very experiences by
which man derives a measure of familiarity also expose him to a
series of estrangements. The first of these is a sense of separation
by abandonment to which corresponds, on the part of the mother, a chilling sense of not being needed; both must be prevented
by the persistent, periodical reassurance of familiarity and mutu-
ality. (p. 605)

Of course, the separation does and must occur, but I agree with Erikson
that the earliest affirmation persists in the recurrent ritual. But the ritual, because it represents the extreme confrontation of the concrete,
precisely defined, individually bordered spatial on the one hand and the
boundary-loosened, psychological, temporal on the other also is the periodic recurrence of the beginning—of the first (tolerated) step.

Elements of the ritual and the ritualistic, thus conceived, are pervasive if not omnipresent. When clinicians and anthropologists have a
closer look at the rituals traditionally studied by each other's discipline,
the similarities of the structural-qualitative characteristics of ritual become more obvious, and the differences are more likely to be seen in
quantitative terms. In all rituals the time-mind-communal/space-
concrete-individual ambiguities are not "overcome," but individuals vary
in their degree of tolerance of the tensions at the border and therefore in
the frequency and manner in which they either must immerse themselves in the experience of a wide or paradoxical reality or must
ritualistically defend against such immersion. Rituals also vary in the
manner in which they deal with the time-mind-communal/space-
concrete-individual tensions and ambiguities. More specifically, the polarity-tension that is the *raison d'etre* and the core structure of rituals
also manifests itself in the evolution of ritual.

To illustrate the broader application of these ideas, an example from religious ritual. With the destruction of the Second Temple and the exodus to Babylon, a significant evolution occurred in the spiritualization of Jewish ritual, which became freed from attachment to concrete sacrifice at a concrete and exclusive site, the Temple in Jerusalem. Judaism became a portable religion of the word (Graetz, 1893). Yet the tension persists in Jewish worship, and the counterforce of the concrete polarity always manifests itself again in those aspects of the concretization of words and ideas that Gabel considers when he discusses "ideology" (Gabel, 1967). Although the concrete site and the concrete sacrifice may be missing, Jewish orthodox ritual insists on the importance of the defined, the circumscribed—for example, the right prayer at the right time, the correct garment, and the yarmulkah. The abstract, the psychological, is again pulled toward concretization, a kind of primitivization of religious ritual.

The tensions in religious groups between traditionalists clinging to more concrete formalities and those who want to de-emphasize them in favor of the spiritual and ideational are always close to the surface. I do not want to use the word *ideological* because of the loading of concreteness that Gabel gives it, but my very avoidance of it reflects the ease with which there is always the "return of the concrete," analogous to the "return of the repressed" of the psychoanalyst. In the evolution of ritual, what is at any one moment considered acceptable is that which is perceived as essentially a subjective equivalent to a former ritual; its repetition reinforces a particular system of equivalences and anchors a view of reality, such as a specific myth of creation. It also serves as a defense against other views of reality.

Clinicians are familiar with such phenomena since patients' rituals can also serve both as an anchor for one reality and as a defense against other views of reality. A vast literature of psychopathology deals with the concrete thinking of schizophrenic patients (Gabel cites much of it). Clinicians who are familiar with this literature are sometimes puzzled by the high-level abstraction manifested by some schizophrenic patients in such areas as mathematics, theory of harmony, and musical composition. As I emphasized in the previous chapter, descriptions of the schizophrenic's objects as either concrete or abstract do not do them justice. Schizophrenics' object constancies, resulting from the mixture of completed and arrested perceptual acts, are idiosyncratic and are sometimes both very concrete and very abstract. ("Heidi-ness" was more constant than any one individual.) The schizophrenics' objects can thus resemble ritual objects, which have a particularly heavy abstract-symbolic *and* concrete-specific loading. While from one perspective Dorothy L, the patient with the reality-anchoring "Heidi-ness" image, was *apparently* involved with an abstraction, she also manifested behavior illustrating schizophrenic concreteness. During one schizophrenic episode she strictly observed a personal taboo that can be understood as a negative ritual. The psychiatrist who was administrator of her hospital unit emphasized patients' personal grooming. If prior to their hospitalization they had gone to a beauty shop once a week, they were urged to do so during their hospitalization. If a patient had shaved her legs at home, she was urged to do so in the hospital. Dorothy L refused to do so, saying she had her "father's legs." In effect, she was asserting a view of reality in which she was not separate from, and controlled parts of, her deceased father. As she emerged from the schizophrenic episode, rituals of adoration of her father took more conventional forms, such as walks in places and at times corresponding to his preferences.

In the usual psychoanalytic work with neurotic patients, the "blinder" functions of ritualistic behavior are the most readily observable in the consulting room. For example, ritualistic repetitions of ways of moving avoid body sensations that are threatening because of unconscious erotic wishes toward the analyst or because they would too easily lead—in unconscious fantasy that is eventually uncovered—to an aggressive act or gesture. Rituals in the consulting room also seem related to phase-specific drives and defenses against them; the ritualistic behavior often seems to be a manifestation of a compromise in this area. More descriptively, certain ritualistically maintained rigidities literally act as blinders. For example, a patient may not be able to look at a painting in the analyst's office because it does not match her view of the analyst's characteristics, a view that she has to maintain and that is consistent with the current stage of transference development.

The idiosyncrasy and repetitiveness of some behavior, its stilted and desiccated characteristics, may lead the clinician to think of it as ritualistic, but it is difficult to draw a line distinguishing it sharply from other symptomatic behavior. The isolation of affect may be particularly striking in behavior that therapists are inclined to label ritualistic because the "dramatic elaboration" (Erikson, p. 614) of the sequence is in such marked contrast to the apparent mechanical nature of the performance. In the clinical setting, what is called ritualistic is often *desiccated drama.* Mr. Brown, the patient mentioned in chapter 1 who moved back and forth between mistress and wife during his analysis, did so in a manner that could be described as desiccated drama. The moves were accompanied by loud dramatic scenes, but they had a pseudoaffective, compulsive, and mechanistic quality. The insight that the moves had something to do with his adoptive parents and his idealized natural parents eventually led to a marked diminution of this particular desiccated drama, to a decrease in ritualistic-manneristic behavior generally, and to an increased sense of continuity in his life and in his relationships. The difficulty of distinguishing the ritualistic from the impulse-defense compromises that are labeled symptomatic behavior—or simply from other behavior, since all socialized behavior contains at least a component of such a symptomlike compromise—lies in the fact that it is only quantitatively more dramatic and more desiccated. Ritual as I conceptualize it, rooted in time-space dualities, saturates human activities and existence.

If ritual has a reality-anchoring function, its ubiquity is no surprise, but what have we gained by this formulation? And how is the desiccated drama of ritualistic behavior in the consulting room related to ecstatic ritual? In one analytic session, a patient experienced some loosening of desiccated drama, isolated affect had begun to acknowledge its object, and he had experienced a sense of greater freedom and autonomy. Afterward he found himself laughing at his own sudden thought while he was waiting on a subway platform. Experiencing a lightening of the psychological weight he carried, he thought, "Even living and dying are not a matter of life and death." This experience, I believe, contained the essence of the successful ritual—a breaking out from the ritualistic.

Although this analysand did not consciously at this moment see himself as a member of a larger group, a link in a generational chain, the lightening he experienced involved a diminution of his sense of isolation, an implicit increase in the sense of connectedness to the rest of humanity. This is what the ritualistic tries for and what the ritual occasionally achieves. It may be that the more complete the achievement, the less often it *must* be reexperienced, and the less successful, the more it must automatically be repeated in dry ritualistic attempts.

The laughing experience that living and dying may not be so serious—not a "matter of life and death"—has some analogy to the mother-infant fusion in which the mother has the delusion that the infant will not fall when he takes the first step. The analysand's sudden laughter on encountering his liberating thought is also reminiscent of Erikson's "*surprise* of recognition which provides a catharsis of affects" (p. 605; Erikson's italics), an element in the earliest ritualization which starts in the mother-infant greeting and recognition.

Through the recapitulative nature of our affectively informed, drive-determined perceptual processes, we continually traverse multiple realities—which may be characterized by confusion or separation of the inner and outer, the animate and inanimate, or time and space—toward a consensually validated commonsense reality. Rituals, in a sense, give public and dramatic recognition to these ongoing individual voyages, which are usually not conscious and generally private. We are only too familiar with the danger of rituals when they validate and value "regressive" primitive reality organizations. Formulations emphasizing the delegation of superego functions and descriptions of projective and introjective phenomena in the rituals of a Nazi rally, for instance, must be supplemented by an examination of the corresponding perceptual "distortions" or different "reality organizations" in such situations. The role of drugs in rituals—such as mescaline in religious rites of some Native American groups—illustrates recognition of the importance of experiencing dramatically and publicly passage through multiple-reality organizations.

Ritual confirms and sustains everyday reality by challenging it in the sense of evoking the prior realities traversed in the evolution of the current one. Its historicity made apparent, everyday reality is imbued with life. Ernst Kris's well-known phrase "regression in the service of the ego" (1952) relates to the freedom, so essential for any creativity, to travel in ascending and descending directions along this recapitulative path. Successful rituals permit and foster in institutionally sanctioned ways the questioning of any one reality, the widest possible travel along this recapitulative pathway. The patterns of subjective equivalence along this path, however, may include some which represent "realities" that for personal developmental reasons are particularly conflict-laden, which correspond to neurotic fixation points. The abortive nature of ritualistic behavior is related to those fixation points, and successful analytic treatment thus transforms the ritualistic into the possibility of successful, enriching, perhaps even ecstatic ritual of an anchoring in an enhanced reality that incorporates the rediscovery of one's development.

In recent decades performance art has introduced the private ritual into a public forum. It is an arena in which it is particularly difficult to separate the ritualistic from ritual. There is no question, however, that the performed rituals of some artists demonstrate rather well the multiple-reality organizations that I have outlined. The performance artist is an individual whose public performances of private ritual are intended to make a statement about who he or she is. Sometimes the performed ritual is also designed as a condensed statement about the personal development of the artist, the genesis of protest, of attitudes and beliefs, about the acceptance (or, more commonly, the rejection) of societal values. The oeuvre of the well-known German artist Beuys, his "rituals" (one can imagine a performance consisting of his standing on a chair in an empty room, wearing a bowler hat and shattering a piece of glass), can be understood as a statement of his need for "ritualization" despite Beuys's disillusionment—in the post-Nazi period—with the meaning of the rituals of all social units: family, religious, and national groups. The ritualization that Beuys has in mind, the personal act, despite its "autistic" character, is intended to be a celebration which we associate ordinarily with formal religious or nonreligious solemnity.

Whether or not we accept such a self-consciously autistic performance as art, the very designation of an individual act with presumably only personal meaning as a ritual (not a ritualistic symptom) strikes us as peculiar—as it is intended to do—and underscores that *ordinarily* rituals are group-related. Rituals may or may not be performed in groups—although there is usually a preference for their performance in a group (the minyan of the Jewish service, for example)—but even the ritual carried out individually indicates concern with, usually adherence to, and, for the performance artist, focused protest against the values or beliefs of the group. The group concerns are of course most clearly illustrated by rituals that mark the entry of the individual into the group (coming-of-age ceremonies), the acceptance of the institution sanctioned by the group (marriage), and the founding of the family.

So far, in our theoretical and rather abstract examination of ritual, the boundary between the individual and the larger social unit occupies a prominent place. The family is the social unit that has received the most careful clinical scrutiny, and it is in the work with a family that its characteristic rituals are most visible to the clinician.

The Patient in the Family

In this chapter, I have endeavored to relate a prominent manifestation of group life, the ritual, to what I have learned in individual analytic treatment about the organization of multiple realities. Because the size of the organism is itself one of the fluctuating elements in the realities under consideration, the term *individual treatment* can also be seen from an enlarged perspective, one that could be conceptualized as a kind of analytically informed systems theory. In discussing the connection between theory and clinical practice, I have thus far focused largely on individual treatment. The connection between theory and clinical practice, however, can also be illustrated in family therapy. For those who specialize in family therapy, there has been a gradual shift away from emphasis on mental illness as a characteristic of the individual to the view that disturbance in one family member is a symptom of the functioning of the entire family. Regardless of whether one adopts that explanatory position, specific aspects of family dynamics are of practical importance in the intensive psychoanalytically oriented treatment of the hospitalized patient whose treatment can be interrupted by the family.

It is commonly said that a patient is often removed from therapy when his improvement threatens to upset the family equilibrium or to lead to the revelation of family secrets. Some family studies concentrate more on the etiologic importance of family dynamics in the development of specific psychopathological pictures (see Lidz and Fleck, 1960); Wynne et al., 1958). Other investigators have emphasized therapeutic aspects of family work (for example, Ackerman, 1963) or both therapy and etiology (Bowen, 1961).

The approach to work with families that will be described here developed gradually in a private psychoanalytically oriented hospital in which all patients receive intensive individual therapy and the patient population comprises a large proportion of chronic schizophrenics. A schematic history of the evolution of work with families in this setting follows.

Initially, the hospital administrators believed that the patient had to be protected from his family, and vice versa. The family, however, had to be sufficiently informed about the patient to continue their financial and other support of the treatment. Another traditional function of the work with families was the use of family members as sources of historical material. Although the patient's therapist, the clinical administrator, and other hospital staff members saw the family occasionally, this function was carried on primarily by the social worker. More intense contact with the family usually occurred in connection with some crisis in the life of the patient or another family member.

As work with the family began to evolve, the emphasis shifted to more detailed and direct study of the family interaction during visits to the hospital plus some direct observation in the family home. The evolving flexible approach was founded on the recognition that, although intensive individual psychotherapy remained the major therapeutic tool, a number of group approaches and milieu therapy could be usefully combined with it. The techniques I will describe developed in a setting in which the salient psychoanalytic therapy was performed by highly individualistic therapists, the functions of the individual therapist and the clinical administrator were usually performed by two different psychiatrists, and the clinical administrators of different units had varying philosophies and styles of administration which meant that they had widely diverging techniques of dealing with families.

The nature of the setting, the patient population, the distance many families lived from the hospital, and the focus on individual treatment all contributed to the development of an extremely flexible way of working with families. In contrast to family therapy as it is often practiced, we did not adopt the stance of considering the entire family as the patient. Despite our frequent recognition of mutually deviant relationships, one hospitalized person was identified as the patient. In what can already be called traditional family therapy, family meetings with the therapist usually constitute the only therapy for all family members, and there is no one-designated patient. In our hospital situation there was a designated patient who was primarily in intensive, individual, psychoanalytically oriented therapy. In traditional family therapy, "the family" is defined at the beginning of treatment. In our work, "the family" was an open-ended concept that could gradually expand to include more peripheral members. In another contrast to the usual family approaches, we did not require all members to come to all sessions; rather, the occurrence and avoidance of particular combinations of family members often had a ritualized rigidity. These fixed patterns were studied as possible indicators of patterns of family dynamics; combinations avoided by the family might be specifically encouraged and attempts made to disrupt the stereotyped and ritualized communication between family members apparently chosen to maintain the status quo.

Instead of structuring the family sessions in terms of length, number, and point of termination, we permitted flexibility in this area, too, with the amount of family involvement perhaps diminishing as the patient progressed toward discharge from the hospital and often toward the status of private patient of his hospital therapist. Instead of insisting, as family therapy usually does, that all information given by family members be shared, "confidential" data given by the identified patient—but not by his or her relatives—could be accepted by the therapist, although the whole family usually shared uncovered data eventually. Instead of the common practice of having one family therapist for the duration of the treatment, we permitted a change if circumstances made that necessary or desirable. For example, in the course of one patient's hospitalization, a social worker and the clinical administrator in effect took turns having the most active contact with the family during various phases of treatment. It must be emphasized, however, that because the staff of the hospital had an extremely low turnover, any staff member who had met members of the family—the individual therapist, the psychiatric social worker, the clinical administrator, and occasionally nursing and activities personnel—could usually be brought into family meetings when this was clinically indicated.

The single most important technical aspect of this work as it developed was the fact that there were meetings of many different combinations of family and staff members. Frequently, the staff made explicit plans concerning the composition of the meetings, and the question of who met whom was itself studied in terms of its dynamic implications. We learned that the tendencies to avoid certain groupings were consistent inside and outside the hospital. It was remarkable how long such patterns could go unnoticed by both the family and the hospital staff until the staff began to focus specifically on the study of such avoidance. In one family, for example, only after several years of work—during which almost all combinations of family members had been seen together—did the staff notice that the patient and her father had never been seen without the presence of another family member; this datum took on special significance in the light of considerable clinical evidence, both from individual and from family therapy, that prior to hospitalization, periods during which father and daughter were alone with each other had been particularly traumatic.

Brody and Hayden (1957) have observed that the intra-team reactions in a clinic may be a re-duplication, diminished in intensity, of the significant family conflicts. These observations were confirmed in our setting, and our permissiveness toward the development of multiple combinations permitted us to observe the parallelism of patterns of avoidance within the family and within the hospital staff. For example, in one situation where the father was ignored by the mother and the patient, the administrator seldom met with the social worker and the therapist. Furthermore, we noted that a family in which the internal power structure was being tested by the family members might also test the power structure of the hospital staff in a parallel way. For instance, a family in which the father's power was being questioned repeatedly tested whether or not the medical director of the hospital would overrule the decision of the unit administrator. When members of the hospital's administrative hierarchy were informed of this family pattern, the resulting changed approach interrupted the family's long-established pattern of moving the patient from one institution to another after brief hospitalizations.

Our study of which combinations of individuals were being formed, dissolved, or avoided also led to an unexpected finding about staff functioning. We did not consistently find that all families attempted to remove the patient when his or her improvement threatened the family equilibrium. Sometimes there seemed to be unconscious collusion between the therapist and family members to take the patient out of the hospital at a time of positive transference. The therapist then blamed the family for the interruption of treatment during a period of apparent improvement. But when our family work reversed the situation and the patient remained in the hospital, the short-lived transference improvement often disappeared; therapists were not always grateful for the work with the families that had thus exposed the incomplete treatment.

One variant of the multiple-combination technique consisted of deliberately introducing a peripheral family member or friend into one of the family meetings, particularly when a patient's apparently psychotic communication in individual therapy had indicated that the peripheral individual was "different"—that is, less fused with other family members. It was our experience that such an individual was likely to reveal a family secret. For example, a visiting aunt, described in the patient's obscure communications as separate from the family, revealed in one session what eight closer relatives had not mentioned in many visits extending over almost five years—namely, that the patient's mother had exerted formidable control over the family by repeatedly and convincingly threatening suicide.

Often the patient's communications about his family made no sense if we dealt only with the manifest family as it presented itself to the hospital.

Our techniques can be seen as attempts to reach the latent elements behind the manifest facade. There are three ways in which the term *latent* can be used in reference to family work. First, it can be used to designate the potential strength of the family, which is expected to emerge if the goals of therapy are achieved. The second meaning is closely related to Murray Bowen's conceptualization concerning the gradually emerging chiefs of a clan, which he presented at a Georgetown University symposium on schizophrenia in 1961. A new chief emerges only when the limits of the old chief's tolerance are reached. The practical task of discovering who in the family can really decide whether or not hospitalization can be supported, financially and otherwise, had long sensitized us to the emergence of the hidden chiefs of the clan. For example, the husband, manifest head of the family, says, "We cannot afford her hospitalization here." At this point, an apparently peripheral uncle-in-law says quietly, "Well, let's have another look at that question later." The atmosphere changes, and clinical matters relating to hospitalization are then discussed.

The third meaning of *latent* refers to idiosyncratic relationships within the family that are not visible on the surface. Our emphasis on this third meaning is related to the observation, in the individual psychotherapy of psychotics in our setting, that the language of schizophrenic patients often reveals and sometimes deals almost exclusively with specific themes of the family mythology. Mrs. W often referred to murderers or killers. She fostered the clinical impression that she hallucinated the voice of her mother and, shortly thereafter, the voice of her sister. We gradually learned, however, that, strictly speaking, neither the mother's nor the sister's voice was hallucinated. In earlier chapters I have pointed out that for a psychotic patient, characteristics of someone may be more stable than the individual. For Mrs. W a perceived characteristic of both the mother and the sister had more stability than either person. This characteristic derived from a prominent theme in the family myth with which Mrs. W was concerned. She believed that there were killers in the family. The parents had decided, after many consultations, that a sibling of the patient should have surgery. When the child died during the surgery, the mother, whom Mrs. W held responsible for the decision, became classified by her as a "killer." Further, a category of "killers in the family" was established in her mind. All those who were considered "killers" were subjectively equivalent to each other, not differentiated from each other. Her mother and sister were subjectively equivalent when the patient was concerned with the killer theme. At one point in therapy, she wondered if she herself was a killer, too.

On the other hand, when she was concerned with the theme of physical appearance, Mrs. W was quite sure that she, brown-eyed and dark-haired, was separate from her sister and mother, both blue-eyed and blonde. Her sister and mother were subjectively equivalent whenever she talked about physical appearance. When she was concerned with the theme of the friendly ones in the family, those who were "warm and make easy contacts," then she and her mother, but not her sister, were subjectively equivalent. Besides the manifest family—the brothers, sisters, husbands, and parents whom the hospital staff meets—there exists in a patient's mind a series of latent families which depends on the context activated in treatment. For the patient different family members may be fused into one if a common characteristic makes them subjectively equivalent. The multiple-reality concept has direct clinical application here. Thus, when patient and family are seen in a variety of combinations, the patient who is concerned with certain basic themes can be helped to form and maintain increasingly stable identities of person as opposed to identities of theme. For example, after a series of multiple-combination family sessions, this patient could sort out identities, saying: "I'm different from you, Mother. I don't kill and I have a nicer figure. You can't even drive a car."

The flexible approach to work with families can thus contribute to increasingly stable feelings of identity in the hospitalized patient. The techniques I have described may also permit the family to tolerate shifts in its equilibrium related to the treatment of the hospitalized member. Premature termination of treatment may thus be avoided.

Characteristics within a family that determine subgroupings, alliances, and the formation of hostile camps have parallels in the family of man. Groupings within families can even be on an apparent "ethnic" basis, with some family members, for example, thinking of themselves as the northern Italian branch and others as the southern Italian branch. Erikson, as we have seen, speaks of ethnic units as pseudo-species (Erikson, 1966) and expresses the hope that they will eventually disappear. I have been impressed, however, by the fact that in the same circles in which nationalism was almost a dirty word about fifty years ago and there was enthusiasm for the ideas of world government and the international language Esperanto, there is now an acceptance of nationalism. To be sure, it is tempered by condemnation of chauvinism and "separate but equal" is the avowed credo but we have learned in racial relations that "separate but equal" is a polite cover for discrimination.

Examination of such changing waves of historical fashions in ego ideals has been a part of the work of the Committee on International Relations of the Group for the Advancement of Psychiatry. A GAP report on *Us and Them: The Psychology of Ethno-Nationalism* (1987) draws on some of the concepts that I have developed about multiple realities, particularly the notions related to primitivization of perception. The "narcissism of small differences" is evident when there is violent strife of closely related groups. To the outsider the difference in beliefs, life-style, even clothing between neighboring tribes may hardly be noticeable. But in the heat of battle the difference in clothing of the enemy tribesman, even if objectively minimal, looms large and is swollen with symbolic significance. Upon closer examination, one can see that primitivization of perceptual process in periods of stress leads to large intrapsychic differences, when completion of perceptual acts, the assessment of the difference in peacetime, would have led to the recognition of the smallness of the difference. Finally, and here I am returning to my basic themes, the differences move from the inner-psychological-temporal-animate to the outer-reified-spatial-inanimate when individual and cultural developments and transitions occur at times of great perceived danger. The extreme situation that may develop is the enemy's loss of the last remnants of recognizable human or even animate qualities. He can be treated and disposed of like so much wood, stone, or dirt.

Chapter 7

Psychoanalysis and Multiple Reality: Compatibility, Clinical Practice, and Prospects

In this concluding chapter, I will move back and forth between clinical and theoretical material, as I have done throughout this book. I will here venture further into theory, however, and I will also include speculations informed by developments in other fields. Partial summaries of ideas presented thus far will be embedded in an examination of their fit with psychoanalytic theory and also in tentative programmatic propositions about how they could be utilized in actual and in "thought" experiments.

In effect, I will be recapitulating the ontogeny of my own perceptions of human behavior, of psychoanalysis, and of relevant ideas and data from such fields as philosophy, epistemology, physics, and neurobiology. As with all such recapitulations, any designation of crisp boundaries between categories tends to distort the cumulative effect of the overlapping areas and their influences on one another. My aim here, which is an outgrowth of my experience in the consulting room and clinic, is to achieve a greater tolerance of ambiguity. In abandoning again and again the comfort of sharp outlines, we can paradoxically find our way to new, more comprehensive, and more precise epistemological, diagnostic, and therapeutic formulations.

The multiple-reality scheme developed here is related to the term *state-specific learning*, which is encountered in contemporary psychiatric literature and had its antecedent in Federn's term *ego states* (1952). Both terms refer to different organizations of mental functioning, organizations that are relatively separate from each other. My conceptualization of multiple realities adds two features to these formulations: (1) it defines dimensions or parameters of the reality organizations, and (2) it specifies an ongoing perceptual process of recapitulation of reality organizations. Together, these features have interacting clinical and theoretical consequences.

Let us first look at the clinical side. Psychoanalysis is not a brief encounter, and, in an enduring therapeutic encounter the limitations, perhaps the falsifications, inherent in some diagnostic classifications become apparent. Over an extended period, each patient seems to have many different "disorders." This observation is not an appeal for the elimination of diagnoses, nor is it simply an appeal to preserve the individual behind the diagnostic category. After all, that would be only a repetition of a universal but usually unheeded cry in this technological age of medicine. In the context of the fluidity of multiple-reality organizations, the structure of diagnostic thinking itself can be somewhat different. The tolerance of such fluidity is at the center of this kind of diagnostic thinking, and it is matched by the extent to which tolerance of fluidity can be modified and increased in treatment; perhaps better, flexible diagnostic thinking centers on the degree to which obstacles to the creative expansion of the patient's tolerance of ambiguity can be removed by appropriate treatment. Concern with the tolerance for change is not very different from concern with "ego strength" or with the "flexibility of the ego," but I have specified some of the dimensions of the multiple-reality organizations in which such an ego must be able to move flexibly.

In the introduction to this book I observed how fashionable it is now to have specialized clinics—depression clinics, premenstrual tension clinics, phobia clinics—as well as specialized, or should I say compartmentalized, treatment facilities for borderline and various psychotic disorders. The very fact that the term *borderline disorder* has come into increasing use, however, may reflect discomfort with diagnostic boundaries that are too rigidly drawn. One could argue that the diagnosis of "borderline" owes some of its relative longevity to its different meanings for different people. For Harold Searles, for instance, it means a syndrome at the border of psychotic and neurotic diagnoses. For others, in particular Otto Kernberg, it indicates a unique symptom constellation and especially the predominance of a specific level of defenses. Still others place borderline diagnoses primarily at the boundary between affective and cognitive disorders. The range of opinions is illustrated by the contributions of twenty-eight authors to *Borderline Personality Disorders*, edited by Peter Hartocollis (1977), which I have critically reviewed (Kafka, 1981).

My discussion of borderline disorders in chapter 4 illustrated how formulations that take multiple realities into account influence diagnostic and therapeutic thinking. For example, particular countertransference tensions are characteristic in work with patients whom the therapist is inclined to diagnose as "borderline." Because for much of the time these patients seem to share everyday reality organization with the therapist and seem to understand and to function in familiar frameworks, their peculiarities, their often infuriating actions and expectations, again and again surprise the therapist. My analysis of such "peculiarities" led to the discovery that the animate-inanimate confusion was particularly prominent for these patients. Recognition that this dimension of the multiple-reality scheme seemed to be in the foreground for them influenced my countertransference reactions and therefore ultimately my technical approach to them. Recognition of this kind helps diminish the confrontational element in the "clarifications" offered by the analytic therapist and influences the timing of interpretations. If it is possible to observe, for example, that the patient's ability to discriminate between animate and inanimate degenerates—becomes more primitive—when he or she is reacting to a particular conflict, then the analyst can shape resultant interpretations in the interests of enhancing the growth and development of such discrimination.

I recognize that my emphasis here on the animate-inanimate dichotomy might lead some analysts, notably Kernberg, to say that I am speaking of narcissistic rather than of borderline patients. In my experience, however, this narcissistic feature is characteristic of borderline patients and is diagnostically central, and I will discuss the issue in some detail later in the chapter. For my immediate purposes, however, it is not crucial whether narcissistic or borderline features of the patients are emphasized, since I wish primarily to illustrate some applications of the multiple-reality scheme and to show how such applications interdigitate with currently accepted psychoanalytic approaches.

The separateness of, the "unbridgeability" between, Federn's ego states and the conditions in which different state-specific learning occurs does have clinical consequences. As I pointed out in chapter 5, Federn believed, for instance, that different therapists should work with the same patient at times when he is flagrantly psychotic and when he is in remission. According to Federn, the therapist who is in contact with the patient during the psychotic period is contaminated by it and by its horror, and another therapist would be better for the "mental hygiene" approach that is appropriate for the patient in remission. Although I agree that there are deeply regressed conditions to which it may be impossible to find bridges during remissions, I have found that one of the essential functions of the therapist of psychotic patients is to enter their object world. He can do so only if he understands the nature of their object formation. As I elaborated earlier, the objects of the schizophrenic patient are understood as resulting from idiosyncratic subjective equivalences, which in turn are the result of a mix of perceptual acts at different stages of completion. Here, too, the multiple-reality scheme has specific clinical applications.

At this juncture we are approaching an area in which the merging of clinical and theoretical issues is particularly complex. I have sought to demonstrate that psychoanalysts do encounter the dimensions of my multiple-reality scheme in clinical work with neurotic patients—for instance, the animate-inanimate issue emerged for Mrs. A who suddenly and transiently experienced her husband as dead, "like a piece of wood." I believe that the moments in which these issues are encountered in the psychoanalytic treatment of neurotic patients are crucial and are related to structural change. Nevertheless, in the treatment of neurotic patients these structural reality issues are in the background most of the time, and the clinical focus is on the usual conflicts, defensive constellations, and transference issues familiar to the psychoanalytic clinician. It is usually only in retrospect that one recognizes the significance of crucial moments such as these I have been emphasizing. The analyst's awareness of such matters, however, may sensitize him to and keep him from neglecting the emergence of pertinent countertransference feelings.

In contrast, in work with some borderline patients and especially in the treatment of schizophrenic patients, the therapist's understanding of these structural reality issues must be in the therapeutic foreground. Here the analysis of the patient's object formation is essential, and this understanding permits the therapist to enter into and become established in the patient's object world.

What is the situation when a therapist has contact with a patient for a truly prolonged period and realizes that the "cross-sectional" diagnoses would be markedly different at various times during the patient's life? My own longest contact with a patient has extended over three decades. The only subgroup of schizophrenic diagnoses that nobody ever applied to her was "hebephrenic," and the range of nonpsychotic diagnoses that could have been applied by a clinician not familiar with her history was very wide. Here I want to emphasize that during periods of remission my work with her could hardly have been differentiated from psychoanalytic therapy with a neurotic patient; during one long period, if one had looked at that segment of the treatment without reference to other segments, the conflicts, the oedipal problems, and the transference configurations observed would have made differentiation from classical psychoanalysis difficult indeed.

I have come to believe that some of our difficulties in functioning as analytic therapists during some periods of work with such patients may be the result of the self-fulfilling prophecy that disaster will strike if we are more "analytic." To the degree to which the analytic therapist has become comfortable with his functioning in what can be considered multiple therapeutic realities, at least some patients can profit by his multiple functioning. Our caution may well be the result of mistakes early in the history of our field when some psychoanalysts attempted unmodified psychoanalysis with patients whose psychosis was only thinly covered. This could indeed have extremely serious consequences. But the situation is different if the therapist is cognizant of the depth of the disturbance and follows the patient's lead during prolonged treatment if and when the patient indicates his or her wish, need, readiness for, and ability to handle exploratory psychoanalytic work.

It may be of interest to reflect on the number of different symptom-oriented clinics to which my long-standing patient could have been sent during this thirty-year period. She would certainly have qualified for clinics specializing in anxiety, phobias and panic, depression, and eating disorders in periods during which she was not particularly eager to talk about her hospitalizations. Of course, the pros and cons of symptom-oriented treatment must be considered in the context of the economics of therapy. Similarly, it is often pointed out that the battle between the champions of the psychiatric revolution that took patients from the attic and put them in institutions and the champions of the subsequent revolution that took them from the institutions and put them on the streets has not yet been decided. Obviously, the economic arguments, which must consider both direct and indirect costs, are complex ("Schizophrenia Costs...," 1986). I want to emphasize here only one point frequently discussed in this context. On the basis of research findings, some psychiatrists recommend that families of chronic schizophrenic patients should be taught to dampen the expression of affect in order to reduce the frequency of relapse and re-hospitalization. Others argue that the cost to the family of such an effort is too great. I would go beyond that and offer the observation that it was precisely the fear of expression of affect, which was thought to be catastrophic or literally deadly to an individual or a relationship, that worsened the tensions within the families of a number of my schizophrenic patients. The pathogenic consequences of the unspeakable have been widely documented, and I am here urging that the usefulness of analytic exploration of both individual and family conflicts not be overlooked in the rush toward cost-effective techniques of dealing with severe mental illness.

When we shift from clinical problems to theory, the most difficult aspect of the multiple-reality approach results from the formulation that the time-space dichotomy is one that itself is a developmental and therefore "temporal" step or achievement. The ongoing perceptual recapitulation of the developmental sequence further complicates the picture, and the time-space dichotomy is thus multiply imbedded in time. As the discussion in chapter 3 has shown, we are here far from common sense.

We are, of course, also a long way from common sense in Longuet-Higgins's model of the central nervous system as a temporal hologram, a "holophone," in which each point in time has information about all other points in time. This is a model, however, that has profound psychological meaning. At each point in time we know something about our present, about our past, and about our projected future, which in turn influences our perception of the present and of the past. I cannot do justice here to the series of highly technical papers that Longuet-Higgins has written (1968, 1969, 1970), but certain questions that he raises will illustrate the pertinence of his work to these concerns. He postulates cells in the cerebral cortex that respond specifically to particular rhythms, just as there are known to be cells that fire only in the presence of specific visible features and arrays of cells that when briefly stimulated discharge rhythmically for some time afterward. He asks whether their thresholds for rhythmic firing can be altered by rhythmic stimulation.

The relevance of such work to my ideas about déjà vu phenomena, for instance, is readily apparent. I have been able to integrate Longuet-Higgins's work with my ideas in combination with Marian Kafka's findings that neurotransmitter receptors have different circadian rhythms altered differentially by psychoactive drugs (M. S. Kafka et al., 1983) and that there are hierarchies of rhythms in neurotransmitter receptors. We have summarized these ideas together with some of the multiple-reality formulations as follows:

> The model of a temporal hologram permits the non-local storage of memory. In the brain fast rhythms include neuronal firing and refractory period; slow rhythms, circadian rhythms. That neurotransmitter receptors have different circadian rhythms altered differentially by psychoactive drugs [and newer findings not involving drugs] supports the idea that rhythmic neuronal events are arranged in hierarchical levels of integration. Object constancies are derived from the subjective equivalence of stimu-

lation patterns which are similar but not identical. Perceptual acts may recapitulate their ontogeny. Stability of equivalence patterns depends on consistency in completing perceptual acts. Disordered temporal relationships of neuronal rhythms, by inconsistently interfering with perceptual act completion, can disrupt equivalence patterns and lead to thought disorder. As depressively tinged affect seems to determine the selection of stimulus-poor reference intervals, only part of the non-local storage bank may be addressed in some depressive disorders with diminished rather than disordered functioning. (Kafka and Kafka, 1983, p. 302)

In this summary, "selection of stimulus-poor reference intervals" refers to the experiment described in chapter 1 (Kafka, 1957a), in which individuals were found to select one out of a series of intervals as a baseline experience with which other experienced durations were then compared. The findings suggested that depressed affect was associated with the selection of the stimulus-poor reference intervals. In the introduction to this book I anticipated the criticism that I was dealing too much with cognition and not enough with affect. I also presented the argument that the affect-cognition dichotomy was not tenable, since drive-state, and therefore affect, determined the scanning activities that underlie perceptual and cognitive processes. But in connection with depressive affect I am now talking about diminished functioning—less or slower scanning apparently related to a state of diminished drive. This raises the theoretical question of the compatibility of these ideas with psychoanalytic formulations of depression.

In connection with my discussion of schizophrenic thought disorder in chapter 5, I remarked that one may have detailed and rather precisely worked out ideas about one aspect of a model and only crude and tentative formulations about other aspects of it. Intuitively, we are inclined to relate affect more directly than cognition to time—the rush of pleasant excitement, the immobility related to the *depth* of depression, or, contrastingly, agitated depression, quiet elation, and other complexities of the phenomenology of time experience explored in earlier chapters.

By itself the notion of diminished expression of drive in depressive affect and depressive illness is not very informative. Consider, however, the following quote from a recent article by Leo Stone, in which he relates rich and differentiated clinical experience to a thorough discussion of early and evolving psychoanalytic theories: "This [depressive illness] is the simple and inclusive term in which one may subsume all those instances in which spontaneous primary affects are *hindered* in their expectable trend toward spontaneous subsidence or toward modification by *affirmative action*" (1986, p. 337; italics mine). Much, if not all, of Stone's paper could be read as a search for the dynamic reasons behind this "hindrance," this inhibition, or perhaps this slowing.[10] His discussion deals with object loss, the fate of narcissistic and anaclitic objects, aggression, conflict, orality, guilt, and much more. Although Stone is always the first to note how the coloring of the individual case transcends limited formulations, the connection of technical vocabulary to clinical data is particularly clear in his presentation. The *hindrance of affirmative action* is, in a sense, a phenomenological description of a central feature of depressive illness, but this is phenomenology intimately related to the genetics, dynamics, and economics of psychic life. My claim is that the phenomenology of perception has equally intimate connections to these determinants of mental functioning. Although I have elaborated the clinical usefulness of understanding these connections, let us look again at the relevant experimental data cited in chapter 5 and at the theoretical possibilities on the horizon.

Smith and Danielsson (1982) and Westerlundh and Smith (1983) have demonstrated that the defensive operations elucidated by psychoanalytic

---

[10] Stone is concerned with unconscious inhibition, unconscious slowing, in depressed patients. A conscious and deliberate defensive manipulation of time can be observed in some patients who are not primarily depressed. Although some such manipulation is common, in my experience it has been of central clinical importance in patients who have suffered from actual early parental physical assaults or who have witnessed such assaults and sought to protect themselves by becoming immobile and "blending into the wall." Inactivity or postponed reactivity after unpleasant experience of thoughts—until, after several days, the perception has faded—may characterize such patients. They may also find it hard to understand why others come so rapidly to conclusions about them. These patients may "hide their light under a bushel" and feel misunderstood, chronically underestimated, because others do not wait until the light is exposed.

theory are essential for the understanding of findings of their experiments on perception. In other words, our familiar defenses operate in the microscopic time frame to which tachistoscopic perceptual experiments permit access. "Masking" is also a technique used in a number of tachistoscopic perceptual experiments. These findings and the pertinent literature are summarized by Holzman (1987). Essentially this technique involves the presentation of at least two different stimuli in succession. By varying the parameters of the various exposures, one can determine the differences in the timing of the second exposure that affect interference or noninterference in the "perception" of the first stimulus. Schizophrenic patients need a greater interval between the two stimuli than control subjects do in order to perceive the first stimulus without interference from the second.

Such a finding is consonant with my clinically derived hypothesis about differences in perceptual processing in schizophrenic patients. Among the parameters that can be varied in such masking experiments, of course, are not only intervals between stimuli and the duration of the stimulus exposure but also the content of the stimulus. The design of the content could variously present not only such "determinants" (as in Rorschach tests) as color and human, animal, or "inanimate" movement but also specific representational scenes (like those in thematic apperception tests) and even individually designed scenes that take into account the individual's development and the development of his defenses. Numerous other experimental possibilities offer opportunities to explore these hypotheses—for example, devices that register eye movement, which permit us to study tracking. The effect of paranoid vigilance on perceptual style could be compared, for instance, to the effect of a hysterical defensive constellation. The combined possibilities of brain visualization techniques, such as PET-scan and magnetic resonance, might permit the localization of cerebral activities when, for instance, specific perceptual processes or *perceptual defenses* are operative. Opportunities for using, confirming, modifying, or extending psychoanalytic theory in the context of sophisticated studies of perception are likely to expand. Clinicians disagree about the relevance of developments in theoretical understanding for psychoanalytic therapeutic technique generally, and it is an open question whether psychoanalytic understanding of perceptual processes in depressed patients will directly influence therapeutic technique with some of them. For me, however, theoretical exploration not only has added a richer background for the clinical work but also has influenced it in subtle ways, even when the immediate connection cannot be so clearly demonstrated as in the case of schizophrenic object formation. The analyst's alertness to previously neglected dimensions, I believe, can permit more correctly attuned responses.

Longuet-Higgins's model of temporally or rhythmically addressable memory is also compatible with the spatial localizations that are becoming more possible through new visualization techniques. But for the moment I would like to turn to some interesting speculations that his model permits concerning the size of organisms, the inner-outer question. Speaking of memories that can be addressed temporally rather than spatially, he evokes the image of banks of oscillators with resonant frequencies and damping constants: "They will behave rather like the strings of a piano, which will be set into oscillation by singing into the piano with the sustaining pedal held down. In this case the air acts as both input and output channel, and one hears afterwards the combined effect of the individual oscillations" (1968, p. 329). Admittedly I am approaching his technical work with considerable poetic license, but his reference to the air acting as both input and output channel brings to mind, for instance, Loewald's discussion of the mother-infant unit, where objects are located, in a manner of speaking, between the two. Arnold Modell's work in *Object Love and Reality* (1968) is also evoked rather vividly. In studying the early cave paintings, he found that prehistoric artists used three-dimensional characteristics of the cave walls, characteristics that suggested the forms of specific animals, as structural parts of their paintings. The object is, so to speak, between whatever created the wall and the creator of the painting. Extending even further the exploration of the question of the size of the organism, who or what does the. remembering when the remembering unit is not fixed but changes its size and temporal configuration? The difficulties discussed in chapter 3, related to our attachment to common sense, never quite leave us.

Since techniques for visualization of the locus of cerebral activities are becoming ever more sophisticated and a model for temporal addressability of memories exists, it is possible that we will be able to localize *spatially* brain regions in which different *rhythms* prevail. There are many opportunities here for research efforts that would integrate local brain visualization, data about differential neurotransmitter activities and rhythms (M. S. Kafka et al., 1986a, 1986b, 1986c), clinical data about phase delays in depression, and psychoanalytically informed behavioral and perceptual studies. I would like, however, to move now from these practicable biological laboratory studies into more speculative territory and consider the whole area of thought experiments that include consideration of spatial and temporal "structures." In doing so, I want to reemphasize the possible connections between structural change in the psychoanalytic sense and the differences between animate and inanimate structures. Sequences that are possible in temporal structures are also profoundly connected with questions of causality and thus with meaning.

Before going further, let me recapitulate some of the more theoretical issues with which I have been dealing. The more philosophical polarity of my preoccupation with time is related to the Zeitgeist derived from modern physics. Commonsense matter has disappeared. Even biology deals with systems of energy—for instance, when molecular biologists discuss the very nature of cell membranes. Let us recall Longuet-Higgins's temporal model of the brain and the observation that the focus on time permits a new perspective on the mind-body problem and fits in with Loewald's radical characterization of time as the inner fiber of mind.

The advantages of clinical attention to the temporal are manifold. The link between clinical and theoretical issues is underlined again when we consider that the meaning of a situation depends on when the situation is perceived as beginning and ending. Attention to idiosyncratic temporal organization and disorganization enlarges the repertoire of possible meanings with which the patient can be heard or observed. The extension of the idea of subjective equivalence to the temporal dimension opens new clinical and theoretical vistas. Although the term *subjectively equivalent stimuli* refers to the content of perception, the concept of subjective equivalence can also be applied to formal temporal characteristics. We know that intervals of different "objective" duration may be perceived as being of equal duration and that "objectively" equal intervals may be perceived subjectively as very different from each other. We do have some information about factors that influence such temporal "distortions." Once again, the need to understand the functioning of affects enters my exposition, which at first seems cognitively oriented. Ever-changing patterns of distortions, patterns of patterns, determine the perceptual temporal texture of our contact with the outer and the inner world. Which "constancies" are maintained, and the very meaning of "constancy," in a world that one approaches with acute temporal awareness are questions that acquire a new depth. My focus on time, however, leads us still further and again into an area where clinic and theory meet.

Psychoanalytic listening is informed by attention to contiguity. The psychoanalyst, by using free-floating (I prefer the term *hovering*) attention, tries also to free himself from that which contiguity sometimes seems intent on imposing. The psychoanalyst, so to speak, continuously changes temporal lenses, which range all the way from zoom to wide angle. He even tries to utilize several lenses at once. Why? First, because he knows that defensive operations—that is, defenses against the emergence into awareness of meanings and affects—utilize temporal tools, temporal disconnections, and false connections. The psychoanalyst, and to some extent every dynamic therapist, must therefore be capable of assuming, with correct "timing," a wider temporal stance than the patient. A widening of the patient's stance is an implicit analytic goal because the very notion of change, of changing awareness, of insight, implies both the development of a sense of connection between matters that previously seemed unconnected and the abandonment of false connections. For example, a patient might be helped to recognize the connection between his sense of guilt and the death of his brother. At the same time the patient can be helped to realize that his baby brother did not die simply because he may have once wished him dead. The discovery of meaning in what had once seemed haphazard and the discovery of the falsity of apparent connections (in a sense, the rediscovery of the haphazard) are essential ingredients of the psychoanalytic venture.

Beyond that, however, the very "meaning of meaning" is deeply rooted in the temporal dimension. Since psychoanalysis has taught us the operations, as it were, through which meaning is discovered and dissolved, since it has opened the door to unconscious meaning, this very expansion of our consciousness and of our self-consciousness regarding our operations has also underlined the question of whether we *ever* go far enough in our connecting, reconnecting, and dissolving of connections. Could it be that the universe is meaningless and chaotic and owes all its apparent causality, order, and meaning to the projection of our needs for those characteristics?[11] In chapter 4, I discussed an experiment (Bavelas, 1970) demonstrating the persistence of erroneous convictions regarding causality, the tenacity with which people refuse to accept randomness of events. The tenacity of such refusal is central in Jacques Monod's thesis (1972) that we live in a chaotic universe upon which we project, impose a false order, that we create, construct, a false causality and attempt to deny essential randomness and chaos.

This is a philosophical issue which we encounter in the laboratories of psychoanalysis and psychopathology, where chaos and disorder can become manifest especially when the belief in one causal connection has been loosened and before another set of beliefs has taken root, when one way of understanding the meaning of the sequence of one's life events is about to give way to another interpretation. New convictions are reached, but the very experience of profound change, the shattering of deeply held convictions when aspects of our development are relived and reinterpreted in the heat of psychoanalytic transference, also underlines at least the theoretical ultimate uncertainty of our convictions. The new experience is how much a new conviction can coexist with a profound knowledge that convictions can change. Shortly before

---

[11] I will not consider here theological arguments that address the meaning of such needs and essentially draw the conclusion that the very existence of the need is proof of the existence of something that corresponds to it.

termination of his treatment, a patient summarized such experiences: "Psychoanalysis is getting out of dead ends."

Order and structure are topics in which clinical and philosophical preoccupations meet. As I commented earlier, in clinical psychoanalysis we encounter the word *structure* in the context of structural change. The study of change in psychoanalysis and an examination of the concept of structure in that context have led me, by way of a retrospective examination of case material, to the facet of the multiple reality theme that I have been describing as the animate and the inanimate object. It is a frequent clinical observation that presenting complaints become less significant as the treatment progresses. Sometimes this may be so because a complaint or a symptom was only the "official," acceptable reason for entering treatment, while other and deeper reasons were close to awareness from the beginning. A shift in the areas in which the "live action" is in treatment, a shift in the themes that are "animated" and those that are "deadly" and uninteresting, may perhaps be traced to the early differentiation between the animate and the inanimate—that is, there may be a connection between structural change in the psychoanalytic sense, the shift from insight to active change, and the early distinction between the animate and inanimate worlds. I am here speaking of inanimate objects as those that either do not react to our actions or at least react differently from those that are "alive." The topic of how the reaction to death may or may not be related specifically to the infant's developing ability to distinguish the animate from the inanimate may also be pertinent here.

Here again the clinical material that I have encountered in my experience and infant research data remind me of more philosophical themes concerning the structure of the animate and the inanimate. I think of Henri Bergson's description of the stone as being different from animate matter because it has only one (unchanging) perception of the universe, which again raises the topic of time. Perception involves making contact with, dealing with, a contrast or at least a difference—hence a temporal movement to and fro. By referring to the stone's unchanging perception, by using a term ordinarily limited to what animate beings can do and by using the term at the absurd limit, Bergson points to the fundamental temporal distinction between the animate and inanimate realms. As I said earlier, Sartre's distinction between "process" and "praxis" deals with the difference between events that result from inanimate occurrences (a thunderstorm, for instance) and those resulting from animate action, be it consciously or unconsciously intended by an animate being.

On this most theoretical level, the nature of this particular structural difference has also led me to the fascinating work of the physicist Ilya Prigogine (1976). He has shown how under certain conditions "new" structures can be formed in physical systems. With extreme differences in temperature in different parts of a liquid, temperature distribution shifts from diffusion to the formation of hexagonal currents. Prigogine believes that his findings are pertinent to the formation of new structures in biological and social systems. Perhaps there is a bridge here to our understanding of animate and inanimate structures and at least a distant connection to the clinically observed switching, the animation and deanimation, that I have discussed.

Among other switching phenomena that have received much attention recently in psychiatric literature, the biology of manic-depressive mood switches in a major focus of interest. The German word *überschnappen* is also relevant here, referring to sudden shifts in mental functioning in a broad sense to becoming crazy or disorganized; it focuses perhaps more on thought disorder, although it does not exclude affective change. In such phenomena, it is usually the analogy between sudden changes in the physical system and sudden changes in the clinical picture that has captured the attention of psychiatrists. Arnold Mandell et al. (1982) speculate that the switches psychiatrists observe may be related to actual shifts in the mode of neuronal transmission. Mandell believes that cellular transmission—that is, neuron to neuron—may under certain circumstances be replaced by a mode of transmission in which the brain, or part of it, suddenly functions as the semiliquid mass that also characterizes its physical reality. If such a view were to receive support from empirical findings, the multiple-reality theme would be anchored in data that were beyond my horizon when I formulated my ideas. Could such switches be connected with shifts from spatial localization to temporal addressability, to my ideas connecting experiential multiple realities, including shifts in the animate-inanimate experience, to different temporal, different rhythmic organizations of the brain?

There is also a palpable connection between the animate-inanimate dichotomy and affective life. The idea of being animate corresponds to the experience of oneself as an autonomous center for the initiation of action. There is an obvious connection to changes in mood, since mood changes are intimately related to shifts in the experience of oneself as powerful or helpless. One patient's high moods were related to identification with a flamboyant father—for example, as a child she had sat on her father's lap and "controlled" a small airplane that he was piloting, even flying upside down, no less. Her low moods were related to falls from grace and experiences of impuissance in the family. Recovery of memories and reconstruction of this material in a long analysis with intense transference developments proved therapeutically effective. This patient's clinical picture descriptively had been indistinguishable from that of patients who are now routinely diagnosed as having an affective disorder and treated with lithium (as my patient had been prior to my work with her) or antidepressant drugs. I believe that in such patients therapeutic approaches may benefit from the simple and explicit recognition of a possible link between the animate-inanimate axis and the polarity of a sense of power (or power over something) and its affective component, on the one hand, and impuissance and its affective component, on the other hand. The wall that had separated the markedly hypo-manic and severely depressed states of my patient with the flamboyant father was a high one indeed. Perhaps different degrees of animation characterize different states—analogous to conditions of state-specific learning and Federn's different ego states.

Let us turn now to an examination of related issues in some borderline and narcissistic patients. Such patients do not differentiate between Sartre's praxis and process, the results of animate volition and of the forces of nature. They force the analytic therapist to deal with this theme when they act as if they were "entitled" to be treated by the forces of nature in a special and individualized fashion. The forces of nature are not "entitled" to be inanimate.

The term *entitlement* is associated with the concept of narcissism, and my reference to borderline patients in this context is not accidental. In Kernberg's schema, narcissistic disorders are a subgroup of the borderline personality disorders. I believe, however, that splitting defenses have such a prominent place in his understanding of the borderline disorders and at the same time are so central in his conceptualization of the narcissistic disorders that his subgrouping runs into some conceptual difficulty. To what extent can the features of "ego weakness" that for Kernberg characterize the borderline disorder be understood—rather than merely described— without reference to the splitting mechanisms that are also the central feature of narcissism? I mention these details of theory here because the idea that ego weakness may have something to do with early difficulties in establishing and maintaining the boundary between the animate and the inanimate is compatible with my approach to these problems.

In the early psychoanalytic literature, narcissistic disorders referred to the psychoses because it was believed that there was a deficiency of (external) object cathexes and an oversupply of narcissistic cathexes. Federn, whose work is now unjustly neglected, saw in psychosis a deficiency of cathexes at the boundary of the ego. In this formulation the psychotic individual was thus unable to discern whether a stimulus had penetrated from the outside or had an internal origin. Hallucinations, for instance, could not be differentiated from perceptions of the "real" world. There is an affinity between this early psychoanalytic formulation and my idea that a lack of the ability to establish or maintain the animate-inanimate boundary—or at least a weakness in it—represents a major issue in psychopathology.

The diagnostic significance of this issue is a complex one, and I emphatically do not want to link all problems of animate-inanimate differentiation with a diagnosis of psychosis. As I hope has been clear from my text. I consider the ability to treat the same object as animate on some occasions and inanimate on others and in other contexts as an essential component of the adaptive and creative use of multiple realities. Nevertheless, a somewhat unexpected bridge may be discovered between the older psychoanalytic uses of the term *narcissistic disorder* and the more current uses of the term if we consider that animate-inanimate boundary difficulties and ways of handling these difficulties characterize both the old and the new diagnostic categories.

The ability to treat the same object as both animate and inanimate is a characteristic that is often discussed in a developmental framework and is related to Winnicott's work on transitional objects. The connections between Winnicott's ideas and mine have been documented in chapters 2 and 4, in studying how a patient may use his or her own body as a transitional object and in the study of rituals. My emphasis on the creative and therapeutic uses of a multiple reality that encompasses the realities of the same object as both animate and inanimate obviously also has considerable affinity with Winnicott's ideas; he emphasizes the creative and therapeutic uses of an object that during particular developmental and usefully regressive moments is neither animate nor inanimate but is both simultaneously, or "transitional" between the two.

My extension or elaboration of the transitional realm goes beyond Winnicott's formulation when I introduce the idea of the transitional between the spatial (or "material") and the temporal, since the spatial is also associated with the inanimate realm and the temporal with the animate one. Gabel's (1967) understanding of ideology as a nonpsychological, spatial, and reified structure that can be contrasted with the temporal characteristics of mental life has led him to consider the similarities between political ideologies and the mind of the schizophrenic patient. In discussing rituals, I have similarly considered mental deposits of the past—and thus perhaps ideologies—as connected with psychopathology, stagnation, and the ritualistic rather than with the genuine ritual, in which transitional experiences can be recapitulated and the connection to root experiences reaffirmed. The ritual object is at the same time the unique, most concrete, specific inanimate material entity and the most condensed symbol of the animus, the spirit, the alive and abstract intentionality of the group, tribe, or ethnic or religious assembly. In contrast, I have emphasized the pathology of the "single reality," the reification and "spatialization" of the psyche. Accordingly, my therapeutic approach focuses on the mobilization associated with multiple realities.

The multiple realities I propose are organized along (1) a spatial-temporal axis, (2) a size-of-organism axis (theoretically, from cellular or even intracellular to the large social unit, but more immediately or prac-tically, from individual to family or group), and (3) an inanimate-animate axis. Certain correspondences, relationships, and perhaps equa-tions exist between the ever-changing positions on the axes of my multiple-reality scheme. As I have stressed throughout this book, more spatial corresponds to more inanimate or reified, and more temporal to more animate, more mental or psychological. The issue of the size of the organism seems to be anchored in a reified spatial dimension, but the person who sees himself as part of the group also at that moment changes his temporal perspective since the unit that determines his "reality" may well extend beyond his individual life span.

The reference to the term *equation* in the paragraph above needs fur-ther elaboration. It is an ambitious term, but I believe it is justified because it deals, after all, with the relationship of the material, the spa-tial, with time. One equation that has changed our world is Einstein's $e=mc2$. The consideration of developments in modern physics when we discuss problems in our field is not new. Marie Bonaparte (1940) in-forms us that the problem did not escape Freud when he considered the timelessness of the unconscious and that he was well aware of what I would call the multiple realities of wave and particle theories. It seems to me that the term *multiple realities* applies when the physicists tell us that certain phenomena can be conceptualized or understood only in the framework of particle theory, whereas others can be managed only in the framework of wave theory. The dichotomy we encounter between the static-reified-spatial-inanimate and the fluid-temporal-animate seems to relate to particle and wave. Despite warnings I mentioned early in this book against facile philosophizing or psychologizing of insights derived from modern physics, perhaps some considerations derived from that discipline can inform psychological perspectives on multiple realities, even though the data that demand such perspectives come from the consulting room. Einstein's equation establishes a relationship between energy, mass, and the square of the speed of light—that is, time. An equation points out that factors do not "exist" in isolation but have a potential for transformation or translation; this phenomenon is not' to-tally removed from the shifts we encounter clinically when a frozen, reified position, a rigid stance, becomes animated or reanimated, becomes fluid, temporal, and psychologically alive. Thus, it is difficult not to think of the probable pertinence of the theory of relativity to the body-mind problem, and thus to our field, especially at a time when Eric Kandel has demonstrated physical structural changes on the cellular level that derive from the experience of the neuron (1983).

Once one decides to consider the world of modern physics as pertinent to work in our field, even wider vistas open up. The equation $e=mc2$ has also been interpreted to mean that mass is frozen energy. Modern cosmology postulates an original energy-cauldron, an "id" that lacks "structure" in the sense that molecules and atoms cannot exist in it. There is, in a sense, a lack of "objects." The expansion of the universe with the accompanying lowering of the temperature leads to the formation of mass, of atoms and molecules, of objects. Perhaps each perceptual act can be understood not only as recapitulating the ontogeny of perception but also as recapitulating the creation of the universe. The perceptual act is the creative expansion from (nonmass) energy to the formation of mass, of structure, of objects. Before I stop my excursion into cosmology, I want to cite an extreme example of the extent to which commonsense efforts to understand the world are being challenged. One serious attempt to help us understand notions of reversed entropy, for example, appeared recently in the daily press. A *Washington Post* article of December 26, 1986, about the physicist Stephen Hawking bore the headline: "Physicist Theorizes on Direction of Time." The idea that the psychological present is informed or formed by a two-directional temporal scheme, the future and the past, is perhaps somewhat less beyond conceptual reach at a moment in history when the reversible time issue hits the newspapers.

It is a somewhat less bold step to relate findings from computer science to aspects of our field. According to Michael Rabin (1977, 1987), the introduction of randomness paradoxically leads to greater order (and better decisions) when large numbers of computers work together on decision-making tasks. Perhaps this is relevant to my critique of the double-bind hypothesis and to the idea that it is the absence of tolerance for ambiguity, not the paradoxical communication pattern, that is likely to be pathogenic. I have described how I went from clinical material to Gödel's formal demonstration of the necessity for ambiguity. When I found that the double-bind theorists had ignored one major component of Russell's *De Principia Mathematica*, Gödel's name was not widely known outside the field of mathematics. Since then, Hofstadter, in his *Gödel Escher, Bach* (1979), has made him an intellectual household word. As psychoanalytic students of the mind, do we need to understand more formal links between Rabin's and Gödel's work, which is central to students of artificial intelligence? Is it possible that the absolute absence of randomness leads to disorder, perhaps even to psychotic disorder?

In at least one sense, grandiose thoughts about the connection between the multiple-reality theme and expansive cosmological parallels are highly pertinent to clinical work. Although it has been said in many different ways that each individual is a universe and creates a universe, an effort to formulate a technical description of its creation, whatever the intrinsic merits or limitations of that description, fosters in the therapist a respect for the details of the individualized processes by which each patient forms both the more ephemeral and the more lasting aspects of his realities. Such added respect colors the atmosphere of the consulting room and underlines the analyst's nonjudgmental stance.

For the analyst, the work is always "in progress." Conceptualization of the patient's problems must always be unfinished as meanings and realities come and go, as connections move from haphazard to persuasive and vice versa. When the analyst finds that he is able to take a position, he recognizes at the same time that it is a contextual position and that it is in response to a change in the patient's contextual position, both temporally and spatially.

Because of such fluctuations, development of the nonjudgmental stance is a truly major component of the psychoanalyst's training. The arguments that a value-free position is unreachable in practice have led some clinicians to downplay the importance of the effort to approximate it. The "moral" questions in psychoanalysis, the questions of intentionality and will (Smith, 1976), are also ultimately questions of "free" will and (psychic) determinism. In discussing this topic from the viewpoint of sociobiology, Wilson (1975) gives the example of the behavior of a bee that is being observed by a scientist who has information about its genetic makeup, its life history, and its environment. While the observing scientist can make accurate predictions about the bee's behavior, presumably the "experience" in the bee's "mind" is one of freedom of choice. Although the cross-species component of the example complicates the picture, the freedom of choice question is reduced by Wilson—as it is in somewhat different ways by many authors—to an "inside-outside" question that is related to the question of the size of the organism. From outside it is "determined" and from inside it is "free." My discussions of perceptual recapitulation in ontogenetic, phylogenetic, and even cosmological terms and of the ever-changing size of the organism being studied (and studying itself) also lead to a less absolute or fixed view of what is outside and what is inside; inside and outside can be understood to be either in constant flux or, if the temporal extension of the discussion is kept in mind, to coexist. Transference-related transactions in psychoanalysis extend the range of the size-of-the-organism experience and thus lead the patient to experiences of autonomy, to possibilities of self-initiation beyond the preanalytic limitations.

As I come to the end of my pendulum swings, moving from clinical data through clinical musing toward theorizing and then back to the epistemological thoughts originating in what I have called "the clinical laboratory of philosophy," I wonder how many familiar chords I have struck in the reader. Has my reader also experienced with regret the lack of bridges—or the lack of *recognition* of bridges—between philosophical and formal logical propositions and psychoanalytic thought, a lack illustrated by the absence of both "Freud" and "psychoanalysis" from the index of Hofstadter's *Gödel Escher, Bach*? A clinical approach that reaches far enough must deal with the organization of the individual's realities—a problem that can go beyond the patently clinical. Essentially no propositions dealing with the nature of reality are too formal if we are to remain profoundly and appropriately receptive to the patient's transitional formlessness when new structures are in the making.

The field of psychoanalysis itself illustrates a context of multiple realities as it simultaneously moves in different directions that expand and enrich both clinical and academic viewpoints. At one extreme, Helmut Thomä and Horst Kächele's recent two-volume survey (1987) of psychoanalytic practice exemplifies sophisticated psychoanalytic scientific empiricism. At the other extreme, Janet Malcolm's description (1987) of current literary psychoanalytic extrapolations—many inspired by contemporary French analysts and philosophers and including transferential analyses of Freud's writings—is no less illuminating to both therapists and humanists. Students of human behavior who can accept such alternate approaches without feeling constrained to choose between them are finding that the mysteries of the resultant more complex world become less forbidding—and even inviting.

Have I struck familiar chords? Freud (1914) said that termination is near when the analysand (the reader?) feels that he has known it all along.

References

Abramson, H. A., ed. (1959). *The Use of LSD in Psychotherapy*. New York: Josiah Macy, Jr., Foundation.

Ackerman, N. W. (1963). Family diagnosis and therapy. In *Current Psychiatric Therapies*, vol. 3. J. H. Masserman, editor. New York: Grune & Stratton.

American Psychiatric Association. (1980). *Diagnostic and Statistical Manual of Mental Disorders (DSM-III)*. 3d ed. Washington, D.C.: American Psychiatric Association.

Anderson, C. M. (1983). A psychoeducational model of family treatment for schizophrenia. In *Psychosocial Intervention in Schizophrenia*, edited by H. Stierlin, L. C. Wynne, and M. Wirsching. Berlin: Springer-Verlag.

Arieti, S. (1963). Studies of thought processes in contemporary psychiatry. *American Journal of Psychiatry* 120:58-64.

Arlow, J. (1959). The structure of the deja vu experience. *Journal of the American Psychoanalytic Association* 7:611-31.

Artiss, K. L. (1962). *Milieu Therapy and Schizophrenia*. New York: Grune & Stratton.

Bakker, C. B., and Amini, F. B. (1961). Observations on the psychotomimetic effects of Sernyl. *Comprehensive Psychiatry* 2:269-80.

Bateson, G., Jackson, D. D., Haley, J., and Weakland, J. H. (1956). Toward a theory of schizophrenia. *Behavioral Science* 1:251-64.

Bavelas, A. (1970). Description of experiment on persistence of erroneous convictions regarding "causality." In *Problem Solving and Search Behavior Under Non-Contingent Rewards*, edited by J. C. Wright. Ann Arbor, Michigan: University Microfilms.

Berlyne, D. E. (1966). Conflict and arousal. *Scientific American* 215:82-87.

Bonaparte, M. (1940). Time and the unconscious. *International Journal of PsychoAnalysis* 21:427-68.

Borges, J. L. (1964). A new refutation of time. In *Labyrinths*, edited by D. A. Yates and J. E. Irby. New York: New Directions.

Boring, E. G. (1933). *The Physical Dimensions of Consciousness*. New York: Century.

Bowen, M. (1961). The family as the unit of study and treatment. *American Journal of Orthopsychiatry* 31:40-60.

Brody, W., and Hayden, M. (1957). Intra-team reactions: Their relation to the conflicts of the family in treatment. *American Journal of Orthopsychiatry* 27:349-55.

Burnham, D. L. (1966). The special-problem patient: Victim or agent of splitting? *Psychiatry* 29:105-22.

Eissler, K. (1953). The effect of the structure of the ego on psychoanalytic technique. *Journal of the American Psychoanalytic Association* 1:104-43.

Erikson, E. H. (1966). Ontogeny of ritualization. In *Psychoanalysis—A General Psychology: Essays in honor of Heinz Hartmann*, edited by R. M. Loewenstein et al. New York: International Universities Press.

Federn, P. (1952). *Ego Psychology and the Psychoses*. New York: Basic Books.

Freud, S. (1913). Totem and taboo. In *Standard Edition of the Complete Psychological Works*, vol. 13. London: Hogarth, 1955.

Freud, S. (1914). Fausse reconnaissance ("déjà raconté") in psychoanalytic treatment. In *Standard Edition of the Complete Psychological Works*, vol. 13. London: Hogarth, 1955.

Freud, S. (1915). The unconscious. In *Standard Edition of the Complete Psychological Works*, vol. 14. London: Hogarth, 1955.

Freud, S. (1919). The "uncanny." In *Standard Edition of the Complete Psychological Works*, vol. 17. London: Hogarth, 1955.

Fry, W. F., Jr. (1968). *Sweet madness: A study of humor*. Palo Alto, Calif.: Pacific Books.

Gaarder, K. (1963). A conceptual model of schizophrenia. *AMA Archives of General Psychiatry* 8:590-98.

Gaarder, K., and Kafka, J. S. (1963). An experimental case study of the effects of Semyl. Presented at *Chestnut Lodge Symposium*, Rockville, Maryland.

Gabel, J. (1962). *La fausse Conscience: Essai sur la Réification*. Paris: Les Editions de Minuit.

Gabel, J. (1967). *Ideologic and Schizophrenic: Formen der Entfrendung*. Frankfurt am Main: S. Fischer Verlag.

Gödel, K. (1931). Über formal unentscheidbare Sätze der Principia Mathematica und verwandter Systeme: I. *Monatschrifte für Mathematik Physik* 38:173-98.

Goodrich, D. W., and Boomer, D. S. (1963). Experimental assessment of modes of conflict resolution. *Family Process* 2:15-24.

Graetz, H. (1893). Geschichte der Juden. Leipzig: Leiner & Lowit.

Green, A. (1977). The borderline concept. In *Borderline Personality Disorders*, edited by P. Hartocollis. New York: International Universities Press.

Green, H. (1964). *I Never Promised You a Rose Garden*. New York: Holt, Rinehart & Winston.

Greenspan, S. I. (1982). Three levels of learning: A developmental approach to "awareness" and mind-body relations. *Psychoanalytic Inquiry* I:659-94.

Grotstein, J. S. (1977). The psychoanalytic concept of schizophrenia: I. The dilemma. II. Reconciliation. International Journal of Psychoanalysis 58:403-52.

Group for the Advancement of Psychiatry. (1989). Us and Them: The Psychology of Ethno-Nationalism. New York: Brunner/Mazel.

Gunderson, J. G., and Carroll, A. (1983). Clinical considerations from empirical research. In *Psychosocial Intervention in Schizophrenia,* edited by H. Stierlin, L. C. Wynne, and M. Wirsching. Berlin: Springer-Verlag.

Handke, P. (1969). *Die Innenwelt der Aussenwelt der Innenwelt.* Frankfurt am Main: Suhrkamp. Eng. trans, by Michael Roloff. New York: Continuum, 1974.

Hartmann, H. (1939). *Ego Psychology and the Problem of Adaptation.* New York: International Universities Press, 1958.

Hartocollis, P., ed. (1977). *Borderline Personality Disorders: The Concept, The Syndrome, The Patient.* New York: International Universities Press.

Hayman, A. (1969). What do we mean by "id"? *Journal of American Psychoanalytic Association* 17:353-80.

Hoch, R. H., Pennes. H. H., and Cattell, J. P. (1958). Psychoses reduced by the administration of drugs. In *Chemical Concepts of Psychosis,* edited by M. Rinkel. New York: McDowell, Oblensky.

Hofstadter, D. R. (1979). *Gödel, Escher, Bach.* New York: Basic Books.

Hohage, R. and Kuebler, J. C. (1985). *The Emotional Insight Rating Scale.* Paper presented at Ülmer Werkstatt, University of Ülm.

Hollos, S. and Ferenczi, S. (1922). *Zur Psychoanalyse der paralytischen Geistesstörung.* Vienna: Internationaler Psychoanalytischer Verlag.

Holzman, P. (1987). Recent studies of psychophysiology in schizophrenia. *Schizophrenia Bulletin* 13:49-75.

Israeli, N. (1936). *Abnormal personality and time.* New York: Science Press.

Jaffe, D. S. (1971). The role of ego modification and the task of structural change in the analysis of a case of hysteria. *International Journal of Psychoanalysis* 52:375-93.

Kafka, J. S. (1957). A method for studying the organization of time experience. *American Journal of Psychiatry* 114:546-53.

Kafka, J. S. (1957). *On the Experience of Duration in Psychotherapy.* Presented at Chestnut Lodge Symposium, Rockville, Maryland.

Kafka, J. S. (1964). Technical applications of a concept of multiple reality. *International Journal of Psychoanalysis* 45:575-78.

Kafka, J. S. (1966). *Practical and Conceptual Developments Concerning Work with Families.* Paper presented at Southern Divisional Meeting, American Psychiatric Association, Hollywood, Florida.

Kafka, J. S. (1969). The body as transitional object: A psychoanalytic study of a self-mutilating patient. *British Journal of Medical Psychology* 42:207-12.

Kafka, J. S. (1971). *A Psychoanalytic Perspective on the Organization and Integration of Time Experience.* Paper presented at panel on the Experience of Time, American Psychoanalytic Association, December 1971.

Kafka, J. S. (1971). Ambiguity for individuation: A critique and reformulation of double-bind theory. *Archives of General Psychiatry* 25:232-39.

Kafka, J. S. (1972). The experience of time. Report on panel, American Psychoanalytic Association, December 1971. *Journal of the American Psychoanalytic Association* 20:650-67.

Kafka, J. S. (1977). On reality: An examination of object constancy, ambiguity, paradox, and time. In *Thought, Consciousness, and Reality. Vol, 2: Psychiatry and the Humanities,* edited by J. H. Smith. New Haven: Yale University Press.

Kafka, J. S. (1981). Review of *Borderline personality disorders,* edited by P. Hartocollis. *Journal of the American Psychoanalytic Association* 29:236-47.

Kafka, J. S. (1983). Challenge and confirmation in ritual action. *Psychiatry* 46:31-39.

Kafka, J. S. and Bolgar, H. (1949). Notes on the clinical use of future autobiographies. *Rorschach Research Exchange and Journal of Projective Techniques* 13:341-46.

Kafka, J. S. and Gaarder, K. (1964). Some effects of the therapist's LSD experience on his therapeutic work. *American Journal of Psychotherapy* 18:236-43.

Kafka, J. S. and Kafka, M. S. (1983). Timing process and mental illness. *Abstracts, Seventh World Congress of Psychiatry.* Vienna.

Kafka, J. S. and McDonald, J. W. (1965). The latent family in the intensive treatment of the hospitalized schizophrenic patient. *Current Psychiatric Therapies,* vol. 5, edited by J. S. Masserman. New York: Grune & Stratton.

Kafka, M. S., Benedito, M. A., Blendy, J. A., and Tokola, N. A. (1986). Circadian rhythms in neurotransmitter receptors in discrete rat brain regions. *Chronobiology International* 3:91-100.

Kafka, M. S., Benedito, M. A., and Roth, R. H. (1986). Circadian rhythms in catecholamine metabolites and cyclic nucleotide production. *Chronobiology International* 3:101-15.

Kafka, M. S., Benedito, M. A., Steele, L. K., et al. (1986). Relationships between behavioral rhythms, plasma corticosterone and hypothalamic circadian rhythms. *Chronobiology International* 3:117-22.

Kafka, M. S., van Kammen, D. P., Kleinman, J. E., Nurnberger, J. I., Siever, L. J., Uhde, T. W., and Polinsky, R. J. (1980). Alpha-adrenergic receptor function in schizophrenia, affective disorders and some neurological diseases. *Communications in Psychopharmacology* 4:477-86.

Katka, M. S., Wirz-Justice, A. and Naber, D. (1983). Circadian rhythms in rat brain neurotransmitter receptors. *Federation Proceedings* 42:2796-2801.

Kandell, E. R. (1983). From metapsychology to molecular biology: Explorations into the nature of anxiety. *American Journal of Psychiatry* 140:1277-93.

Klüver, H. (1933). *Behavior Mechanisms in Monkeys.* Chicago: University of Chicago Press.

Klüver, H. (1936). The study of personality and the method of equivalent and non-equivalent stimuli. *Character and Personality* 5:91-112.

Kohut, H. (1971). *The Analysis of the Self.* New York: International Universities Press.

Kris, E. (1952). *Psychoanalytic Explorations in Art.* New York: International Universities Press.

Laplanche, J. and Pontalis, J. B. (1967). *The Language of Psychoanalysis.* Translated by D. Nicholson-Smith. New York: Norton, 1973.

LeFever, H. (1961). *To Antipodes and Back: Some Observations on the LSD Experience.* Paper presented at Chestnut Lodge Symposium, Rockville, Maryland.

Lichtenstein, H. (1974). The effect of reality perception on psychic structure: A psychoanalytic contribution to the problem of the "generation gap." *In Annual of Psychoanalysis,* vol. 2. New York: International Universities Press.

Lidz, T., and Fleck, S. (1960). Schizophrenia, human integration, and the role of the family. In *The Etiology of Schizophrenia,* edited by D. D. Jackson. New York: Basic Books.

Loewald, H. W. (1960). On the therapeutic action of psychoanalysis. *International Journal of Psychoanalysis* 41:16-33.

Loewald, H. W. (1962). The superego and the ego ideal. II. Superego and time. *International Journal of Psychoanalysis* 43:264-68.

Loewald, H. W. (1971). Some considerations on repetition and repetition compulsion. In *Papers on Psychoanalysis.* New Haven: Yale University Press, 1980.

Loewald, H. W. (1979). The waning of the oedipus complex. In *Papers on Psychoanalysis.* New Haven: Yale University Press, 1980.

Longuet-Higgins, H. C. (1968) . The non-local storage of temporal information. *Proceedings of Royal Society, London* 171:327-34.

Longuet-Higgins, H. C, Willshaw, D. J., and Bunemah, O. P. (1969).Non-holographic associative memory. *Nature* 222:960-62.

Longuet-Higgins, H. C. (1970). Theories of associative recall. *Quarterly Review of Biophysics* 3:223-44.

Luby, E. D., Cohen, B. D., Rosenbaum, G., Gottlieb, J. S., and Kelley, R. (1959). Study of a new schizophrenomimetic drug—Sernyl. *AMA Archives of Neurology and Psychiatry* 81:363-69.

Malcolm, J. (1987). Reflections: J'appelle un chat un chat. *New Yorker,* April 20, pp. 84-102.

Mandell, A., Knapp, S., Ehlers, C. and Russo, P. (1982). The stability of constrained randomness: Lithium prophylaxis at several neurobiological levels. In *The Neurobiology of the Mood Disorders,* edited by R. M. Post and J. C. Ballenger. Baltimore: Williams & Wilkins.

Meyer, J. S., Greifenstein, F., and Devault, M. (1959). A new drug causing symptoms of sensory deprivation. *Journal of Nervous and Mental Disease* 129:54-61.

Modell, A. (1968). *Object Love and Reality.* New York: International Universities Press.

Monod, J. (1972). *Chance and Necessity.* New York: Random House.

Murray, H. A. (1938). *Explorations in Personality.* New York: Oxford University Press.

Nagel, E. and Newman, J. R. (1958). *Gödel's Proof.* New York: New York University Press.

Noble, D. (1951). A study of dreams in schizophrenia and allied states. *American Journal of Psychiatry* 107:612-16.

Novey, S. (1955). Some philosophical speculations about the concept of the genital character. *International Journal of Psychonalysis* 36:88-94.

Olson, D. H. (1969). *Empirically Unbinding the Double-Bind.* Paper presented at the annual meeting of the American Psychological Association, Washington, D.C.

Ornstein, R. E. (1969). *On the Experience of Time*. Baltimore: Penguin Books.

Pollard, J. C., Bakker, C., Uhr, L., and Feuertile, D. F. (1960). Controlled sensory input: A note on the technique of drug evaluation with a preliminary report on a comparative study of Sernyl, psilocybin and LSD-25. *Comprehensive Psychiatry* 1:377-80.

Pribram, K. H. (1986). The cognitive revolution and mind/brain issues. *American Psychologist* 41:507-20.

Prigogine, I. (1976). Order through fluctuation: Self-organization and social system. In *Evolution and Consciousness: Human Systems in Transition*, edited by E. Jantsch and C. H. Waddington. Reading, Mass.: Addison-Wesley.

Rabin, M. (1977). *Handbook of Mathematical Logic, Part C*. Amsterdam: North Holland.

Rabin, M. and Halpern, J. (1987). Logic to reason about likelihood. *Artificial Intelligence* 32: 3:379-405.

Rangell, L. (1981). From insight to change. *Journal of American Psychoanalytic Association* 29:119-41.

Rapaport, D. (1960). *The Structure of Psychoanalytic Theory*. New York: International Universities Press.

Reiser, M. F. (1984). *Mind, Brain, Body: Toward a Convergence of Psychoanalysis and Neurobiology*. New York: Basic Books.

Ringuette, E. L. and Kennedy, T. (1966). An experimental study of the double-bind hypothesis. *Journal of Abnormal Psychology* 71:136-41.

Rose, G. J. (1980). *The Power of Form: A Psychoanalytic Approach to Aesthetic Form*. New York: International Universities Press.

Rose, S. R. (1980). Can the neurosciences explain the mind? *Trends in Neurosciences* 23:2-4.

Ryder, R. G. (1966). Two replications of color matching factors. *Family Process* 5:43-48, 1966.

Ryder, R. G. (1968). Husband-wife dyads versus married strangers. *Family Process* 7:233-38.

Ryder, R. G. (1969). *Three Myths: Brief Ruminations on Interaction Procedures While Contemplating the Color Matching Tests.* Paper presented at the annual meeting of the National Council on Family Relations, Washington, D.C.

Ryder, R. G. (1970). Dimensions of early marriage. *Family Process* 9:51-68.

Ryder, R. G. and Goodrich, D. W. (1966). Married couples' responses to disagreement. *Family Process* 5:30-42.

Ryder, R. G., Kafka, J. S., and Olson, D. H. (1971). Separating and joining influences in courtship and early marriage. *American Journal of Orthopsychiatry* 41:450-64.

Sandler, J. and Joffe, W. (1967). The tendency to persistence in psychological function and development, with special reference to fixation and regression. *Bulletin of the Menninger Clinic* 31:257-71.

Sandler, J. and Rosenblatt, B. (1962). The concept of the representational world. *Psychoanalytic Study of the Child* 17:128-45.

Sartre, J. P. (1960). *Search for a Method.* Translated by H. E. Barnes. New York: Knopf, 1967.

Savage, C. (1955). Variations in ego feeling induced by d-lysergic acid diethylamide (LSD-25). *Psychoanalytic Review* 42:1-16.

Schachtel, E. G. (1947). On memory and childhood amnesia. *Psychiatry* 10:1-26.

Schilder, P. (1935). *The Image and Appearance of the Human Body.* New York: International Universities Press, 1950.

Schizophrenia costs U.S. billions; more research, better care needed. (December 19, 1986). *Psychiatric News*, p. 8.

Schulz, C. G. and Kilgalen, R. K. (1969). The treatment course of a disturbed patient. In *Case studies in schizophrenia.* New York: Basic Books.

Searles, H. F. (1960). *The Nonhuman Environment in Normal Development and in Schizophrenia.* New York: International Universities Press.

Searles, H. F. (1965). On driving the other person crazy. In *Collected Papers on Schizophrenia and Related Subjects.* New York: International Universities Press.

Smith, G. J. W. and Danielsson, A. (1982). Anxiety and defensive strategies in childhood adolescence. *Psychological Issues,* Monograph 52

Smith, J. H. (1976). The psychoanalytic understanding of human freedom: Freedom from and freedom for. *Journal of the American Psychoanalytic Association* 26:87-107.

Smith, J. H. (1983). Rite, ritual and defense. *Psychiatry* 46:16-30.

Squire, L. R. (1986: June 27). Mechanisms of memory. *Science* 232:1612-19.

Stein, M. I. (1949). Personality factors involved in temporal development of Rorschach responses. *Rorschach Research Exchange and Journal of Projective Techniques* 13:355-414.

Stierlin, H., Wynne, L. C. and Wirsching, M., eds. (1983). Psychosocial Intervention in Schizophrenia. Berlin: Springer-Verlag.

Stirnimann, F. (1947). Das Kind und seine früheste Umwelt. *Psychologische Praxis,* vol. 6. Basel: Karger.

Stone, L. (1986). Psychoanalytic observations on the pathology of depressive illness: Selected spheres of ambiguity or disagreement. *Journal of the American Psychoanalytic Association* 34:329-62.

Strachey, J. (1934). The nature of the therapeutic action of psychoanalysis. *International Journal of Psychoanalysis* 15:127-59.

Thomä, H. and Kächele, H. (1987). *Principles.* Vol. 1 of *Psychoanalytic Practice.* Translated by M. Wilson and D. Roseveare. New York: Springer-Verlag.

Turner, V. (1977). Process, system, and symbol: A new anthropological synthesis. *Daedalus* 106(3):61-80.

Unger, S. M. (1963). Mescaline, LSD, psilocybin, and personality change: A review. *Psychiatry* 26:111-25.

Vonnegut, K., Jr. (1969). *Slaughterhouse-Five.* New York: Delta.

Wallerstein, R. S. (1973). Psychoanalytic perspectives on the problem of reality. *Journal of the American Psychoanalytic Association* 21:5-33.

Watzlawick, P., Beavin, J. H. and Jackson, D. (1967). *Pragmatics of Human Communication.* New York: W. W. Norton.

Westerlundh, B. and Smith, G. (1983). Percept-genesis and the psychodynamics of perception. *Psychoanalysis and Contemporary Thought* 6:597-640.

Whitehead, A. N. and Russell, B. (1910). *Principia Mathematica.* Cambridge: Cambridge University Press.

Wilson, E. (1975). *Sociobiology.* Cambridge: Harvard University Press.

Winnicott, D. W. (1958). Transitional objects and transitional phenomena. In *Collected Papers.* New York: Basic Books.

Winnicott, D. W. (1958). Hate in the countertransference. In *Collected Papers.* New York: Basic Books.

Wynne, L. C, Ryckoff, I. M., Day, J. and Hirsch, S. I. (1958). Pseudomutuality in the family relations of schizophrenics. *Psychiatry* 21:205-20.

Part Two

Selected Writings

Theory, Technique, and Psychopathology

Presentation (May 5, 2006). Conference: Freud's Screen Memories in the Light of Contemporary Psychoanalysis and Neurosciences. Czech Psychoanalytical Society. Prague, Czech Republic.

Chapter 8

On Different "False" Memories: From Screen Memories to Déjà Vu

Abstract

Freud never thought that a memory was a precise reproduction of a scene. If memories are not exact reproductions, all memories are "false" memories, *organized amnesias* (Julien Rouart's term). Different kinds of false memories are characterized by being more "amnesic" about content, or about affect, or about the connections between content and affect, or about the time when they are consolidated. Screen memories proper are consolidated long after the event or original experience. Since, however, all memories are *constructed* memories, and all constructions have screening functions, *screen* memories may only differ from other memories by the relative prominence of specific defensive constructions. Memories and screen memories are usually reported as ego-syntonic in the sense that the reporter says "I remember."

On the other hand, the *déjà vu* experience is different. It is also a memory, because "it feels so familiar," but there is an ego-dystonic element inherent in the *uncanny* dissonance between the feeling of familiarity on the one hand, and, on the other hand, the pronounced inability to locate its source in time and space.

Presentation Overview

Here are some of the major points to be developed in the presentation.

1. Studying memory is studying time.
2. Freud thought that understanding the connection between the timelessness of the unconscious and observed change await future philosophical and scientific developments.
3. A discussion of the possible relevance of modern concepts of time in physics to the timelessness of the unconscious.
4. Short-term memory is necessary for all psychic life.
5. The psychological now. Is mind time? Ontogenetic recapitulation and memory in perception and object formation.
6. Screen memories. The prominence of specific defenses in screen memories. From memory construction to confabulation. The trauma of interruption, its effect on implicit memory and the sense of duration.
7. Freud's screen memory explanation of *déjà raconte*.
8. *Déjà-vu* experiences: the synesthetic hypothesis and the temporal lobe.
9. *Nachtraeglichkeit*'s play between aftereffect and hermeneutics. How new information changes not only meaning, but also the memory of experienced past durations.
10. How neurobiological findings correlate with the evolution of memories.
11. Do biological rhythms have an affect on memory construction and does this effect correspond to the aftereffect hermeneutic polarity of *Nachtraeglichkeit*?
12. Psychoanalysis, declarative memory, the unraveling of the condensed, and the construction of time.

Studying memory is studying time. It is obvious, but it must be said: We cannot talk about memory without considering Time. Kurt Eissler[12] writes: (my translation from the German):

---

[12] Eissler, Kurt R. "Tod und Zeit." In: *Der sterbende Patient. Zur Psychologie des Todes.* Stuttgart, 1978.

"Time is always in us and around us: despite this it escapes our grasp. We probably oppose a fundamental resistance to its comprehension, a resistance that reaches much deeper and is more profoundly anchored in us than the resistance that the Ego demonstrates when it defends against an unacceptable aspect of our personality. One can imagine that the Ego would be seized by horror if it would see itself being confronted with the true problem of the nature of time."

Meaning depends on short term memory. Usually, when psychoanalysts discuss memory, they think of relatively long term memory. However, without short term memory, there is no meaning and, without meaning, psychic life does not exist. All meaning, all thinking, all psychological functions are time-linked. Mind and time are intimately connected. Perhaps, the "horror ... of ... the confrontation with ... the nature of time" that Eissler invokes, is the horror of anticipated ultimate aloneness emptied of memory.

Let me give you an illustration of the loss of meaning that accompanies loss of short term memory. Sernyl is a drug that interferes with short term memory. It was once used as an anesthetic for animals and children, but research on the drug continued after its clinical use was stopped. It was given by injection in what, I believe, was the last authorized research project on humans, to Kenneth Gaarder, psychiatrist and psychoanalyst who participated in this research and served as a voluntary subject. Dr. Gaarder was well acquainted with the literature about Sernyl, but had not seen the drug in use. Here is a taped record of Dr. Gaarder's words 10 minutes after the injection.[13]

"...something is going on here and uh-uh-I'm alive-and uh-I'm doing something for some reason, , and I don't know what it is I'm doing and uh-what's happening to me now-and words are things like that what is happening? What is to say what is happening? Is a word-and people talk-and what is talking? And uh-I don't know what's going on......I'm experiencing something and I don't know what's going on, and I don't know what saying what's going on is saying...."

---

[13] Kafka, John S. *Multiple Realities In Clinical Practice*, Yale University Press, New Haven, 1989, pages 64 and 65.

If time is a feature of all psychic activity, the most striking psychoanalytic hypothesis relating to time is the notion of the *timelessness* of the unconscious.

Freud believed that "one day" progress in psychoanalysis and neuroscience would complement each other "in a useful manner." He was deeply interested in the science of mind. Progress in the study of the nervous system was sufficiently rapid in Freud's time that his expectations did not seem outlandish. The basic paradigms for such possible advances were more or less established in the common scientific language. In general, he did not believe that other scientific and philosophical advances might some day also be relevant to psychoanalysis. Freud thought that psychoanalytic understanding awaited fundamental new developments only in its relationship to time. The new developments would have to be fundamental, because Freud could not conceive of them in the framework of the philosophical perspectives or natural sciences of his day.

Freud stated that the unconscious is not affected by time. It is timeless, yet it interacts in some way with a world that knows change. For him, this puzzle had no apparent solution. In one of many references in Freud's works to the timelessness of the id and the timelessness of the system "Unconscious,"[14] he says "There is nothing in the id that corresponds to the idea of time; and no alteration in its mental processes is produced by the passage of time ... Wishful impulses which have never passed beyond the id, ... impressions too which have sunk into the id by repression, are ... immortal ... After the passage of decades they behave as if they had just occurred. ... Again and again I have had the impression that we have made too little theoretical use of this fact, established beyond any doubt, of the unalterability by time of the repressed. This seems to offer an approach to the most profound discoveries. ... Unfortunately, I myself (have not) made any progress here. "

Have there been such developments since Freud's time that "offer an approach to the most profound discoveries?" If so, are they relevant to psychoanalysis as a theory of mind, to psychoanalytic practice or both?

---

[14] Freud, Sigmund. *New Introductory Lectures*, Volume XXII, page 74.

Freud knew about relativity theory, about the uncertainty principle and about quantum physics. Freud did not consider these scientific advances relevant to psychoanalysis and warned against facile use of these concepts in psychoanalysis. The warning against the facile use of the concepts remains justified, but is Freud's skepticism completely justified today? We will touch on this question here, but we will not attempt to pursue it in depth. Philosophers of science and students of time are writing volumes about the question of the relevance for human experience of such concepts as space-time, the uncertainty principle, quantum physics, and emergence.

Today some scientific developments that are not understandable in either "common sense" terms or in terms of classical physics, impact our daily lives more than they did in Freud's time. Today, we use electricity generated by nuclear energy, a development that is an application of Einstein's theories of time-space. Today, some empirical biological research conceives of phenomena in terms of concepts other than those of classical physics. For example and I quote: "Protein -folding....involves the use by biological organisms of quantum computation to solve non-polynomially solvable problems in classical physics."[15]

The central "locality" of our inquiry here is that of psychoanalysis, and more particularly memory and time. Since every psychoanalytic session is implicitly also a laboratory of epistemology, of what we know and how we both the analysand and the analyst know it, we cannot totally ignore some highlights of modern universal philosophical and scientific thought about time. For example, is Gödel's formulation of the non-existence of time pertinent to the psychoanalytic theory of the timelessness of the Unconscious, or is it the ultimate "brain teaser" for a psychoanalyst?

Gödel theorized that maximum curvature in Einstein's space-time leads to our return to the same point in space-time in conceptual time travel. If we find ourselves at the same point in space-time, he reasoned, time does not exist as a"physical" reality. This notion suggests that all

---

[15] Turner, Frederick, "Interdisciplinary Research Opportunities: Limits and Constraints." In: *Time's News*, No. 37, February 2006.

time-related psychological activity, (and there is no time independent psychic activity), including memory is constructed by us. The Sernyl[16] experiment described previously, illustrated the loss of meaning that accompanies the loss of short term memory. Even the word "now" lost its meaning. A now without short term memory is meaning -less. It has no psychological existence; it is mind-less.

The psychological moment, the existence of a psychic reality needs short term memory to exist and the psychic reality of the moment is a building block of later memories. Therefore our study of memory is inescapably linked to the study of the building of psychic reality. Psychoanalysts are careful to avoid "reification"of their concepts, but nevertheless the term "object" has some connotations of solidity, of "separate" tangible existence.

In this connection, I would like to summarize here some ideas that I have developed in much more detail elsewhere.[17] In general psychology, the concept of object permanence, or object constancy, refers to observations of the kind that a table is perceived as the same table when viewed from different angles despite the fact that the retinal projections of the table are different when the viewing angles change. In the context of our study of memory and the recognition that memories are not reproductions of a scene, nor of an object, it is essential to note that time is involved in the movement from one position to another in viewing the table that will be a (permanent) object. This notion is not absent from psychoanalytic understanding of object constancy. Psychoanalysts just do not explicitly focus on it. Psychoanalysts focus on affect and meaning when considering that object constancy has been achieved when the nourishing and the withholding mother are recognized as the same person, but mother seen from different angles and in different physical positions also has different retinal projections. I emphasize that even object constancy has both a hermeneutic and a "tangible, as it were

---

[16] Kafka, John S. *Multiple Realities In Clinical Practice*, Yale University Press, New Haven, 1989, pages 64 and 65.

[17] Kafka, John S. *Multiple Realities In Clinical Practice*, Yale University Press, New Haven, 1989.

physical reality " component, because this theme will be important when we discuss *Nachtraeglichkeit.*

This discussion of object constancy leads to the conclusion that our psychological "object world" consists of subjective equivalences of different objects. Different time intervals may also be subjectively equivalent. There is also ample evidence that the same "linear" time interval may be experienced as shorter or longer, and that different time intervals may be experienced as similar or identical, depending on many different factors, including time linked affective factors, expectations, hopes, and fears. From this perspective, psychic reality consists of processes of forming networks of spatial and temporal subjective equivalences. "Object" loses some of its "Solidity."

I have hypothesized in the past that every perceptual process, every psychic process is a recapitulation of the onto-genetic developmental process. To illustrate this hypothesis, I have used the story that the drowning individual (after he is saved) recounts that he experienced his whole life "in a flash." This conscious experience may correspond to the unconscious micro- or nano- second recapitulation of the development of the individual's perceptual processes.

Freud often dealt with recapitulation. For instance in his article on déjà vu and déjà raconté, he stated that when a patient says that he has known "it" all the time, the end of the analysis is near. Although phylogenetic and ontogenetic recapitulation are closely connected, I will limit myself here to a discussion of ontogenetic recapitulation.

Now to look at what is being recapitulated. There is an ever expanding literature on the perceptual processes of infants and children. I have focused on a developmental sequence of the discrimination between outside and inside, the discrimination of the animate from the inanimate, the synesthetic from the sensory-specific, and the priority of temporal or of spatial ways of organizing sensory data. The latter point needs clarification. My awareness of such a priority derives from work with schizophrenic patients. A patient described how the distance between two buildings had shrunk. I observed that she walked faster, but such observations with schizophrenic patients made me aware to what extent we usually give priority to spatial organization. I have more fully developed elsewhere how these developmental stages are recapitulated in "object formation." I have also described a certain congruity between, on the one hand, animate, inside, temporal, and synesthetic, and, on the other hand, inanimate, outside, spatial , and sensory-specific, on the other hand. Tachistoscopic experiments, the study of perception of stimuli exposed for extremely short periods permit a kind of temporal dissection of the recapitulative process. There is support for the idea that extremely short exposure led adults to have responses that have characteristics in common with those of very young children and that longer exposures correspond to responses of older children.

I would like to return to "subjective equivalence" in object formation. If the psychic objects are not "real, tangible objects, " but represent subjective equivalences of different perceptions, then each perceptual act represents a travelogue -and therefore a micro-memory trail -through different "object formations." If the recapitulation of developmental processes is "complete" in each perception, the subjective equivalences form"objects" that are recognizable by and can be shared by others. If the recapitulations of some perceptions are incomplete, interrupted by trauma or for other reasons, subjective equivalences between completed and partially completed perceptions form "bizarre" objects. In any case, we arrive at the conclusion that the "now" that may be remembered is itself a process of object formation, but the *nachtraeglich* recapitulation of this object formation may be particularly difficult if it were interrupted and led to "bizarre" objects, distortions of memory that are particularly hard to trace and to understand.

Memory is a processing of a process. The concept of *Nachtraeglichkeit* has long been neglected in the English-speaking psychoanalytic world because the term had been poorly, at least very incompletely translated as "deferred action." An attempt has been made to clarify the concept by speaking of "retroactive attribution of meaning," Kettner[18], who has studied Freud's use of the concept, finds that Freud sometimes gave it a hermeneutic meaning, referring to changes of interpretation of memories, and sometimes a "causal" meaning. The latter can be thought of in terms of the

---

[18] Kettner, Matthias. "Das Konzept der Nachtraeglichkeit in Freud's Erinerungstheorie." *Psyche* 4 (53. Jahrgang, April 1999).

aftereffects, like a chain of effects on a series of billiard balls. Kettner finds that psychoanalysis operates in the "*Spielraum*" the place between these two meanings.

This *Spielraum* is also the area of confluence of unidirectional linear time linked to traditional causality and of bidirectional temporal processes. Bidirectional processes escape the narrow structure of a mechanical billiard-ball causality chain and involve the alterations of meaning produced by seeing old material in the light of new information and vice-versa.

In only a brief discussion of *Nachtraeglichkeit*, I want to point to the similarity of Kettner's *Spielraum*, between the concrete and the hermeneutic, to the *Spielraum* between unidirectional linear time and bidirectional hermeneutic time. In this connection, I'd like to mention the work of Matte Bianco who distinguishes symmetrical and asymmetrical mental processes. "John is the brother of Paul" is symmetrical because Paul is also the brother of John. "Paul is the brother of Mary" is asymmetrical because Mary is not the brother of Paul. "Yesterday is before today" is asymmetrical because today is not before yesterday. The Unconscious, says Matte-Bianco, does not distinguish between the symmetrical and the asymmetrical, and is in this way timeless. In this context, I again refer to the possible relevance of Gödel's hypothesis of "non-existence of time."

The other aspect of *Nachtraeglichkeit* that I want to discuss, is a relatively neglected one, the *nachtraeglich* modification of the sense of duration. Shifts during psychoanalysis in what is understood as meaningful, be it in one analytic session or in a perspective on life developed during psychoanalysis, have profound consequences for our experience of time, because the judgments of the duration of intervals in which "meaningful" things happen differs from the judgments of duration of intervals of "accidental" events. An experimental demonstration[19] (Ornstein reference in Kafka, Multiple Realities) of the retroactive effects of new information on judgment of past duration is the following:

---

[19] Kafka, John S. *Multiple Realities In Clinical Practice*, Yale University Press, New Haven, 1989.

Subjects in one experimental group learned a series of apparently random numbers and then were asked how long it took them to learn the series. Subjects in another group learned the same series and then were given a code that transformed what was apparently a random series into an ordered one before being asked (to estimate) how long it took them to learn the series. The subjects, who were given the code and whose actual learning period was the same, estimated the learning period as shorter than did the subjects who were not given the information that would have permitted them to reorganize –recode– their experience retrospectively. It is well established that ordered numbers are learned more rapidly than random ones. Subjects given the code that transformed the apparently random series into an ordered one after learning them estimated their learning period as though they had known the ordering code at the time of learning. New information had had a retroactive effect on judgment of past duration.

The findings of this experiment are relevant to clinical psychoanalysis, to the topic of memory, false memory and, because a distorted sense of past duration can itself have a screening function, perhaps especially to screen memory. All memories can have screening functions. In his article on screen memories, Freud often refers to similarities between other memories and memories that he designates as screen memories. I think this is a device to highlight some characteristics, most of which are present in all memories, but are more prominent in some. They include sensory intensity and the delay in developing the screen memories (his own screen memory refers to events that occurred when he was three years old and to a screen memory that was formed when he was 17). Freud also emphasizes that the wish he encounters in this screen memory is the wish to change the past rather than a wish for the future. He emphasizes that he returns to a past nostalgia. My own preferred graffiti is "Nostalgia ain't what it used to be." Nevertheless, Freud's technique of analyzing his screen memory is not fundamentally different from the technique he employs in analyzing other memories.

Freud locates the source of his screen memory at age 3 when the financial collapse of the family's business leads to a quite sudden and unexpected move to Vienna. For analysands, a screen memory is accepted by the subject as a "real" memory, but Freud and other students of screen memories emphasize to what extent the sensory intensity, (the yellow flowers, for instance) , is particularly fresh, and current and, as it were, factually verifiable. The narrative of the screen memory is, however, particularly unlikely. The manifest story is false, although analyzing it as one would analyze a dream, may make it understandable. While all memories are constructions, the more evident falseness of the screen memory, makes of it a confabulation. The psychiatric definition of confabulation is: "Replacement of a gap in memory by a falsification that the subject accepts as correct. "

I think that Freud's choice of the trauma of a particularly unexpected interruption as the source of his emblematic screen memory, is not accidental. "Implicit" memories permit us to perform daily tasks without conscious focused attention. Implicit memory involves (the unconscious memory of) the correct timing in which these tasks have to be performed in a specific setting. Sudden changes of setting disrupt our expectations, force us to pay conscious attention where it was not needed previously, and disrupt the continuity in our sense of duration. This leads to pronounced gaps in narrative memory coexisting with particularly clear and vivid memory of sensory impressions, the hallmarks of screen memories. In discussing *Nachtraeglichkeit* in memory formation, we have located this *Nachtraeglicheit* "between billiard ball"—like concrete aftereffects and hermeneutics, meaning and changes of meaning. In screen memories the center of gravity of the usual mid-space *Nachtraeglichkeit* is shifted to the concrete and away from meaning and narrative, where the gaps of memory are particularly pronounced. This discrepancy is especially conducive to confabulation and screen memory formation. The individual, however, locates the screen memory, the confabulated story, in a specific point in time. This is one feature that distinguishes it from the déjà vu experience.

In his paper, *Fausse Reconnaissance (Déjà Raconté) In Psychoanalytic Treatment*[20], Freud reviews some of the earlier literature on the déjà vu subject, including an "anatomical" one put forward by Wigam in 1860. I will return to this "anatomical" idea later because of its relevance to a

---

[20] Freud, Sigmund. *Standard Edition*, 1914. Volume 13, pages 201-207.

modern biological hypothesis. Primarily, however, Freud speaks of an "unconscious" earlier experience that explains the present feeling of déjà, the sense of familiarity. Freud gives credit to Gasset for this idea, but explains that he did not know of Gasset's work when he first formulated his own explanation. Freud makes an especially interesting link between déjà raconté and screen memory when he explains that a patient's false certainty that he had already told him of a memory, turned out to be correct in the sense that he had told of the remembered event in the form of a screen memory. Arlow[21] has described how a déjà vu experience can be analyzed with the usual techniques of dream analysis.

I have emphasized the uncanny nature of déjà experiences and related it to simultaneous contradictory convictions such as "I am sure I have seen this, or I have been there" and I am sure I have never been there.[22] Here, in brief, is my hypothesis which is supported by neurobiologic findings. Contradictory convictions are the result of the repetition of the same pattern of stimulation, but in different sensory compartments. Synesthesia is the blending of different sensory compartments. A synesthetic pattern may be the same as a sensory compartmentalized pattern. Think of an oscilloscope that has the same wave pattern whether it represents an auditory, a visual or a synesthetic stimulus pattern. Neuroscientific support for this hypothesis derives from the importance of temporal lobe functions in integration and differentiation of sensory "compartments" and the fact that individuals with temporal lobe abnormalities are often inundated by ongoing déjà experiences. In this connection, the "anatomical" hypothesis put forward by Wigam in 1860, the hypothesis that Freud cites, is quite remarkable. Wigan thought that déjà phenomena resulted from an absence of simultaneity in the functioning of the two cerebral hemispheres.

Earlier in the presentation, I described my hypothesis that each perceptual act represents an unconscious recapitulation of the ontogeny of

---

[21] Arlow, J., "The Structure of the Déjà Vu Experience." *Journal of the American Psychoanalytic Association* 7:611-631, 1959.

[22] Kafka, John S. (1989). *Multiple Realities In Clinical Practice*, Yale University Press, New Haven.

perception, and that, developmentally, synesthetic perceptions antedate sense specific (visual, auditory etc.) perceptions. Interruptions of some micro-temporal recapitulations lead to the subjective equivalence of completely and of incompletely recapitulated perceptions and therefore to the formation of bizarre and uncanny "objects." (As an aside: This has led me to study the psychotic's "atmospheric" objects. Imagine being immersed in an unending series of déjà experiences. Some psycho-biological schizophrenia research currently focuses on temporal lobe functions.)

In *Déjà Vu*, a micro-temporal memory dysfunction leads to a loss of autonoetic awareness. In déjà experiences the memory, the uncanny familiar feeling cannot be localized in time and place. Neurobiologists use the term "autonoetic" to describe "self-in-time" awareness. I believe that this loss of "self-in-time" awareness in déjà vu experiences is the result of interruptions of some micro-temporal recapitulations, i.e., micro-temporal breaks in the unconscious memories of the chain of perceptions involved in "object" formation.

To recapitulate, we have developed so far: We cannot talk about memories without talking about time. Some modern conceptions of time are perhaps relevant to psychoanalysis, particularly to the notion of the timelessness of the unconscious. In any case, memories are not copies of the past. Episodic memories are constructions. In that sense, all memories are false. We have examined different ways in which they are false and how episodic memories unroll what has been temporally condensed. (Freud says that when the patient says "I have known this all along, the end of the analysis is near.) The concept of *Nachtraeglichkeit* has received special attention. Clinical psychoanalysis and memory formation function in the *Spielraum* "playroom" (or"playtime") between the concreteness of mechanical aftereffects, on the other hand, and hermeneutics, i.e., meaning and change of meaning resulting from new information, on the other. And it is here, somewhat surprisingly, that *Nachtraeglichkeit* and neurobiology may encounter one another.

There is no attempt in this presentation to deal with the vast topic of the neurobiology of memory. There have only been some brief references to temporal lobe function and to the currently possible visualization of the movement of brain activation that may correspond to psychological recapitulative processes in perception. But now, I want to mention two points made in a neuro-biological paper that seem particularly relevant to our discussion. The paper is titled "What are the memory sources of dreaming?"[23] The first point deals with the correspondence between movement of brain activity from one brain area to another and psychological movement between two elaborations of a memory. The second point deals with the constraints imposed on memory formation by chronobiological factors.

The simple naming of specific areas of the brain as centers of a specific affective or cognitive function, may strike us as only a kind of internal phrenology and thus of limited interest. The situation is different when a shift in cerebral activation and the timing of the shift corresponds to interesting psychological developments. Nielsen and Stenstrom have observed that a different brain area is activated when an individual recounts a dream he had yesterday and when he talks about the same dream one week later. "...the dependence of newly acquired memories on the hippocampus decreases over time whereas their dependence on neocortical structures, such as the medial prefrontal cortex, increases in a complementary fashion. Memories are...relocated over time from the hippocampus to the neocortex..." The authors describe corresponding qualitative changes, in essence from "day residue" to cognitive elaboration, to emotionally relevant episodic memories. Here is a neurobiological finding connected to the construction of meaning, to the hermeneutic pole of *Nachtraeglichkeit*. The finding that chronobiological factors at several levels influence the selection of memory sources, corresponds to "aftereffect," the "billiard ball" external, mechanical, and concrete pole of *Nachtraeglichkeit*. The timing and the rhythms of cerebral functions in general correspond to linear clock time, precisely, the linear clock time in which billiard balls have their aftereffects. These "external" rhythms are gate keepers to provide or deny access, at any one moment, to a multitude of cerebral activities.

---

[23] Nielsen, Tore A. and Stenstrom, Philippe, "What are the memory sources of dreaming?" *Nature*, 4/7, October 2005, pages 1286-1289.

The brain itself functions with the polarity between aftereffect and hermeneutic transformations. This kind of polarity of brain functioning is congruent with our psychoanalytic work. The fixed clock time of the beginning and ending of the psychoanalytic session forms the frame in which the hermeneutic search of the unconscious unfolds itself, an unfolding necessary for the construction of personal psychological time, an unraveling of the ultimate condensed timeless into the thread with which we weave our memories and our lives.

References

Arlow, J. (1959). The Structure of the Déjà Vu Experience. *Journal of the American Psychoanalytic Association* 7:611-631.

Eissler, Kurt R. (1978). Tod und Zeit. In: *Der sterbende Patient. Zur Psychologie des Todes*. Stuttgart.

Freud, Sigmund. *New Introductory Lectures*. Volume XXII, page 74.

Freud, Sigmund. *Standard Edition*, Volume 13, pages 201-207.

Kafka, John S. (1989). *Multiple Realities In Clinical Practice*. New Haven: Yale University Press.

Nielsen, Tore A. and Stenstrom, Philippe, (2005). What are the memory sources of dreaming? *Nature* 4/7, October 2005, pages 1286-1289.

Turner, Frederick, (2006). Interdisciplinary Research Opportunities: Limits and Constraints. *Time's News*, No. 37, February 2006.

Published in Dutch Translation in Festschrift for Han Groen-Prakken,
Chapter 7, Hanfest, Amsterdam, January 1998.

Chapter 9

The Analyst's Autonomy:
Individuation and Flexibility of Technique

A paper dealing with the development of the analyst's autonomy and individuation is necessarily a most personal one. As I try to write it, I am aware to what extent the struggles for my own autonomy and my efforts at psychoanalytic individuation are never-ending. Daily analytic work, observations of, and interchange with colleagues and supervisees, and the writing of this paper are powerful stimuli to self-examination.

Ernst Ticho[24] makes a distinction between life goals and analytic goals. What happens to this distinction when we apply it to the personal analysis of the future analyst, his or her training analysis? Ticho points out that overcoming obstacles to further growth and individuation is an *analytic* goal that opens the door for post-analytic work on *life* goals for all patients. Ticho does not address explicitly the topic of training analysis. He seems, however, to recognize implicitly that the development of his or her "analytic function" may be a life goal for the future analyst when he says: "Sometimes we even confuse our professional model of a good analyst with what the individual goals of the (non-trainee) patient

---

[24] Ticho, E. (1972). Termination of Psychoanalysis: treatment goals, life goals. *Psychoanalytic Quarterly* 41:315-33.

should be." (p. 318.) Some candidates discover in their analyses that the path that leads them to further individuation also leads them away from an analytic career. For others, however, those who do become analysts, there is a relatively good fit between their individuation and their desire and ability to function as analysts.

The preoccupation with this particular fit between life and work emerges as a common element in the psychoanalytic self-portraits published in the series *Psychoanalyse in Selbstdarstellungen.*[25] When I was asked to write a contribution[26] to this series I dreamt that the sheets of paper handed to me were already completely covered with text. My first thought upon awakening was that I didn't want to go through all this again. I had already lived it. I have theorized that one constantly recapitulates (in microseconds) features of one's own development, including the history of the development of one's perceptual processes.[27] I think that these recapitulative condensations are the result of much *previous* conscious and unconscious psychic work. To write a psychoanalytic self-portrait that others, not privy to my condensations could understand, I had to do much of the difficult psychic work again. I was faced with the task of deconstructing my personal recapitulative condensations to present a credible publicly acknowledgeable story of events; hence my resistance. Perhaps I also feared that my condensations contained some personal myths that might be threatened if the deconstructed elements could not be reassembled into the old mold.

In the psychoanalytic self-portrait that I wrote, I described how the analytic task of empathic resonance with the patient's experience dovetailed with my personal history of great demands on me to comprehend and live in different worlds, cultures and realities. Such demands in addition to the emotional consequences of losing my father at an early age played a big part in my seeking analysis in the first place. How early pa-

---

[25] *Psychoanalyse in Selbstdarstellungen*, ed. Hermanns, L., édition diskord, Tuebingen, Vol. I, 1992; Vol.II, 1994; Vol.III, 1995.

[26] *Psychoanalyse in Selbstdarstellungen*, ed. Hermanns, L., édition diskord, Tuebingen, Vol. I, Volume III, pp. 141-187, 1995.

[27] Kafka, J. (1989). *Multiple Realities in Clinical Practice.* New Haven: Yale University Press.

rental loss, disruptions, and emigrations complicate individuation and the stages of achieving degrees of autonomy need hardly be spelled out. Disruptions can make one more dependent. Attachments, even attachments to some psychoanalytic ideas, may become tenacious. Awareness of this tendency can lead one to reactively emphasize and constantly fight for autonomy. The fear of being too readily influenced can lead to intellectual rebellion. Idealizations of ideas and of those who promote them are often followed by exaggerated rejections of ideas and of past heroes. After such a sequence the development and the maintenance of psychoanalytic autonomy then involves efforts to decontaminate ideas from such overreactions.

Authoritarian psychoanalysts and authoritarian analytic institutes make the candidates' task of analytic individuation more difficult. Han Groen-Prakken has written about this problem.[28] Fortunately many of us have witnessed an anti-authoritarian evolution of our institutes. In countries emerging from repressive regimes, where individuation and personal autonomy had been anathema, psychoanalysis has a powerful appeal. As analysis reawakens there, the personal and institutional struggles against overt or disguised expressions of authoritarian attitudes are intense. Han Groen-Prakken's involvement in, and profound understanding of these issues form the basis for her outstanding success in fostering the development of psychoanalysis in Eastern Europe.

I want again to turn closer to home, to the topic of psychoanalytic individuation. Again, I will be autobiographical, but I believe that much of what I describe characterizes the development of the majority of colleagues, those whose psychoanalytic development is a continuing process.

I have observed a few general trends that increasingly characterize my work with most patients. I will give two examples.

(1) Although my attention to transference and countertransference developments is as alive as ever, the overall frequency of my *explicit* transference interpretations has diminished markedly. At first I tended

---

[28] *The Psychoanalytical Society and the Analyst. With special reference to the history of the Dutch psychoanalytical society.* Dutch Annual of Psychoanalysis, ed. Groen-Prakken, H. & Ladan, A., volume I, pp.13-37. Amsterdam/Lisse. 1933.

to make them later and later in my analytic work and then found that the patient's own discoveries made them unnecessary.

(2) I think that most analysts, on the basis of their clinical experience develop hypotheses and theories for which they seek further confirmation. Theories I have formed and that I wish to be confirmed have a general influence on my listening. I have hypothesized, for instance, that an early developmental difficulty of differentiating animate from inanimate sources of stimuli is related to some adult patients' sense of "entitlement" because they expect the inanimate environment to be as responsive as the animate world to their needs. Since I am conscious of my wish for confirmation of this idea, I have to be on guard against neglecting other clinical data when the possibility of such confirmation is in the wings.

Despite some general trends in the development of my analytic technique, it is primarily the *variations* in my technique with different patients, and with the same patients at different periods in their treatment, that have increased over the years. While it may be a banal observation that one's work becomes more differentiated with experience, it is striking how long it takes and how difficult it is to wean oneself from certain technical shibboleths. The warnings, for instance, against so-called "intellectualizing" became one of those sticky "rules" for me. I became especially aware of this when I worked with a patient who insisted on a practically mathematical demonstration of the validity of any point, but who also postponed judgment for an unbelievably long time during which he carefully considered every argument offered and, to my surprise, also worked them through on a hidden but deeply emotional level. I learned not to worry about the heavy intellectual features of my interventions after I understood that there was no other access to my patient. My comments or interpretations, even transference interpretations with "usual" content were phrased with "unusual" care. I had to overcome theoretical and technical "prejudices" before I could let the clinical situation guide my technique, my phrasing, my timing and my tempo as well as the content of my interventions. There are a number of other "teachings," widely held beliefs that are justified in most instances, that I now also consider to be theoretical and technical "prejudices."

They concern such issues as the connection between certain diagnoses and analyzability, the analyst's responsiveness to the patient's questions, and notions about acceptable duration of treatment.

The variability of my general activity and apparent passivity with different patients, and during different phases of treatment with the same patient, has greatly increased over the years. There are fewer and fewer technical stereotypes. I am aware of pronounced variations in my speed of talking, my tolerance of silence, my tolerance of defensive talking (although I recall an instance in which I asked a patient to consider being silent until he had something to say), the frequency with which I ask questions, whether I obtain minimal or detailed histories and the frequency with which I use extra-analytic transference comments. I have already referred to a general decrease in my explicit transference interpretations, but even here my work with different patients varies greatly.

My retrospective genetic, dynamic and economic formulations may explain and justify these technical differences. Something else, however, plays the most prominent role in the ongoing clinical work. When I think of specific patients, I find that my way of working with each patient has characteristics that match an inner portrait I have of him or her. This inner portrait determines a *typical* style that characterizes my work with each patient, discernable despite my recognition of the unpredictability of the clinical situation encountered in each new session with that patient.

I have already described the task that faced me when I was asked to write a psychoanalytic *"Selbstdarstellung."* I have referred to my theory that one recapitulates in microseconds the history of the development of one's perceptual processes. A further hypothesis[29] is that early perceptual processes are synesthetic, i.e. not clearly differentiated into hearing, seeing, feeling etc., but rather characterized by sensory blending. Internal self-portraits and internal portraits of others that are operative in the psychoanalyst's and in the analysand's mind are rich in synesthetic components, because the regressive features of psychoanalytic work

---

[29] Kafka, J. (1989). *Multiple Realities in Clinical Practice*. New Haven: Yale University Press, pp.41,77.

bring them to the surface. When analytic regression begins, the patient's "presenting problems" become transformed into psychoanalytically experienced—and conceptualized—issues. When defenses, condensations and displacements in a transferentially bathed self-observing atmosphere are alive, internal portraits of self and others, as well as portraits of events can have what I have called "abstract expressionist" features.[30] By this I mean that a simple pictorial element conveys and stands for vast information and great depth of affect. I have observed abstract expressionist dreams in middle phases of analytic work. One example was a dream of a moving line with a minute dip. The dreamer "knew" the meaning of the dream. The line represented the course of history and the dip represented the Holocaust. The meaning of the moving line with its minute dip, had been transformed, expanded, exploded and deepened. Such transforming work, I believe, closely resembles artistic creation.

Our analyzing function resembles artistic work when it involves the formation and use of these "condensed" portraits. They are condensed because much psychic work has led to the formation of symbolic and metaphoric touch-stones that carry vast information. One brings these condensed portraits to each psychoanalytic session, but during the session they expand like a condensate that is being hydrated. The portraits we bring to, and further develop during analytic sessions, resemble those of the artists who, influenced by characteristics of the subject, create realistic, symbolic, impressionist, abstract, romantic, expressionist, cubist, abstract expressionist or musical portraits.

Good portraiture and good analysis involve empathic resonance with the subject's history. There is surface and depth to the work, and a special relationship between model and artist. Sometimes the portraitist or the analyst paints, i.e. projects some of his or her own features onto the model or onto the analysand. But the work is ruined if this projection goes too far and cannot be corrected as the work progresses. The individuation of the analyst and of the artist, their respective struggles for

---

[30] Kafka, J. (1989). *Multiple Realities in Clinical Practice.* New Haven: Yale University Press, p. 61.

autonomy have much in common. Analyst and artist must have a solid self-picture, the ability to refer to what I have described as a solid inner "condensed" self-portrait to make possible their work of creative transformation.

A manifest theme in Freud's 1908 paper "Creative Writers and Daydreaming" is the limited ability of analysts to comprehend the creative process. I believe, however, that Freud is somewhat disingenuous and that we find the essence of the psychoanalytic process precisely where Freud finds the probable locus of the elusive creative process. In order to develop my argument, I must quote the following passage from the final section of Freud's paper:[31]

"...the daydreamer carefully conceals his phantasies from other people because he feels he has reasons for being ashamed of them. I should now add that even if he were to communicate them to us he could give us no pleasure by his disclosures. Such phantasies, when we learn them, repel us or at least leave us cold. But when a creative writer presents his plays to us or tells us what we are inclined to take to be his personal daydreams, we experience a great pleasure, and one which probably arises from the confluence of many sources. How the writer accomplishes this is his innermost secret; the essential *ars poetica* lies in the technique of overcoming the feeling of repulsion in us which is undoubtedly connected with the barriers that rise between each single ego and the others. We can guess two of the methods used by this technique. The writer softens the character of his egoistic daydreams by altering and disguising it, and he bribes us by the purely formal—that is, aesthetic—yield of pleasure which he offers us in the presentation of his phantasies. We give the name of *incentive bonus*, or a *fore-pleasure*, to a yield of pleasure such as this, which is offered to us so as to make possible the release of still greater pleasure arising from deeper psychical sources. In my opinion, all

---

[31] Freud, S. *Standard Edition of the Complete Psychological Works of Sigmund Freud*, vol. 9, Hogarth Press, London, 1953.

the aesthetic pleasure which a creative writer affords us has the character of a fore-pleasure of this kind, and our actual enjoyment of an imaginative work proceeds from a liberation of tensions in our minds. It may even be that not a little of this effect is due to the writer's enabling us thenceforward to enjoy our own day-dreams without self-reproach or shame. This brings us to the threshold of new, interesting and complicated enquiries; but also, at least for the moment, to the end of our discussion."

In Freud's sentence "the essential *ars poetica* lies in the technique of overcoming the feeling of repulsion in us which is undoubtedly connected with the barriers that rise between each single ego and the others," I propose to substitute *ars poetica and psychoanalytica.* Condensation and displacement, elements that Freud recognizes as important features of the artistic creation, are prominent as analysis gets underway. Even more relevant, however, is Freud's brief, but striking reference to the problem of "the other," the negative charge of the "outside." It is not only the poet and the artist who have to "overcome" the narcissistic barrier, it is precisely also the essential task of the psychoanalyst. Freud says that creating aesthetic pleasure involves the "technique of overcoming the feeling of repulsion in us which is undoubtedly connected with the barriers that rise between each single ego and the others." The aesthetic element also plays an important role in psychoanalysis. The high degree of individuation and autonomy of artist *and* analyst makes the "outside" less dangerous and permits the unthreatening resonance with public or patient in which " the other's" aesthetic pleasure and individuation can unfold.

Freud's almost casual comment in this essay, that "...the ...feeling of repulsion (*abstossend* in Freud's text)... is connected with the barriers...between each single ego and the others" is a powerful early statement about narcissism. It invites discussion in its own right, especially because it foreshadows later developments in the theory of narcissism. Treuerniet, describing Freud's thought after 1914, says, "As the blows to our narcissism always come from reality, we can frequently observe a hatred of certain aspects of reality: what is hated is the evidence of the limitations of our omnipotence, the feeling of narcissistic mortification."[32] I am, however, focusing on parallels between artistic and psychoanalytic work in the context of the maturation of the analyst's and the artist's autonomy. While this topic certainly involves the psychic management of narcissism in both, I want to call attention to a text of Freud written probably about three years before "Creative Writers and Daydreaming." It supports my contention that Freud's modesty concerning psychoanalytic understanding of creativity is somewhat disingenuous since in this paper he specifically relates therapeutic to artistic work. In "Psychopathic Characters on the Stage"[33] he points out that a play gives aesthetic pleasure only if the stage characters fulfill three conditions: 1) The hero's psychopathology is not present from the outset, but develops in the course of the play. 2) The repressed impulse is one which is similarly repressed in all of us; this repression is shaken up by the situation that confronts the hero in the play. 3) The impulse that is struggling into consciousness is never given a definite name. In the spectator the process is carried through with his attention averted. He is in the grip of emotions and does not, at the moment, take stock of what is happening. Freud makes a specific parallel between the lowering of resistance through similar means in analytic treatment and successful stage productions. But Freud's parallel between treatment and artistic creation goes further. He says that we do not understand (initially) the sick neurotic patient who brings us a ready-made picture of his illness. But when we learn to understand the patient's conflict, we forget that he is sick, as the patient himself, when he understands his conflict, ceases to be sick. Freud says that it is the task of the *Dichter*, the playwright, to make us, the audience, sick, to induce in us some of the character's sickness, to guide us through the development of the conflict, and thus to our, (and the patient's) comprehension of this conflict. Freud clearly recognizes

---

[32] Treuerniet, N. (1991). Introduction to "On Narcissism"; Introduction to an Introduction, chapter in *Freud's "On Narcissism: An Introduction"*, ed. Sandler, J., Person, E., Fonagy, P. International Psycho-analytic Association, p. 82. London: Hogarth Press.
[33] Freud, S. (1942). *Standard Edition of the Complete Psychological Works of Sigmund Freud*, vol. 7: 305. Hogarth Press, London, 1942.

the parallel between the processes of identification in art and in treatment *and* the parallel of the tendency to "repulse", to *abstossen* the not understood patient *and* the stage character with whom one cannot identify. A transformation has to occur in art and in treatment before the feeling of repulsion toward the "other" is laid to rest.

Identificatory processes are necessary, but not sufficient for the transformation that characterizes artistic creation *and* successful psychoanalysis. As I have tried to show earlier in this paper, the progressive sharing of recapitulative processes make possible condensations that can again and again expand into rhythmic resonances between analyst and analysand, between spectator, audience and artist. In *fausse reconnaisance ('déjà raconté') in psychoanalytic treatment*[34] Freud writes that when the patient says about some recent "insights" that he has known this all along, the end of the analysis is near. I believe that at that particular moment the analysand makes a reference to the knowledge that existed before the analytic transformation when the knowledge was narrower and isolating and flat. It is with the creative and the analytic transformation that knowledge acquires greater depth and perspective. Three dimensional perspective, in turn, depends on each participating individual's ability to conceive of the other as the center of his or her own universe.[35] This ability to tame his own narcissism that is essential for the artist and for the analyst fosters a similar development in the public and in the patient. Knowledge and self-understanding can then exist in the psychological presence of "the other", in the presence of mutual autonomies.

---

[34] Freud, S. (1914). *Standard Edition of the Complete Psychological Works of Sigmund Freud*, volume 13: 201. Hogarth Press, London, 1953.
[35] Kafka, R. (1897). Weltanschauung und Perspektive. Chapter in *Die Gesellschaft, Monatschrift für Litteratur, Kunst u. Sozialpolitik*, ed. Conrad, M. and Merian, H. Leipzig: Hermann Haacke, pp.15-26.

Psychiatry (1983) 46:31-39.

Chapter 10
Challenge and Confirmation in Ritual Action

C*linicians* are concerned with ritualistic behavior, and anthropologists with rituals. Both involve repetition. Hans Loewald, in a paper on repetition and the repetition compulsion (1971), makes the point that not all repetition is a manifestation of repetition compulsion. He elaborates the difference between a compelled tacit repetition and active repeating, working through what is being repeated. In his paper, "The Waning of the Oedipus Complex" (1979), he elaborates the idea that the same problematic is recurrent, not disposed of but reworked in different developmental stages and in the context of different life tasks. This distinction is pertinent to the difference between *ritual* and the *ritualistic.*

Rituals can produce a feeling of completeness—a whole act, a finished sequence, the achievement (at least for a while) of satisfaction, satiation, perhaps serenity. But sometimes, as in "ritualistic behavior," they may instead generate a feeling of mechanical repetition or the absence of a meaning achieved, the sense of being enmeshed in an endless series of aborted sequences. I will develop the theme that both of the behaviors, the ritual and the ritualistic, emerge from a concern with boundaries such as those between the individual and the group, what is within and what is without, the concrete or concretized-spatial and the psychological-temporal. Ritual and the ritualistic address these divisions—which are central to our understanding of psychological reality—not consciously, perhaps, but in a particularly focused manner. My thesis is that ritual differs from the ritualistic by both confirming and challenging the shared, commonsense, everyday reality.

*   *   *

The rituals with which a psychoanalyst is concerned in daily clinical work are manifestations of obsessive-compulsive urges. While the degree of ego dystonicity of such urges and acts may vary, they are often considered symptoms by the analysand and may be the overt reason why an individual seeks psychoanalytic treatment. The psychoanalyst, as work with the patient continues, may soon think of many other aspects of almost any patient's behavior as ritualistic. The way he or she enters the consultation room, a particular way of reclining on the couch, of rising from it with a characteristic jerking or with a slow rolling motion, greetings or avoidance of greetings, may have for the analyst's eyes a ritualistic quality, not recognized as such by the patient but eventually of importance in understanding the patient and in the formulation of interpretations. The extent to which such rituals can be seen as related to those which the anthropologist studies depends on our fundamental conceptualization of the nature of both kinds of ritual. The analyst, both through contact with persons whose behavior does not conform to social norms and through a growing understanding of the personal dynamics of conformity, may be especially aware of the ritual component of behavior within a given society. My own concept of the nature of ritual leads me to believe that despite some surface differences, the term *ritual* signifies the same fundamental characteristics to the clinician and to the anthropologist. Both fields understand the structural role of ritual as in some way related to the attempt to maintain the psychological homeostasis necessary for the individual's functioning in a social context.

Much information about rituals is obtained through the study of rites of passage. Birth, puberty, marriage, and death are the major transitional events around which rituals are organized. In my view, the occurrence of rituals at these times derives from the basic stabilizing function of ritual in situations with the potential for instilling dystonic feelings ranging from discomfort to terror. The following characteristics of cultural rites also emerge in clinical counterparts: (1) Precision of performance of the ritual act, in which the emphasis on the concreteness of the ritual object coexists with emphasis on an abstract symbolism—the nonconcrete mental or spiritual charge with which the ritual performance or event is invested. Thus, the ritual is the condensed encounter of the material and psychological extremes. (2) Ritual confrontation of the issue of the boundary of the individual and the relationships between the individual and the other, the inside and the outside.

In biology, what we consider a unit is in some sense arbitrary. For example, it is unclear whether certain marine organisms should be considered colonies of unicellular organisms or individual animals. The anthropologist encounters the boundary question in the study of rites of passage when the individual "becomes a part" of the society. The clinician frequently comes to understand rituals as connected with the patient's struggles to define or to protect his own boundaries. It seems to me that anthropologists might agree—as one example, see Victor Turner's central concern with liminality (1977)—that the rituals they study also concern, first, transcendence of the concrete, the material, the body, and second, the boundary between individual and societal entities.

Having introduced the notion that ritual is related to the concrete-psychological boundary and to the individual-group boundary, I will discuss the former more specifically, although our perspective on the latter will be greatly affected by the considerations offered. Developments in modern physics that have made inroads on our commonsense understanding of matter, energy, and time have no doubt contributed to the *Zeitgeist*, playing some role in contemporary explorations of perennial questions involving the linkage of the psychological and the temporal. Various authors who have approached this issue from very different angles have independently concluded that the study of mind and the study of time are intertwined. In a paper in which he develops the theme of the presence of the active past and future in the now, psychoanalyst Hans Loewald has gone so far as to equate time and mind (1962). Hugh Longuet-Higgins proposes a model of the brain based on the model of the holograph, but giving a temporal rather than a spatial meaning to the terms in the mathematical formulae describing its physics (1968). In holography, each point in space has *some* information about all other points in space; in the temporal analog, each "point" in time has some information about every other point in time (past and future). Longuet-Higgins' treatment of the brain in temporal terms—rather than in commonsense, "material," concrete terms—perhaps brings us close to Loewald's trenchant statement "mind is time." (1962, p. 268)

A whole literature deals with the pathogenic consequences which result when the *temporal* psychological event undergoes a transformation through reification, concretization, *spatialization*. Much of this literature is summarized by Joseph Gabel in *La fausse conscience—Essai sur la ré ification* (1962). Here he develops the theme that estrangement, common to "ideology" (I will later amplify his use of this word) and schizophrenia, is grounded in this reification, the spatialization of the temporal. Gabel's concept of ideology thus has a clearly negative connotation.

On the surface, but I believe only on the surface, this contrasts with Erikson's initially positive reference to the ideological element, "the element providing a coherence of ideas and ideals" which "become part of formal rites" in the ontogeny of ritualization (1966, p. 617). Erikson says that only after the addition of the ideological element "can man be said to be adult in the sense that he can devote himself to ritual purposes and eventually be trusted to become the '*everyday ritualizer*' in his children's life" (p. 617; italics mine). Erikson starts out by studying human ritualization in contrast and in relation to animal ritualization as described by the ethologist. His positive evaluation of ritual derives from its roots in the mother-infant recognition, such as the appreciation conveyed by a greeting, which fosters a sense of self in the infant and helps maintain it in the mother. He introduces a more negative element when he discusses human ritualization as being largely related to the existence of human pseudospecies—tribes, clans, classes—which consider all outsiders as enemies, and he foresees the possibility that humanity will succeed in diminishing its pseudospecies divisiveness. I believe that for Erikson ideology thus also implies a certain concretization. The positive aspects of evaluation of the ideological by Erikson result not so much from a view of ideology essentially different from Gabel's, but rather from Erikson's view that—to a certain extent and at our current state of development—roots in a somewhat concretized group must coexist with individualism that would otherwise risk being autistic. Such dialectic conflicts are characteristic of all of the developmental phases described by Erikson.

A discussion of individual-group boundaries calls for a brief comment on current attempts in psychoanalysis to distinguish "self" from "ego." A self-psychology, which attempts to clarify issues related to the experiencing or self-representations of the image of the self, has had a prominent place in recent psychoanalytic literature. The influence of Kohut (1971) is considerable in this literature. Freud's ambiguous usage of "*Das Ich*" is often critically cited in this connection. While the concept of self-representation is clinically useful, I believe that on a more theoretical level the ego-self differentiation can be a pseudo-solution— that is, it can slide over a problem which is more interesting if its unsolved paradoxical nature is squarely faced. In their discussion of *Ego,* J. Laplanche and J.-B. Pontalis mention the history of the usage of "*Ich*" in psychoanalysis and the conceptual problems involved:

> "some authors have sought, for the sake of clarity, to make a conceptual distinction between the ego as agency, as substructure of the personality, and the ego as love-object for the individual himself. ... . Hartmann, for example, has suggested a way of getting rid of the ambiguity which arises in his view from the use of terms such as 'narcissism' and 'ego-cathexis' (*Ich-Be-setzung*). ... in using the term narcissism, two different sets of opposites often seem to be fused into one. The one refers to the self (one's own person) in contradistinction to the object, the second to the ego (as a psychic system) in contradistinction to other substructures of personality. However, the opposite of object cathexis is not ego cathexis, but cathexis of one's own person, that is, self-cathexis; in speaking of self-cathexis we do not imply whether this cathexis is situated in the

id, in the ego, or in the superego. ... It therefore will be clarifying if we define narcissism as the libinal cathexis not of the ego but of the self." [Laplanche and Pontalis 1967, p. 131]

Laplanche and Pontalis go on to say:

"In our view this position builds upon a purely conceptual distinction, running ahead of a real solution to some essential problems. The danger of proposing a usage of 'Ich' which is taken to be exclusively psycho-analytical by contrast with other more traditional senses is that the real contributions of the Freudian usage may be lost. For Freud *exploits* traditional usages: he opposes organism to environment, subject to object, internal to external, and so on, while continuing to employ 'Ich' at these different levels. What is more, he plays on the ambiguities thus created, so that none of the connotations normally attaching to 'ego' or 'I' ('*Ich*') is forgotten. It is this complexity that is shunned by those who want a different word...." [pp. 131-32]

While there is ambiguity in the notion of self-observation, it is the concreteness and spatialization of a self-observing self which makes the ambiguity so difficult and motivates those who want to eliminate it. I believe that the advantages of the Freudian ambiguity which Laplanche and Pontalis also want to preserve lie in the fact that it avoids a one-sided concretization (of *Ich*) which is essentially spatial and incompatible with our groping for a new understanding of psychological reality—an understanding which has already achieved some distance from common sense in recognizing mind as time.

In discussing some aspects of the development of psychological reality, I will focus on my belief that the rituals observed by clinicians and anthropologists both have essentially a reality-anchoring function. For example, when Erikson discusses the recognition-greeting ritual of mother and infant, he emphasizes the formation of the individual's sense of his own existence and of a reality that, through generational "cogwheeling" (Erikson using David Rapaport's phrase), links it to the reality of the group.

In developing my formulations based on clinical data, I have drawn inspiration from the experimental work of Heinrich Klüver. In experiments in which an animal trained to jump to a green circle rather than a red square subsequently had to choose between a blue oval and a yellow triangle, he might consistently choose the blue oval. Klüver's study of such "subjectively equivalent stimuli" (1936) had a profound impact on several areas of experimental psychology, especially comparative psychology. The concept is especially useful in the clinical study of psychotic persons, but I have found that its more subtle aspects have also contributed to my understanding of other kinds of patients and eventually to the formulation of my broader ideas about the nature of psychological reality. (Kafka 1964, 1977, 1979)

To elaborate these ideas briefly, drive states determine which characteristics of the environment are "taken in"—that is, what is selected by perceptual scanning depends on need. Percepts related to satisfaction of needs form clusters of subjectively equivalent stimuli, which function as the building blocks of subjective reality, constant "objects." The term "object constancy" is used differently in experimental and general psychology and in psychoanalysis. In the former context, it refers to such matters as the recognition of a table as the same when it is seen from different angles—that is, to constancy despite the different retinal projections. In psychoanalysis object constancy refers to the ability to continue to love someone when he or she has become frustrating (Anna Freud, 1971). The psychoanalytic-psychodynamic usage of the term *constancy* can be said to presuppose the psychological, but I believe that the implication of drive states in all perceptual scanning, all perception, further diminishes the distance between the two kinds of object constancy. The rapprochement of the two meanings becomes clearer when we examine in greater depth the loading of the word *constancy* with time.

Scanning implies a temporal dimension. Motivational intensity influences scanning speed; the greater the hunger, the more intense and rapid the searching activity. Furthermore, time experiences—time sensations and judgments—are profoundly affected by drive states and affects. Time judgments are based on *subjectively equivalent temporal intervals*, and dominant affects and moods determine the selection of the reference interval

(Kafka 1957, 1972). My emphasis on the importance of *subjectively equiva-lent intervals,* and of the ever contracting and expanding temporal grids of psychic activity is in harmony with such authors as Gabel, who contrasts the *temporal* fluidity of psychological processes with "alienating," essentially nonpsychological, concretization and *spatialization.*

Here we have moved toward an equation of the most "pure" psycho-logical processes with temporal processes, an idea which matches Loewald's conclusion "mind is time," although he reaches it from a somewhat different starting point. Our common sense finds this equa-tion difficult to accept. Regardless of our exposure to and degree of understanding of the modern physicist's revolutionary conceptions of "matter," time, and other aspects of reality, and regardless of our grasp of the idea of subjective equivalences, our practical need to deal with a concrete reality renders the mind-time translation persistently difficult. Facing this difficulty permits us to make explicit a feature which is im-plicit in some of Erkison's remarks on developmental ritualization.

As mentioned, Erikson links a necessary ritualization (to avoid autism) that is part of generational "cogwheeling" to the development of a feeling of belonging to groups, clans, and other human "pseudo species." In Gabel's terms, the operational concrete-ness implied by *pseudo species* would be seen as psychologically "false," for Gabel considers projection of "bad aspects of myself feeling as spatialization of the psychological (temporal). I will show below that when Erikson relates ritual to the basic individual-group dichoto-my, the structure of this dichotomy is similar to that of the psychological-concrete (temporal-spatial) dichotomy as it is discussed by Gabel.

Thus, if ritual is concerned with the boundary of the individual and the group, it is also concerned with the boundary of the psychological (temporal) and concretized (spatial). Questions of ambiguity on one boundary correspond to the same questions at the other boundary. Erik-son discusses ambiguity as it relates to ritualization, to self and other, to individual and group. In summarizing basic elements of ritualization, which starts with the greeting-recognition of mother and infant, he says:

> "Its mutuality is based on the *reciprocal* needs of two quite *unequal* organisms and minds; yet, it unites them in *practical reality* as well

as in *symbolic actuality.* It is a highly *personal* matter, and is yet *group-bound;* by the same token it heightens a sense both of *belongingness* and of personal *distinctiveness.* It is *playful,* and yet *formalized,* and this in *details* as well as in the whole *procedure.* Becoming *familiar* through repetition, it yet renews the *surprise* of recognition which provides a catharsis of affects. And while the ethologists will tell us that ritualization in the animal world must, above all, provide an *unambiguous* set of signals so as to avoid fatal misunderstanding, we suspect that in man, *the overcoming of ambivalence* is an important aim of such ritualization. [1966, p. 605; Erikson's italics]

Note in Erikson's text the juxtaposition of the question of the *ambiguity of signals* and the topic of the *overcoming of ambivalence.* Since ambivalence refers to good and bad feelings toward the same object, it takes for granted an antecedent degree of object constancy, a certain solidity (concreteness) of the borders of the self, a solidity of the boundary between inside and outside.

In studying the development of ambivalence, I have examined the formal logical structure of ambiguity and, on a more clinical level, I have found that parental fear of ambiguity may be a pathogenic element leading the offspring to experience estrangement and alienation when confronted with the ineluctable ambiguities and paradoxes of life (1971).

With that in mind, let us return to Erikson's emphasis on the relationship, in ritualization in animals and man, between the need for an *unambiguous* set of signals and the *overcoming of ambivalence.* I have written elsewhere (1964) that in order to tolerate the infant's first step, the mother must for the briefest moments have the delusion that the infant will not fall. This delusion occurs at a moment of psychological lack of separation of the two individuals involved. In a sense, it is the mother's ability to laugh at herself and at her delusion when the fall occurs but has no serious injurious consequences, that permits the infant's further development. I would now add that it is this delusion which permits the mother, for a moment, to give an unambiguous set of signals that the first step should be attempted. The signal is unambiguous at the moment when the definition of the individual is ambiguous, when the boundaries between mother and infant are blurred. (It should also be noted here that psychoanalytic theory offers a conceptual bridge between ambivalence and the ambiguity of what is the unit in the mother-infant dyad. Since the infant equates good with the satisfaction of his needs and bad with the lack of satisfaction–that is, with "need," something he cannot himself satisfy–the differentiation of inner and outer in a sense corresponds to the birth of good and bad.) It is the phase-appropriate degree of ease with which the mother can cross the fusion-differentiation (from her infant) barrier which indeed forms the foundation of what Erikson calls *"the overcoming of ambivalence"* that is "an important aim of ... ritualization."

While "overcoming of ambivalence" is a term which succeeds in conveying a readiness to act, it is a somewhat misleading term. Ambivalence is not "overcome," it is tolerated. Erikson himself writes:

> "What we love or admire is also threatening, awe becomes awfulness.... Therefore, ritualized affirmation, at first playfully improvised, becomes indispensable as a periodical experience and must find new forms in the context of new development actualities. Its perversion or absence, in turn, leaves a sense of dread or impoverishment.... the earliest affirmation soon becomes reaffirmation in the face of the fact that the very experiences by which man derives a measure of familiarity also expose him to a series of estrangements. The first of these is a sense of separation by abandonment to which corresponds, on the part of the mother, a chilling sense of not being needed; both must be prevented by the persistent, periodical reassurance of familiarity and mutuality." (p. 605)

Of course, the separation does occur and it must, but I agree with Erikson that the earliest affirmation persists in the recurrent ritual. But the ritual, because it represents the extreme confrontation of the concrete, precisely defined, individually bordered spatial on the one hand, and the boundary-loosened, psychological, temporal on the other, also is the periodic recurrence of the beginning—of the first step.

Elements of the ritual and the ritualistic—thus conceived—are pervasive if not omnipresent. When clinicians and anthropologists have a closer look at the rituals traditionally studied by each other's discipline, the similarities of the structural-qualitative characteristics of ritual become more obvious, and the differences are more likely to be seen in quantitative terms.

In all rituals the time-mind-communal/ space-concrete-individual ambiguities are not "overcome," but individuals vary in their degree of tolerance of the tensions at the border and therefore in the frequency and manner in which they either must immerse themselves in the experience of a wide or paradoxical reality or ritualistically defend against such immersion.

Rituals also vary in the manner in which they deal with the time-mind-communal/ space-concrete-individual tensions and ambiguities. More specifically, the polarity-tension which is the *raison d'etre* and the core structure of rituals also manifests itself in the evolution of ritual. For example, with the destruction of the Second Temple and the exodus to Babylon, a significant evolution occurred in the spiritualization of Jewish ritual, which became freed from the attachment to a concrete sacrifice at a concrete and exclusive site, the Temple in Jerusalem. Judaism became a portable religion of the word (Graetz 1873). Yet the tension persists, and the counterforce of the concrete polarity always manifests itself again in those aspects of the concretization of words and ideas which Gabel considers when he discusses "ideology." The abstract and the psychological is again pulled toward concretization, a kind of primitivization of religious ritual.

The tensions in religious groups between traditionalists clinging to more concrete formalities and those who want to deemphasize them in favor of the "spiritual" and ideational are always close to the surface. I do not want to use the word "ideological" because of the loading of concreteness which Gabel gives it, but my very avoidance of it reflects the ease with which there is always the "return of the concrete," analogous to the "return of the repressed" of the psychoanalyst. In the evolution of ritual, what is at any one moment considered acceptable is that which is perceived as essentially a "subjective equivalent" to a former ritual; its repetition reinforces a particular system of equivalences and anchors a view of reality, such as a specific "myth" of creation. It also serves as a defense against other views of reality.

The patient's ritual also serves to anchor a view of reality and as a defense against other views of reality. For example, one woman, during a schizophrenic episode, strictly observed a personal taboo which can be understood as a negative ritual and refused to shave her legs, saying she had her "father's legs." In effect, she was asserting a view of reality in which she was not separate from and controlled parts of her deceased father. As she emerged from the schizophrenic episode, rituals of adoration of her father took more conventional forms, such as walks in places and at times corresponding to his preferences.

A vast literature of psychopathology deals with the "concrete" thinking of schizophrenic patients (Gabel cites much of it). Clinicians who are familiar with this literature are sometimes puzzled by the manifestations of high-level abstraction by some schizophrenic patients in such areas as mathematics, theory of harmony, and muscial composition. Here, too, I have found Klüver's ideas about subjective equivalence useful. I have described elsewhere (Kafka 1964) a schizophrenic patient who apparently had the delusion that a certain blond nurse with a foreign accent was the Swiss fictional character Heidi. Emerging from the acute phase of her psychotic episode, the patient was able to explain to me that she had never really thought the nurse was the little Swiss girl, but that the book *Heidi* had been extraordinarily important in her formative years. The *concept* of "Heidiness"—arrived at by such equivalence-determining characteristics as the blond hair and a foreign accent—had had infinitely more stability, more constancy, than any one *person*. Individuals had merged, changed, and transformed into each other constantly during the acute psychotic episode. A personal Heidiness *cult* had served a reality-anchoring function, defending her against massive confusion and total disorganization because "Heidiness" had the necessary "concrete" object constancy for her. The abstraction stayed steady.

In the usual psychoanalytic work with neurotic patients, the *blinder* functions of ritualistic behavior are the most readily observable in the consulting room. For example, ritualistic repetition of ways of moving avoid bodily sensations that are threatening because of unconscious erotic wishes toward the analyst or because they would too easily lead— in unconscious fantasy which is eventually uncovered—to an aggressive act or gesture. Rituals in the consulting room also seem related to phase-specific drives and defenses against them; the ritualistic behavior often seems to be a manifestation of a compromise in this area. More descriptively, certain ritualistically maintained rigidities literally act as blinders. For example, a patient may not be able to look at a painting in the analyst's office because it does not match the view of the characteristics of the analyst which the patient has to maintain and which is consistent with the current stage of transference development.

The idiosyncrasy and repetitiveness, the stilted and desiccated characteristics of some behavior may lead the clinician to think of it as ritualistic, but it is difficult to draw a line distinguishing it sharply from other symptomatic behavior. The isolation of affect may be particularly striking in behavior which we are inclined to label as ritualistic because the "dramatic elaboration" (Erikson, p. 614) of the sequence is in such marked contrast to the apparent mechanical nature of the performance. In the clinical setting, what is called ritualistic is often *desiccated drama*.

For example, all the trappings of drama, performed and described *loudly*, but somehow mechanistically repetitious, accompanied a middle-aged analysand's many moves away from wife and toward mistress and vice versa. A dream in which, from a corner room, he could see in *two directions* ushered in a change. The patient was an adopted child and he came to understand his view of the absent companion as related to his view of the idealized natural parents. This insight eventually led to a marked diminution of this particular desiccated drama, to a decrease in ritualistic-manneristic behavior generally, and to an increased sense of continuity of his life and of his relationships.

The difficulty of distinguishing the ritualistic from the impulse-defense compromises that are labeled as symptomatic behavior—or simply from other behavior, since all socialized behavior contains at least a component of such a symptom-like compromise—lies in the fact that it is only quantitatively more dramatic and more desiccated. Ritual, as I conceptualize it rooted in time-space dualities, saturates human activities and existence.

If ritual has a reality-anchoring function, its ubiquity is no surprise, but what have we gained by this formulation? And how is the *desiccated drama* of ritualistic behavior in the consulting room related to ecstatic ritual? In one instance, after an analytic session in which there had been some loosening of desiccated drama, isolated affect had begun to acknowledge its object, and the patient had experienced a sense of greater freedom and autonomy, he found himself laughing at his own sudden thought while he was waiting on a subway platform. Experiencing a lightening of the psychological weight he carried, he thought: "Even living and dying is not a question of life and death." This experience, I believe, contained the essence of the "successful" ritual—a breaking out from the ritualistic. This is what the ritualistic tries for and what the ritual occasionally achieves. It may be that the more complete the achievement, the less often it *must* be re-experienced, and the less successful, the more it must automatically be repeated in dry ritualistic attempts.

The laughing experience that living and dying may not be so serious—not a "question of life and death"—has some analogy to the mother-infant fusion in which the mother has the delusion that the infant will not fall when he takes the first step. The analysand's sudden laughter on encountering his liberating thought is also reminiscent of Erikson's "*surprise* of recognition which provides a catharsis of affects" (p. 605; Erikson's italics), an element in the earliest ritualization which starts in the mother-infant greeting and recognition.

One more word needs to be said about the reality-anchoring function. There is some evidence that each perceptual act recapitulates the ontogenetic development of perception (Stein 1949). Individuals asked to describe what they saw after viewing Rorschach cards exposed for extremely short intervals may say that they can say nothing about that "flash." When pressed to describe what they saw, their responses indicate that they perceived what very young children see when they have an unlimited time to look at the Rorschach cards. What adults see in slightly longer "flashes" corresponds to what slightly older children perceive with unlimited exposures. The effects of slight increases in the exposure time for the adults correspond to the effects of months or years on the responses of children. If we apply the subjective equivalence technique to these brief "tachistoscopic" exposures, the clusters of subjectively equivalent stimuli produced are different from those which are established when there is no similarly imposed time constraint on the exposure. We thus pass again and again through a series of "realities"—a series which may well be not only an ontogenetic recapitulation but a phylogenetic one.

The reality which is established at the end of each series is that of one, everyday, commonsense, practical reality. Boundaries between objects are relatively firm and so is the boundary between subject and object. Ritual simultaneously sustains and challenges such practical, pedestrian reality. One might say that ritual confirms and sustains everyday reality *by* challenging it in the sense of evoking the prior realities traversed in the evolution of the current one. Its historicity made apparent, everyday reality is imbued with life.

Synesthetic phenomena (Kafka and Gaarder 1964; Kafka 1977), the *blending* of visual, auditory, olfactory, and tactile experiences, probably play a significant part in determining the equivalence patterns and thus the realities traversed earlier during the recapitulation inherent in each perceptual act. Ernst Kris's well-known phrase "regression in the service of the ego" (1952) relates, I believe, to the freedom, so essential for any creativity, to travel relatively freely—and in ascending and descending directions—along this recapitulative path. Successful rituals permit and foster in institutionally sanctioned ways the questioning of any one reality, the widest possible travel along this recapitulative pathway. It is an anchoring in the enriched reality, the rediscovery of one's development.

The patterns of subjective equivalence along the recapitulative path may include some which represent "realities" that for personal developmental reasons are particularly conflict-laden, which correspond to neurotic "fixation" points. The abortive nature of ritualistic behavior is related to those fixation points, and successful analytic treatment thus transforms the ritualistic into the possibility of successful, enriching, perhaps even ecstatic ritual.

References

Caruso, I. A. (1967). Zu Joseph Gabels Theorie des falsehen Bewufsteins. In: J. Gabel, *Ideologie und Schizophrenic: Formen der Entfremdung (Ideology and Schizophrenia: Forms of Estrangement)*. Frankfurt am Main: S. Fischer Verlag.

Erikson, E. H. (1966). Ontogeny of Ritualization. In: R. M. Loewenstein et al., eds., *Psychoanalysis—A General Psychology: Essays in Honor of Heinz Hartmann*. International Universities Press.

Freud, A. (1971). Address to the International Psycho-Analytic Congress, Vienna.

Gabel, J. (1962). *La fausse conscience—Essai sur la réification*. Paris: Les Editions de Minuit.

Graetz, H. (1873). *Geschichte der Juden*. Leipzig.

Kafka, J. S. (1957). A Method for Studying the Organization of Time Experience. *American Journal of Psychiatry* 114:546-53.

Kafka, J. S. (1964). Technical Applications of a Concept of Multiple Reality. *International Journal of Psycho-Analysis* 45:575-78.

Kafka, J. S. (1971). Ambiguity for Individuation: A Critique and Reformulation of Double-Bind Theory. *Archives of General Psychiatry* 25:232-39.

Kafka, J. S. (1972). The Experience of Time. Panel Report: *Journal of the American Psychoanalytic Association* 20:650-67.

Kafka, J. S. (1977). On Reality: An Examination of Object Constancy, Ambiguity, Paradox, and Time. In J. H. Smith, ed., *Thought, Consciousness, and Reality*, Vol. 2 of *Psychiatry and the Humanities*. Yale University Press.

Kafka, J. S. (1979). Psychic Effort, Drift and Reality Structures: Observations from Psychoanalytic Work with Neurotic, Borderline and Schizophrenic Patients. In: C. Muller, ed., *Psychotherapy of Schizophrenia*. Proceedings, 6th International Symposium on the Psychotherapy of Schizophrenia, Lausanne. Amsterdam-Oxford: Excerpta Medica.

Kafka, J. S., and Gaarder, K. R. (1964). Some Effects of the Therapist's LSD Experience on His Therapeutic Work. *American Journal of Psychotherapy* 18:236-43.

Klüver, H. (1936). The Study of Personality and the Method of Equivalent and Non-equivalent Stimuli. *Character and Personality* 5:91-112.

Kohut, H. (1971). *The Analysis of the Self.* International Universities Press.

Kris, E. (1952). *Psychoanalytic Explorations in Art.* International Universities Press.

Laplanche, J., and Pontalis, J.-B. (1973). *The Language of Psychoanalysis* (1967). Translated by D. Nicholson-Smith. Norton.

Loewald, H. W. (1962). The Superego and the Ego Ideal. II. Superego and Time. *International Journal of Psycho-Analysis* 43:264-68.

Loewald, H. W. (1980). Some Considerations on Repetition and Repetition Compulsion (1971). The Waning of the Oedipus Complex (1979), in: H. W. Loewald, *Papers on Psychoanalysis.* Yale University Press.

Longuet-Higgins, H. C. (1968). The Non-local Storage of Temporal Information. *Proceedings of Royal Society* 171:327-34, London.

Stein, M. I. (1949). Personality Factors Involved in Temporal Development of Rorschach Responses. *Rorschach Research Exchange and Journal of Projective Techniques* 13:355-413.

Turner, V. (1977). Process, System, and Symbol: A New Anthropological Synthesis. *Daedalus* 106(no. 3):61-80.

Lecture (April 4, 1983). Annual Frieda Fromm-Reichmann Lecture. Washington School of Psychiatry. Bethesda, Maryland.

Chapter 11

How Do We Change?

It is appropriate that a memorial lecture deals with the topic of change, since we wish to preserve the memory of powerful agents of valued change. Robert Cohen (1982) and Sylvia Hoff (1982) have recently written about Frieda Fromm-Reichmann and the lasting effects of the changing perspectives we owe her. First and foremost, she thought that psychoanalytic understanding is pertinent for treatment of severe psychopathology. (I think I should add a personal note. I'm among those who really came to this area because of Frieda Fromm-Reichmann and her influence. She died just a few months before I actually started working at Chestnut Lodge, but she still interviewed me and essentially hired me. She interviewed me twice. Once, when I was thinking of coming here and once when I formally applied. I think the total interview time was around seven hours and there was very little about me that she didn't know. I don't know what it means that after all this time she thought I should also talk to Dr. Weigert before I actually got the job.) Of all the things she said about change and resistance against change, her description of a patient who had emerged from psychosis—became essentially symptom free—but held on to one symptom comes particularly to my mind. Efforts to understand the persistence of this one symptom, the peeling of skin from her heel, failed until the patient explained the importance of the maintenance of the symptom as a bridge to her former self. Fromm-Reichmann touches here on one aspect of the topic: change as trauma because it involves loss—a theme forming a backdrop to all psychoanalytically-informed discussion of change in life and treatment. Every clinician is always a student of repetition and a student of change. The hope to *not* only repeat what others have said prompts my immediate introduction of clinical material, of necessity greatly disguised and more than usually condensed, but perhaps solid enough to serve us as an anchor. My title sounds more ambitious than what I will do. I simply tried to free myself temporarily from theoretical preconceptions and see what central themes might emerge for me now when I look retrospectively at some cases in which significant change had occurred in the course of treatment. I will be long on clinical material and somewhat sketchy on some aspects of theory.

Mrs. A, around 40, married since her early twenties and mother of four boys, has been greatly concerned about her husband's health in recent years. Her anxiety seems to have been somewhat contagious to both Mr. A and some physicians, and Mr. A was hospitalized twice for diagnostic work-ups which, however, resulted in a clean bill of health. Marital dissatisfaction of recent origin—she apparently found him much more aggressive and sarcastic than previously and he found her more anxious, provocative and critical—had led to their seeking couples therapy at her initiative. Marital tension continued to increase, however, a mutual accusatory pattern could apparently not be broken, and the couple's therapist in this instance recommended some form of individual treatment to both. According to Mrs. A, her husband had become vehemently opposed to any treatment for anybody, by the time her increasing depression and difficulties—now also in her relationship with her sons and many of her friends—led her to seek some consultations and the eventual decision to enter psychoanalysis. In and through this analysis the following story emerged. As you hear the story, you can probably imagine where the areas of major resistance were and reconstruct for yourself the approximate sequence of its unfolding.

Mrs. A was the youngest of a large number of children, all girls. When she was between four and five years old, a brother was born who died at the age of two. Mrs. A became an attractive adolescent and young woman;

she had many dates whom she usually brought home to meet her family. Her future husband was studying the same narrow subspecialty of the technical field in which her father worked. Of all the young men she brought home, he was the only one with whom her father had lengthy conversations, the only one with whom her father developed a genuine relationship, which continued and prospered after Mrs. A's marriage. Mr. A's career was successful. The A's, as I have already mentioned, had four sons who grew and developed well. Mrs. A apparently experienced, and in any case, gave no *signs* of experiencing dissatisfaction with her life. Her concern for her husband's health, the complaints and symptoms which led to couples' therapy and eventually to her entering analysis, followed by a few months her father's death. This information, I might add, was somewhat slow in emerging because of a sequence of "errors" made by Mrs. A in giving and elaborating on her history. Eventually, however, she described how one morning, not long after her father's death, she had awakened and had looked critically at her sleeping husband, had experienced him briefly as a stranger and then had the thought—I quote—"What am I doing being married to *that*?" You can imagine, on the basis of this action. We do have with these concepts at least a framework for a psychoanalytic description of change.

Has there been "structural" change? I believe that a link between "structure" is the psychoanalytic sense—superego, ego and id—and concepts of "structure" which have emerged in other fields, can and should be attempted. For the present, however, let us return to the clinical situation.

A great part of Mrs. A's life had been organized around her guilt connected to her brother's death. One could say that her psychic reality was that she had killed him, a psychic reality reactivated in the heat of the transference. One could also say that in a sense life had played a cruel joke on Mrs. A, that she had unconsciously organized a good portion of her life as if she had killed her brother and that psychoanalysis had helped her to chance from, escape from the role of victim of a cruel joke in part by illuminating the "adult" reality that she had not killed her brother. Perhaps one could say that she learned in analysis just how much she had wanted to kill her brother in the context of her derepressing various aspects of her wishes, including sexual ones, for her father. Perhaps, her learning in analysis something about the intensity of her death wish on different developmental levels (i.e., Greenspan's schema built on Piaget's foundation involving somatic learning, consequence learning, and representational-structural learning). In any case, this learning was more important for change, possibly for "structural change," than her learning that she had not actually killed her brother nor anybody else. It is accurate, but insufficient and too simple, to speak of her discovering in a situation laden with transference affect that wish and deed are not identical, a differentiation which was not solidly established at the time of her brother's death. I wish briefly to remind you of her admission, i.e., admitting to consciousness the thought: "What am I doing—being married to *that*?" I have gradually learned to pay attention to the literal meaning here: *that* was not human. *That* was not animate. *That* was a thing. The frenetic activity which followed, the hypochondriasis for her husband, were efforts to breathe some life onto the scene.

I am moving toward the exposition of my thesis that a crucial factor in motivation for, and the coming about of "structural" change is some contact during the course of treatment with life and death issues in a form which may hark back to the dawning of awareness in the infant of the differentiation of the inanimate and animate worlds. (In one sense "dead" can only be applied to that which was once "alive," but anyone who has seen childrens' encounters with death, will appreciate how formidable is the task to eventually perceive the dead as inanimate.) This is the area of the uncanny—only briefly touched more or less explicitly in treatment by some—like Mrs. A—and an area of recurrent or prolonged immersion during the treatment for other patients. These others include, but are *not* limited to, patients who are generally considered to have more severe psychopathology. While my central thesis connects change in treatment, i.e., also changed insight to the re-experience during psychoanalytic regression of early contact with the animate-inanimate border, developmental variations in coming to terms with this border could explain differences in the readiness to take action.

The change in Mrs. A's life is easily visible even in a brief presentation of the case because she *acted*—after acquiring insight—to alter her situation. Rangell (1981) has tried to understand psychoanalytically the difference between patients whose response to insight is "So what" and "I see this, but shall I do now" from those who move autonomously from insight to the initiation of change. Rangell refers to Walder's statement that "analysis offers patients "a possibility of working out a viable, non-neurotic, solution," but the limits of current formulations of the difference between those who also act from those who only understand, are illustrated by Rangell's need to include unspecified constitutional factors in the formation of more or less action-prone "executive egos." It is my hypothesis that vicissitudes in the development of the individual's ability to differentiate the animate from the inanimate contribute through the formation of self representations as animate—implying action initiating—to this behavioral dimension. Despite its importance in the background and possible emergence at nodal points of change, material related to the animate-inanimate differentiation may either not be noticed at all, or in any case, will not usually demand focused attention in the analysis of a patients with a relatively uncomplicated developmental history of this differentiation. I believe that this was the case for Mrs. A and is characteristic for many patients with so-called good "executive ego" function. I believe, however, that Mrs. A, as is the case with many patients without major "ego deficits," was spurred into action in treatment and then in life, not only through a transferentially activated confrontation with destructive wishes, but also in this context, a regressive brief encounter with the uncanny breakdown of the inanimate-animate boundary—when her husband had been transformed into "that." Inasmuch as he had, in a deep sense, been a quasi-inert instrument of contact with her father who was the real object of her live cathexis, the experience of her husband as "that" was of course accurate.

The following example also illustrated what I have come to consider a significant encounter with the animate-inanimate boundary in treatment. In one session, a brilliant and highly creative young scientist was discussing his doubts about whether or not to marry his girlfriend, the possibility that she may be pregnant, and related issues which could justify a considerable degree of emotional turmoil. Yet his agitation and, at times, bewilderment in the session seemed somehow disconnected from the content. The analyst commented on that impression and inquired about other areas in the patient's life. In response, the patient was flooded with tears and suddenly recalled a dream. He was flying over a beautiful city which he described in exquisite detail. It was, however, as he discovered when he flew lower and lower over the city and searched for signs of life, an absolutely dead city. No bustling activities downtown, no children in the school yards, no life in the residential areas. His associations led to his work. In a creative storm—working night and day—he had just solved a very fundamental problem, a problem which had been recognized for over a hundred years, about which many books had been written and about which there had been many lively controversies. He had found a simple and elegant solution to the old problem, he could fly over the city now, but the intense life around a basic scientific question, an area of research and agitation in which he had been a major participant, had come to an abrupt end. The problem was dead. The significance of the patient's achievement (and "achieving" also means killing incidentally) was soon widely recognized and led to a meteoric rise in his career. It was also noted by his colleagues that his writing sytle at this point changed radically. Although working in a rigorous and highly abstract scientific field, he was often complimented thereafter about a change from a dry style, similar to the one usual in his field, to a remarkably readable animated style which conveyed with simple elegance the growth and unfolding of his thought.

This patient had practically been raised by his father on fierce chess battles which were closely connected to his subsequent scientific intensity. Rich analytic material illustrated how his scientific breakthrough was related to oedipal issues and his ability to deal with an oedipal victory. This information does not, however, detract I believe from the significance for—and at the moment of profound change—of his contact with the uncanny boundary of the lifeless, perhaps with the *structural* difference of animate and inanimate.

Freud discusses this encounter primarily in his cultural and antropological works, although these interests are, of course, not segregated for him from clinical concerns. The topic is a central one in his paper on "The Uncanny" (1919), but in *Totem and Taboo* (1912) he already touches on the connection of the uncanny experience with the animate-inanimate boundary. "We appear to attribute an 'uncanny' quality to impressions that seek to confirm the omnipotence of thoughts and the animistic mode of thinking in general, after we have reached a stage at which, in our judgement, we have abandoned such beliefs." (Freud, Standard Edition, Vol. XIII, p. 86.)

In the two clinical examples given so far, the intrusion, the shock, was the appearance of the inanimate in an animate world. I also have an example of a patient referred to analysis because of fugue-states during which she experienced inanimate objects as strangely alive. Searles has collected rich clinical material in his work on the non-human environment. For my patient, this pseudo-animism, reexperienced in mini-fuges during analytic sessions, proved to be defensive against the reliving of a particularly unexpected encounter with death in a situation when she had made light of potential danger.

Until recently I have thought that I was simply using Winnicott's transitional object theory when I was dealing with the animate-inanimate border. The transitional object, however, is for Winnicott precisely that object which is at the same time treated as animate and inanimate. It's ambiguity, and Winnicott emphasizes that point, is unchallenged. The child, who ferociously dismembers a mama or a papa doll in play therapy, senses some anxiety in the therapist and turns around to say, "Don't worry, I know it's a doll" has at that moment integrated the transitional object in its non-challenged territory. The fugue state of our patient is the mark of the lack of integration. Schematically, animism is a defense against the encounter with the inanimate, and when this defense fails in the face of violent death wishes and death fears, when the truly inanimate threatens, the defense of dissociation may be activated.

Under the title "The Body as Transitional Object: a psychoanalytic study of a self-mutilating patient," I have previously described the work with a patient who had a severe skin disorder during the language learning period and whose later symptomatology included repeated cutting of her skin when she experienced herself as inanimate (Kafka, 1969). She stopped each cutting episode when she felt it—and she felt it—and that was unfortunately not as soon as the incision began. Today I would modify my discussion of this case somewhat, would focus more on the encounter with deadness, would emphasize more the failure of the transitional object and her compulsive search for a functioning transitional object, a search which also manifested itself in her decorating practically every inch of her room with fur. The failure of a transitional sphere to protect against absolute destruction might account for this patient's recurrent dream, a falling dream which was unusual in that she did not, as is generally the case, wake up just before reaching bottom. This patient in the dream experienced the impact of her being smashed.

The question of the essential structural differences between the animate and the inanimate has received the attention of philosophers and scientists for a long time, but before sketching in briefly some pertinent theoretical vistas, I would like to once more return to a situation in which the animate-inanimate problem presents itself perhaps most frequently and typically in psychoanalysis and psychotherapy.

A young divorcee starts her Monday morning hour with a barrage of complaints centering on her inability to cope with a baby who cries all hours of the night, a boyfriend in whom she is more interested than he in her, and without any differentiation in her tone between the things which happen to her and things which she does. She continues to complain about her own bad driving, her over-eating, over-smoking, and her wish to kill her baby. The whole thing is presented as an attack on the analyst, who has not helped her with any of these problems. She continues "It is not safe for me to drive. I have had some vague thoughts of killing myself and the car seems to agree with me. Wouldn't start."

You will recognize in this brief sketch features which some clinicians would refer to as "entitlement," a label which is frequently applied when what is the result of action, consciously or unconsciously volitional, is not differentiated from events which are external, events not related to anyone's intentionality. The therapist's problem in such situations has to do with the ego syntonicity for the patient of this lack of differentiation, the fact that it does seem so natural to the patient not to differentiate between her complaint that she smokes too much, that the car wouldn't start, or that there was a thunderstorm. Sartre in his later work, which has largely been ignored by psychoanalysts, (Ref to *Discours sur la methode*) has emphasized the distinction between praxis (actions resulting from intentionality) and the processes related to inert matter. An important axis on which change occurs, if the therapeutic efforts with the patient I described are successful, deals with the formation in the patient of a differentiation between the results of "*praxis*" on the one hand, and the inert processes or the haphazard on the other hand.

A close look at the process in the analytic session may illustrate a direct technical application of some ideas developed here. Because her car wouldn't start the patient took a taxi. This woman, whose friend had recently been mugged, experienced acute anxiety in the taxi when the driver took her over an unfamiliar route and through a part of the city where there were few people on the street. At the time of this session, several years into an analysis, the analyst had learned that any confrontation with the fact that she treated events which she had *caused* in the same manner as events with which she had apparently nothing to do was unproductive. So, having learned a lesson, the analyst asked if she had thought about the mugging while in the cab. The patient replied that she had indeed and that she had also thought about some murders she had read about in the newspaper. The analyst's next intervention was based on the idea that the danger in the atmosphere, so to speak, should be addressed rather than the location of the source of the danger since the patient's difficulties were seen by the analyst as having their roots in an uncompleted differentiation of who or what can initiate action, that is, ultimately what is animate from that which is acted upon, i.e., the inanimate. Very carefully choosing his words, the analyst said: "You have been in touch with a lot of murderous feelings since our last session. You had murderous feelings against your baby, and you had thoughts about murderous feelings directed against you." Again, what was important, I believe, is the analyst's *not* confronting the patient with his, the analyst's differentiation of praxis and process, of not differentiating for the patient the actor from the acted upon, but rather to watch carefully over the develop- ment of this differentiation in the patient. (Note however also the analyst' differentiation of "feelings" on the one hand and "thoughts about feelings" on the other.) It does not advance the work if the analyst, feeling unfairly accused and held responsible for everything that goes wrong in the patient life, might be tempted to respond, or, more realistically to retaliate with confrontation, in effect saying that the patient *should* be big enough to differentiate between what she is doing and what happens to her.

How then does such a change occur? A few months after the session described above, the patient again spoke of a series of unfortunate developments in her life. She had had a bad night. For various reasons the analyst believed that the patient was not reporting a dream. He asked: "In this terrible night, did you have any dreams?" The patient becomes restless and says: "Yes, but I can't remember." Restlessness continues and patient says after a fairly long pause: "Well, there were people, and I was literally coming apart. The buttons on my blouse wouldn't stay closed." "Too many demands pulling you apart," the analyst says. "But it is not exactly like that," the patient continues, "there was something sloppy about it. Self demeaning. I'm getting fat." Note that the patient is not attacking, does not blame the analyst for her overeating. There are some indications of embarrassment. She uses the neutral way of phrasing which had been characteristic of the analyst's way of doing it: "There was something sloppy about it." She moves to "self demeaning" which is followed by "I am getting fat." She is en route to the autonomous experience that she eats too much and that she can initiate eating less. The patient proved to be en route to more autonomous experience generally. (I won't go into how this can be reconciled with some definitions of Strachey's about change. He talks about it in terms of identifying with the analyst: how she's taking in small doses of reality about the analyst.)

In any case, becoming conscious changes process to praxis. Let me elaborate: she says she "wanted" to come to her analytic session and thought that the stalling engine was a process phenomenon, the fault of inert matter. Suppose, however, that in analysis it becomes clear that her neglect of her car is related to the ambivalence which she harbors vis-a-vis her treatment. Then the process has been changed to praxis. The unconscious transforms much that is "accidental" into meaningful sequence. Slips are no longer haphazard (a cornerstone of psychoanalytic thinking). Our discovery of the uncertainty of the boundary between the meaningful and the haphazard has its consequences however. We do not trust the border any more. Is there meaning everywhere or is there meaning nowhere?

The transformation of process into praxis also has obvious clinical consequences. If nothing is haphazard, there is either omnipotence or paranoia.

The connections between the animate-inanimate dichotomy and the usually more visible issues of boundary between inner and outer are often most clearly visible in our study of schizophrenic phenomenology, but are frequently quite visible in non-schizophrenic patients with many different diagnoses. Still, the animate-inanimate problem seems to be near the psychotic, the autistic, core. A young man who had been hospitalized for years with flagrant schizophrenic pathology, has apparently made a remarkable recovery. The degree of his insight and his descriptive abilities are considerable. He described his emergence from psychosis. He characterized his first transitory moment of feeling normal again as "feeling that he was feeling." "Feeling that he was *not* feeling" was his characterization of his abnormal state. His surroundings at that time, the walls, cars, rugs, etc., were not real, were placed there perhaps to fool him he thought, to make him believe that there was something. At times, he seemed to succeed however in a kind of "*cogito ergo sum.*" Then, he existed, but there was no possibility of having any kind of effect on what was around him. There is, he said, no possibility that what exists can have any impact on what does not exist. I interpret this as an absence of an integrated feeling of oneself as animate. His descriptions brought to my mind science fiction stories about isolated heads or perhaps brains existing in nutrient solutions. The patient said that "what saved his life" (I translate "what made him feel alive") was a psychiatric aide saying to him "you are somebody, you can do what you want." I do not know what factors were responsible for the patient's ability to *hear* at that particular moment, to experience himself as an autonomous center of action which can "connect," which can have an impact on what surrounds him. When only he existed and the other existences around him were pretend, he was not truly animate. Anima means breath, animate means movement, or the potential of a movement that connects and that in connecting establishes if the other is inert matter or is another animate center of autonomous action.

I now come to the mere theoretical part of my presentation. I would like to more specifically deal with the question of structural change and considerations of the concept of structure. I quote from Loewald (1960, p. 16), "If structural changes in the patient's personality means anything, it must mean that we assume that ego-development is resumed in the therapeutic process in psycho-analysis." For Loewald the analyst is a *new* object in the patient's life. Loewald does think of the analyst as a sculptor, but we must specify a sculptor whose vision of the finished statue is influenced by the characteristics of the marble. He frees the form which is kept captive by the stone. There are several problems with this analogy, which I will not discuss here. Loewald's conception however offers me a convenient platform for my own speculative ideas because of his emphasis on a cooperative venture and the formation of a new structure. I prefer a temporal analogy to the spatial one. Longuet Higgins has developed the conceptual model of a phonogram, using the mathematical formulae of the hologram, but substituting the time values for the space values used in the formulae. (Many of you, I'm sure, are familiar with holography. If you have a picture of a man and you cut it in two, you don't get an upper and a lower picture of the man, but rather two pictures of the whole man that are a little bit less distinct. Every point in space has some information about other points in space. In Higgin's model, temporal concepts are substituted for spatial concepts, so we have a model where each point in time has some information about all other points in time: a psychologically useful model because in our psychological present we indeed have some information about our past and some information about the future, at least the planned future.) In this model, the memory access bank is based on rhythmic, i.e., temporal structure rather than on spatial one. The structure, the new structure which is being created in the psychoanalytic work, resembles a symphony more than it does a sculpture. (In connection with temporal models of the nervous system, I would like to mention the finding by Marian Kafka, working with Dieter Naber in Germany and Anna Wirtz in Switzerland, of definite and distinct rhythms of neurotransmitter receptors.)

Although I prefer the concept of a temporal structure to that of a spatial one, Loewald's formulation of structural change remains applicable:

"The interpretation takes with the patient the step towards true regression, as against the neurotic compromise formation, thus clarifying for the patient his true regression-level which has been ... made unrecognizable by ... defensive ... structures ... by this very step it mediates to the patient the higher integrative level to be reached." The possibility for freer interplay between the unconscious and preconscious systems is thus created by the interpretation. The analytic process then consists in certain integrative experiences between patient and analyst as the foundation for the internalized version of such experiences: reorganization of ego, 'structural change' (1960, p. 25).

Elsewhere I have developed in considerable detail the notion that our subjective realities depend on object constancies, which are in turn dependent on the speed with which we scan the environment to select patterns of stimuli, patterns which are 'judged' to be subjectively equivalent. For such subjective realities of analyst and analysand to match, to overlap to a certain extent, for a certain agreement about an 'objective' reality to exist, there may have to be also some shifts in the reality organizations of the analyst. As Loewald puts it, "The analyst in his interpretations reorganizes, reintegrates unconscious material for himself as well as for the patient." To arrive at a common wave-length, the rhythms organizing reality may have to shift for both analyst and analysand in the analytic or therapeutic dyad.

At this point in the development of my ideas I would like to briefly describe an experiment by Bavelas, an experiment which I believe to be of considerable interest for our understanding of the process of change. The experimental subject is confronted with a board of which there is an array of buttons. The subject is to discover the correct pattern of pushing the buttons, and success is to be rewarded with the sound of a bell. After a while a bell sounds indeed and the subject is told to punch the correct pattern again. This time the bell sounds after a briefer interval. The process is repeated several times until the subject is interrupted and asked to describe the correct pattern. Usually the subject will describe an intricate pattern and when the experimenter tells him that there was no correct pattern, that the intervals between bell soundings were based on a theoretical learning curve, the subject simply will not believe the experimenter.

The only way to convince the subject is to have him discover that another naive subject will discover a completely different pattern and will be equally convinced of its correctness and distrustful of the former subject, now experimentor, when he informs him of the coupling of the bell intervals to a theoretical learning curve. The experimental subject is of course correct when he says he has been lied to. The only error is the timing of when he was lied to. The lie was when he was told there was a correct pattern of pushing the buttons. I think it is an experiment of some interest to all therapists. Although we could profitably discuss this experiment in terms of its implications that role changes are necessary for alteration in belief systems and how such role changes may be related to the flow of transference and countertransference, trial identifications, etc., there may be a more profound way of looking at the experiment of Bavelas. A perhaps somewhat oversimplified statement of the views of Jacques Monod is that the universe is chaotic and that our perceptions of order, or our hopes of discovering ever greater, more encompassing and fundamental laws of nature, are vain. If this is so, if there is no ordered structure, then the establishment of any shared views of reality, any possibility of communication, any common wave-length between analyst and analysand—in our context—is truly remarkable. We really do create our own structures, and to some extent structures which we can share with each other, in a universe, which, if Monod is correct, is unstructured.

Whether or not, however, the universe is ultimately chaotic, a shared structure is formed between the mothering figure and the infant, an area of shared realities without which communication would be impossible. It is Loewald's—and also my—view that shared realities, which again make communication possible where it had previously been crippled, are constructed in the interaction process between analyst and analysand. This is the structural change, which can be expressed in such conventional psychoanalytic terminology, for instance, as "a change from an archaic, severe superego to a more benign one."

A few more words about the nature of structure in our field. David Rapoport, recognizing that the term "structure" could lead to a reification which is counterproductive to our theory building, developed the notion that structure differs from function only in their respective rates of change. Structure is not static. The order of magnitude of the rate of change of a psychological structure compared to the rate of change of what we commonly call psychic function corresponds to the differences between the rate of change of geological epochs compared to the rates of change, for instance, of a fast runner.

The de-reification, the de-materialization of structure also receives support from Ann Hayman's study of how psychoanalysts actually use a structural concept such as id. In her paper "What do we mean by id?" she describes her finding a practically exclusive adjectival use of the concept. Patients talk more or less "iddish."

A brief mention should also be made here of a recent development in the understanding of structural change in physics, a development which several psychiatrists, including Ciompi in Switzerland and Arnold Mandel in San Diego, believe to be relevant to our field. Prigogine's dissipative structures deal with such matters as heat diffusion in liquids and the fact that under certain circumstances there is a sudden switch from conduction to convection, the emergence of a structure, the formation of regular, mostly hexagonal convection cells, a kind of streaming molecular cooperation replacing the speeded up random molecular activity. The possible direct applicability of the physical findings to groups of nerve cells—a semi-liquid mass—is being studied by some, while others are exploring the possible behavioral and psychiatric analogies, mood switches and switches into psychosis, using the mathematical tools developed in connection with Prigogine's work. It is in any case not surprising that psychiatrists are interested in work dealing with the formation of new structures. Could the formal description of a system permitting the formation of new structures (apparently a system in which the second level of thermodynamics does not hold) be pertinent to the formal description of animate structures? Bipolar fluctuations are involved in Prigogine's physics and our thinking about psychic structures seems always to involve polarities, even when we return to clinical ground from such abstract speculations.

The distinction between self and other, between inside and outside is closely linked to the differentiation between animate and inanimate, yet I believe, it is not the same.

At this point, my working hypothesis remains that the animate and the inanimate are "representational structures" which serve as anchors in our organization of ourselves, and thus as anchors in the interpersonal network which makes communication possible. The structural differences between the animate and inanimate are, I believe, fundamental. This difference must be learned on all levels, and the learning on all levels must be integrated to avoid the danger of *action* contamination of our ideational contact with and use of the inanimate. When there has been a wrong hook-up, so to speak, when a human is experienced as inanimate, a true regression in the analysis occurs and a restructuring is not only essential but may be precipitated by the encounter.

Research on infancy is a particularly active field at present—Joseph Lichtenberg has surveyed much of it recently—and in such work the development of the differentiation of the animate and inanimate is bound to receive considerable attention. Much of Piaget's work, (especially on decentering), being increasingly integrated with analytic thinking, is pertinent and I believe that clarification of the development of the animate-inanimate differentiation will contribute to our understanding of the process of change in treatment. Margaret Mahler has called my attention to some early research on the infant's reaction to, differential grasp of a proffered finger, a gloved finger, a glove without finger and a stick. This is some research by Sternamen in 1947 in which the infant differentiates between these stimuli in the first hours of life. As usual, a fairy tale has already dealt with our topic. The "raw-cooked," the fundamental cannabilistic anxiety of the animate-inanimate boundary is dealt with in the story of Hansel and Gretel. The witch in Hansel and Gretel obviously cannot make the distinction between the animate and the inanimate and it is this characteristic which permits Hansel and Gretel to survive, since the witch, mistaking stick for finger, believes the children are not yet fat enough to eat. If we were to psychoanalyze the witch and the distinction integrated on all levels of learning between animate and inanimate were again possible for her, her cannibalistic tendencies would undoubtedly become confined to the ideational or fantasy level and she would be much less prone to act like a witch.

References

Cohen, Robert (1982). Notes on the Life and Work of Frieda Fromm-Reichmann. Psychiatry 45(#2): 90-98.

Hoff, Sylvia (1982). Frieda Fromm-Reichmann, The Early Years. Psychiatry 45(#2): 115-121.

Kafka, John (1969). The Body as Transitional Object: A Study of a Self-Mutilating Patient. British Journal of Medical Psychology 42: 207-212.

Loewald, Hans (1960). On the Therapeutic Action of Psychoanalysis. International Journal of Psycho-Analysis 41: 16-33.

Rangell, Leo (1981). From Insight to Change. Journal of the American Psychoanalytic Assn. 29: 119.

Archives of General Psychiatry 25: 232-239

Chapter 12

Ambiguity for Individuation:
A Critique and Reformulation of
Double-Bind Theory

From the Family Development Section. Child Research Branch. National Institute of Mental Health, the Department of Psychiatry, George Washington University School of Medicine, and the Washington Psychoanalytic Institute, Washington. DC. Presented in part at Chestnut Lodge in 1963 and 1965, at the National Institute of Mental Health in 1966 and 1969, and at the Double-Bind Symposium of the 77th annual meeting of the American Psychological Association, Washington, DC. September 1969.

C linical observations suggest a link between dissociative experiences in adult patients and underexposure to ambiguous communications during certain developmental phases. Formal characteristics of ambiguous and paradoxical communications are examined in detail. A theory is proposed which connects parental fear and intolerance of ambiguity with the offspring's inability to integrate paradoxical aspects of reality. This theory is contrasted with the double-bind theory which states that an abundance of certain paradoxical communications is schizophrenogenic. The "therapeutic double-bind" is seen as a "replacement" of essential paradoxical communications which were scarce and inadequate rather than overabundant during crucial developmental phases.

Thoughts concerning a number of separate clinical and theoretical projects can be profitably considered under the general heading on positive aspects of ambiguity, the significance of the hunger for, and the tolerance of, ambiguity. In order to organize these thoughts, it is necessary to consider the formal definition of ambiguity. Although in everyday language information is often said to be ambiguous when it is conflictual, in the language of formal logic information is ambiguous only when the conflicting data are of different "logical type," ie, are on different levels of abstraction. Formally, ambiguity is an abbreviation of the expression "ambiguity of types" or—more completely—"ambiguity of logical types." A paradoxical communication can always be shown to consist of conflicting data which are on different levels of abstraction. Although psychologically we associate uncertainty with ambiguity more than with paradox, ambiguous and paradoxical communications are logically synonymous.

The formally best developed aspects of double-bind theory emphasize that overexposure to paradoxical communication is pathogenic or, more specifically, schizophrenogenic. Since clinical observation suggested that the exposure to ambiguous situations which is unavoidable in daily life was less tolerable, more "dissociative," and more "uncanny" for those who had early underexposure to paradoxical communications, I found myself in apparent opposition to the main tenet of double-bind theory. Furthermore, this underexposure of the offspring to ambiguity during crucial developmental phases seemed related to parental fear of paradox.

Double-bind theorists also refer to "therapeutic double-binds" which are, however, formally similar to the pathogenic variety. They are described as occurring in a more benevolent interpersonal atmosphere, but their formal similarity creates conceptual difficulties and is an obstacle to the research application of the theory.

In addition to the clinically based interest in ambiguity, the search for concepts useful in the design of longitudinal family research has also led to a detailed examination of double-bind theory. The infinite variety of the content of communications is difficult to manage in any research design. A theory proposing the identification of pathogenic communications on the basis of formal characteristics which transcend content is therefore of great interest. If it had indeed been possible to identify such

pathogenic double-bind communications on the basis of formal characteristics alone, it would have been relatively easy to locate young parents
who have a tendency to communicate in this fashion, and their offspring
could have been contrasted later with those of parents not prone to issue
such double-bind messages. Difficulties encountered in objective studies
using the double-bind concept have recently been reviewed by Olson.[1]
Our own difficulties in identifying "pathogenic double-binders" were
related to the problem of discriminating between benevolent "therapeutic" vs pathogenic binds, to the ubiquity of paradox (for instance, wives
asking husbands to be spontaneously more affectionate[2]), to the observation that in human communication the level of abstraction is in
constant flux, and to the finding that shifts in levels of abstraction could
probably not be differentiated from shifts in role relationship. While
double-bind theory was not directly useful for the intended research
design, the analysis of the difficulties and a critical examination of the
theory contributed to a reformulation.

Critical Evaluation of Double-Bind Theory

What, more precisely is double-bind theory? It states that a history of exposure to inescapable traps is schizophrenogenic, and attempts to explain the
patient's feeling of being trapped, an experience to which the therapist has
easy empathic access. Bateson et al[3] give recognizable examples such as that
of a "young man who had fairly well recovered from an acute schizophrenic
episode (and who) was visited in the hospital by his mother. He was glad to
see her and impulsively put his arm around her shoulders, whereupon she
stiffened. He withdrew his arm and she asked, 'Don't you love me any
more?' He then blushed, and she said, 'Dear, you must not be so easily embarrassed and afraid of your feelings.'" The patient has received the
messages that he must, and that he most not, show his affection to her in
order to keep his ties with his mother. Impressed by and sensitized to such
"impossible no win" situations, the clinician seemingly encounters them
everywhere. The father of a schizophrenic girl, for instance, has made major changes in his career in order to pay for her treatment in a private
hospital. Despite a recent heart attack, this clergyman has left his pulpit, has

become a hard driving nationally prominent lecturer and author. During a visit to the hospital he explains both to his daughter and to the staff that he owes his new-found energy, this renewal in his life, to the financial needs of her expensive hospitalization. One could say, on the basis of these data, that the patient is caught in a double-bind. If she makes successful efforts to recover rapidly, she deprives her father of the reported renewal in his life. If, on the other hand, she fails to improve sufficiently to be discharged from the hospital, the associated financial need imposes a "killing" workload on father. On the face of it, she is in a no-win situation.

A similar trap apparently characterizes the following case: The musically talented son of a conductor has received communications from his family throughout his early life to the effect that the only truly valuable lifetime activity is to be a musician. In the same breath he has been told again and again about tragedies associated with sons of musicians attempting to follow in their fathers' footsteps. Not only is the competitive effort destructive to the son, but he was told it is usually also destructive to the family name, to father's fame. Despite his fervently expressed wish for musical training, such an education was withheld from him in this musically saturated household. At the age of 6 or 7, he developed a peculiar mannerism of running to his father, making a "staccato" contact, briefly throwing his arms around him and then running away from him as fast as he could. Prominent features of the clinical picture were an extreme vacillation from notions of grandeur to feelings of abject worthlessness, a fractionation of self-representation and a general ideational lack of continuity. We will later amplify this and other case material, but these examples show that the "damned if you do and damned if you don't" situation described by the double-bind theory offers a seductively elegant and immediately plausible framework in which to place clinical observations.

While Bateson et al[3] have heavily emphasized the pathogenic double-bind, they have observed "therapeutic double-binds"; "benevolent" binds in therapy which they illustrate with the following example: The patient informs the therapist of her delusional god. The therapist, Frieda Fromm-Reichmann in this instance, tells the patient that she, the therapist, does not believe in this god and then instructs the patient to ask her delusional god for permission to work in therapy with the doctor.

The therapist has her patient in a "therapeutic double-bind." If the patient is rendered doubtful about her belief in her god then she is agreeing with Dr. Fromm-Reichmann, and is admitting her attachment to therapy. If she insists that god is real, then she must tell him that Dr. Fromm-Reichmann is "more powerful" than he—again admitting her involvement with the therapist.

The "therapeutic," like the "pathogenic" double-bind is formed by conflicting information involving a shift in the level of abstraction. The similarity of the formally best defined features of therapeutic and pathogenic binds greatly complicates attempts to identify them differentially for research purposes in the study of actual communication sequences, *if one conceives of and looks for paradoxes which may "promote individuation"* and in this sense could perhaps be called "therapeutic"—in nontherapy situations.

Bateson and his co-workers focus, however, on the role they ascribe to the double-bind in the etiology of schizophrenia when they indicate that the necessary ingredients for a double-bind situation involve: (1) two or more persons, ... (2) repeated experience, ... (3) a primary negative injunction, ... (4) a secondary injunction conflicting with the first at a more abstract level (italics mine) and like the first, enforced by punishment or signals which threaten survival, ... (5) a tertiary negative injunction prohibiting the victim from escaping from the field. ... What most specifically, pointedly, and most interestingly distinguishes this from other conflict theories is the focus of the shift in the level of abstraction. Such qualitatively different conflicts are paradoxes. How does a paradox, a term synonymous with "ambiguity of type," differ from a contradiction? Watzlawick et al.[4] illustrate a contradiction by a stop sign to which is nailed another sign saying "no stopping at any time." In this contradictory situation one has the choice to obey one or the other of the two injunctions. Presumably a father asking his son not to tattletale and also inviting him to report how his younger sister got into trouble corresponds to such a contradictory request. Presumably the son can *choose* which injunction to obey, but the role relationship between father and son is different in the context of the "no tattletale" injunction and in the context of the request for information about sister. The latter request may carry the implication "son, you are in this particular situation seen more like an adult, like me, and should help me to protect and educate a child." The question of the possible correspondence between shifts in role relationship and shifts in levels of abstraction raises doubts about the existence of *pure* contradictions in ordinary communication. It certainly is another factor complicating the identification of paradoxes as opposed to contradictions when actual communication sequences are analyzed for research purposes. Watzlawick et al. formally illustrate a paradox by a photograph of an overpass spanning a roadbed. To this overpass is attached a sign saying "ignore this sign." This sign "(a practical joke, we assume)" is formally not "contradictory," but ". . . creates a true paradox through its self-reflexivity: in order to obey the injunction of ignoring it, one first has to notice it. But this very act of noticing it is in disobedience of the injunction itself. Therefore, this sign can only be obeyed by disobeying it." The nature of such paradoxes, Bateson et al. point out. has been studied by Whitehead and Russell.[5] Russell's theory of types deals with the observation that paradoxes involve different levels of abstraction which are not immediately apparent. The above "ignore this sign" paradox, for instance, contains such a hidden shift since the word "sign" and the actual material sign on which the word is written involve different levels of abstraction. Whitehead and Russell would say that in the above sentence I have made explicit the hidden shift in "logical types," I have communicated about the paradoxical communication, i.e., I have "meta-communicated" and have thus escaped the paradox. The relevance of this aspect of a formal logical approach to a theory postulating that the future schizophrenic individual is inundated by paradoxical communications, coupled with taboos against "meta-communicating" about these paradoxes, is apparent. There is, however, another aspect of Whitehead and Russell's work which is more congruent with the reformulation which is here being proposed.

Reformulation

The reformulation focuses on the *effects* of relative parental avoidance of expression of paradox and of poor parental tolerance of ambiguity: These effects are experiences of dissonance for the developing offspring who is confronted by other experiential data which are ambiguous, full of paradox, and which all have to be somehow included in his "reality." In contrast, parental tolerance of the child's relatively free, unchallenged, and playful travel in the no-man's land in which irreconcilable paradoxes coexist, in which one is compelled both to notice and not to notice them, permits relative "integration" of parental, and gradually evolving individual, formulations of realities. Such integration aids the acceptance of parents as "objects" in the psychoanalytic sense of the word—and makes possible a necessary degree of accommodation to paradoxical systems which are to represent reality.

While this thesis is primarily derived from and will be supported by clinical observations, even the following briefly summarized excursion into modern formal logic reveals the forceful emergence of a similar, or at least congruent, theme.

Formal Basis of Reformulation

While Bateson focused on Russell's techniques for escaping paradoxes, Whitehead and Russell recommend the use of their escape technique only after one has been caught in a trap. They specifically warn, however, against too much caution to avoid traps. They point out that reasoning would have to come to a standstill if attempts were made to rigorously avoid the possibility of paradox even in the most formal logical chain. Specifically they talk of the necessity of ambiguity of types in order to ". . . make one chain of reasoning applicable to any of an infinite number of different cases, which would not be possible if we were to forego the use of typically ambiguous words and symbols." Thus, even the classical syllogism contains some "ambiguity of types." Oversimplifying almost shamelessly the concepts involved, let us consider the syllogism, "All men are mortal. Socrates is a man. Therefore, Socrates is mortal." Not quite so, would say Russell: we do not know that Socrates is mortal until he is dead. While Whitehead and Russell describe their observations concerning the necessity for ambiguity, this is a part of their work in which they do not present formal proofs. In this respect, Kurt Gödel "has gone beyond them by proving formally the necessity of paradoxes in nontrivial systems by demonstrating the necessary incompleteness of a finite system. What Gödel formally proved (Nagel and Newman, 1958) is that". . . if arithmetic is consistent, its consistency cannot be established by metamathematical reasoning that can be represented within the formalism of arithmetic."

Nagel and Newman, who have made Gödel's work accessible to the non-mathematician, point out (p. 98) that Gödel's argument does not eliminate the possibility of strictly finitistic proofs that cannot be represented within arithmetic. But no one today appears to have a clear idea on what a finitistic proof would be like that is not capable of formulation within arithmetic. What is significant about Gödel's work in connection with the proposed reformulation, is his demonstration that one has to jump to ever more inclusive levels of abstraction even in formal logical procedures in order to avoid triviality. He thus offers formal support to Whitehead and Russell's more impressionistic warning not to avoid the possibility of paradoxes. This is congruent with a clinically based reformulation emphasizing the psychological necessity of appropriate exposure to ambiguity. Gödel's demonstration may also facilitate a sharpening of conceptual focus in this reformulation: The developing individual, who must operate in an open system, experiences dissonance for which he has not been prepared when his parents operate and communicate as though a closed system were the only one in existence.

If self-consistency in a closed system is associated with triviality in modern logic, reduction to one level of abstraction is, in operational terms, unthinkable in living systems, especially in human experience and communication. The study of our very perceptual process seems to indicate that with each perception we pass rapidly through various stages and levels of organization. Tachistoscopic presentation of Rorschach cards8 shows that we recapitulate our perceptual history—the briefest exposures resulting in the most "concrete" responses resembling those of a child and longer exposures involving higher levels of abstraction, adult responses. Thus, after having been so rigorous in our distinction of contradiction which involves one level, and paradox which involves more than one level of abstraction, we can relax a bit—a conversation, words spoken and heard, any living communication on one level of abstraction is indeed unthinkable. Strictly speaking, any live contradiction is a paradox, but what created our sharp "paradoxical experience" with the "ignore this sign" sign was the degree of our unpreparedness for the nature of the shift in the levels of abstraction involved.

(Certain transitional periods, such as courtship and early marriage, involve considerable shifts—for which one may be poorly prepared—in role relationships and in the levels of abstraction which have to be bridged. If the magnitude of the shifts makes it necessary, semiritualized intervention of "third parties" permits bride and groom to have a discontinuity of experience before they are presented with a "new reality." Some social factors which help bridge experiences of discontinuity have been considered in a study of "Separating and Joining Influences in Courtship and Early Marriage.")

Our excursion into formal logic was useful and, I believe, necessary. Our psychological "reality" depends on our abstracting level of the moment. Klüver (1933-36) had noticed that the traditional experimental study of the smallest difference between two stimuli to which the organism can respond led to psychologically uninteresting findings. He therefore studied how great the differences between stimuli can be before a subject would fail to recognize similarities. This method determines the parameters of stimuli which the individual abstracts and the greatest distance of the levels of abstraction within which there is subjective equivalence. The notion has been developed in a previous publication (1964) that such patterns of "subjective equivalence," the patterns of organization, of abstraction, are the very building blocks of our realities, of our patterns of "object constancy" as the term is used both in experimental psychological and psychoanalytic literature. If one individual's "reality possibilities" are thus tied to the range of his levels of abstraction, his communication to another depends on some degree of correspondence between his and the other's range of levels of abstraction. We constantly gauge the level of abstraction to which any partner in a conversation will carry our words—our timing depends on it— and Searles' (1965) clinical descriptions imply veritable acrobatics in shifts of levels of abstraction.

There are distances in levels for which we are prepared and there are distances for which we are not prepared. The differences between these are objectively quantitative, but they lead to subjectively experienced qualitative differences. Psychologically, the former range of distances are associated with experiences we may continue to call contradictions, and the latter is associated with experiences we may continue to call paradoxes. The former are related to "ambivalence" and the latter to a somewhat uncanny feeling, a mild form of which we experience when we think of ourselves as trapped (when in a mood in which we cannot quite laugh it off) by the "ignore this sign" sign.

Our use of the terms ambiguity and paradox in further clinical discussions will reflect the above considerations. A patient, for instance, who cuts herself to find out whether or not she is alive, is trying to escape from *ambiguity* and not a simple contradiction since the distance between the levels of abstraction involved in experiencing "aliveness" and "deadness" is not one for which she is, at that moment, prepared.

Clinical Basis of Reformulation

The very interest in paradoxical communications led to the observation that they were ubiquitous. This in turn led to a questioning of their specific schizophrenogenic role, even when the qualifications specified by double-bind theory for their pathogenicity were considered. On closer analysis, the impression was gained that there might even be a relative paucity of ambiguous expression in some families of schizophrenic patients. Ringuette and Kennedy (1966) have found that a group of experts, i.e., individuals who had been involved in the development and formulation of the double-bind concept, had a poor inter-judge reliability in identifying double-binds in letters written by mothers of schizophrenic patients. In our experience, when clinicians tend to agree on the existence of a double-bind, they are referring to situations in which patients, and more typically parents of patients, have made striking and bizarre defensive maneuvers when confronted with the paradoxes they had expressed. Compared to random clinical material the paradoxes themselves are often not particularly unusual, but it is the response to confrontation which forces the issue into the therapist's awareness. The letters in the Ringuette and Kennedy study do not permit the clinician to observe such responses to confrontation with paradoxes.

The paradox itself is actually not so unusual in the example of the clergyman who communicated to his hospitalized daughter and to the staff that her expensive hospitalization was forcing him to adopt a "never more happy" lifestyle and a pace which, while leading to success and self-discovery, was also "killing him." No set of clinical vignettes can be fully convincing, but in this and many other instances the impression was gained that the response to confrontation with the paradox—which involved the issue of the clergyman's life or death on one level and the quality of his life on another level of abstraction—was unusual. In a late afternoon interview, the family consultant at the hospital made an initial attempt to "play back" to the father the "no win" situation in which this communication was apparently placing his daughter. An appointment was made to explore the matter further the next morning but, when the family consultant arrived for that interview, he was given a message that father had suddenly left town. Father's message indicated that his presence in another city was suddenly required because his other daughter who lived there had telephoned him and informed him of a suddenly disturbed and involved relationship with her psychiatrist. Shortly thereafter the patient's family transferred our patient to another hospital, and father never responded to the family consultant's efforts to communicate with him.

Sometimes the intolerance of ambiguity is revealed by a rigidity, tending to the bizarre, with which family myths are maintained. In the previously mentioned example of the conductor's son, a decade of intensive analytic work with this patient, a decade during which the therapist also had some direct contact with members of his family, revealed the rigidity of several family myths and the extent to which father was a frozen mythical figure. While the grandeur and the untouchability of this paternal figure, the assignation of the only and ultimate value to it on the one hand, and the taboo against emulating it on the other, were impressive, this paradox is nevertheless not so unusual if we consider it against the background of a patriarchal culture from which this family came. Any attempts by the therapist to discuss more or less directly with the patient's mother the no-win situation in which her son was placed was met by blank stares and total incomprehension. It was simply not in the accepted script. When the therapist then attempted to approach the matter more indirectly by discussing the lives of various family members, he encountered repeatedly the style of defending the untouchability of the myth which is illustrated by the following example: The patient's mother was describing how her now deceased husband had been determined to follow his own inspired musical career despite the tremendous pressure placed on him by his own family to follow a technical one. The same day, she said with much emphasis, on which he was supposed to register for a technical course (in his home town) he went to register in the musical conservatory in the city of X. The therapist indicated that the clarification of minor matters can sometimes be of importance in connection with therapy. Was it possible that he registered a few days later since the city of X is a great distance from the home town? "No," she said again emphatically, "he took a plane so he could do it the same day." Although this supposed event occurred long before the era of commercial aviation, the "same day" of registration was part of the literal and verbatim untouchable family myth and could therefore not be tampered with even if the recital of surrounding circumstances had to be distorted). Mythical structures cannot be approached with playful ambiguity to which they are particularly vulnerable. Herein lies the connecting link between the life and death seriousness of the defense of the family myth and the problem of tolerance of ambiguity. The child prepared to deal only with myths is ill prepared to deal with living beings and live experiences.

In a sense the timeless rigidity of the mythical being or object is the opposite of the fluidity of play, of the toy, of the transitional object.[16] A lack of preparation for the necessary integration of ambiguous experience was also the common element of two cases which were reported in detail elsewhere.[12,17,18] The *uncanniness* which characterized the experiences of a patient who had many déjà vu sensations and also the experiences of a self-mutilator could be traced to paradoxical experiences for which they were especially ill prepared.

The security blanket belonging to Linus of comic strip fame corresponds roughly to the concept of the "transitional object" as described by Winnicott. In the previously published study of the psychoanalytic treatment of the self-mutilating patient,[17] the theme was developed that she used her own body as such a transitional object. For Linus, the security blanket is half alive, transitional between animate and inanimate; in the inner world of fantasy it can be treated as if it were alive, and in the external world of reality it is not alive. Problems related to touching and skin sensitivity were prominent since the patient's infancy when she was gravely ill during the first year of her life with a generalized dermatitis. As a young adult she treated her own body as if it were still repeatedly on the brink of becoming experienced as alive. She experienced anesthesia at the beginning of each cutting episode which she terminated as soon as she experienced pain. Self-mutilation was used repeatedly to deal with her profound unconscious doubts about the aliveness of her body and her preoccupation with the unfinished work of differentiating external from internal reality. Genetically, the intensity of the early contact hunger, and the pain when there *was* contact, was conceptualized as a traumatic fixation point, an area of still strikingly unfinished business when analysis began, an area in which the "task of keeping inner and outer reality separate yet interrelated"[18] was particularly difficult. The probability that a rather dramatic connection existed in this case between the early skin disease and the later symptom may offer a lead. It was speculated that, although less dramatically, early traumatic fixation points, relating particularly to the formation of the membrane of the body scheme, may play a part in the developmental history of other patients with the cutting syndrome.

Uncanniness (ref 19) is an appropriate term to describe the experiences the patient conveyed about her state just prior to cutting. This uncanniness was related to equally strong convictions that she must somehow be alive, but that she did not feel alive. Cutting was an escape from this intolerable burden of ambiguity. I have now come to see her treatment of her body as a transitional object as a special case of an attempt to work on what Winnicott calls the "perpetual human task of keeping inner and outer reality separate yet interrelated." Winnicott's development of the theme that a "neutral area of experience which will not be challenged" is important during specific development phases—he says the pattern of transitional phenomena begins to show at about four to six to eight to twelve months—(p. 232) is congruent with the theme being developed here. The "lack of challenge," or I would say the tolerance of ambiguity, permits the gradual formation of a membrane which is ego-syntonic to the extent to which it was not prematurely and externally imposed but individually established through much active exploratory crossing and recrossing of the culturally poorly or ambiguously defined border territory. In my work with this patient I experienced some sadistic feelings which I believe were at times an escape for me from *my* uncanny experiences which were triggered by my contact with her. These uncanny experiences were related, I believe, to the patient's "undigested," dissociated transitional states involving the animate vs "inanimate" nature of her own body. I now consider the above as one, and the case material which follows as another, special case involving experiences of ambiguity for which the individual was poorly prepared.

A patient who reported many *déjà vu* experiences and who came to psychoanalysis in connection with some hysterical fugue states experienced minor repetitions of such states during her sessions. In these hours, characterized by a somewhat trance-like atmosphere, references to ongoing experiences of synesthesia were prominent. A shiny object in the office, for instance, would be experienced and described as a "shrill (sounding) object." At this point a experience would be reported and frequently a comment made about the uncanniness or *déjà vu* awesomeness of the moment. After several minutes of "heavy" silence, an early memory of the "atmosphere." ie, a synesthetic blending of the sounds, sights, rhythms, tastes, smells, etc, of a certain place and/or time would emerge. A fragmented image from a fugue episode could then be traced to either a fact or fantasy associated with the time or place characterized by the remembered "atmosphere."

Impressed by the association of synesthetic and *déjà vu* phenomena,[18] I have previously proposed the following formulation in an attempt to explain this connection: To present the idea schematically, let us imagine that a certain wave pattern on an oscilloscope can represent visual, auditory, or tactile stimuli. A responding organism or electronic scanning machine may be asked if this is a familiar pattern, be it visual, auditory, or tactile, or it may simply be asked if this is a familiar *visual* pattern. Obviously, if the response is to the pattern, whatever the sensory modality involved, the likelihood that it will be familiar is much increased. In other words, if a certain pattern of stimulation, let us say a visual pattern, occurs at a time when the sensory compartments are particularly interwoven, particularly blended, the chances that this pattern will arouse a feeling of familiarity are multiplied since a *déjà vu* or related sensation will be aroused if the pattern of the visual stimulation evokes an echo in *any* other sensory compartment, if it corresponds to a previous pattern of stimulation, be it auditory, tactile, etc. Schachtel (1947) has eloquently developed the theme that infantile amnesia is related *not* to the content of early infantile experiences but to the fact that the schemata of experience are different from the adult ones. Synesthesia is more characteristic of early, and sensory compartmentalization is more characteristic of later, experiences. Elsewhere I have reported clinical evidence that the "*déjà vu* patient" had experienced premature demands for task oriented behavior involving sensory compartmentalization at times when playful "dreamy" synesthetic experience was wished for and would have been more appropriate. I came to conceptualize some of her difficulties as related to insufficient opportunity to cross and re-cross without challenge the "transitional" area between synesthesia and sensory compartmentalization. The uncanny affect of the *déjà vu* experience ("I just caught myself experiencing something as familiar which I know is not familiar") has a similarity to the slightly uncanny affect one experiences after having been trapped by reading the sign "ignore this sign." If feelings of uncanniness are understood as occurring when typically ambiguous experiences of about equally convincing strength are present simultaneously, we can see that this condition is met in the *déjà vu* experience. One doubts one's senses, one has trouble with one's "me-ness." I no longer believe that synesthesia is necessarily involved in *déjà vu* experiences. What I still believe is that *some* ambiguity, be it sensory blending vs sensory compartmentalization, animate vs inanimate, linear vs nonlinear systems of "causality," or some other source of ambiguity, may be particularly strange and unacceptable to individuals of whom well-compartmentalized ego functioning was demanded at a time when normally a parent more adequately fulfills this function and permits the child to indulge without danger in the richness of blending or other ambiguous experiences. Without describing here the course of therapy, it is possible to indicate that for the self-mutilator and for the patient with fugue states and *déjà vu* experiences, therapy involved processes of re-acceptance of, or perhaps acceptance of, or more specifically a *learning to be less unfamiliar with, feelings of estrangement*. In work with hospital-ized patients, [21,22] the risk that the patient will be removed from treatment by a parent most intolerant of ambiguity has led to approach-es to the work with families which combine necessary myth-breaking with precautionary measures. These techniques include contact with a large number of family members and the selective joint interviewing of individuals who have avoided being alone with each other.

Comment

Formal and clinical considerations of two kinds of conflicting commu-nication, contradictions which theoretically involve one, and paradoxes or ambiguities which involve more than one, level of abstraction, have led to the belief that human experience and interaction always involve more than one level of abstraction. *Subjectively*, the handling of conflict-ing data, which involves distances in levels of abstraction for which we are prepared, is seen as contradictory and may be associated with feel-ings of ambivalence particularly when the contradictory pulls are of approximately equal strength. Conflicting data involving distances in levels of abstraction for which we are *not* prepared are seen as paradoxi-cal or ambiguous and, particularly when the conflicting data are of approximately equal strength (as in *déjà vu*), are associated with experi-ences or dissonance, of uncanniness, various degrees of loss of feelings of "me-ness," or depersonalization.

Living involves considerable paradoxical experience and struggle with paradoxical systems which represent reality (from mild *déjà vu* sensations to wave vs particle theory). More centrally, individuation without alienation involves the development of personal "realities" which incorporate paradoxical discontinuities of the personal from maternal or parental realities. Parental tolerance of ambiguity which is communicated in a style, to a degree and with timing more or less appropriate for the developmental level of the child, is conceptualized as necessary for the offspring's individuation and for the prevention of "pathologic" degrees of "splitting," alienation and dissonance. (Although I am not prepared to say schizophrenia as such.) Such a beneficial, non-pathogenic tolerance is seen as embedded in a communication system in which an anchoring in a reality common to parent and child has been achieved—an overlap in the child's, the family's, and the larger society's "subjective equivalences" or in their levels of abstraction.

Such formulations relating to the positive aspects of ambiguity have implications for research and therapeutic conceptualizations. Attempts to identify parents or parents-to-be who are "pathogenic double-binders" were not successful—probably because of difficulties inherent in double-bind theory. Ryder, Goodrich et al.2-[23-27] have, however, generated interaction test data concerning modes of behavior of couples who are confronted with irreconcilable information. Subjects in these experiments may decide, for instance, that their spouses or the experimenters are tricking them, or they may doubt their own functioning, they may to varying degrees leave the question open, they may or may not communicate about their doubts or tentative conclusions. On the basis of the formulations advanced in this paper, couples and/or individuals whose task performance deteriorates when they are confronted with irreconcilable data and who do not meta-communicate about the paradoxical situation in which they find themselves, could be expected to deal poorly with their individuating offspring who will confront them with reality experiences paradoxical to their own. Any such prediction concerning parental help or interference with individuation would, of course, hinge on the extent to which performance in a laboratory task with one's spouse is predictive of naturalistic behavior with one's child. Attempts to rate ambiguity tolerance in interview material are still crude, but may be of some limited use. Some adaptations of Berlyne's[28] experimental techniques to determine the optimum ambiguity range—optimum for the maintenance of interest—might also be useful in locating parents with wide and narrow optimum ranges.

In the framework of the reformulation which is being proposed here, the *"therapeutic double-bind"* is conceptualized more parsimoniously than in the original theory as a kind of replacement in therapy of what was missing during crucial developmental phases, i.e., adequate exposure to paradoxes which prepare the person for life as a separate and unique individual, paradoxes which are conceptualized as an essential component of the very process of individuation. This therapeutic application of ambiguity does not refer, however, to any planned or calculated use of paradox or irrationality, but rather to the ambiguities which naturally emerge in the flow and counterflow of transference and countertransference in a relationship in which communications and meta-communications are appropriate to the mixture of developmental levels which characterize both the patient and the therapist.

(Alex Rosenberg, professor of mathematics at Cornell University, called my attention to the work of Kurt Gödel.)

References

1. Olson, D.H. (1969). *Empirically unbinding the double-bind.* Read before the 119th annual meeting of the American Psychological Association, Washington, DC.

2. Ryder, R.G. (1970). Dimensions of early marriage. *Family Process* 9:51-68.

3. Bateson, G., Jackson, D.D., Haley, J., et al. (1956). Toward a theory of schizophrenia. *Behavorial Sciences* 1:251-264.

4. Watzlawick, P., Beavin, J.H., Jackson, D.C. (1967). *Pragmatics of Human Communication.* New York: W.W. Norton & Co, Inc.

5. Whitehead, J.N., Russell, B. (1910). *Principa Mathematica.* Cambridge, Mass.: Cambridge University Press.

6. Gödel, K. (1931). Uber formal unentscheidbare Satze der Principia Mathematica und verwandter Systemie: I. *Mschr Mathematik Phxjsik* 38:173-198.

7. Nagel, E., Newman, J.R. (1958). *Gödel's Proof.* New York: New York University Press.

8. Stein, M.I. (1949). Personality factors involved in temporal development of Rorschach responses. *Rorschach Research Exchange & Journal of Projective Techniques* 13:355-414.

9. Ryder, G., Kafka, J.S., Olson, D.H. *Separating and joining influences in courtship and early marriage.* Unpublished.

10. Klüuver, H. (1936). The study of personality and the method of equivalent and non-equivalent stimuli. *Character Personality* 5:91-112.

11. Klüver, H. (1933). *Behavior Mechanisms in Monkeys.* Chicago, University of Chicago Press.

12. Kafka, J.S. (1964). Technical applications of a concept of multiple reality. *International Journal of Psycho-analysis* 45:575-578.

13. Kafka, J.S. (1957). *On the Experience of Duration in Psychotherapy.* Read before the Chestnut Lodge Symposium, Rockville, Maryland.

14. Searles, H.F. (1965). On driving the other person crazy. In: *Collected Papers on Schizophrenia and Related Subjects.* New York: International University Press.

15. Ringuette, E.L., Kennedy, T. (1966). An experimental study of the double-bind hypothesis. *Journal of Abnormal Psychology* 71:136-141.

16. Winnicott, D.W. (1958). Transitional objects and transitional phenomena. In: *Collected Papers.* New York: Basic Books Inc.

17. Kafka, J.S. (1969). The body as transitional object: A psychoanalytic study of a self-mutilating patient. *British Journal of Medical Psychology* 42:207-212.

18. Kafka, J.S. (1966). *Deja vu phenomena: Observations and a theory.* Read before the 119th annual meeting of American Psychiatric Association. Atlantic City, NJ.

19. Freud, S. The uncanny. In: *The Complete Psychological Works of Sigmund Freud,* Volume 17. London: Hogarth Press.

20. Schachtel, E.G. (1947). On memory and childhood amnesia. *Psychiatry* 10:1-26.

21. Kafka, J.S., McDonald, J.W. (1964). The latent family in the intensive treatment of the hospitalized schizophrenic patient. In: Masserman, J.S. (ed). *Current Psychiatric Therapy*. New York: Grune & Stratton.

22. Kafka, J.S. (1966). *Practical and conceptual developments concerning work with families*. Read before the Southern Divisional Meeting of American Psychiatric Association. Hollywood, Florida.

23. Goodrich, D.W., Boomer, D.S. (1963). Experimental assessment of modes of conflict resolution. *Family Process* 2:15-24.

24. Ryder, R.G., Goodrich, D.W. (1966). Married couples' responses to disagreement. *Family Process* 5:30-42.

25. Ryder, R.G. (1966). Two replications of color matching factors. *Family Process* 5:43-48.

26. Ryder, R.G. (1968). Husband-wife dyads versus married strangers. *Family Process* 7:233-238.

27. Ryder, R.G. (1969). *Three myths: Brief ruminations on interaction procedures while contemplating the color matching tests*. Read before the annual meeting of National Council on Family Relations. Washington, DC.

28. Berlyne, D.E. (1966). Conflict and arousal. *Science American* 215:82-87.

Selected Writings

Psychoses, Schizophrenia

Journal of the American Psychoanalytic Association 58:27-47, 2011

Chapter 13

Chestnut Lodge and the Psychoanalytic Approach to Psychosis

The study of psychosis has a long history in psychoanalysis and so does the debate about the suitability of psychoanalysis for treatment of schizophrenia. For decades, Chestnut Lodge was not only a hospital but also a clinical research and educational institution. A unique patient-staff ratio—about 20 analytic therapists for 100 patients—made possible prolonged and intense clinical work with schizophrenic and other severely disturbed patients. Interstaff discussions were encouraged and facilitated. This quasi-academic approach to in-depth individual case studies led to clinical findings and theoretical formulations that had a significant impact on developments in American and international psychoanalysis, both here and abroad. Many of these findings and theoretical formulations are relevant to the current studies and treatments of psychotic and nonpsychotic patients.

The study of psychosis has a long history in psychoanalysis and so does the debate about the suitability of psychoanalysis for treatment of schizophrenia. Nathaniel London (1973) in his "An Essay on Psychoanalytic Theory: Two Theories of Schizophrenia," contrasted the view that psychosis is on a continuum with neurotic disorders, (a conflict theory of schizophrenia) with the idea that specific ego defects characterize psychosis. Freud thought the schizophrenic cannot be treated psychoanalytically the narcissistic libidinal withdrawal typical of the disorder prevents the development of transference. That seems to have remained Freud's basic position but Ping-Nie Pao (1973) has called attention to some of Freud's other ideas about schizophrenia, ideas dispersed in various papers: "Freud did not seem to have dealt with thought disorder adequately. This deficit, however, was supplemented in two later papers (1915), (1917), in which he distinguished thing-presentation and word-presentation of an object and suggested that, in schizophrenia, *words* and not things are subjected to the primary psychic process" (p 470). Though Freud remained interested in the theory of schizophrenia, his belief in the unanalyzability of schizophrenic patients led to his lack of interest in the first psychoanalytic hospital organized by István Hollós, an analysand of Paul Federn.

In contrast to Freud for whom the schizophrenic's basic pathology consists in the withdrawal of libido from external objects, Federn (1952) theorized that in the disorder the ego *boundary* is insufficiently cathected. With too few border guards, the ego cannot differentiate which stimuli came from the outside or which originate internally—that is, whether they are perceptions or hallucinations. Federn, one of the early analysts to be interested in work with psychotic patients, based his clinical approach on this theory. It is hardly, then, surprising that one of his analysands, István Hollós, made the first attempt to operate a psychoanalytically-informed hospital for psychotic patients. Co-founder with Ferenczi of the Hungarian Psychoanalytic Association, István Hollós directed such a hospital before World War I. "Already in the 1910's he was convinced that the "liberation" of the mentally ill from the chains of their stigmatization will only become possible if society arrives at a psychoanalytic understanding of its own madness, if nurses are taught that there is meaning in psychotic talk, and if caregivers analyze *their* Unconscious...and integrate the "mad" parts of themselves." (Pestalozzi et al. 1998, p.xx). Federn's approach to the treatment of psychotics implied that psychotics had sane parts that could be used therapeutically. Nevertheless, he thought that the therapist who treats the patient during the psychotic episode might be afterward be viewed by the patient as contaminated by psychosis for the patient and that subsequent treatment is better conducted by a new, uncontaminated, analyst. At Chestnut Lodge, we found it preferable *not* to change therapists.

The vision of those who started treating schizophrenic patients at Chestnut Lodge resonated with the philosophy of the first psychoanalytic hospital. At Chestnut Lodge, from the very beginning, there was also a belief that there were sane parts to the psychotics that could be used in the therapeutic work with these patients.

The Early History of Chestnut Lodge and its Move toward Psychoanalyically Informed Treatment of Psychosis

How did Chestnut Lodge evolve? How did it become a center for psychoanalytically informed treatment of severe pathology, eventually becoming a unique institution.

Dr. Ernest Bullard had been a superintendent of a state hospital for the insane in Wisconsin. Wanting to establish a hospital of his own, he bought the Woodlawn Hotel in 1908 and by 1910 Chestnut Lodge was born. Ernest Bullard was the only physician until 1925 when Dexter arrived. From then on, Dexter was in charge. His formal psychiatric training had consisted of two months at the Boston Psychopathic Hospital. In 1935, he hired Frieda Fromm-Reichmann. Julia Waddell (1964), who became the chief nurse, writes that, when she arrived on May12,1935, the nursing staff consisted of a superintendent of nurses, two RNs and five aides: "Orientation was unknown...I was expected to go on night duty that evening ... Some medical students had been hired to "cover" night duty in exchange for room and board and they would call for me at 4 o'clock to ... meet the patients. A week or so later, about two o'clock in the morning I heard someone come onto the porch ... 'I'm Dr. Dexter Bullard. You must be Miss Blankenhorn (Mrs. Waddell's maiden name) ... glad to have you here' ... The admission of patients was handled quite differently (at that time). We got no preview of what was coming ... one night I was told a patient was to be admitted ... the doorbell rang. The medical student and I went to the door and a mother and her 21-year-old son were standing on the porch arguing ... the son said "Mother, I can't leave you here." The mother said, 'I certainly can't leave you in a place like this.' Which was the patient? I could not decide. So I kept them both all night. Dr. Bullard could settle this in the morning. The next night, when I came on, neither was there" (p 123).

Dr. Douglas Noble (1963), describing a somewhat later phase in the development of Chestnut Lodge: "Underlying the therapeutic program was the theory that the schizophrenic patient because of early hurts to his ego required a long period of affectionate care in which his trust in another person would be restored and intensive psychotherapeutic work would then become possible. In accordance with this concept, patients were encouraged to self-realization and exposed to very little frustration in the hospital. The patient was always right. This led to much frustration of the nursing personnel and staff, especially since the method was obviously susceptible of exploitation. Patients' privileges were reviewed frequently, sometimes by different doctors with not a little crossing of wires. Frieda Fromm-Reichmann and Dexter Bullard were remarkably faithful to their therapeutic concepts, often at the cost of great discomfort to themselves. In an early paper, Dexter Bullard describes a session with a patient who hurled an ash tray at him; there was another occasion on which he sat at the door of a room of a patient in a panic because the patient had a sheet of glass which he broke into pieces and threw at the therapist. Dr. Frieda Fromm-Reichmann tells of sitting on a bench beside a patient for an hour daily for several weeks while the patient remained silent. Then one day, he placed a newspaper in her accustomed seat saying that he did not wish her to dirty her dress. Most of the work, however, was less dramatic than these episodes would indicate. Dr. Bullard was at work every morning at eight o'clock for his first hour and saw several patients daily in analysis. I recall Freida From-Reichmann's trudging up the stairs to the fourth floor every night for weeks to see a schizophrenic patient who would not talk with her at any other time. There was, in other words, great interest but much drudgery. Some of the things that were done were later discarded but they were learned the hard way" (pp 93-103).

From such beginnings, Chestnut Lodge developed into a unique institution: a place with about hundred patients and about twenty psychiatrists who had four to five sessions a week with each patient; a place where patients and psychiatrists met at least once a week among themselves; a place where senior staff members supervised junior members;

where the psychiatrists, most of whom were psychoanalysts or were in psychoanalytic training, met at least once a week in staff conferences with nursing and psychiatric aides staff, social workers, one or two psychologists, the recreational staff, occupational, art, and dance therapists; and one weekly all hospital meeting for patients and staff together! Add to this that there was quite an active social life among staff members, making Chestnut Lodge a hotbed of interpersonal activity. Work with psychotic and other severely disturbed individuals stirred up existential and deep intrapersonal issues and contributed to an intellectually and emotionally charged atmosphere experienced by staff members.

I was a staff member from 1957 to 1967 although I continued to work with a few of my patients for several more decades. In retrospect, I think that those of us, who were interested in being therapists of psychotics in some way resembled a group of anthropologists who wanted to understand and to find a way of communicating with the inhabitants of psychosis-land. Perhaps, we also shared with anthropologists the temptations and the dangers of going native. I believe the unique culture of Chestnut Lodge, with its structure of supervision and small- and large- group discussions, offered an emotional and intellectual supportive framework—an arena to work through, or at least on, the profound countertransference feelings engendered by intense involvement with psychotic patients.

Dr. Noble's comment make it clear that some of the lessons learned in the early phases of his work at Chestnut Lodge were learned the hard way. These hard lessons consisted precisely in the findings of what does not work in the long run, even if it seemed successful for the moment. Findings—negative and positive—from very extended longitudinal studies may be quite different from more time-limited studies. Staff members who published what they learned are those who are known to the wider psychoanalytic community but there were others who learned much and taught much to the rest of us and who never published. Milton Hendlich, for instance, remarkably successful in treating extremely traumatized patients, conveyed to us his therapeutic strategy of spending a great deal of time with patients exploring every detail of their positive, untraumatic, memories.

The freedom to experiment with group and individual therapeutic approaches eventually led to a menu of theories and practices of Chestnut

Lodge that included just about all the diverse approaches to treatment of severely disturbed patients described in "Psychoanalytic Psychotherapy in Institutional Settings" (Pestalozzi, et. al. 1998, p xvii), for instance, the Cassel hospital, with which Chestnut Lodge was associated, emphasized the psychosocial nursing approach. Chestnut Lodge also worked with a halfway house. Work with families was expanded by including families who lived at a great distance from the Lodge. Together with the social work staff, I was allowed to start a program in which visiting families could stay for several days in the Frieda Fromm-Reichmann cottage. I mention these developments now because they resonate with the radical shift in the asylum system that was created in Italy. Indeed, some of its architects were acquainted with the work done at Chestnut Lodge. In the Italian system, the program for each patient was to be "tailor made." This was true to an even greater extent at the Lodge. Here is a brief description of the Italian system: "New patients are treated with different sorts of "tailor-made" provision on a home and community basis, according to four different models as models as previously defined by Janssen: the *bifocal* model, with emphasis on a dual therapeutic relationship, *the small integrated -group model,* based on individual intervention involving the interaction of several professional figures and models, including, for instance, psychotherapeutic, pharmacological, and rehabilitative; the *community model,* based on the tradition of the "therapeutic community"; ..." (Pestalozzi, et. al. 1998, p xvii).

At Chestnut Lodge, all these models were applied with variations in emphasis and timing tailor-made for each patients. Individual therapists at the Lodge experimented with many approaches that are now often parceled out as "educational or rehabilitative" modalities. The mainstay of treatment, however, was always individual psychoanalytic therapy four or five times weekly.

The Development of Therapeutic Approaches to Psychosis

Despite the intense interaction of the Chestnut Lodge staff members, the large body of their publications cannot be called the work of a Chestnut Lodge *school.* The books and papers are very much the product of individuals with different theoretical and technical ideas and styles. There are, however, some common elements: all Chestnut Lodge authors recognized, on the one hand, the importance of using the healthy part of the individual patient and, on the other hand, the importance of following the patient into his/her psychotic world. The latter was seen as a prerequisite for establishing contact with such patients. Readers of the literature by Chestnut Lodge authors may note, however, that they differed in their focus on one or the other of the polarities: the "healthy" or the psychotic parts. For instance, references to classical ego psychology, for instance, are especially elaborated in Ping-Nie Pao's papers (1973, 1983), whereas immersion in the world of psychosis is prominent in the writings of Harold Searles (1963). These divergent emphases not only reflect differences in personal style; they may also echo the psychoanalytic theories of psychosis as *defect* or *conflict* (London 1973; Kafka 1997).

A theoretical discussion of these two views was never a central concern of Frieda Fromm-Reichmann, whose name is most closely associated with Chestnut Lodge. A refugee from Nazi Germany, she had a broad background in psychiatry, neurology, and psychoanalysis, and had on her arrival in 1935 already published neurological and psychoanalytic papers. Jarl E. Dyrud (1989) has shown how these earlier experiences influenced her later work, during which she published and lectured widely. On the occasion of her fiftieth anniversary at the Lodge, her patients, students, supervisees, and colleagues contributed to a festschrift in her honor, *Psychoanalysis and Psychosis* (Silver 1989). This volume, which also includes verbatim transcripts of some of her remarks in staff conferences, gives a vivid picture of her personality, her style, and her work. Frieda is described as forceful, intensively engaged, and direct, and in particular as explicitly addressing the 'healthy' and the psychotic parts of the patient at the same time. According to Jacob Arlow (1989), "Hers was a special ability to understand a patient's metaphoric language but, more than that, she had the ability to communicate the understanding in a way that helped to create for her patients a bridge that led from metaphor to simile to objective communication. It was her special gift not only to understand the nature of the unconscious conflicts hidden behind the patient's delusion and metaphors, but also to use language that indicated to the patient that he was being understood. This perhaps was the first step on the road to recovery" (pp 181-182).

Interviewed by Laurice McAfee (Silver 1989), Joanne Greenberg, the author of *I Never Promised You a Rose Garden* and perhaps Frieda's best known patient, indicates that from her perspective, "the personalities have to fit in therapy and if the symptoms are metaphors, the therapist has to be someone who understands those metaphors or at least is amenable to learning them so that when they appear in the therapeutic dialogue, the right amount of weight is given to them" (p 523). Concerning the polarity of the sane and psychotic parts, Joanne Greenberg's comments are particularly informative. Fromm-Reichmann told her that "you must take me with you," that she, Frieda, knows nothing about mental illness and that Joanne has to be her teacher (p 515-516). But Greenberg speaks also about the danger of being understood on the psychotic level. "People would tell you what perceptive things a patient had said. The thing is I want to choose my perceptions. I don't want them to come out of some kind of unconscious soup. I want it to be something I choose to say, not something that says me." Joanne adds that, being understood in that state, felt horrifically dangerous: "I don't know how Frieda got around that. I remember the danger. ... It's bigger than you are. It's more powerful. It can kill." (p 528) "Maybe the strongest thing I'd like to say ever to anybody is that creativity and mental illness are *opposites,* not complements. It's a confusion of mental illness with creativity. Imagination is, includes, goes *out,* opens out, learns from experience. Craziness is the opposite: it is a fort that's a prison" (p 527).

We should note that this is Greenberg's retrospective view. There is no reason to believe that Fromm-Reichmann could have made any contact with a patient without acknowledging and following her into her psychotic world. What is striking is that, from the very beginning of treatment, Fromm-Reichmann functioned in both the non-psychotic and psychotic worlds. This is a useful approach that I discovered and elaborated by noting that the schizophrenic patient may move in and out of psychotic mental organization very rapidly from second to second and that the therapist who speaks on the psychotic and non-psychotic level is more likely at some point to be on target. I also believe that the patient may be reluctant to let the therapist know, at least early in the therapeutic work, when he is more or less psychotic. This is an area where the patient, aware of his inadequate functioning generally, may feel that he can be "one up" on the therapist.

The great part of the literature emanating from Chestnut Lodge describes the efforts of the therapists to comprehend psychotic functioning and the counter-transference developments while working with such disturbed patients. This is a dominant feature in Harold Searles' work. In (1963), "Transference psychosis in the psychotherapy of chronic schizophrenia," he describes his " ... realization that even the most deep and chronic symptoms of schizophrenia .. emerge ... (as) the manifestations of ... (an) unconscious effort ... of the patient ... to maintain, and to become free from, modes of relatedness which held sway between himself and other persons in his childhood and which he is now fostering unconsciously ... in ... his relationship with his therapist" (p 249). In Searles' view, the utter helplessness that the therapist feels may reflect the patient's helplessness in dealing with a disturbed parent. "Even the most ... 'crazy', manifestations of schizophrenia come to reveal meaningfulness and reality-relatedness not only as transference reactions to the therapist, but, even beyond this, as delusional identifications with real aspects of the therapist's own personality" (p 280). My personal reaction to Searles' moving descriptions of counter-transference developments is influenced by my experience of having been supervised by him for many years. At times, he spoke of how important it is for therapists of psychotic patients to assure their own emotional survival. One function of the kind of countertransference examination that Searles described made prolonged work with psychotic patients tolerable. The scope and depth of Searles' countertransference explorations permitted him contact with patients who otherwise were nearly inaccessible. The "no-holds barred" search he encouraged for my own raw emotional reactions proved valuable in my work with both nonpsychotic patients, as well as with the more disturbed patients I was treating. Searles' writings on countertransference resonated deeply with analysts including many who did not work with severely disturbed patients. Countertransference reactions may be related to the patient's experiences in childhood but Searles' implied view that those experiences are a major etiological factor for schizophrenia is today not now widely accepted. Willick (2001), for instance, has argued that as an etiological factor in schizophrenia " ... very serious inadequacies in the care taking person ..." have not stood the test of time (p 27). It should be noted also that Searles referred to schizophrenic patient's efforts "to become free from, modes of relatedness which held sway between himself and other persons in his *childhood* (p 249; emphasis added). Here Searles speaks essentially of a schizophreniogenic parent and does not dissociate himself from that etiological view.

Other Chestnut Lodge authors do not propose a primary etiological theory of schizophrenia. Donald Burnham (1969), for instance, wrote that the schizophrenic's personal need for contact and his concomitant fear of it make up a central dynamic that the therapist also experiences in his countertransference reactions. In his forward to Burnham, Gladstone, and Gibson's (1969), *Schizophrenia the Need-Fear dilemma*, Robert Cohen noted that " ... the authors are not proposing a primary etiological theory of schizophrenia. We ... do not know ... how the ego defect develops. It may be inherited, constitutional, experiential, or the result of some biological imbalance. What the authors attempt to explain is the nature of the human experience of the schizophrenic individual, and they offer a structural psychological theory to account for his observed behavior and reported feelings, relating these to vicissitudes in the course of personality development. Any theory of schizophrenia which purports to be complete must include a consideration of these issues, and must take into account the schizophrenic's adapted as well as his mal-adapted behavior" (p xv).

Joanne Greenberg's comments about the danger of being responded to on the psychotic level and the need to be contacted at that level is an expression of this "need-fear dilemma," the need, and the fear, of contact with psychosis. Joanne Greenberg said "I feared that when I would not be sick, that if I gave that up, since madness and creativity were equated in my mind at the time, I would have to give the latter away and then not have anything" (In McAfee 1989, pp. 517-518). As I have mentioned,

Paul Federn thought that a therapist who works with the patient in the most psychotic regressed phase of his illness becomes "contaminated" with psychosis and therefore recommended that another therapist worked with the patient once that phase has passed. This definitely was not the experience at Chestnut Lodge. The patient who was not abandoned during descent into, and escape from, a deep psychotic state may feel that he can convey about that experience to the therapist, that he can, as one of my patients put it, "train,"the therapist.

In some psychoanalytic presentations and panels on psychosis, no clear distinction is made between patients in deep psychotic states and relatively well-functioning patients with "psychotic aspects" of the personality. This lack of distinction contributes to confusion and seemingly contradictory views regarding the connection (if any) between psychosis and creativity.

Joanne Greenberg insisted that there is nothing creative about psychosis. When Donald Burnham (1973) studied the psychotic episodes of Strindberg in great detail and made a connection between psychosis and creativity, he did so by emphasizing the creativity it takes to *transform* (my italics) the psychotic experience into a new and broader vision (Burnham 1973; see also Kafka 2009).

Ping-Nie Pao (1983) is particularly clear in differentiating three levels of psychosis and provides examples of each interviews with patients. In two cases—"Apparent Contact With Reality But Severe Thought Disorder" (pp 147-154) and "Intermittent Loss of Reality Contact and Visible Panic" (pp 154-161)—he counts on the patient's creativity and metaphoric understanding, while in the third—"Lack of Reality Orientation and Almost Mute" (pp 161-167)—his concern is primarily with understanding the patient's panic and helping her to become less frightened.

I have discussed works by Fromm-Richmann, Searles, Donald Burnham, and Ping-Nie Pao, but can hardly do justice here to the wealth of books and papers originating at Chestnut Lodge. Many papers presented at the Chestnut Lodge's annual symposium were collected in private booklets and were not published more widely. Among other papers written by staff members are the studies of McGlashan McGlashan (1984a,b, 1986), an ambitious project widely cited to discredit the value of psychotherapy in the treatment of psychosis. Many articles followed, spin-offs of the three main papers describing the methodology and results of the follow-up and long-term outcomes of patients suffering from schizophrenia, the affective disorders, and borderline personalities. The papers are complex. Although McGlashan is far from condemning all interpersonal, dynamic, or psychoanalytic therapies, his conclusion, that intensive psychotherapeutic work with chronic schizophrenic patients is not effective, had considerable impact. McGlashan (1984) wrote:

"The most striking findings relate to our schizophrenic population. These findings are clear: two of every three schizophrenic patients treated at Chestnut Lode were chronically ill or marginally functional at follow-up. The result is distressingly familiar; schizophrenia in its chronic form tends not to respond to treatments of known effectiveness with other difficulties. This outcome certainly did not derive from inadequate effort, at least in the psycho-social sphere where treatment was an active, intense, and prolonged endeavor. The psychopharmacologic aspects of treatment, on the other hand, were undoubtedly inadequate by today's standards since psychoactive drugs were not used systematically until well into the 1960s. Nevertheless, the results are clear; by and large the treatment as it was constituted failed to alter the momentum of this disease toward lifelong disability.

"The findings are not unequivocally negative. Recoveries and functionally adequate outcomes occur in one of every three of the schizophrenic patients studied. Furthermore, this has been observed among some of the most chronic and "hopeless" cases in the hospital. These developments, of course, are of particular interest, including the degree to which they can be predicted and/or related to particular therapeutic interventions. These developments may also justify trials of intensive residential treatment in schizophrenic patients who have run the gamut of therapeutic interventions to no avail" (p 600).

The phrase "not unequivocally negative" is perhaps somewhat mislead-ing. If one considers that we are dealing with a population of deeply psychotic individuals who had not improved with any other treatment and for whom hospitalization at Chestnut Lodge was "last resort," rela-tively positive outcomes in one-third of this population could be considered remarkable.

Brigitte Bechgaard (2003), chief psychologist at the Copenhagen University Hospital, has criticized McGlashan's work in the aggressively titled, "Lessons in How to Ruin a Study in Psychotherapy Effectiveness: a Critical Review of the Follow-up Study from Chestnut Lodge" (pp 119-139). While she mentions various Chestnut Lodge research publications on psychotherapy The phrase "not unequivocally negative" is perhaps somewhat misleading. If one considers that we are dealing with a popu-lation of deeply psychotic individuals who had not improved with any other treatment and for whom hospitalization at Chestnut Lodge was "last resort," relatively positive outcomes in one-third of this population could be considered remarkable.

Brigitte Bechgaard (2003), chief psychologist at the Copenhagen University Hospital, has criticized McGlashan's work in the aggressively titled, "Lessons in How to Ruin a Study in Psychotherapy Effectiveness: a Critical Review of the Follow-up Study from Chestnut Lodge" (pp 119-139). While she mentions various Chestnut Lodge research publications on psychotherapy that McGlashan has coauthored with Dingman, Gedo, Goodrich, Fritsch, Keats, Miller and Nayfack, she directs sharp and de-tailed criticism at McGlashan's second paper, on the long-term outcomes for schizophrenia and the affective disorders (1984a): "Originally, the follow-up study was intended as a study of the psychotherapeutic pro-cess and its outcome. While widely referred to as a follow-up study, it is not possible to make conclusions about psychotherapy from the study. Data about the psychodynamic aspects of therapy have been collected but never analyzed. Additionally, the study does not fulfill the require-ments of a psychotherapeutic outcome study. The conclusion of the current review is that as the study turned out, it only allows one to draw conclusions about different kinds of illness courses and predictor fac-tors" (abstract, p 119).

I cannot describe here the merits and limitations of McGlashan's study or of Bechgaard's critique, but it is clear we cannot claim that, looking at results statistically using Kraeplinian criteria, the work at Chestnut Lodge led to the *cure* of a majority of chronic schizophrenics by psychotherapy alone. It is the *individual case* that yielded Chestnut Lodge's richest fruit yields both personal and conceptual. What all of us who worked at Chestnut Lodge learned are the personally transforming self-searching effects of profound contact with raw psychosis and the consequent opening, deepening, and widening of therapeutic range with all of our patients. We could communicate some of these attitudes and skills to students and colleagues. Depending on our individual interests, we also had the opportunity to harvest the more conceptual fruit of unusually intensive, detailed, and prolonged single case studies, and clusters of such studies. Indeed, McGlashan (1984) recognized that "adequate outcomes ... among some of the most chronic and hopeless cases . . . are of particular interest" (p 600). This brings to mind Heinrich Klüever's influential lectures, which I attended at the University of Chicago, in which he stressed that most major advances in any field emerge from the study of *exceptions*. These lectures were influential precisely because they were addressed to an audience of statistically oriented psychologists. And at Chestnut Lodge, we were given the opportunity to study the unique characteristics of each patient.

It was clear to us just how different from each other were patients with the same formal diagnosis. Ian Hacking (2009), writing in "Humans, Aliens and Autism," about the many forms of autism being studied, says, "If you know about one autistic person, you know about *one* autistic person" (p 46). We could equally well say, "If you know about one schizophrenic person, you know about *one* schizophrenic person." Saying this, of course, does not diminish the importance of studying any features that may characterize most or all schizophrenics.

Chestnut Lodge provided an unique opportunity to observe, in great detail, patients during the periods of *transition*—in and out of the most severe psychotic states. Where short hospitalization periods and early discharge are practiced, these particularly interesting moments of transition are not seen. Furthermore, we could continue to treat our patients when they were functioning on a relatively good level. Elsewhere, treatment would have been stopped, curtailed, or reduced to "medication management." At the Lodge, we could explore what kind of treatment was desirable and possible during periods when the patients functioned on a nonpsychotic, frequently high (even highly creative) level. Sometimes, during such periods, psychoanalysis without "parameters" was the treatment of choice though overall the course of treatment would not fit with the description of "classical" psychoanalysis because of the modifications invoked at times of psychotic crisis.

These moments of transition are of such particular interest because, at least, some patients, especially those who function at times on a very high level, are interested in teaching us something about *their* experiences and about *their* world. When one such patient, after many years of treatment, was discharged and moved to another city, I referred her to a colleague there. She would not accept this referral and insisted on coming to see me although it had to be at a reduced frequency. She told me, with the apparent lack of humor of some schizophrenic patients, "It took me so long to train you."

The Schizophrenics' Objects

Following is a condensed formulation of a theory based on what Chestnut Lodge patients have taught me. This theory and related theories are elaborated in my book, *Multiple Realities in Clinical Practice* (Kafka 1989) and my paper, "The Romantic and Classic Visions in the Therapy of Psychosis: a Personal Perspective and an Evolving Theory of Schizophrenia" (Kafka 1997). The central theory deals with the schizophrenic's object world.

I have made a brief reference to Nathaniel London's review (1973) of the history of psychoanalytic efforts to understand schizophrenia, in which he distinguishes a unitary and a specific theory of the illness: "The Unitary Theory asserts an essential continuity between schizophrenic and neurotic behaviors. ... and considers intra-psychic conflict and defense as primary determiners ..." "Such an assertion, ... strains our available knowledge of these mental states so disparate in phenomenology and likely aetiologies. ..... The Specific Theory is focused on a deficiency in mental representation" (p 190).

My work with schizophrenic patients also led me to focus on mental representations, the schizophrenic objects. My observations at the Lodge led me to disagree with Arieti's influential theory of a specific different schizophrenic *logic* (1963, p 59) which led in turn to my hypothesis that schizophrenics apply our common logic to specific schizophrenic objects. Schizophrenic patients have taught me that *combinations of characteristics* can be more constant than any "person," self or other, any "object" in the usual psychoanalytic sense. They have taught me that to comprehend them it is useful to decipher these combinations of characteristics as their own, their idiosyncratic, relatively more constant objects—their "atmospheric objects," as I call them. An example is a female patient who, during an acute psychotic episode, had called a particular nurse, "Heidi." After emerging from this acute episode, she explained to me that she never thought the nurse was "Heidi" but that the combination of being blonde and having a foreign accent had evoked in her an atmosphere she could hold on to, the atmosphere of the book *Heidi* that she had loved since her childhood. She could not hold on to the identities of actual people, not mine, not her own. In psychoanalytic language, the "object constancy" of common or commonsense objects was missing or, at least, was less stable. It might be countered that, after all, there must have been such constancy, as she always called the same nurse, "Heidi" (Kafka 1989, pp 28-29). But, if we keep in mind the rapid fluctuations of levels of psychic organization and disorganization that we observed in our Lodge patients, the relatively greater stability of "atmospheric objects" becomes comprehensible. All object formation, all "object permanence," involves the acceptance as "identical," of patterns of stimuli that are not exactly the same. Patterns of stimuli that differ in some respects from each other are accepted as subjectively equivalent and thus all psychological objects are based on subjective equivalences. Even the psychological existence of "a table" requires the subjective equivalence of the different visual patterns that result when the table is seen from different angles. This is usually called "object permanence." Psychoanalytically understandable defenses play a role in more complex emotionally charged object constancy, such as a constant mother image that includes the *bad* withholding mother and the *good* giving mother. We know that affect influences our experience of time, that objectively identical intervals can be subjectively different and that vice versa. Our psychological object world, therefore, is an ever changing web of spatial and temporal subjective equivalences, a model that fits well with current neuroscientific findings.

Still pertinent to the topic of object formation, including the schizophrenic's object formation, is a hypothesis that perceptual acts recapitulate the ontogeny of perception. Studies of percept-genesis support the idea that developmentally early perceptions are more synesthetic and less sensory-specific than later perceptions. Adult perception—as shown in the microtemporal dissection of the process in tachistoscopic experiments—recapitulates autogenetic developments. Ordinary object formation involves more or less complete recapitulative cycles that lead to subjective equivalences—objects—that are our "commonsense" objects. I hypothesize that schizophrenic objects represent subjective equivalences resulting from a mixture of completed and aborted recapitulative perceptual cycles involving rhythmic distortions. It is possible to think of a conflictual basis for aborted perceptions but it is at this juncture that disturbances in biological rhythms—perhaps genetically based—play a role in the etiology of schizophrenia. Effects of psychopharmacological agents may be due to changes they induce in biological rhythms. I believe that many schizophrenic patients shift rapidly between different levels of psychic organizations, for instance, between an atmospheric object organization (as exemplified by the Heidiness vignette) and a more specific *personal* world. A therapist, however, who assumes that the patient experiences these extremely rapid changes in levels of functioning and who therefore approaches the patient on multiple levels (of functioning) at the same time, is more likely to be "on target." At Chestnut Lodge, our therapeutic approach was informed by the recognition that some schizophrenic patients had not only these microtemporal fluctuations in levels of functioning, but that some were able to comprehend and feel at ease in highly complex and abstract domains while at the same time they may have been severely deficient in problem-solving abilities needed for daily functioning. This has specific implications for therapeutic technique. I would work with a patient on cognitive problems involved, say, in ordering in a restaurant or using a telephone while, at the same time, dynamically exploring, for example, the connection between the patient's emotional history (close ties and identification with her father) and the peculiar body sensations she has when informing me that she has her father's legs and therefore could not shave them.

We must confront the fact that there are states in which some schizophrenic patients, with or without the use of medication, are unreachable. These are the times when we can only wait. But the therapist's presence—again and again—at moments of entry and exit from the psychotic episodes, forms a bond which may permit the patient to communicate, however subtly, the need for hospitalization. A patient who had been discharged telephoned me to say that she wanted to visit the Lodge and complain to Dr. Bullard about her previous hospitalization which had been against her will. Her violence had forced her family to admit her to the hospital with the help of several attendants. Her phone call essentially informed me that now she sought voluntary hospitalization.

Psychotic Processes and Contemporary Psychoanalysis

Most analysts would agree that the question if there is a continuum between neurosis and psychosis has essentially been answered, at least in the sense that conflict theory alone does not explain schizophrenia. Psychoanalytic therapy based only on conflict theory is not an effective approach to treating psychotics.

I have already discussed the clinical use of the "atmospheric object" concept in work with schizophrenic patients. Once alerted to the "atmospheric objects" of psychotic patients, an awareness enhanced by the work at Chestnut Lodge, we discovered transference and countertransference to the "atmospheric object" elements with all our patients. For example, I offered an early Monday morning session to a patient with marked obsessive-compulsive features whose passive-aggressive characteristics played havoc with his professional career. He said, "Monday morning is my father—get to work—you never finish anything and you never finish anything right." I had become the atmospheric Monday morning demand. Perceptual recapitulation is always at work. We are both atmospheric and more personally defined objects to many of our patients and they are both to us. As the range of pathology of our psychoanalytically treated patient population expands, we find that some function primarily in the atmospheric transference realm, whereas for others we are so personally real that we never assume a more atmospheric resonance that would be useful in their lives. This widening and deepening of our comprehension of deeply disturbed patients at Chestnut Lodge refined our approach to patients with lesser degrees of similar "ego defects."

The atmospheric object, as observed in the schizophrenic patient, gives us a conceptual bridge to the understanding of features of some nonpsychotic patients. Much of contemporary psychoanalytic literature deals with such patients for whom interpretation is insufficient. The focus is often on the analysand's sense of self, its vicissitudes, and the sense of reality. An object—in the usual psychoanalytic meaning—is *personified* and so is a "self object." A person experiences himself as having the power of agency, whereas an atmospheric object does not have a sense that it can make decisions and influence "reality." The existence of the link between "personified" objects—including self objects—and reality is best illustrated by observing the effects of a lack of a personified self-object. A patient told me, "There are thoughts and feelings around but I don't know whose they are." Descartes' "*cogito, ergo sum*" (I think; therefore, I am) does not hold. The same patient told me that he had to close the door on his finger to make sure that the car and his finger in fact existed. The same patient told me that he wanted to travel to California to assure himself that California existed and was not just a patch on a map. Working with patients, whose sense of self and commonsense reality is deeply disturbed but who maintain a sense of atmospheric reality through which we can make contact with them, can help us in our treatment of patients who have less severe, less persistent but qualitatively similar "ego deficits."

Conclusion

Work with the psychotic patient as an unique individual confronted the therapists with the profound questions about our emotional and intellectual lives. Chestnut Lodge provided an opportunity to deal with these questions in depth because it recognized and fostered the importance of the single case, the single individual. The Chestnut Lodge legacy of the importance of the single case is in sharp contrast to the regressive tendency in much of current psychiatry to focus on the single *symptom*. In an article on Freud's Schreber's case, McGlashan (2009), in a *Schizophrenia Bulletin* article, wrote "A case like Schreber's is sufficiently removed from our contemporary clinical scene to be useful in germinating questions that would otherwise never ever occur to us as we run from one modern patient to another" (p 480). But the psychoanalytic therapist at Chestnut Lodge *did* see cases like the Schreber's. That is why some questions occurred to the them: questions that they could pass on to a wider psychoanalytic and psychiatric community. Pursuing these questions in conditions quite different from Chestnut Lodge need not deprive any "modern psychiatric patient" of access to basic humanistic psychiatry. Some understandings of severe pathology gained at Chestnut Lodge and related therapeutic strategies are also valuable in the treatment of nonpsychotic patients in a psychoanalytic patient population with an ever widening range of pathology.

References

Arieti, S. (1963). Studies of thought processes in contemporary psychiatry. *American Journal of Psychiatry* 120:58-64.

Arlow, J. A. (1989). Delusion and metaphor. In: *Psychoanalysis and psychosis*, Ann-Louise S. Silver, M.D., editor. Connecticut: International Universities Press, Inc., pp 173-182.

Bechgaard, B. (2003). Lessons in how to ruin a study in psychotherapy effectiveness: a critical review of the follow-up study from Chestnut Lodge. *Journal of the American Academy of Psychoanalysis and Dynamic Psychiatry* 31:119-139.

Burnham, D.L. (1973). Restitutional functions of symbol and myth in Strindberg's *Inferno*. The Sixteenth Annual Frieda Fromm-Reichmann Memorial Lecture. *Psychiatry* 36:229-243.

Burnham, D.L., Gladstone, A.I., & Gibson, R.W. (1969). *Schizophrenia and the need-fear dilemma*. New York: International Universities Press.

Dyrud, J.E. (1989). The early Frieda, and traces of her in her later writings. In: *Psychoanalysis and psychosis*, Ann-Louise S. Silver, M.D., editor. Connecticut: International Universities Press, Inc., pp 483-494.

Federn, P. (1952). *Ego psychology and the psychoses*. New York: Basic Books.

Fonagy, P. and Target, M. (2007). Playing with reality: IV. A theory of external reality rooted in intersubjectivity. *International Journal of Psychoanalysis* 88:917-937.

Hacking, I. (2009). Humans, aliens and autism. *Daedalus, Journal of the American Academy of Arts and Sciences,* 138 (Summer 2009):44-59, page 46.

Kafka, J.S. (1987). On the question of insight in psychoanalysis. Presentation: Symposium of Psychoanalysis and Psychosis. *American Academy of Psychoanalysis*, 1987:18-28.

Kafka, J.S. (1989). *Multiple realities in clinical practice*. New Haven and London: Yale University Press.

Kafka, J.S. (1992). Consciousness and the shadow of time. In: *Two Butterflies on My Head. Psychoanalysis in the Interdisciplinary Scientific Dialogue*. Leuzinger-Bohleber, M., Schneider, H., Pfeiffer, R., editors. Springer—Verlag, Berlin, 1992, pp. 87-95; and IPSO Newsletter Anniversary Edition, Summer 1991.

Kafka, J.S. (1997). The romantic and classic visions in the therapy of psychosis: a personal perspective and an evolving theory of schizophrenia. *Psychiatry* 60:209-221, Fall 1997.

Kafka, J.S. (2009). Commentary on 'restitutional' functions of symbol and myth in Strindberg's *Inferno*.' On schizophreniform crisis and on schizophrenia. *Psychiatry* 72(2):139-142.

Libet, B. (2004). *Mind time: the temporal factor in consciousness*. Cambridge, MA: Harvard University Press.

London, N. (1973). An essay on psychoanalytic theory: two theories of schizophrenia. Part I: Review and critical assessment of the development of the two theories. Part II: Discussion and restatement of the specific theory of schizophrenia. *International Journal of Psychoanalysis* 54(2):169-193.

McAfee, L.I. (1989). Interview with Joanne Greenberg. In: *Psychoanalysis and psychosis*, Ann-Louise S. Silver, M.D., editor. Connecticut: International Universities Press, Inc., pp 513- 533.

McGlashan, T. (1984). The Chestnut Lodge follow-up study. I: Follow-up methodology and study sample. II: Long-term outcome of schizophrenia and the affective disorders. *Archives of General Psychiatry* (1984a) 41:573-601.

McGlashan, T. (1986). The Chestnut Lodge follow-up study. III: Long-term outcome of borderline personalities. *Archives of General Psychiatry* (1986) 43:20-30.

McGlashan, T. (2009). Psychosis as a disorder of reduced cathectic capacity: Freud's analysis of the Schreber case revisited. *Schizophrenia Bulletin* 35(#3):480.

Noble, Douglas. (1963). Early days at the 'The Lodge'. *The Ninth Annual Chestnut Lodge Symposium*, Friday, October 25, 1963, Rockville, Maryland. Privately published., pp. 93-103.

Pao, Ping-Nie. (1973). Notes on Freud's theory of schizophrenia. *The International Journal of Psychoanalysis* 54:469-476.

Pao, Ping-Nie. (1983). Therapeutic empathy and the treatment of schizophrenia. *Psychoanalytic Inquiry* 3:145-167.

Pestalozzi, J., Frisch, S., Hinshelwood, R.D., Houzel, D., editors. (1998). *Psychoanalytic Psychotherapy in Institutional Settings*. The EFPP Clinical Monograph Series. London: Karnac Books for the European Federation for Psychoanalytic Psychotherapy in the Public Health Services, page xx.

Searles, H. F. (1963). Transference psychosis in the psychotherapy of chronic schizophrenia. *The International Journal of Psychoanalysis* 44:249-281.

Silver, Ann-Louise, ed. (1989). *Psychoanalysis and psychosis.* Connecticut: International Universities Press, Inc.

Stern, D.N., Sander, L.W., Nahum, J.P., Harrison, A.M., Lyons-Ruth, Morgan, A.C., Brushweilerstern, N., & Tronick, E. Z. (1998). Noninterpretive mechanisms in psychoanalytic therapy: the 'something more' than interpretation. *International Journal of Psychoanalysis* 79:903-921.

Stoerig, P. (2006). The impact of invisible stimuli. *Science* 314:1694-1695.

Waddell, J. (1964). The evolution of nursing at Chestnut Lodge. *The Tenth Annual Chestnut Lodge Symposium,* Friday, November 6, 1964, Rockville, Maryland. Privately published, page 123.

Wegner, D. M. (2002). *The Illusion of Conscious Will.* Cambridge, MA: MIT Press.

Willick, M.S. (2001). Psychoanalysis and Schizophrenia: a cautionary tale. *Journal of the American Psychoanalytic Association* 49:27-56.

Psychiatry 60:262-274, 1997

Chapter 14

Romantic and Classic Visions in the Therapy of Psychosis: A Personal Perspective and Evolving Theory of Schizophrenia

Note: A panel titled "The Treatment of Schizophrenia and Severe Psycho-pathology: Its History and Practice in the Washington Psychoanalytic Community" took place in Washington. D.C. on June 12,1994 as part of the International Symposium for the Psychotherapy of Schizophrenia. Some material from the panelists' and formal discussant's panel presentations is included in the first section of this paper. The panel consisted of Dexter Bullard, Jr., M.D.. Donald Burnham, M.D., Robert Cohen, M.D., Clarence Schulz. M.D.: discussant Marco Conci, M.D.. and John S. Kafka, M.D.. chair. Tapes of the panelists' and formal discussant's presentations are available from Goodkind of Sound. Inc., North Carolina. Tapes 5A and 5B.

I.

As I reflect from current perspective on decades of work with schizophrenic patients, Strenger's (1989) recent paper contrasting the classic and romantic visions in psychoanalysis comes to mind. Strenger related these contrasting *psychoanalytic* visions to the literary and philosophical romantic and classic visions in the 18th and 19th centuries, visions that "have one value in common: that of autonomy. But their understanding of what autonomy consists of is profoundly different . . . Hegel, the great representative of the classic vision in the nineteenth century, sees autonomy in the individual's recognition that he is but an aspect of the general structure of reality and (in) the submission to the laws of the whole. As opposed to that, Kierkegaard, one of the great figures of the romantic view, considers autonomy in the individual's ability to attain his own subjective truth" (p. 596). In the 1940s and 1950s those of us who were interested in the psychoanalytically oriented treatment of schizophrenic patients were determined to comprehend the subjective truth, the nature of the thought processes, and the affects of these puzzling human beings, our schizophrenic patients. Although we did struggle with theories about the nature of schizophrenic "defects," and though we did not necessarily make the mistake of idealizing pathology, we were perhaps also not completely free from the notion that schizophrenic patients could have some features in common with Rousseau's "noble savages," a romantic notion par excellence.

All of us who followed the call of Dexter M. Bullard, Sr. to Chestnut Lodge shared the romantic vision that no human being is so different from us as to be inaccessible, incomprehensible, permanently isolated, and unresponsive. If only our efforts to make contact were heroic enough we would be able to alleviate suffering and isolation. This "romantic" vision had its antecedents (e.g., Cohen 1994) in the longstanding humanistic and humanitarian tradition in psychiatry. In the first decade of the century the neuroanatomist Meyer (Cohen 1994) "recognized that there would always be a residuum where etiological classification would be impossible, but before one turned to heredity there should be a search of the patient's own life" (Cohen 1994). White, who became superintendent of St. Elizabeth's Hospital in 1903, was fascinated by Freud's early work. White was a prodigious worker and through both his own professional work and his publishing was instrumental in spreading psychoanalytic and dynamic ideas. Because he was also involved in publishing a volume on Jung, he earned Freud's enduring disapproval.

Harry Stack Sullivan and Frieda Fromm Reichmann, who were invited to Chestnut Lodge by Dexter Bullard, Sr., are central in our story. Sullivan's interest in the social sciences and the contributions they could make to achieving and maintaining contact with patients who seemed difficult to reach contributed to a therapeutic and, in our sense, romantic optimism that permeated the atmosphere. Bullard invited Sullivan to lecture at Chestnut Lodge, and his ideas influenced Frieda Fromm Reichmann who saw a patient, "not as a victim in the family drama but as an actor in its transactions" (Cohen 1994). The autonomy of the patient, of the *actor* in the transactions of the family, is closer to the romantic autonomy of the individual who finds her or his own subjective truth (Kierkegaard) than to Hegel's classic view of autonomy as submission to the *general* (here the family's) structure of reality. Frieda Fromm Reichmann had come to pay increasing attention to responses to anxiety. She had become particularly concerned with the elucidation of defenses that had delayed an ego development and believed that it was important to use language that indicated to the patient that he or she was being understood. In this romantic tradition there is less emphasis on treatment techniques than on a "philosophy of tradition based on the therapist's relative security in the face of uncertainty" (Cohen 1994).[36]

The importance of countertransference is also part of the romantic tradition because it emphasizes the *personal*—the therapists', not *general,*—reality. Searles' (1965) prodigious writings on this subject are well known. Anne Louise Silver (1993) has written about the history of this focus on countertransference phenomena.

In the framework of a romantic-classic polarity, the romantic and highly individualistic vision emphasizes a longitudinal life-history approach. In contrast, a cross-sectional approach, the focus on a patient's symptomatology at a given moment, corresponds more to classic emphasis on the *general structure* (rather than the development) of reality. Exclusive cross-sectional focus can become a clinically useless *tunnel vision* of the patient. Therapists who work for many years with a patient discover that the patient might have been diagnosed differently at various cross-sectional points. The romantic vision's caricatured-but today sometimes all too real-opposite attitude would lead to some current treatment approaches that, despite being labeled biopsychosocial, employ a

---

[36] Cohen's profound knowledge of the evolution of treatment of schizophrenia in the greater Baltimore-Washington area is of course rooted in the fact that in his long career he had participated in and shaped much of that evolution.

reductionistic biological approach and ignore the complexities of the life of the individual patient. In settings in which there is a requirement to immediately treat the patient with medication, the therapist who, in some instances may have preferred to observe the effects of other interventions on the unmedicated patient, is no longer able to do so. This can lead to limitations and mistakes in assessment, treatment, and research strategies and to misguided efforts at nosological reformulation. Too narrow a focus on description may result in interrater reliability but may ignore the heterogeneity of schizophrenia. Focus on description and behavior may discourage inference, formulation of theory, and abstract conceptualization. What may be similar on a superficial descriptive level can be the outer manifestation of very different dynamics. Romantic single-case reports often offer information that is missed in studies using blind matched controls (Schulz 1994). In several European countries practitioners are now more successful than their colleagues in the United States in limiting the influence of reductionistic thinking and in maintaining some therapeutic and research strategies influenced by the individualistic romantic tradition (Conci 1994). Conci, who was the formal discussant of our panel, reported that interpersonal therapeutic approaches to schizophrenia are currently widely practiced in some European countries, especially Italy, Switzerland, and in the Scandinavian countries. Levander and Cullberg (1993) described a Swedish case finding study of schizophrenic patients being treated psychotherapeutically and state that in 1991 "some 200 cases were reported from 130 therapists" (p. 284).

Strenger (1989) noted that "the essence of the tension between the classic and the romantic attitude is ultimately the tension between identification with one's own perspective and the detachment from it. It is the expression of the fact that as human beings we have the ability to experience ourselves from within and to reflect about ourselves from without" (p. 606). Trial identification, momentary identification with the patient's perspective, and some degree of detachment from it, in order to *comprehend* it, to view it *also* from the outside, from the broader stance that the therapist assumes, is also the essence of the tension inherent in psychoanalysis generally. In psychoanalytically oriented work with schizophrenic patients, this tension, unless the therapist has tenaciously defended against it, is greatly magnified. What happens to these trial identifications when we work with patients whose thought processes and behaviors are so different from ours? The perspective "We are all more human than otherwise" is part of a romantic vision to which we cling. As romantically tinged therapists we defend ourselves against the possibility that an abyss may separate us from these patients, by projecting our own meanings onto their behavior. A mute patient's repetitive arm movements, forming, as I see it, an angle in the air, pauses after each repetition of the gesture and looks at me with a questioning look. Eventually I hazard, "You mean-what's my angle?" The patient's gestures stop. For a moment I wonder if I have understood, but not for long. Perhaps my effort to understand has had an impact? I still wonder about the latter interpretation, but I am no longer under the illusion that I have correctly interpreted the gesture's meaning. It is hard to accept not knowing, being in the dark. The wish to negate or at least to minimize the differences between the workings of my mind and those of my schizophrenic patient is great.

Nathaniel London (1973) made a major contribution in a two-part essay on the unitary and the specific psychoanalytic theory of schizophrenia. London wrote about the dangers of over-extending and under-extending theories generally and psychoanalytic theory in particular. He brilliantly described the struggles of Freud and of some other early and recent psychoanalytic authors to hold on to a parsimonious unitary psychoanalytic theory in the face of data that support a specific theory of schizophrenia. I believe the reluctance in theory building to abandon the unitary theory corresponds to the reluctance I experience in acknowledging my own lack of comprehension of my patient when I use my *common* sense, the sense that I deeply feel we *should* share, we should have in common. London stated, "The Unitary Theory asserts an essential continuity between schizophrenic and neurotic behaviors. Such an assertion, while possible, strains our available knowledge of these mental states so disparate in phenomenology and likely aetiologies. The Unitary Theory also considers intrapsychic conflict and defense as primary determiners (the independent variable) of schizophrenic behaviors. The Specific Theory is focused on a deficiency in mental representation" (p. 190). A unitary theory of schizophrenia could be fully congruent with a romantic vision. A specific theory of schizophrenia would necessitate some modifications of the romantic vision.

If schizophrenic patients have a defect, or defects, if there are "biological" differences, what happens to the romantic vision? Must it be abandoned, or is there a place for it in a specific theory of schizophrenia? On the practical level, can advances derived from the romantic vision be safeguarded in a modern hospital? Many demands push the hospital in the direction of the classic view that defines the patient's autonomy as his willingness and ability to adapt and submit to a "general," commonsense reality (Bullard 1994). The findings of the Chestnut Lodge follow-up study that a large number of patients did not do well after prolonged treatment (McGlashan 1984a, 1984b), and especially the economics of health care, played a major role in bringing about some changes at Chestnut Lodge. New antipsychotic medications have played a major part in helping many patients to adapt to the demands of society. The hospital operates in a climate in which the efficacy of psychodynamic approaches to schizophrenia is seriously questioned. Although seasoned clinicians have long been concerned with similar questions, current research focuses on them in a more rigorous fashion. "What distinguishes schizophrenic patients who engage and remain in E IO-type (insight oriented) therapies," and do they have "a history of more, not less, prior treatment" with other modalities (Gunderson 1993). At Chestnut Lodge the patient population has changed. Patients are younger, and the proportion of severe borderline patients has increased whereas the number of schizophrenic patients has decreased. In the past, schizophrenic patients who had been treated with no or little success with all available methods in other institutions had been accepted at Chestnut Lodge. There is less focus on individual psychotherapy now. Although the attention to the milieu has always been a feature of Chestnut Lodge, it now receives more attention than ever. The use of medication has increased, residential care, social therapies, and rehabilitation are emphasized.

A treatment goal for and of the patient may well be the development of a tolerance of the ambiguity inherent in the tension described by Strenger (1989): "the ability to experience ourselves from within and to reflect about ourselves from without" (p. 606). The challenge for the modern hospital may be whether or not it can tolerate this tension.

Donald Burnham (1969) has emphasized that the "need-fear dilemma"- the need for, and the fear of, closeness, the danger of an isolating, impenetrable, or an unprotecting barrier that threatens any separate autonomous existence—is a central issue that must be addressed in the treatment of schizophrenia. Burnham's focus on this dilemma can be seen as an attempt to deal with Stranger's (1989) romantic-classic tension, that is, the tension between an extreme individualism that cuts off contacts with others or that leads to total merging and dissolution of the self. It is Burnham's (romantic) effort to get in touch with the long-range fluctuations (not a cross-sectional approach) of the patient's conflicts that led him to the formulation of the need-fear dilemma. But is the *intensity* of the need-fear dilemma explained by the history of the individual's conflicts, or are there also nonconflictual etiologic factors for schizophrenic patients? I believe this question may still be open. Burnham has pointed out that the perspective of the need-fear dilemma may be useful in studying and influencing a patient's compliance (and that can be seen as the classic adaptational polarity) with a medication regimen. In any case, if the romantic vision implies a *continuity*, despite all the emphasis on individual variations, a qualitative commonality of the therapist's and the patient's conflicts and experiences, then the need-fear dilemma certainly qualifies as congruent with the romantic vision. We all experience the dilemma, but with more or less intensity. Burnham's need-fear dilemma offers a framework in which the romantic-classic tension can exist.

II.

I will now describe how I have tried to integrate a classic perspective with my own romantic views. In the sense in which London (1973) used the term, I have gradually and reluctantly also formulated a specific theory of schizophrenia. My own work with schizophrenic patients has also led me to focus on the nature of the schizophrenic's mental representations. I now believe that the most salient feature of schizophrenic thought disorder (and I am among those who believe that the thought disorder is the most salient feature of schizophrenia) are the schizophrenic's *objects*. These objects, however, are neither commonsense objects, such as a table, nor quite objects in the usual psychoanalytic sense, such as a mother, the "constant object," that represents the coalescence of the two original separate images of the frustrating and the gratifying mother. Furthermore, the existence of these schizophrenic objects does not mean that the common and commonsense objects cannot coexist with them for the patient. To spell out more clearly my hypothesis concerning schizophrenic thought disorder and schizophrenic "objects" I must briefly sketch ideas that have been developed in more detail elsewhere (Kafka 1989) about "ordinary" object formation. In contrast to Arieti (1963), I do not believe that thought-disordered schizophrenic patients use a logic different from that of individuals who are not schizophrenic; rather, they use the same logic applied to different objects.

The major lesson that patients have taught me about schizophrenic objects is that combinations of characteristics can be more *constant* than any "person", self or other, and "object" in the usual psychoanalytic sense. They have taught me that in order to comprehend them it is useful to decipher these combinations of characteristics, their own, their idiosyncratic relatively more constant objects, their "atmospheric objects," as I have come to call them. An example I have used concerns a patient who, during an acute psychotic episode, had called a particular nurse "Heidi." After emerging from this acute episode, she had explained to me that she never thought the nurse was "Heidi" but that the combination of being blond and having a foreign accent had evoked in her an atmosphere she could hold on to, the atmosphere of the book *Heidi* that she had loved since her childhood. She could not hold on to the identities of actual people, not mine or her own. In our language the object constancy of common or common-sense objects was missing, or at least less stable. It can be objected that after all there must have been such constancy because she always called the same nurse Heidi. But if we keep in mind the rapid fluctuations of levels of psychic organization and disorganization, the relatively greater stability of atmospheric objects becomes comprehensible (Kafka 1989).

Arieti's (1963) investigations of schizophrenic thought processes have been very influential. Arieti quoted Von Domarus's principle, which stated: "Whereas the normal person accepts identity only upon the basis of identical subjects, the schizophrenic may accept identity based on identical predicates" (p. 59). Arieti wrote: "If ... a schizophrenic happens to think, 'The Virgin Mary was a virgin, I am a virgin,' she may conclude 'I am the Virgin Mary.' ... For normal persons a class is a collection of objects to which a concept applies ... In paleological thinking ... a class is a collection of objects which have a predicate or part in common" (p. 59). The difficulty with Arieti's statement is that this essentially grammatical approach may have little to do with psychic reality. Arieti fails to point out in this context that what is part and what is whole, what is subject and what is predicate, are not building blocks of experience but are themselves the results of experience. When a patient has experienced a characteristic of a person as being more fundamental, more lasting, more "identical" over time than the person as a whole, this characteristic acquires qualities of the subject, and the person, then merely a personification of the more stable idea, acquires qualities of the predicate.

Although I disagree with Von Domarus's and Arieti's ideas concerning the nature of the "identities" involved in schizophrenic object formation, it is clear that all object formation, all "object permanence" involves the acceptance as "identical" of patterns of stimuli that are not exactly the same. Patterns of stimuli that differ in some respects from each other are accepted as subjectively equivalent, and thus all psychological "objects" are based on subjective equivalences. Even the psychological existence of a table requires the subjective equivalence of the different visual patterns that result when the table is seen from different angles.

Tachistoscopic experiments, that is, perceptual studies utilizing extremely brief exposures of stimuli (Smith and Danielson 1982), support the hypothesis that perceptual acts recapitulate the ontogeny of perception. Palmquist (1996) has recently studied perceptual processes of schizophrenic patients and control subjects by means of tachistoscopic percept-genetic experiments in which the exposure time needed for correct perception and the distortions with brief exposure times are compared. He found that "a feature of the average schizophrenic ... in this study is the inability to discriminate figure from ground, thus *stalling* [italics added] the perception of the human figures. This might be due to an inborn/acquired deficit or to the fact that the motifs presented generate such a level of anxiety that the defence against this becomes a kind of refusal... perhaps negation (or) regressive fragmentation of the entire percept-building sequence, or, a combination (p. 224).

In line with such experimental data, my hypothesis described more fully previously (Kafka 1989) is that ordinary object formation involves more or less complete recapitulative cycles that lead to subjective equivalences objects that are our commonsense objects. I also hypothesize that schizophrenic objects represent subjective equivalences resulting from a mixture of completed and aborted recapitulative perceptual cycles. Note that Palmquist (1996) left open the question of whether the perceptual "stalling" has an inborn biological cause, a dynamically understandable cause, or if it results from a combination of both. Later in this article I consider possible biological mechanisms, but I too consider the question still open, although interaction between these possible etiologies seems the most likely. Whatever their origin, such disordered rhythms, lead to idiosyncratic schizophrenic object formation and this, in my view, is the basis of schizophrenic thought disorder.

Because the discrimination of animate and inanimate stimulus sources may not be established in very early developmental phases, such discriminations may be absent in aborted recapitulative perceptual cycles. This may explain some strange features of schizophrenic objects. I want to focus, however, on the importance of synesthetic phenomena during the perceptual recapitulative cycles. The neurologist Richard Cytowic (1996) has reviewed current knowledge of the phenomenology and neuropsychology of synesthesia and concluded that the stimulation of one sensory modality reliably causing a perception in one or more different senses is a normal brain process. Synesthetes are described as individuals in whom this normal brain process is *prematurely* displayed to consciousness. Cytowic found that the hippocampus is critical for the experience of synesthesia, that seizure discharges in the hippocampus of the limbic system produce synesthesia in persons who are not ordinarily synesthetes, that seizures confined to the hippocampus produce simple synesthesias, but that spread to the cortex of the temporal lobe produces elaborated synesthetic perceptions.

My notion that formation of the common (and commonsense) object requires completion of perceptual recapitulative cycles is also congruent with Cytowic's thoughts about the perceptual process. He stated that, by analogy, the consensual image we see on the television screen corresponds to the terminal perception, but interception between the studio camera and the TV screen would reveal an analog to synesthesia. Cytowic found that synesthetes as a group seem more prone than the general population to "unusual" experiences as, for instances, *déjà vu*, precognitive dreams, clairvoyance and a feeling of a presence, all experiences that are frequently also described by schizophrenic patients.

I hypothesize that an explanation for the unusual experiences described by Cytowic's subjects and those of schizophrenic patients can be found in the mixture of complete and incomplete perceptual cycles, that is, some cycles that are arrested during the synesthetic phase and some of which go to the point when sensory compartmentalization is achieved. Some synesthetes, although they find it difficult to describe their experiences, do not interpret them, however, as unusual, otherworldly, and bizarre. I hypothesize that the uncanny interpretations may be linked to a connection between synesthesia and *déjà vu* and other *déjà vu* experiences that may be so pervasive in at least some schizophrenic patients that they contribute significantly to uncanny disorientation and derealization. I have hypothesized that a deja vu experience may occur when a present and a past perception are *identical* if these perceptions are processed synesthetically, whereas these same perceptions, processed with the usual sensory compartmentalization, are *different*. "Imagine that a particular wave pattern on an oscilloscope represents visual, auditory, or tactile stimuli. A responding organism or electronic scanning machine is then asked if this is a familiar *visual* pattern. Obviously, if the response is to the *pattern*, whatever the sensory modality involved, the likelihood that it will be familiar is much increased. That is, a *déjà vu* or related sensation will be aroused if the pattern of the visual stimulation evokes a corresponding echo in *any* other sensory compartment, be it auditory, tactile, or the like. In other words, if a certain pattern of stimulation, let us say a visual pattern, occurs at a time when the sensory compartments are preconsciously particularly interwoven, particularly blended, the chances that the pattern will arouse a feeling of familiarity are multiplied" (Kafka 1989, p. 46). If at the same time, the sensory compartments are separate on the conscious level, the uncanny feeling tone associated with *déjà vu* experiences can be understood as resulting from the disorienting simultaneous convictions that the situation is both *familiar* and unfamiliar.[37] My thoughts about the uncanny interpretation of synesthesia-related and temporal lobe-related *déjà vu* experiences form a bridge between what has been viewed conventionally as psychological and biological approaches to the phenomenology of schizophrenia. On the basis of structural, magnetic resonance imaging (MRI), and event-related potential (ERP) studies, integrated with functional findings from the basic neuro-sciences and with clinical data, McCarley et al. (1993) believe that the psychology of schizophrenia and the biology of temporal lobe abnormalities are closely related and that this relationship will be a central component of the data-based pathophysiological characterization of schizophrenia.

In any case, if, as I hypothesize, brief intermittent runs of synesthesia-related *déjà vu* experiences contribute to the movements in and out of psychotic disorganization that can take place within fractions of a second, no therapist can hope to follow these movements accurately. The therapist, however, who assumes that the patient experiences these extremely rapid changes in levels of functioning, and who therefore approaches the patient on multiple levels (of functioning) at the same time, is more likely to be "on target." At Chestnut Lodge our therapeutic approach was informed by the recognition that some schizophrenic patients had not only these micro

---

[37] Such a chain of reasoning based on the clinically derived hypothesis concerning synesthesia leads to empirically addressable questions about which neurotransmitters and receptors in what brain areas mediate sensory compartmentization and synesthesia. Do antipsychotic drugs bind preferentially to these receptors?

temporal fluctuations in levels of functioning but also that some were able to comprehend, and feel at ease in, highly complex and abstract domains whereas at the same time they may have been severely deficient in problem-solving abilities needed for daily functioning. This has specific implications for therapeutic technique. Then, and now, I would work with a patient on cognitive problems involved in ordering in a restaurant or using a telephone and at the same time dynamically explore, to give a specific example, the emotional history of her peculiar body sensations when she informs me that she "has her father's legs and therefore could not shave them." Liberman and Corrigan (1993) wrote: "Just as a stroke victim undergoing physical therapy must learn to use a cane or walker in order to resume ambulatory skills, persons with schizophrenia may also need the 'cognitive prosthesis' of the deliberate and systematic application of the problem-solving steps to negotiate ... everyday life" (p. 246). Although the modules of the psychosocial treatments they describe include much that was also done alongside the psychodynamic treatment of these patients, it is both the institutional systematic application of these instructional and cognitive techniques and the investigations of their effectiveness that are new. Some of these more cognitive approaches to schizophrenic patients resemble techniques employed with brain-injured patients. It is interesting in this context to note that Paul Federn (1952), probably the first psychoanalyst working with schizophrenic patients, felt that they needed, during phases of their illness, a *mental hygiene* approach that involved helping the patients recognize the special features of their cognitive and perceptual processes in order to minimize the effects of these "defects." Federn thought in rather biological terms that a boundary defect accounted for the inability to differentiate external and internal stimuli and that this lack of differentiation of outer and inner sources of stimulation could explain hallucinations. The term *atmosphere* also denotes a degree of suspension of the question of external or internal origin of an experience, of a mood, and this question may also be suspended in the schizophrenic's atmospheric object.

It is not an idealization of the misery of schizophrenia to recognize that these atmospheric objects may have a certain poetic beauty that both patients and therapists can value. They can share this broad romantic vision.

Patients and therapists can sometimes recognize the need for a coexisting "narrowing," and sometimes the possible usefulness of medication for "narrowing" their concepts, for making them more utilitarian. To elaborate, I believe every therapist who uses medication has a hypothesis (sometimes quite private, not verbalized, and occasionally not yet verbalizable) about the mode of action of the medication. One of my hypotheses involving the narrow-wide dimension is that some antipsychotic medications interfere with synesthetic experience, the blending of sensory modalities, and that some medications facilitate sensory compartmentalization. Cytowic's (1996) references to convulsive foci and synesthesia suggest a possible mode of antipsychotic action of some anticonvulsive medications. Other psychoactive drugs may interfere with the spread from the limbic system to the temporal lobe.

Whether or not *déjà vu* phenomena or synesthesia play a part in a particular case, a schizophrenic patient with whom I worked "psychodynamically," but whom I also taught how to use a telephone and how to order in a restaurant, asked me, "Should I talk broad or narrow today?" She and other patients have expressed to me their fear of losing richer concepts, their fear of loss of the overtones of sounds, as opposed to *utilitarian* sound that may have little or no harmonic and melodic development.

Mueser (1993), in their commentary on Liberman and Corrigan (1993), discussed research on the interaction between psychopharmacological treatment and social-learning approaches. They pointed out that pharmacological treatment only blunts the effects of interpersonal stress that may lead to re-hospitalization. Additional behavioral family therapy and cognitive social skills training of patients play an important part in reducing relapse. Mueser et al. referred to findings that a lowering of affective intensity saves money by reducing re-hospitalization rates.

At first a romantic vision of schizophrenia and its treatment seems hard to reconcile with a focus on the economic advantages of diminished affectivity. Failures of treatments aiming at a general affective blunting of family and patient may be explained, however, by seemingly paradoxical interpersonal stresses that occur when the characteristics of a particular family, the individuality of the patient, and their interaction, are neglected. It is important that knowledge of the cognitive defects of schizophrenics inform some aspects of the treatment, but such techniques can coexist with the romantic notion of the value of an individualized approach that requires dynamic understanding. In this sense Reiss' (1995) work exemplifies the marriage of classical and romantic vision. He illustrated the complexities of such a conceptual marriage by writing that "genetic evidence clarifies the magnitude of nongenetic environmental influences on pathogenesis. Second, genetically-informed designs can specify ... the type of environmental influences which may be operating ... the distinction between characteristics . .. common to sibs in a family ... and factors .. . unique to each sib. Third, genetically-informed designs search for genetic influences on environmental factors which may be critical components of the mechanisms of gene expression ... heritable characteristics of children influence the level of adversity of parental treatment of them" (p. 3). Reiss pointed to research designs that explicitly and systematically deal with issues with which a clinician who works intensively with a particular family and a particular patient may be in touch empathically and less explicitly.

With or without the use of medication, we have to confront the fact that there are states in which some schizophrenic patients are unreachable. These are the times when I can only wait. But the therapist's presence-again and again-at those moments of entry and exit from psychotic episodes form a kind of bond and may permit the patient to communicate to the therapist in a subtle manner the need for hospitalization by a reference, for instance, to an event from a previous hospitalization. Much distress, violence, and trauma often associated with hospitalization can be avoided if such cues are attended to. Patients have taught me about the connection between their "unreachableness" and the problem of *consciousness*, a problem more mysterious than that of the unconscious. A patient says, "There are thoughts and feelings around, but I don't know whose they are." Descartes's "*cogito, ergo sum*" does not hold. Is there a temporal element involved? In order to feel that the thoughts and feelings that are "around" are one's own, must the experience of these thoughts and feelings and the experience of one's self occur within a time limit defined as *now*? At the dawn of experimental psychology, the psychological *now* was defined as the time interval that is neither over-estimated nor underestimated, because very short periods are generally overestimated and longer ones underestimated. The study of perceptual recapitulative cycles and the possibility that the experience of *now* may be linked to the experience of *I* have led me to focus more and more on the temporal aspects of mental functioning. When we talk about time, our usual mind-matter dichotomies tend to evaporate. That rhythmic pat-terns and coincidences play a part in the experience of consciousness is an idea that now finds an echo in a number of neuroscientific investigations. Jonathan Winson (1985) for instance, has suggested that consciousness may be related to the time it takes for specific feedback circuits to process a stimulus. He cited the experiments carried out by Libby on neurosur-gical patients. The interval between the sensation of having one's hand touched was longer when the cortex (cortical projection area of the hand) was stimulated directly than when the stimulus was applied to the hand, a condition in which the sensation was almost simultaneous. In Winson's view, the *delay of awareness with direct cortical stimulation* could correspond, could have some eventually definable relationship, to the neuronal circuitry underlying consciousness.

Again and again we must use "spatial" words in our attempts to *de-scribe* temporal experiences and phenomena. Consciousness, as we have discussed it, is an "in-sight," perhaps the fundamental insight, but we have to use the spatial *seeing from the outside in*, to describe this tem-poral double take. There are, however, some literally spatial expressions that we experience more "temporally." Although "surprise" (literally, "take from above") is a spatial term, it provokes a temporal resonance, probably because it contains movement, therefore time. Actually, sur-prise deals with a double take of time, a kind of "two-timing," an expectation of one kind of timing and the occurrence of another kind of timing. The German word is *überraschen*, literally, "rushing beyond." Consciousness is a kind of overtaking oneself, a temporal split, a *décalage*, a micro-jet lag, a catching up with one's shadow.

The schizophrenic patient who had not known that the "thinking that was around" was his own also told me that he believed that im-provement had started the moment one psychiatric aide told him that he had a *choice*. I, however, think that his improvement manifested itself in the fact that he was *able* to hear this communication at that moment, to comprehend it, to conceptualize himself as a center of autonomous action, to be conscious of self, to be *conscious*. At this point we do not know what factors cause, or perhaps even consistently contribute to, this emergence from the deepest psychotic states, these particular "disorders of consciousness." Perhaps a change of timing in the neuronal circuitry, a change in the rhythmic activities of neurotransmitter receptors, or a change in the patterns of circuitries involved brings the lag necessary for the double take of consciousness within the acceptable limits for psychologies now (Kafka 1992). Perhaps, and this is one of my working hypotheses concerning possible modes of action of some anti-psychotic medications, they modify the timing in the neuronal circuitry and have an effect on consciousness and accessibility.

Both my hypotheses about schizophrenic object formation and about consciousness and accessibility thus involve timing and brain rhythmicity. Marian Kafka and I in 1983, using Longuet-Higgins's (1969) ideas about a temporal hologram, described a temporal model of the brain in which shared rhythmicities were more important than brain localization. Current research substantiates these speculations (Schechter 1996). Summarizing recent findings, Schechter wrote: "The shape of an apple ... is recognized by the neurons in one portion of the visual cortex and its color by another portion ... Researchers believe that the solution to the binding problem lies in regular rhythms in the brain which seem to become synchronized whenever separate regions are responding to the same apple (p. 339)."

Another area in which clinically derived ideas are congruent with current research data concerns my critique of the double-bind hypothesis (Kafka 1971). The latter stated that paradoxical communication from parent to offspring could be a pathogenic, perhaps especially a schizophrenogenic element. My work with patients and their families has led me, however, to the hypothesis that it was parental paralysis, when confronted with paradoxical communications, that could be a pathogenic factor (Kafka 1989). It is the absence of ambiguity tolerance that has pathogenic consequences. This conclusion is congruent with the findings of Tienari et al. (1985, 1987) suggesting that ambiguity tolerance of adoptive families may be a powerful protective factor against the development of schizophrenic symptomatology even in individuals who are particularly vulnerable on the basis of biological genetics (Reiss et al. 1991).[38]

Let us once again return to Strenger's (1989) contrast between the romantic and the classic perspectives in psychoanalysis, the romantic vision anchored in the subjective—the optimistic view from within, the perfectibility of the unique, a fountain, he says, as contrasted with a bucket that has limits, the Kantian given framework, a relatively pessimistic view of humanity. London's (1973) contrasting between the unitary theory and the specific theory of schizophrenia is congruent with Strenger's romantic-classic dichotomy. A unitary theory that postulates fundamental similarities in the basic conflicts of schizophrenic and nonschizophrenic individuals also postulates similarities in appropriate psychoanalytic approaches. From one perspective this, however, *is* a view from the outside, the more classic perspective emphasizing communality. Yet initially this very hope for communality between the mental processes of schizophrenic patients and our own was the basis for a kind of romantic and optimistic therapeutic zeal. The specific theory of schizophrenia, on the other hand, underlines differences, a "*deficiency* [italics added] in mental representations" (London 1973, p. 190).[39] For me there was, however, an evolution, a reconciliation of perspectives. Although the atmospheric schizophrenic objects may be the result of a "deficiency," as seen from the outside, the therapist struggling to *understand* these idiosyncratic, not commonsense objects, to comprehend them also from within (the patient), has a romantic vision by virtue of the intense focus on this particular inner reality of the individual. The classic outside view, the recognition of the schizophrenic "deficiency" coexists with the respectful search for the individual's inner truth.

In summary, the evolution of the romantic vision of schizophrenia has taken me—and many of my colleagues—from a stance emphasizing

---

[38] In an important article David Reiss has pointed out that even in those conditions in which biological genetic factors have been clearly recognized, they account for less than 50% of the variance.

[39] London, incidentally, did not exclude the possibility that biological factors may be more or less etiological factors here.

the similarity of our own and our schizophrenic patients' mental processes to a recognition of differences. Yet our work entails the search for some common elements in our mental processes. I have shown why I believe that the logic of schizophrenic patients and our own is the same. If there were no common element, the hopes for communication with each other would be minimal indeed. But if only the objects to which the logic is applied, are different, thoughtful contact with our patients often permits us to learn much about their idiosyncratic atmospheric objects, and communication becomes possible.

Because I see the problem of consciousness and consciousness of self as a central issue in our study of schizophrenia, a metaphor comes to mind that opens a bridge between neuroscience and a romantically tinged poetic image. Perhaps neuronal change in timing of the circuitry involved "brings the lag necessary for the double take of consciousness within the acceptable limits for psychological *now*. For our schizophrenic patient the intervention of the psychiatric aide (who told him that he had a choice) was like the appearance of sunlight that permits a sundial (that translates space into time) to function; it is the split between the object and its moving shadow that gives us consciousness and that gives us time" (Kafka 1992, p. 94).

The hypotheses concerning schizophrenic pathology which have been outlined in this article have specific implications for therapeutic techniques and for a therapeutic stance when working with such patients. Furthermore, because the exploration of schizophrenic pathology has led to hypotheses about differences and similarities between psychotic and nonpsychotic mental processes, these hypotheses have implications for a wider patient population. The hypothesis that incomplete perceptual recapitulative cycles lead to idiosyncratic objects that can become understandable has its most specific therapeutic implication for work with some schizophrenic patients and with some brain-injured patients. I now believe that the "entitlement" of some borderline and narcissistic patients may be the result of a stalled perceptual development involving the differentiation of animate and inanimate sources of stimulation. Such patients may expect that the inanimate environment is as responsive as the animate environment; hence, their peculiar entitlement that can lead to such negative countertransference reactions and unproductive confrontations in which the therapist emphasizes the patient's responsibility for an act or an event. A therapeutic approach informed by the hypothesis concerning animate-inanimate differentiation sensitizes the therapist to this issue. This may help the therapist to take advantage in a non-confrontive manner of moments in which the blending of the animate and inanimate worlds is not complete and ego-syntonic for the patient. Experience with schizophrenic patients has alerted me to the fact that for some neurotic patients cognitive approaches can be productively integrated with the more usual psychoanalytic and psychodynamic strategies. In a psychoanalytic therapeutic frame, cognitive approaches need not lead to unproductive defensive intellectualization. Finally, the focus on the temporal aspects of mental processes as considered in perceptual recapitulation, in synesthesia and *déjà vu* phenomena, and ultimately in hypotheses about the very nature of consciousness, has wide-ranging therapeutic implications. Through their effects on neural timing, psychoactive drugs may be crucial for the accessibility of some schizophrenic patients. Calling patients' attention to issues of timing may be a relatively nonthreatening component of cognitively tinged interventions with many kinds of patients. One example is a suggestion to a patient to "linger" on a thought or feeling before rushing on, a simple example of an often useful intervention that is informed by the therapist's attention to the complexities—including the defensive uses—of thinking.

We have known a honeymoon and a post-honeymoon nostalgia for a period in which a romantic vision, as I have described it, influenced our treatment philosophy of schizophrenia. We went beyond this, however, and new conceptual vistas, research, and treatment possibilities have opened up. Bridges built with new sophistication and without simplistic reductionism will connect new and old thinking. The humanistic psychiatric tradition that informed the psychoanalytic and psychodynamic approach to schizophrenia need not be lost.

References

Arieti, S. (1963). Studies of thought processes in contemporary psychiatry. *American Journal of Psychiatry* 120:58-64.

Bullard, D., Jr. (1994). *History and current practice of treatment of schizophrenia at Chestnut Lodge.* Paper presented at the International Symposium for Psychotherapy of Schizophrenia, Washington, D.C. June 1994.

Burnham. D., Gibson. A. W., and Gladstone. A. (1969). *Schizophrenia, the Need/Fear Dilemma.* International Universities Press.

Cohen, R. (1994). *History of treatment of schizophrenia.* Paper presented at the International Symposium for the Psychotherapy of Schizophrenia. Washington, D.C. June 1994.

Conci, M. (1994). *Formal Discussion of panel at the International Symposium for the Psychotherapy of Schizophrenia.* Washington, D.C. June 1994.

Cytowic, R. (1996). *Neurology Side of Neuropsychology.* MIT Press.

Cytowic. R. *Syesthesia: Phenomenology and neuropsychology.* A review of current knowledge. *Psyche* URL: ftp "//herl.open.ac.uk/pub/psyche/ (Paper version MIT Press: Cambridge]

Federn, P. (1952). Ego Psychology and the Psychoses. Basic Books.

Gunderson, J. (1993). Commentary: Schizophrenic patients. *Psychiatry* 56(3):308.

Kafka, J. (1971). Ambiguity for individuation-A critique and reformulation of double-bind theory. *Archives of General Psychiatry* 25:232-239.

Kafka, J. (1992). Consciousness and the shadow of time. In M. Leuzinger-Bohleber, H. Schneider, and R. Pfeiffer, eds.. *Two Butterflies on My Head. Psychoanalysis in the Interdisciplinary Scientific Dialogue,* pp. 87-95. Springer.

Kafka, J. (1989). *Multiple Realities in Clinical Practice.* Yale University Press.

Kafka, J., and Kafka, M. (1983). *Timing and mental illness.* Presentation, VII World Congress of Psychiatry. Austria: Vienna. July 1983.

Levander, S., and Cullberg, J. Sandra (1993). Successful psychotherapeutic work with a schizophrenic woman. *Psychiatry* 56(3):284-293.

Liberman, R., and Corrigan, P. (1993). Designing new psychosocial treatments for schizophrenia. *Psychiatry* 56(3):238-249.

London, N. (1973). An Essay on psychoanalytic theory: Two theories of schizophrenia. Part I: Review and critical assessment of the development of the two theories. Part II: Discussion and restatement of the specific theory of schizophrenia. *International Journal of Psychoanalysis* 54(2):69-178.

Longuet-Higgins, H., Willshaw, D., and Buneman, O. (1969). Non-holographic associative memory. *Nature* 222:960-962.

McCarley, R., Shenton, M., O=Donnell, B., and Nestor, P. (1993). Uniting Kraeplin and Bleuler: The psychology of schizophrenia and the biology of temporal lobe abnormalities. *Harvard Review of Psychiatry* 1:36-56.

McGlashan, T. (1984a). The Chestnut Lodge follow-up study. I: Follow-up methodology and study sample. *Archives of General Psychiatry* 41: 573-585.

McGlashan, T. (1984b). The Chestnut Lodge follow-up study. II: Long-term outcome of schizophrenia and the affective disorders. *Archives of General Psychiatry* 41:586-601.

Mueser, K., Bellack, A., Douglas, M. S., and Morrison, R. L. (1991). Prevalence and stability of social skill deficits in schizophrenia. *Schizophrenia Research* 5:167-76.

Mueser, K. (1993). Commentary on Liberman and Corrigan. *Psychiatry* 56(3):250-253.

Palmquist, D. A. (1996). *A study of critical variables in the anxiety of schizophrenics by means of structured clinical interview and percept-genetic experiment.* University of Lund, Department of Psychology.

Reiss, D. (1995). Editorial: Families and schizophrenia redux. *Psychiatry* 58(l):1-5.

Reiss, D., Plomin, R., and Hetherington, E. M. (1991). Genetics and psychiatry: An unheralded window on the environment. *American Journal of Psychiatry* 148(3):283-291.

Schechter, B. (1996). How the brain gets rhythm. *Science* 274:339-340.

Schulz. C. (1994). *Evolution of current treatment of schizophrenia*. Paper presented at the International Symposium for the Psychotherapy of Schizophrenia, Washington, DC, June 1994.

Silver, A.-L. (1993). Countertransference, Ferenczi. and Washington, DC. *Journal of the American Academy of Psychoanalysis* 21(4):637-654.

Smith, G. J. W., and Danielson, A. (1982). Anxiety and defensive strategies in childhood adolescence. *Psychological Issues* (1982) Monograph 52.

Strenger, C. (1989). The classic and the romantic vision in psychoanalysis. *International Journal of Psychoanalysis* 70(4):563-610.

Tienari, P., Lahti, L, Sorri, A., Naarla, M., Moring, J., Whalberg, K.-E., and Wynne, L. C. (1987). The Finnish adoptive family study of schizophrenia. *Journal of Psychiatric Research* 21(4): 437-445.

Tienari, P., Sorri, A., and Lahti, I. (1985). Interaction of genetic and psychosocial factors in schizophrenia. *Acta Psychiatric Scandinavica* 71:19-30.

Winson, J. (1985). *Brain and Psyche: The Biology of the Unconscious*. Anchor Press.

Journal of The American Academy of Psychoanalysis, 18(1), 18-28, 1990

Chapter 15

On the Question of Insight in Psychosis

We are discussing psychoanalytic approaches to psychosis at a peculiar time in the history of our field. Let me quote from a recent article in *Science* on schizophrenia research:

> "Scientific leads have been a long time coming, in part because of the grip of psychoanalytic theories of mental illnesses which did not loosen until the 1970s when the revolution in biological psychiatry finally unseated psychosocial factors as the primary etiological suspects for schizophrenia." (Barnes, 1987)

Distortions of history sometimes are the result of the choice of the moment at which one thinks a particular story has its beginning. The search for the "organic" causes of schizophrenia has a much longer history than the psychoanalytic search for an understanding of the disorder and the psychoanalytic approaches were the result of the failures of the organic approaches. New levels of biological sophistication should, however, not blind us to the dangers of reductionism and to the premature jettisoning of the results of psychoanalytic work.

A review of current issues in biological research on schizophrenia demonstrates to what extent this research may be hampered by a lack of consensus on what is meant by psychosis and by schizophrenia, a question to which psychoanalytic work has much to contribute. When we study the question of insight in psychosis, into what are we seeking insight? Lest we, as psychoanalytic and psychodynamic investigators, by comparing our understanding to that of more biologically focused workers, develop feelings of inadequacy, it is important to consider the current state of biological research.

In the above-cited review article in *Science*, Kenneth Kendler says,

> "If you put everything that is known about schizophrenia into a pot and boiled it down, you would come up with three things—it seems to run in families, neuroleptics [drugs that interact in some way with the brain's dopamine system] make it better, and there may be something structurally abnormal in the brains of schizophrenics."

The article goes on to say that "Researchers continue to debate whether schizophrenia represents a discrete mental disorder, or is just one component of a spectrum of mental illnesses." Ming Tsuang of Harvard Medical School thinks that the current data favor the former, traditional concept of two discrete, major psychoses. One is schizophrenia, which starts during adolescence and usually becomes worse; the other includes affective disorders, which occur in episodes and are less likely to incapacitate the patient. But he says, "to really nail this down, we need to have molecular genetics studies to show whether the two diseases are different at the molecular level."

Timothy Crow (a prominent British researcher) sees affective illnesses and schizophrenia as opposite ends of a continuum of psychotic disorders, rather than being separate disease entities. At one end of the spectrum is depression, followed by manic depression, mixed schizophrenia and affective disorder, and schizophrenia without accompanying affective disorder. Crow emphasizes that "the people in the middle of the spectrum are much more common" than those at either extreme. Steven Matthysse (of McLean Hospital in Massachusetts) emphasizes the uniqueness of the thought disorder in schizophrenia. Although both manic-depressive patients and schizophrenics have disturbed thinking, the way schizophrenics think is special. ... It is so distinct that it may be used to define the disorder."

In connection with the question of the inheritance of this undefined disorder, it is pointed out that 90% of relatives of schizophrenic patients are *not* schizophrenic, and there are conflicting hypotheses of a single major gene locus or of multiple genetic causes. Methodological questions and questions of interpretation surround possible findings of structural lesions in the limbic system and parts of the neocortex (but here there is perhaps rapid progress), inconsistencies in the findings of enlarged ventricles are legion and most if not all of the findings reported are not specific to schizophrenia. Some findings of task related decreased blood flow to the prefrontal cortex (i.e., decreased blood flow only at the time when the patient is asked to perform specific tasks) offer especially great problems in interpretation since the issues of motivation and effort enter the picture. I expect that the question whether certain developmental processes in the brain that take place around puberty may be related to schizophrenia, will be discussed later during today's program. The recent review article summarizes the picture as follows, "For every point of view about the biology of schizophrenia there is a counterpoint." This then is not the time, in my opinion, in which to discard the hard-to-come-by phenomenologically descriptive, and psychoanalytically conceptual data about psychosis.

One of the issues which has been prominent in psychoanalytic discussions of schizophrenia is whether or not we are dealing with a distinct primary disorder with secondary compensatory defensive or restitutional processes or if psychoanalytic conflict theory is sufficient to account for the development of schizophrenic symptoms (London, 1973). One of the earliest psychoanalysts working with schizophrenic patients, Paul Federn, postulated a primary disorder which, in an oversimplified way, was characterized by insufficient *cathexis* at the border of the ego. If there are insufficient troops at the border, the ego cannot distinguish perceptions or ideas which originate outside the border from those that originate inside and, therefore, for instance, perceptions cannot be distinguished from hallucinations. It is conceivable that an updated model of Federn's ideas, a model using data from receptor studies, could guide some biological research.

Dr. Marian Kafka and I have proposed a model in which certain disrhythmias of transmittor receptor functions are related to perceptual and thought disorders of schizophrenic patients (Kafka, 1983). My ideas about schizophrenic thought disorder are summarized in a chapter, "The Schizophrenic's Objects" in the Ping Pao Memorial Volume edited by David Feinsilver (Kafka, 1986) and they are more fully developed in my book, *Multiple Realities in Clinical Practice* (Kafka, 1989).

The central hypothesis is that constant objects of schizophrenic patients have specifiable differences from those established during ordinary object-constancy formation. A certain characteristic or attribute shared by several individuals in the patient's environment may be, for instance, the constant object for him or her, while the persons themselves may not have such object constancy. The schizophrenic applies ordinary logic to idiosyncratic objects. Furthermore, the study of the ontogeny of perception offers clues concerning the formation of these idiosyncratic object constancies. (a) Normally, each perceptual act recapitulates the ontogeny of perception. (b) The psychological constancy of the object is based on the subjective equivalence of different percepts, and is dependent on the relative completion of each perceptual act. (c) Idiosyncratic object constancies occur when some perceptual acts are carried to relative completion, while other perceptual processes are interrupted at various earlier stages in the micro-development of the perception. (d) There could be psychodynamic or "biological" explanations for these perceptual disrhythmias.

Time thus plays an important part in the hypotheses concerning schizophrenic thought disorder formulated until now. Ideas about thought disorder may, however, be of little use to us when we deal with a patient in the depth of psychotic inaccessibility. In the discussion section below I will suggest that a temporal factor will not only help us in our understanding of the thought disorder, but will propose a possible mechanism of temporal discrepancy that may be essential for consciousness.

We will soon turn to an autobiographical account of a schizophrenic patient in order to deal with our subject on a less abstract level. I hope to demonstrate that typical clinical accounts support the following notion: The primary disorder is closely related to or consists of the patient's "feelings not being connected to a sense of self." If this is so, the task confronting biological researchers of schizophrenia is nothing less than to elucidate the biology of the sense of self, which is, I believe, the biology of consciousness itself.

"Insight," in the American College Dictionary is defined as follows:

"1) a sight had or given into something: (example) this little insight into the life of the village. 2) penetrating mental vision or discernment; faculty of seeing into inner character or underlying truth: (example) a man of great insight. 3) (the technical) Psychological (meaning is) a. the sudden grasping of a solution: configurational learning. b. the ability to see oneself as others see one; self-knowledge. c. (Specific meaning in psychiatry) the capacity of a mental patient to know that he is suffering from mental disorder."

Note that the definition—as it relates to psychosis—concerns insight into a *process*, whereas the other definitions relate more to mental *content*.

Psychoanalysis spells out specific mechanisms of how some of the insights described above (insights related to mental content primarily) are obtained, by focusing on shifts in the meaning of connections. Insight into the meaning of a slip of the tongue occurs when the apparent (i.e., unconnected to motivation) slip becomes connected to a motivation of which the individual had not been aware previously. On the other hand a person may have felt guilty because he connected his unconscious death wish with the actual death of an individual. I have illustrated this point elsewhere by showing how an analysand's unconscious belief that her death wish at age 4 toward a brother killed him determined major aspect of her later life and how "insight" into this led to major changes in her life. The false causal connection can be dissolved when the wish becomes conscious. The wish, when seen in the light of day, did not kill.

Following are some autobiographical notes of a schizophrenic patient. The patient is a man in his mid-30s, and he has a history of long hospitalization. He has been out of hospital for over 5 years and has not been on medication for the past 4 years. As you read, I invite you to distinguish insights into what you consider psychotic phenomena from other insights. Are there connections between "psychotic" and non-psychotic insights? Are there some insights which, at least in their formal characteristics, apply across the board? What is your sense of the clinical importance of some of the insights expressed?

NOTES from Dr. Kafka: The patient has given permission for the use of this material. Grammar and spelling have been generally preserved. Words that could not be deciphered with certainty are marked.

"I would like to relate on my previous condition to you as before hospitalization on how I related to the world or my state of reality. First off there are a number of things one must assume. That is I had no sense of my being as self, that is I wasn't aware that my feelings were related to myself. I had no sense of worth or really care about myself. I always tried to please the other fellow or think that I was, that was the problem. Actually I wasn"t communicating in a sane way so nobody had a way of telling me that I was off my rocker. But I'm getting ahead of myself. I"ll try to start at the beginning. As far back as I can remember I felt that I was worthless. I always felt that I could read other people's minds and that they could read mine. This lead, as one may imagine to intense paranoia. I compensated for it by hiding everything- all my emotions thoughts and what I really felt like doing was suppressed. For example, if I felt I wanted a glass of water I would have to test the environment (by that I mean asking others or by getting some ["upleat"? complete?] answer from some sign that it was alright for me to drink water at that time. This is just an example but I think it clarifies what was going on inside.) If it wasn't the right time of day or the sunset wasn't pretty enough or something so silly as that I would not drink. This applied to other things as well. Certain topics were forbidden to bring up. (Maybe the earth would open up and swallow me who knows the reasons.) However I did not even think about what was on my mind always trying to get in touch with that nebulous sign in the environment that give me the "okay" symbol. All the while I was depressed and insecure on the inside. I was coherent but felt like there was something pressed against my brain most of the waking hours and think I first saw a sociologist when I was in the eighth grade. Also, (I'm skipping around just trying to relate what comes up) I had a most horrible relationship with every member of my family.

"Due to what was oppressing me or my depression I also engage in a type of testing my environment. I remember I felt extreme guilt and sensed I hadn't had enough pain in my life. This was probably physical hurt though I also felt that that applied to emotional hurt. The incredible thing about mental dicess [?] (I hesitate to call it a disease) is that one doesn't realize he's going through a lot of strain, as I didn't. I thought and felt that it was normal to be the way that I was. I know I had a few problems, but until now when I am completely better did I, or rather should I say do I realize the depth of my problems. I believe that my reality was distorted and I didn"t realize that my reality was distorted.

"The guilt that I felt was overwhelming. I felt guilty to be alive while others were dieing, guilty to have food while half the world was hungry, guilty about my parents' lifestyle and most of all guilty about sin. I knew that men were all worthless and totally useless to God as I was. This lead me to a search for God. I knew that he existed for someone had to made a semblance of reasonableness out of my life. I'll get into more of that later. But my guilt about sin was terrible. I felt that I hadn't had enough pain in my life and started to think that I needed some more. To gratify this desire I started dropping shelves on my feet and halfway slamming car door on my hand. I didn't do it too hard, I just closed the door on it enough to hurt. The shelves I also didn't drop from too great a height, just enough to do temporary damage. But I felt I had this coming, it was a sort of eminent feeling that if I didn't do this to myself, some sort of "higher power" would do it for me.

"There were three ways in which I tested my environment, being (1) people (2) things as the shelves and drawers indicate and (3) idea or imagination which usually lead to testing with people or things. All of this or a lot of it started when I was in college or first dropped, flunked out. However I remember being very young and practicing piano, when I got real upset I used to bite the keys, as if they were the problem and bite the paper of books when they doesn't make sense, I figured that at least I had average intelligence and if I couldn't understand it, then no one could and it didn't deserve to be written.

"The way I tested people were many and varied. First off I was sort of abrasive to most everyone. I never really got along with my parents. I thought that I had made a major revelation when I was about 17. I decided that not I or anyone else cared about any other person. Everybody was on this planet to use others or to be used. Now that can be argued philosophically but practically, if I had hit on a truth I abused it to the tilt. I got mad at people easy, but didn't always express it, cursed at them and just got along with my small group of friends. We banded together as one against the world. This is during the "hippie" revolution and everyone was stressing peace and love on the outside but repressing anger on the inside. I was anyway.

"My relationships with my parents was pretty awful most of the time. I never talked to my father about anything that most fathers talk to their sons about. He would come home about 5 o'clock and have a couple drinks and the fighting would begin. It would either end by me walking out of the house, he or my mom throwing me out or both. There was rarely any peace around when I lived at home around the summer and winter of '73. At that time I was talking to a shrink but I don't remember too much of that time due to what was later to happen to me.

"I seemed to put people in categories according to the lines on their face. All this is kind of crazy I know now, but not so crazy as to not have a partial truth mixed in to a pretty disturbed area. I thought that the chin was a sign of caring whether is was clefted or not. The clefted people were the ones who used people and didn't care about them. There were others who were fools but really didn't know that they were being fooled. I know it's somewhat difficult to follow but there were other rules such as the clefted individuals always knew what they were talking about or made sense while the others (fools) didn't. Now there were even more clever people who could carry on the game further and acted like they cared when in the real sense they were just using the fools to a higher degree. An example would be for me to tell you (a fool) to build me a big structure and use all of your money and efforts to accomplish this. Then when it was almost completed I'd tell you that it didn't really serve as my purpose and you did all that hard work for nothing. That was my one great fear. That I wasn't afraid of work wasn't the issue. It is just that I would do all of this for naught. And someone would come along and say "you idiot, now you really blew it" and they would laugh at my folly. This is what was going on inside my head at that time. I was one of the fortunate individuals who caught on the game and whose mission it was to express it. My father was one of these "parasitic" people who tried to continue the game acting as if nothing was ever wrong, but never letting any of their own feelings come out of. Actually I wasn't that far off as far as people's uncaring goes, just it was carried to ludiciosity by my paranoia.

"By the way I think that "mental disease" is a misnomer. A disease is biological and can be diagnosed. Most patients don't have the problem that easily nailed down so it can be pointed out specifically as being "this" and not "that." In other words some psychological terms such as paranoia, schizophrenia and so on are so nebulous that that really carry no weight. Also some of the symptoms seems to overlap a lot. Who says that this thought of killing someone is paranoid and not psychotic? Where does one get the audacity to label a catatonic person as such, maybe it's extreme depression? I want to paint this out for several seasons. One being that when one gets "better or well" (both terms I despise) one realizes that throughout the day in normal society it's perfectly "normal" to many about that young man following your home from work. One does feel down in the dumps and gets depressed. The hardest thing about becoming a true person or back into reality is extrapolating the definite qualities of genuine difficulties and separating from them the "fantasy" or made-up problems which you're just coming out of. In other words in reality, there are times to exhibit signs which if they were in a mental patient, would deem that that person is no worse off than I am or was.

"A breakdown is hard to define. Some people exhibit qualities of them everyday yet handle them. The stress of life is tremendous and causes us to take a break for hours each day known as sleep. However what I'm trying to discern specifically is that there are several steps to mental sickness and the first step is to as they say recognize things are going haywire which is a very humbling and humiliating thing to do. For me to say "yes, I'm crazy I can't handle things, lock me up" is a very heavy thing in and of itself. The expression "you have to get worse before you get better" is applicable here. What I think they're referring to is to let yourself really get depressed and "let it all hang out" and get the "stuff" out of your system onto the table so we can examine it. It's probably more condusive to do this in a controlled environment so they intended mental hospitals.

"My philosophy of hospitalization (mental wards) is not particularly appealing to a modern day money grabbing psychiatrist, but I'll explain anyway. I heard a preacher say one time that mental illness is nothing but irresponsibility and laziness. Get the person out of that situation-- threw him out on the street if need be--but that would be the "kick in the pants" he needs. I agree.

"I was brought up (if I said before I don't remember) having a maid, not doing own laundry, just doing a few chores around the house, not paying rent--I could have, had my own credit card at age 19, or, and free gas living at home. I did work: worked hard on construction, loading trucks, scrubbing steel "I" beams but I didn't had to provide for myself. At this time I was pretty much out of myself or out of touch with reality and knew something was wrong but didn't care. I just wanted to make it from day to day hoping to find a reason for life and maybe some clue as to how to get in touch with people. I knew that my conversations were put, an act and that I really wasn't getting through to anybody about where my head was really at. I felt that if I said or did the wrong think the world would open up and enclose me. Yet, there were feelings I knew I had to get out. I knew that everybody didn't go through paranoia. I felt as it there was a dagger going through my head much of the time even though I did not realize this till much later.

"I was hospitalized for the first time during the winter. I was there for a short time, yet it was terror filled and drug induced. I was put an Lithium, Haldol, Melerill [sic] at various times of my encampment. Then there was the eighteen . . . antiquated method of torture known as shock treatment or electro-convulsive therapy. Being put to sleep was bad enough and even though I don't remember much about those times I'll try to explain what I do remember. I remember waking up after each ECTC electro-convulsive therapy / and finding a little less of my memory remaining. I couldn't remember my friends in high school, my distant or immediate past was less clear to me. I almost forgot what I was doing in the hospital or friends there. It was supposed to eradicate bad memories, yet the treatment showed no discrimination. I don"t know why I signed up for them, only I guess they gave them to a lot of patients there regardless of the damage that done.

"I remember making few friends and getting into a lot of fights. Whenever there was a special show on TV or I felt that it was "special" I had to see it. I couldn't be distracted from it and had to indulge every minute otherwise I wouldn't be fulfilling my destiny or something weird like that. I couldn't self actualize myself unless I did or said certain things at just the right time (when the right person was reading my mind or vice-versa.) I felt that there were inlaid obstacles to my completing these task.

"I remember a semi-final game. This was one of those special times. My parents were visiting and I had get very emotional or pent-up for the game which didn't require much effort. Well, there was a guy sitting there who I happened to like. However, during the game, he asked me to be quiet. This really set me off since he was counter-acting my scene. So I got really upset with him and a fight almost ensued. This was how important the game was to my life. There's just no way to explain how games either Super Bowl, world series or academy awards or whatever affected my well-being. Part of my world was entrap with them.

"Just like in high school, I was thought of as a clown and really was though of course I was hurting on the inside. Going back further to junior high I remember that I was picked on by a guy a lot. He had a couple of friends who joined in. This usually took place during gym. I was a skinny awkward ugly guy growing-up if I'm honest with myself. My self-esteem was always being lowered by constant reinforcement from my parents or my enemies at school. My mother later asked me how come I never told her about my problems at school or about my later marijuana usage. The answer, I suppose is the same as to why we had the terrible type of relationship we had. That is, there was no trust on my part and no communication at all. Now looking back on it, it seems like there was something I could have or that they could have done to alleviate the situation. But also it seems that hind sight is always 20-20. The same problems with them I'm sure contributed to my continuous distortion of reality and other family situations such as their own break-up.

"I remember my father would came home and have a couple of drinks and he couldn't hold his liquor very well and at the dinner table he would say something or I would take it the wrong way and words would be exchanged and even sometimes blows. I remember feeling really threatened by him, like I said before that he was either out to get me or to trick me in some devious way. It's amazing how one person could hold in this much anger over a period years without "doing something about it." Of course, I did do things about it, that weren't in my best interests, to say the least.

"Getting back to my past high school years, there was a group of friends that I usually hung out with whom I got to know very well and whose house I would go over to get stoned. As I said since I had free rent, free gas and free car the money I obtained from work was used on my friends and sometimes vice-versa, that is they used me a little. I really wonder if that life of semi-luxury was all it was crapped up to be. After all I didn't seemingly have any worries, just sit around watch TV, get stoned get horny get to bars--it kind of makes me sick right now to think."

Discussion

On the basis of my own work with schizophrenic individuals, I believe, this patient immediately focuses on the central characteristics of psychosis and therefore on the central insight. "First off there are a number of things one must assume. That is I had no sense of my being as self, that is I wasn't aware that my feelings were related to myself." You will agree that this is a powerful statement.

The second characteristics which strikes one immediately as psychotic relates to the "signs," the signs which give permission and the sign of the clefted chin. In my chapter on the "schizophrenic's objects"--and in earlier papers--I developed the idea that certain characteristics, such as for instance "chin cleftedness" can have greater "object constancy" than the "object" of the person, one self or the other, but that the logic applied to the idiosyncratic object is comprehensible. For the psychotic patient and for the neurotic patient, insight involves the recognition that some connections which were thought to be meaningful, are not and that some connections which were thought to be haphazard, do have some causal--unconsciously motivated--connections. What distinguishes the psychotic individual, however, is the fact that the person, the self does not have a privileged position in the object world. "I wasn't aware that my feelings were related to myself," my patient says. A "self" that has feelings does not come experientially first. Feelings are therefore somehow in the atmosphere and the "signs" result from a search for organization in the absence or lack of predominance of this experientially central "I".

Jonathan Winson (1985), a professor of neuroscience at Rockefeller University, develops a hypothesis concerning "off line processing" ("the acquisition of input information and its temporary storage ... until ... processing components are available" (p. 206) during sleep. Psychoanalytic dream theory and psychoanalytically obtained data informs the work of this neuroscientist. Although he does not believe that the psychoanalytic study of psychosis has been productive, I think that his ideas of considerable interest to us if we keep in mind the centrality for our understanding of psychosis, the patient's statement, "I wasn't aware that my feelings were related to myself."

Winson writes,

"there is consciousness, the immediate, undeniable "I" in each of us that perceives, think, feels, and acts. This is the last frontier of neuroscience, probably the most difficult realm of the mind to explain on the basis of brain function, ... Libet's approach may provide a path for investigation."

Libet's important experiments on human surgical patients show temporal discrepancies involving the moment of becoming conscious that one's hand has been touched when (1) the hand has actually been touched or (2) the corresponding spot on the sensory cortex is being stimulated. Paradoxically, the actual touching on the hand perceived simultaneously while the direct cortical stimulation is perceived with a delay of half a second. For our purposes it is sufficient to note Winson's suggestion that a temporal split may be the neuroscientist's entry into the study of consciousness.

In my own language I would say that indeed consciousness is a *double-take*, the "*cogito ergo sum*," Descartes' "I think, therefore I am." The patient "I feel, therefore I am" was not a given.

The patient dates the beginning of his recovery with his hearing a psychiatric aide telling him on one occasion "You have a choice. You can do what you want." The beginnings of insight into the psychotic process are in this double-take, the *you* (or I) on the one side and the *do* or *want* on the other side. Our research must focus on the issue why the message could be heard at that particular moment by our patient.

My own guess is that affect, finding expression in subtlety of timing of emotional fusion and separation play a part. I do not, however, exclude the possibility that some pharmacological agents expand or contract neurobiological rhythms into a range which facilitates an empathic resonance leading to the double take of consciousness, the beginnings of insight into the psychotic process.

References

Barnes, D. (1987). Biological issues in schizophrenia. *Science* 235:430-433.

Holden, C. (1987). A top priority at NIMH. *Science* 235: 431.

Kafka, J. S. (1986). The schizophrenic's objects. In: D. Feinsilver (ed.), *Towards a Comprehensive Model for Schizophrenic Disorders: Psychoanalytic Essays in Memory of Ping-Nie Pao, M.D.* Analytic Press, Hillsdale, N.J.

Kafka, J. S. (1989). *Multiple Realities in Clinical Practice.* Yale University Press, New Haven.

Kafka, J. S. and Kafka, M.S. (1983). Timing process and mental illness. *Abstracts, VII World Congress of Psychiatry*, Vienna, p. 302.

London, N. (1973). An essay on psychoanalytic theory: Two theories of schizophrenia. Parts I and II. International Journal of Psycho-Analysis 54:169-193.

Winson, J. (1985). *Brain and Psyche, The Biology of the Unconscious.* Anchor Press, Doubleday, New York.

Chapter 6: 99-110. In J. M. Natterson (Ed): The Dream in Clinical Practice. J. Aronson, New York (1980).

Chapter 16

The Dreams In Schizophrenia: Problems In Assessing The Dreams Of Schizophrenics

W hen I was asked to contribute this chapter on schizophrenic patients for *The Dream in Clinical Practice*, I agreed to do so only if a somewhat personal, partly impressionistic contribution were acceptable rather than a more scholarly paper which would include a review of the literature. So many questions about schizophrenia and its treatment remain unanswered that I consider a chapter dealing with the clinical use of dreams something of a *tour de force*. Nevertheless, despite vast areas of ignorance and uncertainty, we are working clinically and psychotherapeutically with schizophrenic patients, and therefore some thoughts which have crystallized out after several decades of experience are perhaps worth reporting. Two further initial cautions are in order: (1) Since areas of uncertainty tend to foster the influence of idiosyncratic factors, elements of one's personal work history must be spelled out; (2) I do not *generally* consider the clinical use of dreams of central importance in the therapeutic work with schizophrenic patients. Some thoughts about when it may be important, the extent to which it may be important, and similarities and differences between ways of using dream material in the treatment of schizophrenic and other patients will be explored below.

The following elements of my work history are pertinent to my perspective on the psychotherapy of schizophrenia and the use of dreams in this context. For many years I spent a significant portion of my time working with extremely ill schizophrenic patients in a psychoanalytically oriented hospital. I continued to work with a few of these patients after I stopped my formal affiliation with this hospital and concentrated on a psychoanalytic practice and teaching activities. My views thus largely result from observations of a few patients with whom I have had contact, and usually fairly extensive contact, for up to two decades. Consultative work on a schizophrenia research unit, which in recent years has concentrated more on biological questions, has also contributed to my perspective. Prior to medical, psychiatric, and psychoanalytic training, I was educated as a psychologist, and I am aware that an interest in some perceptual problems, which dates from that period, still contributes to my approach. I also wish to state emphatically that psychoanalytic treatment of neurotic patients and also of patients with character disorders is radically different from "psychoanalytically informed" psychotherapeutic work with schizophrenic patients.

Dreams and the "Bridging" Therapeutic Approach

In referring to the personal work history, I want to stress the continuity of my work with schizophrenic patients during acute phases, during prolonged states of regression or "decompensation," and during long periods when there is no psychotic state, at least of the kind which requires hospitalization. The attempt to provide continuity, to offer a bridge from the flagrantly psychotic to the other stages, has always been a major component of my therapeutic strategy. This is not to be taken for granted even for therapists who are psycho-dynamically and psychoanalytically oriented. Federn (1952), many of whose insights I profoundly appreciate, thought, for instance, that it might be better for some patients to have another therapist take over after the patient emerged from an acute psychotic state. His view had something to do with the thought that the first therapist might be in a sense "contaminated" with the terror of the psychotic experience, and that this contamination would interfere with the treatment in other phases. The fact is that even if one works with them long enough, some relapses for some of the patients occur, whichever of the now available treatments are used. Furthermore, some of these relapses are not, at this point, understood, whether we try to understand them "biologically," psycho-dynamically, or through combined approaches.

If I had written this article earlier in my career, I would have announced some "understandings" which I do not now claim. This is because over the years too many different "understandings" were required for the same kind of relapse in the same patient. Overall it is my current opinion that a "bridging" therapeutic approach has played a part in avoiding relapses in some patients, very probably in diminishing their frequency in other patients, in diminishing their duration, and certainly in diminishing the impact of recurrences on their lives and also on the lives of family members. It is in connection with the bridging approach in the work with schizophrenic patients that dreams have their most explicit application.

The topic of the continuity of the content of the psychosis in dream material was developed by Douglas Noble (1951) and by Clarence G Schulz (1969). While I wish to refer the reader to such discussions of the etiology of schizophrenia as are summarized in the two-part article by James S. Grotstein (1977), some relatively simple ideas have determined many aspects of my day-to-day therapeutic work. Clarence Schulz (1969) writes about his work with a severely disturbed schizophrenic patient who began to relate dreams after about five months of psychotherapy: "As his behavior began to improve, his psychotic thinking decreased and he began to report dreams" (p. 20). Three themes which were prominent in this patient's psychosis were: "(a) Violence and Fear, (b) Depression, and (c) Identity Diffusion ..." (p. 53). One aspect of the history of Schulz's patient was that his two siblings had died under tragic circumstances in separate accidents. 1 will return shortly to the use of dreams in the psychotherapy of schizophrenic patients with a fairly obvious traumatic history of this kind.

Evacuation Function of Dreams in Schizophrenics

I would like to refer to a few other ideas in the literature which have evoked an echo in my own clinical experience. One concerns the function of "evacuation." I have found applicable in work with schizophrenic patients, at times and with reservations which will be spelled out gradually, what Andre Green (1977) says about work with borderline patients:

> "dream analysis ... is, as a rule, unproductive. . . . Dreams do not express wish-fulfillment but rather serve a function of evacuation. . . . The dream barrier is an important function of the psychic apparatus. .. . Even though the dream barrier is effective, the dream's purpose is not the working through of instinct derivatives, but rather the unburdening of the psychic apparatus from painful stimuli... . The dreams ... are not characterized by condensation but by concredzation. One can also observe dream failures in these patients: wakening in order to prevent dreaming or to find themselves surrounded by a strange, disquieting atmosphere, which constitutes a transitional dream state akin to a nightmare. In more successful instances, dreams are actualizations of the self in the dream space, attempts to reformulate traumatic experiences. ... In such instances, the most significant thing in analyzing a dream is not the dream's latent content but the dreamer's experience." [p. 38]

Trauma in the Life and Dreams of Schizophrenics

Whatever our eventual understanding of the etiology of various schizophrenic disorders, for immediate therapeutic and practical working purposes, I do find that I function as though I believed that trauma was etiologically more important for some schizophrenic patients than for others. I think, for instance, of a patient, Eleanor M, who had her first acute episode after she had obeyed her mother's request and arranged to be present in the operating room in which her mother was "opened up" and found to have a widespread malignancy. Eleanor was also the main caretaker of her dying mother, and the notion that a sedative which she gave her mother killed her was at times an important element in her delusions. Without giving a more complete case history, I do want to indicate that she was diagnosed as schizophrenic on the basis of all the usual criteria by the staff of several hospitals and showed particularly flamboyant pathology. Hallucinating, wildly agitated, she was denudative, smeared herself and the walls of seclusion rooms with menstrual blood, and was destructive of property and sometimes assaultive. During more than fifteen years of psychotherapeutic work with her, I found the role of dreams in treatment an important one, as I shall describe below. She was eventually able to leave the hospital, the frequency and the severity of acute episodes diminished radically, and during the last eight years only one brief hospitalization was necessary. (Medication, on the whole, did not play a significant role in her management and treatment.) When she did not need to be hospitalized, Eleanor's functioning was usually of a rather high caliber as a wife, mother, and participating member in community affairs. Her preoccupation with violence in her waking life was limited to a fascination with crime and criminals, wars, and catastrophies. Her selection of movies and television shows, her reading of newspaper and magazine articles, was almost exclusively based on such interests. Her dream life was characterized by prolonged periods during which she reported hundreds of more or less repetitive dreams dealing with amputations, mutilations, and bloody scenes.

Thus, Eleanor presented the contrasting picture of being prim and proper when not psychotic, but of having a dream life and psychotic periods full of gore. Over the years of working with her, I developed a technique of using "gory" language in talking about her dreams and impulses. I also commented, however, again and again about my reasons for doing so, spelling out the idea that the attempt at compartmentalization of such material in her case might contribute to the psychotic episodes. I would like to repeat that I draw a sharp line between doing psychoanalysis and conducting psychotherapeutic work with such schizophrenic patients, although there may be times when the technique of working with such a patient has some superficial resemblances to psychoanalytic technique. A thorough grounding in psychoanalytic concepts is important for understanding both the analogous techniques and the approaches that might be useless or destructive.

In this instance there were long periods when the therapy resembled some of the therapeutic work done with cases of "battle fatigue" during and after World War II. I am referring, for example, to the actual showing of war movies to soldiers who had experienced major dissociative episodes in battle. Showings of these movies were interrupted from time to time, and when the lights went on Red Cross girls offered tea to the soldiers. Despite the use of such techniques, recognition of transference elements and the genetics of the conflict had their place in the treatment. The emphasis was, however, as Andre Green put it, "not [on] the dream's latent content, but the dreamer's experience."

Repair of Psychosis Through Dreams

From the literature on dreams in schizophrenia and psychosis, I will cite one further notion which is in harmony with my own clinical use of dreams with these patients. In Eissler's paper, "The Effect of the Structure of the Ego on Psychoanalytic Technique" (1953), there is a reference to a psychotic patient, who in her dreams repairs the psychosis, so to speak. It is as if the dreaming ego were nonpsychotic while her waking ego was psychotic. Eissler also refers to similar observations made by Freud. Furthermore, Eissler refers to Freud's notion that "reality" appears like an instinct derivative in dreams of psychotics. That is, it was Freud's belief that the psychotic individual had constructed for himself a world which was so different and distinct from "reality"—I would now (Kafka 1977) say commonsense reality—that ordinary reality broke through into dreams in the same way in which material related to "instinct" broke into the dream of the non-psychotic individual. Although oversimplified, these references to Eissler's and Freud's notions are related to the following clinical observations.

I accidentally discovered many years ago that when I woke a hospitalized schizophrenic patient with a complex paranoid delusional system, for five or ten minutes he was apparently free of delusions. I could never obtain from the patient any confirmation that he was dreaming, and any possible "repair" of the psychosis could have been the work of merely the "sleeping" and not necessarily of the "dreaming ego."

I would also like to refer to the work with another male patient, John M, who had been diagnosed as schizophrenic during several prolonged hospitalizations and who had at one time prior to my acquaintance with him, received a series of electroconvulsive treatments. Without getting into a discussion of diagnostic criteria, I would simply like to say that some clinicians would consider him as having a severe borderline disorder with pronounced narcissistic features. He did have frankly psychotic periods during my years of work with him, and brief hospitalizations were required, although drug abuse made it difficult to identify the precipitating factors. Dreams were also important in my work with John; but in this instance I worked more analytically, and my clinical use of dreams did not differ significantly from psychoanalytic dream interpretations. One feature of his reporting of dreams may, however, relate to Eissler's observation. He often spoke with great emphasis about the fact that his dreams now contained some "distortions." A room in which he lived or a landscape which he remembered from his childhood differed from the way it "really" was. Ordinarily, non-psychotic dreamers consider such distortions as part of the usual fabric of the dream. John emphasized these distortions, for him "unusual," which he compared with what he considered his normal dreams. During psychotic episodes, he had apparently experienced dreams in which there was much "undistorted" reality. Clinically he was able to use my observations relating to such fluctuations in his dreams in a "bridging" fashion. My observations served as an introduction to part of normal living, namely, normally distorted dreams. Furthermore, I learned to use the degree of distortion reported by him about his dream material as an indicator of his "distance" from a psychotic episode, and such observations helped in his "management."

On the other hand, I have also encountered in a patient, Robert S, specific fear of a psychotic reaction when the vividness of the dreams was extreme—for instance, when he not only saw his own face as that of an animal, but also in his dream touched his face and discovered that his skin possessed the texture of an animal's skin. Robert never actually was psychotic, but several family members had been hospitalized with a diagnosis of schizophrenia, and his fear of psychosis was never far from the surface.

Another patient, about whose schizophrenic diagnosis there was no doubt but who lived most of his life outside a hospital, found that he had made all kinds of commitments, had pledged charitable contributions, and had accepted invitations when he had actually answered the telephone, but had believed that he was dreaming the whole thing. By the time I started working with him, he had already developed a method to circumvent this problem. Since he did not know if he was awake or dreaming—he had multiple dreams within dreams—and since "pinching himself" didn't do the trick, he had learned to always ask, "What is your number? I'll call you back."

"Intellectual" Approach to Dreams

Some of the above observations tend to move away from the clinical use of dreams in the therapy of schizophrenic patients. They are nevertheless pertinent. For some patients there seem to be common elements in dreams and psychotic experience, or at the very least, there are fears that certain dream characteristics herald psychotic experiences. In working therapeutically for prolonged periods with such patients, the therapist is likely to discover characteristics of dream reports which are indices of the closeness to the surface of some psychotic phenomena. An index may be valid for only one particular patient because it depends not only on general characteristics of schizophrenic and dream processes, but also on such personality variables as intelligence and intellectual style, and various characteristics of patient and therapist which determine their relationship and communication. If one works long enough, even with deeply regressed, chronic or "deteriorated" patients, one often discovers periods of relatively greater accessibility during which both content and formal elements of dream experiences can be considered collaboratively with the patient. Despite my overall recognition of the general uselessness of too much "intellect" in therapeutic endeavors, I have become less afraid of an "intellectual" approach with some patients at such junctures. It connotes a respect for formal characteristics of the patient's thought—a respect which has a therapeutic function in itself.

My goals are often rather modest and frequently turn out to be only a hope for better self-management of psychosis. Such better self-management occurred with a patient who on previous occasions had been brought to the hospital in a police ambulance, with sirens wailing and half a dozen aides needed to restrain her agitated behavior. After a prolonged therapeutic effort, this patient experienced herself as disturbed while on vacation, hallucinated my office in her vacation home, heard me telling her that she had better go to the hospital, and did so on her own initiative. Discussion of form and content of dream material has been, for me, one of the tools useful in facilitating such a development—that is, previous discussion with the patient of form and content of dreams enhances the patient's ability to observe critically some of the psychotic experiences, even with the therapist only psychologically present.

Primary Process, Dreams, and Psychotic Phenomena

I do not wish to enter here into a more theoretical discussion of the degree to which the primary-process concept may have different explanatory power in elucidating the formation of dreams and of psychotic thought content. Nevertheless, an understanding of primary process can clarify for the therapist such practical problems as, for example, the equivalences and fusions of various family members in the mind of the waking schizophrenic patient (Kafka and McDonald 1964).

Certain characteristics of the dreams of schizophrenic patients can also give the therapist information about the patient's control techniques or methods of self-management. Robert S—the patient with the telephone-answering difficulties—on many occasions had "geological" dreams. While geology was one of his daytime interests, it was the immensely long and slow time scale of geological events that was the clue to his self-management style. One day I told him that I was reminded of the puzzle which one citizen of Berne—whose inhabitants have a reputation for slowness—poses to another. "What is this?" asks the Swiss from Berne, while very slowly drawing an angular line in the air. The correct answer is "lightning." Very, very slowly the patient dared to break—or, should I say, "melt"—into a smile. After this it was possible for me to comment on certain catastrophic geological events in his dreams and to relate them in a therapeutically meaningful way to events in his life.

While one could discuss the nature of the obsessive elements in the defensive structure of Robert S, I would like to focus on the relative *completeness* of his slow-motion perception and his slow-motion self-perception, and the relative completeness and appropriateness of his gradually developing affective responses. Elsewhere I have developed the notion that perceptual acts recapitulate the development of perception, so that what is perceived in and as a "flash" by the adult corresponds to what a child may perceive in a more "lingering" perception (Kafka 1977,1979). I have also developed the idea that certain qualities—for instance, "suspendedness"—can have for certain patients and under certain conditions an "object constancy" which is in a sense more "solid" than the objects which we usually associate with the notion of object constancy (Kafka 1979).

Concreteness Versus Abstractness in Dreams and Thoughts of Schizophrenics

This work has a possible connection to the question of concreteness or "concretization" versus abstract qualities in dreams of schizophrenic patients—and perhaps also in schizophrenic thinking generally. In writing about "abstract expressionist dreams" (Kafka and Gaarder 1964), we gave an example in which a reported dream consisted of a continuous line with a small squiggle. It was perfectly clear to the dreamer, a "normal" individual after an LSD experience, that the line represented the course of history, and the squiggle represented the Holocaust. I have come to believe that this kind of dream experience corresponds in large measure to the waking experience of many schizophrenic patients for whom certain "abstractions" carry a bewildering but convincing richness of meaning or meanings. As I indicated earlier, I have been impressed by the contrasting concreteness and vividness—"the reality"—of certain "schizophrenic" dreams (always remembering that in the most acute phases dreams are not reported and the question is thus irrelevant for therapeutic purposes) If "abstract expressionist" elements in waking experience have been recognized by the therapist, this may facilitate the patient's reporting, at stages of considerable improvement, the reversal in dream characteristics that I mentioned earlier—namely, a dream "atmosphere" in dreams and more "concreteness" in daily living.

As an elaborated example of this kind of reversal, one month after a psychiatric hospitalization a schizophrenic patient, Amanda T, reported dreaming that her mother was dead, her father was alive, and another woman was embracing him. The patient's actual life situation was that her *father* was dead and her *mother* was living. She emphasized that the scene reminded her of some Picasso paintings of the Blue Period, and further commented, "It's an interesting dream; the female figure is of undetermined age." Her sexual interest in her father had been an explicitly recognized theme in my prolonged work with her. During acute psychotic episodes, she also was fused with, transformed into, or partially blended with her father. At one time, for instance, she made a point of not shaving her legs because "I have father's legs." I want to underline in the present context the patient's emphases on the Blue Period and the atmospheric qualities of the dream. Some of her other associations involved her daughter who liked Picasso, a period in her daughter's life when she was developing breasts, a visit to a relative who was divorcing her husband, and the patient's wish that her father had divorced her mother. In many respects these dream elements were understood by Amanda and were interpreted by her in a fashion similar to that in which a neurotic patient after prolonged insight-oriented therapy or analysis might comprehend her own dream material. She explained, however, that she could have such a dream now "because last month has been going very well. My husband did not go on any trips. He cooked a lot of dinners." She then talked about her father's flirtations, but discussed "love" very explicitly in terms of who fed whom. Mother did not feed father well; therefore, she did not love him. Amanda made precise equations in energy terms. She could have this dream now because she was well fed during the last month and consequently had enough energy to work on the old problems of her father's death.

"Dreamlike" Dreams as a Sign of Improvement

In my experience, when a schizophrenic patient can talk about atmospheric conditions—that is, in essence the *dreamlike* qualities of a dream—and does not see everyday reality as the intruder in the dream, then the patient is most removed from a psychotic ego organization. In prolonged psychotherapeutic work with a schizophrenic patient, such a period should not be ignored. That is, the therapist can at such a moment explicitly deal with the apparently "neurotic" conflicts which are being presented and dealt with in the dream, but the therapist can also at such a moment introduce a discussion of the changes which such material undergoes during psychotic episodes. With Amanda, for example, the topic of her wish to be close to her father, to be with her father, and its shading into her wish to *be* father or at least to have *parts* of father, could be introduced in an effort to form the bridge between the current and the psychotic states. It is my belief that such an approach in the long run permits the patient to utilize the image of the therapist in the "bridging" management of her own psychosis.

Pharmacological Interventions and Dreams in Schizophrenics

Thus, despite our uncertainties in understanding schizophrenic phenomena, despite the observation that the most clearly schizophrenic patients—when they are most clearly schizophrenic—do not report dream material, it is apparent that dreams can be used in the treatment of schizophrenia. Recently, as a psychoanalytic consultant on a biologically oriented schizophrenia research unit on which various vigorous pharmacological interventions are being studied, I have noted that in some patients whose condition changes and fluctuates rapidly, the reporting of dreams can occur almost immediately after emergence from the most severe disorganization. Dream material may be reported when delusions are still very active. The overlapping of acute psychotic manifestations and the reporting of dreams is greater here than I have observed where no such forceful pharmacological interventions are attempted. I would, therefore, not exclude the possibility that the study and perhaps the therapeutic use of dreams in schizophrenia may become of interest to clinicians with a variety of theoretical orientations.

References

Eissler, K. R. (1953). The effect of the structure of the ego on psychoanalytic technique. *Journal of the American Psychoanalytic Association* 1:104-143

Federn, P. (1952). *Ego Psychology and the Psychoses*. New York: Basic Books.

Green, A. (1977). The borderline concept. In *Borderline Personality Disorders*, P. Hartocollis, editor. New York: International Universities Press.

Grotstein, J.S. (1977). The psychoanalytic concept of schizophrenia: I. The dilemma. II. Reconciliation. *International Journal of Psycho-Analysis* 58:403-452.

Kafka, J.S. (1977). On reality: an examination of object constancy, ambiguity, paradox, and time. In *Thought, Consciousness, and Reality. Psychiatry and the Humanities*, vol. 2, ed. J>H. Smith. New Haven, Conn.: Yale University Press.

Kafka, J.S. (1979). Psychic effort, drift and reality structures: Observations from psychoanalytic work with neurotic, borderline and schizophrenic patients. In: *Psychotherapy of Schizophrenia*, ed. C. Miller. Proceedings of the 6th International Symposium on the Psycho-therapy of Schizophrenia, Laussane: *Excerpta Medica,* Amsterdam-Oxford.

Kafka, J.S. and Gaarder, K.R. (1964). Some effects of the therapist's LSD experience on his therapeutic work. *American Journal of Psychotherapy* 18:236-243.

Kafka, J.S. and McDonald, J.W. (1964). The latent family in the treatment of hospitalized schizophrenic patients. In *Current Psychiatric Therapy*, ed. J.S. Masserman. New York: Grune and Stratton.

Noble, D. (1951). A study of dreams in schizophrenia and allied states. *American Journal of Psychiatry* 107:612-616.

Schulz, C. G., and Kilgalen, R. K. (1969). The treatment course of a disturbed patient. In *Case Studies in Schizophrenia*. New York: Basic Books.

Selected Writings

Time and Memory

Chapter 10, pp. 197-214. Volume 15 (2016) International Society for the Study of Time

Chapter 17

Psychoanalysis and the Temporal Trace

Abstract

Deepening one's self-knowledge in psychoanalysis involves reviving one's memory traces and exploring one's distorting or forgetting of them. These processes involve one's experience of time and one's conscious and unconscious manipulation of time. This essay provides an overview of the relevance of time-related concepts in classical psychoanalysis while also extending to—and casting a new light on—some concepts based on the treatment of psychotic patients.

Keywords
déjà vu—Ketamine—memory—Nachtraeglichkeit—object formation—perception—psychoanalysis—screen memories—Sigmund Freud—Sernyl—timelessness of the unconscious

Introduction

Time is a central theme in psychoanalysis as a theory of the *sequences* in human development and as a historical perspective that concerns itself with unconscious temporality, the unconscious motivations of the individual and of societies. As a specific psychotherapeutic method, psychoanalysis

375

takes time, and it is not limited to a brief encounter because its aims are not limited to symptomatic change. The aims of psychoanalysis include change through self-knowledge, resulting from new and more inclusive perceptions of self and others that in turn lead to freedom from compulsive repetitions of self-damaging thoughts, actions, and destructive relationship patterns. *Transference*, emotionally charged repetitions between analyst and analysand of earlier relationship patterns in the analysand's life, is a key element in the psychoanalytic method. Transference thus involves memory and time, as well as distortions of memory and of time.

Time is also of essence in the very arrangement of psychoanalytic treatment. Sessions begin and end at a fixed time, but within that time period, the analysand is encouraged to "free associate," to suspend judgment about the *correct* sequential connectedness between different thoughts that come to his mind. The analysand is asked to function in a tight conscious and a loose unconscious mode. This temporal polarity and the movements between these poles, given the obstacles to and limitations of these movements, is at the core of the psychoanalytic process, which strives to modify them. I will explore various aspects of time from this psychoanalytic perspective. I also will examine connections between earlier and recent psychoanalytic and wider recent philosophical and scientific views on time. In addition to the more familiar "classic" psychoanalytic perspective, I will also introduce ideas that are based on my psychoanalytically-informed work with psychotic, especially schizophrenic, patients. Their pathology challenges us to focus on temporal disorientation and the connection between time experience and the sense of reality and unreality.

The earliest and most widely known connection between psychoanalysis and the topic of time is Freud's notion of *timelessness of the unconscious*. Freud believed that the unconscious knows no time and that whatever has been repressed leaves permanent traces in the unconscious (Freud 1923-25, 225ff.). Late in his life, Freud wrote that he had not solved the paradox of this unchanging state that can be modified when the analysand retrieves it from the unconscious. Freud thought that "the solution to this puzzle would have to wait for further scientific and philosophic development" (Freud 1932-36, 74). Some such recent developments may contribute to the solution of this puzzle.

From a historical perspective, Freud's most explicit reference to the concept of a temporal *trace* is his paper on the "Mystic Writing Pad" [*Wunderblock*, literally, the "Miraculous Pad"], a forerunner of Etch-A-Sketch (Freud 1923-25, 225ff.). On a Mystic Writing Pad, one writes on a covering surface, leaving a *temporary* trace on that cover. This trace disappears when the cover is lifted from the underlying surface; however, the writing has also left a permanent trace below. Freud used the Mystic Writing Pad as a concrete representation of his early views on the functioning of the perceptual apparatus of the mind. The Mystic Writing Pad illustrated how permanent *traces* are laid down while a perceptual conscious system is ready to receive new stimuli (perceptions) on what seems to be a blank page. The *trace* on one layer of the pad seemed at that time to solve the problem of combining the functions of a permanent and a temporary memory. One limitation of the Mystic Writing Pad model is, however, that experienced memories are not exact reproductions of the past. Thus, even if we could conceive of a psychological method that would correspond to lifting the Mystic Writing Pad's covering sheet and exposing the original impression, such a feat would not lead us to a replication of living memory in which some traces are subject to repression and alterations.

What does the temporal trace contribute to the formation of the living memory, to its plasticity and its modifiability? After a general discussion of time and memory, I will focus on and re-examine some specific psychoanalytic concepts that address this question, the concepts of *Nachtraeglichkeit* or *après coup* and of screen memory.

Studying Memory and the Temporal Trace is Studying Time

All study of memory is a study of time. Meaning depends on the traces of short-term memory. Usually, when psychoanalysts discuss memory, they think of relatively long-term memory. However, without short-term memory, there is no meaning, and without meaning, psychic life does not exist. All meaning, all thinking, all psychological functions are time-linked, as the following illustration of the loss of meaning that accompanies loss of short-term memory confirms.

Sernyl is a drug that interferes with short-term memory. It was once used as an anesthetic for animals and children, but research on the drug continued after its clinical use was stopped. In an experiment that I conducted (which was probably the last authorized research project on humans involving the drug), Sernyl was given by injection to Kenneth Gaarder, a psychiatrist and psychoanalyst who participated in this research and who served as a voluntary subject (Kafka 1989b, 62ff.). Dr. Gaarder was well acquainted with the literature about Sernyl, but had not seen the drug in use. Here is a transcript of the taped record of Dr. Gaarder's words 10 minutes after the injection:

> [S]omething is going on here and uh-uh-I'm alive-and uh-I'm doing something for some reason, and I don't know what it is I'm doing and uh—what's happening to me now—and words are things like that what is happening? What is to say what is happening? is a word- and people talk-and what is talking? and uh-I don't know what's going on [. . .] I'm experiencing something and I don't know what's going on, and I don't know what saying what's going on is saying. . . . (Kafka 1989b, 65)

From this illustration of the loss of meaning linked to the experience of *timelessness* induced by the short-time memory loss, let us return to Freud's most well-known psychoanalytic hypothesis relating to time. It is the notion of the so-called *timelessness* of the *unconscious*, and the ensuing paradox of the existence of change, a puzzle that Freud could not solve (as he admits in the quote above). An important recent development in psychoanalytic theory that is relevant here is the work of psychoanalyst and mathematician Matte-Blanco, in particular his understanding of this so-called timelessness (Matte-Blanco 1988). Matte-Blanco distinguishes symmetrical and asymmetrical mental processes. "John is the brother of Peter" is symmetrical because Peter is also the brother of John. "Peter is the brother of Mary" is asymmetrical because Mary is not the brother of Peter (Matte-Blanco 1959, 2). "Yesterday is before today" is asymmetrical because today is not before yesterday. The unconscious, according to Matte-Blanco, does not distinguish between the symmetrical and the asymmetrical, and is, in this way, timeless (Matte-Blanco 1988, 43ff.). Of particular relevance to psychoanalysis and the psychoanalytic interpretation of dreams is that, in dreams, there is no directionality of time, no consistent before and after.

It will be helpful at this point to step back from psychoanalytic theory and practice and turn to physics and time studies more broadly conceived. Freud knew about relativity theory, about the uncertainty principle, and about quantum physics, but he did not consider these scientific advances relevant to psychoanalysis and warned against facile use of these concepts. But a complex, non-reductive theory of time (including its evolution and conflicts) such as J. T. Fraser's can assist us in working through the vexed problem of time Freud leaves us with. For example, Matte-Blanco's psychoanalytic view of the unconscious is congruent with Fraser's *eotemporal umwelt*, the shaft of an arrow representing events that are countable and orderable without a preferred direction (Fraser 1981). J. T. Fraser writes:[40]

"[W]hen psychoanalysts deal with time in the psychoanalytic situation, they assume the existence of an objective temporal matrix in which psychic processes take place and to which the subjective

---

[40] Editors' Note: J.T. Fraser developed what he called a hierarchical theory of time's conflicts according to which time assumes (at least) five canonical forms. The model is evolutionary as well as hierarchical in that each higher level emerges as the result of the incompleteness evident in the conflicts generated in the level beneath it, but without cancelling out any lower level. In the work cited here, Fraser (1981) identifies the five forms (and illustrates each with regard to the image of the arrow of time) as, in order of decreasing complexity: the nootemporal, the level of the mature human mind with its symbol-generating capacity (the full arrow with head and tail clearly drawn); the biotemporal, or world of living organisms (just the arrow's head, representing consciousness of the immediate present and past but without long-term anticipation or memory); the eotemporal, the abiding present of directionless time (only the shaft of the arrow); the prototemporal, the fragmented time of elementary objects (the arrow disintegrated into slivers of wood); and the atemporal, the world of electromagnetic radiation in which time blends with space (a blank sheet of paper on which the image of an arrow could be drawn). Fraser later began to develop the concept of the sociotemporal as a response to the conflicts of nootemporality.

time of the patient is gradually attuned. A desirable result of therapy is an identification of the subjective time of the patient with the assumed, objective physical time. Psychoanalytic theory may, therefore, be seen as endorsing that view of time which was proposed by Issac Newton in 1687. He wrote that "absolute, true and mathematical time, of itself, and from its own nature, flows equably without relation to anything external, [that is, anything other than itself] and by another name is called duration . . ." But this understanding of time must be rejected, though not at all for reasons that come from post-Newtonian physics but rather because of reasons that stem from evolutionary biology and from psychoanalytic insight." (Fraser 1981, 3)

The relationship between the hierarchical levels of time and psychoanalytic approaches to time is the central subject of Fraser's 1981 paper "Temporal Levels and Reality Testing." Fraser's work can be considered the new philosophical and scientific development that provides an answer to Freud's puzzle. One hierarchical level involves an unchanging state and another accommodates modifiability. In Fraser's system, no previous or "lower" level of organization is lost. They are constantly recapitulated and co-exist although they may be in conflict with each other. This is congruent with Freud's view that permanent traces of the past in the unconscious are constantly recapitulated. But, as mentioned, change in the unconscious that knows no time remains a puzzle for Freud while Fraser's system accommodates co-existence despite conflict.

Another scientific and philosophical development that postdates Freud and is relevant here is Gödel's conclusion that time is not a "physical reality." Gödel theorized that the maximum curvature in Einstein's space-time leads to our return to the same point in space-time in conceptual time travel (Gödel 1931, 173ff.). If we find ourselves at the same point in space-time, he reasoned, time does not exist as a "physical" reality. This notion suggests that all time related psychological activity (and there is no time-independent psychic activity) is constructed by us. In Fraser's theory, we construct all hierarchical levels of time in the course of evolution.

The human construction of time is the construction of mind, the construction of meaning. The Sernyl experiment described previously illustrated the loss of meaning that accompanies the loss of short-term memory. Even the word "now" lost its meaning. A "now" without short-term memory is meaningless. It has no psychological existence; it is mind-less.

Psychic Reality

The psychological moment, the existence of a psychic reality, needs short-term memory to exist. The psychic reality of the moment is a building block of later memories. Therefore, our study of the memory trace is inescapably linked to the study of the building of psychic reality. Psychoanalysts are careful to avoid "reification" of their concepts, but nevertheless the psychoanalytic term "object" has some connotations of solidity, of a separate, tangible existence.

In this connection, I will summarize here some ideas that I have developed in much more detail elsewhere (Kafka 1989a). In general psychology, the concept of object permanence, or object constancy, refers to observations of the kind that a table is perceived as the same table when viewed from different angles despite the fact that the retinal projections of the table are different when the viewing angles change. In the context of our study of memory and the recognition that memories are not reproductions either of a scene or of an object, it is essential to note that time is involved in the movement from one position to another in viewing the table that figures as a (permanent) object. This notion is not absent from the psychoanalytic understanding of object constancy, but psychoanalysts focus on affect and meaning when considering that object constancy has been achieved, for example, when the nourishing and the withholding mother is recognized as the same person. But here, too, the term "mother" refers to a physical presence that, seen from different angles and in different physical positions, also has different retinal projections. I emphasize that even object constancy has both a hermeneutic and a physically real, tangible component, a theme to which we will return when discussing *Nachtraeglichkeit*.

This discussion of object constancy leads to the conclusion that our psychological "object world" consists of subjective equivalences of different objects. *Different* time intervals may also be subjectively equivalent. As is well known, an identical "linear" time interval may be experienced as shorter or longer, and different time intervals may be experienced as similar or identical, depending on many different factors, including time-linked affective factors such as expectations, hopes, and fears. From this perspective, psychic reality consists of processes of forming networks of spatial and temporal subjective equivalences. "Object" loses some of its "solidity." (Note that I speak about processes of forming subjective equivalences that, I believe, recapitulate ontogenic development.)

Freud thought that past traces in the unconscious are permanent and are always available for repetition and recapitulation. In Fraser's system, as stated above, levels of organization are not lost but recapitulated, co-existing even if they are in conflict with each other. Reports of—and by—drowning individuals (after they were saved) that they experienced their whole life "in a flash" may serve as an illustration of my hypothesis that every perceptual process is a recapitulation of the onto-genesis of perception. This conscious experience may correspond to the unconscious micro- or nano-second recapitulation of the development of the individual's perceptual processes. What is being recapitulated? In Fraser's theory, as already mentioned, all hierarchical levels coexist or are available for recapitulation. My clinical work with *schizophrenic* patients has led me to focus on a developmental sequence of the discrimination between outside and inside, the discrimination of the animate from the inanimate, the synesthetic from the sensory-specific, and the priority of temporal or of spatial ways of organizing sensory data. A patient described how the distance between two buildings had shrunk. I noticed that she walked faster. Such observations made me realize to what extent we usually give priority to spatial, over temporal, organization (Kafka 1989a, 14). These developmental stages are recapitulated in "object formation" (Kafka 1989a, 26-50). Furthermore, there is a congruity between, on the one hand, animate, inside, temporal, and synesthetic, and, on the other hand, inanimate, outside, spatial, and sensory-specific objects. Tachistoscopic experiments, the study of perception of stimuli that one is exposed to for extremely short periods, permit a kind of temporal dissection of the recapitulative process. Extremely short exposure led adults to have responses that have characteristics in common with those of very young children; longer exposures correspond to responses of older children (Westerlundh and Smith 1983, 597ff.; Kafka 1989a, 41ff.).

Returning to "subjective equivalence" in object formation, if the psychic objects are not real, tangible objects, but represent subjective equivalences of different perceptions, then each perceptual act represents a travelogue—and therefore a micro-memory trail—through different object formations. If the recapitulation of developmental processes is complete in each perception, the subjective equivalences form objects that are recognizable by and can be shared by others. If the recapitulations of some perceptions are incomplete, as they may be in psychotic thought disorder, subjective equivalences between completed and partially completed perceptions form "bizarre" objects or what we may call atmospheric rather than sensory-specific objects. Here is a clinical example of the latter. During an acute psychotic phase, a patient insisted on calling a nurse "Heidi" although that was not her name. After this acute phase, the patient explained to me that people were not the same for her from day to day. This nurse, however, was blond and had a foreign accent. The patient had loved the Swiss book *Heidi* since her childhood and a combination of characteristics, a kind of "Heidiness," permitted her to hold on to something—and incidentally something pleasant—during a time of distress, disorientation, and loss of her sense of self. Atmospheric objects are more synesthetic than sensory-specific. It was only in retrospect (*nachtraeglich, après coup*) that the patient understood the source and reasons for her misnaming the nurse.

Nachtraeglichkeit

The concept of *Nachtraeglichkeit*, Freud's term for the retroactive modification of memory traces, has long been neglected in the English-speaking psychoanalytic world because the term had been poorly (or at least very incompletely) translated as "deferred action." An attempt has been made to clarify the concept by speaking of "retroactive attribution of meaning." M. Kettner, who has studied Freud's use of the concept, finds that Freud sometimes gave it a hermeneutic meaning, referring to changes of interpretation of memories, and sometimes a "causal" meaning. The latter can be thought of in terms of aftereffects, like a chain of effects on a series of billiard balls. Kettner finds that psychoanalysis operates in the *Spielraum* (latitude, literally "space for play") between these two meanings (Kettner 1999). This *Spielraum* is also the area of confluence of unidirectional linear time linked to traditional causality and of bidirectional temporal processes. Bidirectional processes escape the narrow structure of a mechanical billiard-ball chain of causality and involve the alterations of meaning produced by seeing old material in the light of new information and vice versa, in the *Spielraum* between the concrete and the hermeneutic.

Another aspect of *Nachtraeglichkeit* is a relatively neglected one, the *nachtraeglich* modification of the sense of duration. Different senses of duration leave behind traces. Shifts during psychoanalysis in what is understood as meaningful, be it in one analytic session or in a perspective on life developed during a course of psychoanalysis, have profound consequences for our experience of time, because the judgment of the duration of intervals in which "meaningful" things happen differs from the judgment of duration of intervals of "accidental" events. The following experiment demonstrates the retroactive effects of new information on judgment of past duration: Subjects in one experimental group memorized a series of apparently random numbers and then were asked how long it took them to memorize the series. Subjects in another group memorized the same series and then were given a code that transformed what was apparently a random series into an ordered one before being asked to estimate how long it had taken them to memorize the series. The actual memorization period of each group was the same, but the subjects who were given the code estimated its duration as shorter than did the codeless group: the new information about the code permitted them to reorganize—recode—their experience retrospectively. It is well established that ordered numbers are learned more rapidly than random ones. Subjects given the code that transformed the apparently random series into an ordered one after memorizing them estimated their period of memorization as though they had known the ordering code when they committed the series to memory. New information has had a retroactive effect on judgment of past duration (Kafka 1989c, 18).

The sense of duration is influenced by cognitive information, but it is more profoundly influenced by affective elements. During a German-speaking conference on time, I was asked what I thought was the opposite of *Muße*, a hard-to-translate term referring to the experience of peaceful, utterly relaxed free time. I was surprised that what came to my mind was *boredom*. In effect, boredom is a problem for the military in certain situations when troops are not active. In a cease-fire situation (not after a peace accord) when opposing troop encampments remain facing each other, soldiers have to be on the alert for any sign of a possible violation. At the same time, they must make sure not to do anything that the enemy could interpret as a threat. This is the perfect situation of inhibited aggression which, I believe, is the deep source of boredom, the utterly *not*-relaxed free time. In psychoanalytic treatment, attention to the quality of experienced duration can contribute much to the understanding of emotional conflicts. This was the case in the psychoanalytic treatment of a man who was trying to decide whether to stay with his wife or to marry his mistress. It gradually emerged that a conflict between a situation in which he experienced *Muße* (with his mistress) and one of inhibited aggression (with his wife) best described his situation. This clarification permitted the patient to contextualize his current conflict, to recollect, re-examine and re-evaluate it *nachtraeglich* in the light of current understanding of some past situations.

Screen Memories

The concept of "screen memories" deals more explicitly than *Nachtraeglichkeit* with the polarity of overall actual temporal traces and living memory. In addition, however, screen memory also deals explicitly with false memories. In his article on screen memories (Freud 1893-1899, 299ff.), Freud often refers to similarities between other memories and memories that he designates as screen memories. I think this is a device to highlight certain characteristics that may be present in all memories, but are more prominent in some. They include sensory intensity and the *delay* in developing the screen memories. Freud himself reports a screen memory that refers to events which occurred when he was three years old, and one that was formed when he was 17. Freud also emphasizes that the wish he encounters in this screen memory is the wish to change the past rather than a wish for the future. He emphasizes that he returns to a past nostalgia. (My own favorite graffito is "Nostalgia ain't what it used to be.") Nevertheless, Freud=s technique of analyzing his screen memory is not fundamentally different from the technique he employs in analyzing other memories. He emphasizes that the concept of screen memory owes its value as a memory not to its own content but to the relation existing between that content and some other that has been repressed. While this may be particularly salient in the analysis of screen memories, it is indeed part of all psychoanalytic study of memories.

Freud locates the source of his screen memory at age three when the financial collapse of the family's business leads to a quite sudden and unexpected move to Vienna (Freud 1893-1899, 309). For analysands, a screen memory is—or, I would say, was once—accepted by the subject as a "real" memory, but Freud and other students of screen memories emphasize to what extent the sensory intensity (the yellow flowers in his screen memory) appears particularly fresh and current and, as it were, factually verifiable. The narrative of the screen memory is, however, particularly unlikely. The manifest story is false although, as already mentioned, analyzing the story as one would analyze a dream may make it understandable. While all memories are constructions, the more evident falseness of the screen memory makes it a confabulation. Psychiatrically, confabulation is considered a replacement of a gap in memory by a falsification that the subject accepts as correct.

I think that Freud's choice of the trauma of a particularly abrupt interruption as the source of his emblematic screen memory is not accidental. "Implicit" memories permit us to perform daily tasks without conscious focused attention. Implicit knowledge involves the unconscious memory of the correct timing in which these tasks have to be performed in a specific setting. Sudden changes of setting disrupt our expectations, force us to pay conscious attention where it was not needed previously, and disrupt the continuity in our sense of duration. This leads to pronounced gaps in narrative memory coexisting with particularly clear and vivid memory of sensory impressions, the hallmarks of screen memories. In discussing *Nachtraeglichkeit* in memory formation, we have referred to both the billiard-ball-like mechanical aftereffect of events and to hermeneutics, meanings, and changes of meaning. Intermixed, all of these play a role in memory formation and our search to reconstruct the past. This is relevant to the analyst's listening during a psychoanalytic session. The psychoanalyst's suspended way of listening differs from the focused attention of ordinary listening. The analyst may even suspend the distinction between the recital of a dream and the description of real events. She may listen to everything as though it were a dream or a screen memory. In such a listening mode, the analyst's attention may shift back and forth to a focus on the description of the sensory experience and away from the analysand's story line that may be confabulated.

Déjà Vu

The individual experiencing and describing a screen memory locates it, the confabulated story, in a specific point in time. This is one feature that distinguishes it from the *déjà vu* experience, another elaboration of a memory trace. There is, however, also a close connection between the concept of screen memory and the *déjà vu* phenomenon. It is the emphasis on sensory experience. In the *déjà vu* experience, the individual is convinced that the same sensory features were present in the past and are present now—the same location, the same colors, the same landscape. Yet, as we shall see, in a sense, *déjà vu* is the opposite of the screen memory. My hypothesis is that the apparent sameness of a past and current situation is based on the resemblance of formal patterns, precisely *not* the same sensory experience.

I have emphasized the uncanny nature of *déjà vu* experiences (Kafka 1966; Kafka 1989a, 46-B47) and related it to simultaneous contradictory convictions such as "I am sure I have seen this, or I have been there" and

"I am sure I have never been there." My hypothesis, which is supported by neurobiological findings: *Contradictory convictions are the result of the repetition of the same pattern of stimulation, but in different sensory compartments.* Synesthesia is the blending of different sensory compartments. The *pattern* of a synesthetic perception may be the same as a pattern of a compartmentalized perception. Think of an oscilloscope that has the same wave pattern whether it represents an auditory, a visual, or a synesthetic stimulus pattern. Neuroscientific support for this hypothesis derives from the importance of temporal-lobe functions in the integration and differentiation of sensory "compartments" and the fact that individuals with temporal-lobe abnormalities are often inundated by ongoing *déjà vu* experiences. In this connection, the "anatomical" hypothesis put forward by Wigan in 1860, the hypothesis that Freud cites, is quite remarkable: Wigan thought that *déjà vu* phenomena resulted from an absence of simultaneity in the functioning of the two cerebral hemispheres.

A Clinical Example of *Déjà Vu* and Fugue States

A middle-aged woman without any previously observed psychiatric pathology rather suddenly was frequently absent from home, sometimes for several days. She could not give any explanations for this and apparently had no memory of her activities during these days. When I saw her for an evaluation, she described frequent and somewhat disorienting *déjà vu* experiences. Her family had traced her absences and found that she, very active in women's clubs, had given several well-received lectures at women's clubs in other cities. As mentioned, she was amnesic of these trips and activities. Temporal-lobe abnormalities have been linked with fugue states (altered states of consciousness in which a person may move about purposely and even speak but is not fully aware of having done so) and great frequency and intensity of *déjà vu* phenomena. I referred her for a neurological evaluation that revealed a very large tumor involving the temporal lobes. My work with schizophrenic patients has led me to believe that ongoing, steady immersion in *déjà vu* experiences may play a role in the profound temporal disorientation. Also, in connection with the study of schizophrenic thought disorder, I have already described the hypothesis that each perceptual act represents an unconscious recapitulation of the ontogeny of perception, and that, developmentally, synesthetic perceptions antedate sense-specific (visual, auditory, etc.) perceptions. Interruptions, however, of some microtemporal recapitulations lead to the subjective equivalence of completely and of incompletely recapitulated perceptions and therefore to the formation of bizarre psychotic uncanny "objects."

Conclusion

We cannot talk about memories, about memory traces, without talking about time. Some modern conceptions of time are relevant to psychoanalysis, particularly to the notion of the timelessness of the unconscious. In any case, memories are not copies of the past. Episodic memories are constructions. In that sense, all memories are false. We have examined different ways in which they are false and how episodic memories unroll what has been temporally condensed. (Freud says that when the patient says "I have known this all along," the end of the analysis is near [Freud 1913-14, 207].) The concept of *Nachtraeglichkeit* has received special attention. Clinical psychoanalysis and memory formation function in the *Spielraum* (space—or time—for play) between the concreteness of mechanical aftereffects on the one hand, and hermeneutics, i.e., meaning and change of meaning resulting from new information, on the other. And it is here, somewhat surprisingly, that the psychoanalytical concept of *Nachtraeglichkeit* and neurobiology may encounter one another.

The simple naming of specific areas of the brain as centers of a specific affective or cognitive function may strike us as only a kind of internal phrenology and thus of limited interest. The situation is different when a shift in cerebral activation and the timing of the shift correspond to interesting psychological developments. Tori Nielsen and Philippe Stenstrom have observed that a different brain area is activated when an individual recounts a dream he had yesterday and when he talks about the same dream one week later: "[T]he dependence of newly acquired memories on the hippocampus decreases over time whereas their dependence on neocortical structures, such as the medial prefrontal cortex, increases in a complementary fashion. Memories are [. . .] relocated over time from the hippocampus to the neocortex [. . .]." The authors describe corresponding qualitative changes, in essence from "day residue" to cognitive elaboration, to emotionally relevant episodic memories (Nielsen and Stenstrom 2005, 1286ff.). Here is a neurobiological finding connected to the construction of meaning and to the hermeneutic pole of *Nachtraeglichkeit*. The finding that chronobiological factors at several levels influence the selection of memory sources corresponds to "aftereffect," the "billiard-ball" external, mechanical, and concrete pole of *Nachtraeglichkeit*. The timing and the rhythms of cerebral functions in general correspond to linear clock time, that is, the linear clock time in which billiard balls have their aftereffects. These "external" rhythms are gatekeepers that provide or deny access, at any one moment, to a multitude of cerebral activities. The brain itself functions within the polarity of aftereffect and hermeneutic transformations, a polarity that can be conceptualized as existing in Fraser's hierarchical levels. This polarity of brain functioning is also congruent with our psychoanalytic work. The fixed clock-time of the beginning and ending of the psychoanalytic session forms the frame in which the hermeneutic search of the unconscious unfolds, an unfolding necessary for the construction of personal psychological time, an unraveling of what is initially condensed and timeless into the thread with which we then proceed to weave our memory traces and our lives.

References

Arlow, Jacob. (1959). The Structure of the *Déjà Vu* Experience. *Journal of the American Psychoanalytic Association* 7:611-631.

Eissler, Kurt R. (1955). *The Psychiatrist and the Dying Patient.* New York: International Universities Press, Inc.

Eissler, Kurt R. (1993). On the Possible Effects of Aging on the Practice of Psychoanalysis. *Psychoanalytic Inquiry* 13:316-332.

Fraser, J.T. (1981). Temporal Levels and Reality Testing. *The Internation-*

al Journal of Psychoanalysis 62:3-26.

Freud, Sigmund. (1893-1899) . Screen Memories. In Freud 1953-1974, vol. III: *Early Psycho-Analytic Publications (1893-1899)*: 299-322.

Freud, Sigmund. (1909). Analysis of a Phobia in a Five-Year-Old Boy. In Freud 1953-1974, vol. X: *Two Case Histories ("Little Hans" and the "Rat Man") (1909)*, 1-150.

Freud, Sigmund. (1913-1914). Fausse Reconnaissance ('Déjà Racontee') in Psycho-Analytic Treatment. In Freud 1953-1974, vol. XIII: *Totem and Taboo and Other Works (1913-1914)*, 199-207.

Freud, Sigmund. (1923-1925). A Note Upon the "Mystic Writing Pad." In Freud 1953-1974, vol. XIX: *The Ego and the Id and Other Works (1923-1925)*, 225-232.

Freud, Sigmund. (1932-1936). New Introductory Lectures on Psycho-Analysis. In Freud 1953-1974, vol. XXII: *New Introductory Lectures on Psycho-Analysis and Other Works (1932-1936)*, 7-182.

Freud, Sigmund. (1953-1974). *The Standard Edition of the Complete Psychological Works of Sigmund Freud.* Translated from the German under the general editorship of James Strachey, in collaboration with Anna Freud, assisted by Alix Strachey and Alan Tyson. 24 vols. London: Hogarth Press and the Institute of Psycho-Analysis.

Freud, Sigmund. (1971). Screen Memories. In *Abstracts of the Standard Edition of the Complete Psychological Works of Sigmund Freud*, edited by Carrie Lee Rothgeb. 28. Rockville, Maryland, National Institute of Mental Health (Philadelphia, PA: Scientific Literature Corporation, Philadelphia).

Freud, Sigmund. (1985). *The Complete Letters of Sigmund Freud to Wilhelm Fliess 1887-1904*, edited by J.M. Masson. Cambridge, Mass. and London: Harvard University Press.

Gödel, K. (1931). Über formal unentscheidbare Sätze der Principia Mathematica und verwandter Systeme: I. *Monatshefte für Mathematik und Physik* 38: 173-198.

Kafka, John. (1966). Déjà Vu Phenomena—Observations and a Theory. Paper presented at the annual meeting of the American Psychoanalytic Association.

Kafka, John. (1989a). *Multiple Realities in Clinical Practice*. New York: Yale University Press.

Kafka, John. (1989b). Déjà Vu, Drugs, Synesthesia. In Kafka 1989a, 51-78.

Kafka, John. (1989c). Time, Timing, and Temporal Perspective. In Kafka 1989a, 18-25.

Kettner, M. (1999). Das Konzept der Nachträglichkeit in Freud's Erinnerungstheorie. *Psyche* 4: 309-342.

Lestienne, Rémy. (2013). On the Limits of Time in the Brain. *KronoScope* 13, no. 2:228-239.

Matte-Blanco, Ignacio. (1959). Expression in Symbolic Logic of the Characteristics of the System Ucs or the Logic of the System Ucs. *The International Journal of Psychoanalysis* 40: 1-5.

Matte-Blanco, Ignacio. (1988). *Thinking, Feeling, and Being: Clinical Reflections on the Fundamental Autonomy of Human Beings and World*. New Library of Psychoanalysis 5. London and New York: Tavistock/Routledge.

Murrough, James W.; Iosifescu, Dan V.; Chang, Lee C.; Al Jurdi, Rayan K.; Green, Charles E.; Perez, Andrew M.; Iqbal, Syed; Pillemer, Sarah; Foulkes, Alexandra; Shah, Asim; Charney, Dennis S.; Mathew, Sanjay J. (2013). Antidepressant Efficacy of Ketamine in Treatment-Resistant Major Depression: A Two-Site Randomized Controlled Trial. *American Journal of Psychiatry* 170: 1134-1142.

Nielsen, Tore A. and Philippe Stenstrom, (2005). What Are the Memory Sources of Dreaming? *Nature* 437 (27 October): 1286-1289.

Smith, David L. (2000). The Mirror Image of the Present: Freud's Theory of Retrogressive Screen Memories. *Psychoanalytische Perspectieven* 39: 7-29.

Watts, Vabren. (2013). Ketamine Shows Rapid Action in Treatment-Resistant Depression. *Psychiatric News* September 10: 1, 23.

Westerlundh, B. and Smith, G. (1983). Percept-genesis and the psychodynamics of perception. *Psychoanalysis and Contemporary Thought* 6: 597-640.

Yourgrau, Palle. (2005). *A World Without Time. The Forgotten Legacy of Gödel and Einstein.* New York: Basic Books.

Chapter in Two Butterflies on My Head; Psychoanalysis in the Interdisciplinary Scientific Dialogue, M. Leuzinger-Bohleber, H. Schneider, R. Pfeifer, (eds.), Springer-Verlag, Berlin 1992

Chapter 18
Consciousness and the Shadow of Time

Abstract

The hypothesis of this paper is that each perceptual act recapitulates the ontogeny of perception, that it recapitulates the early development of the distinctions and discriminations that underlie the perceptual repertoire. Furthermore rapid replays of the developmental history of conflicts occur in the perceptual processes that take place in a transferential frame during psychoanalytic treatment. The study of this temporal phenomenon (recapitulation), led to the recognition of the centrality of time in psychic activity and eventually to the notion of the equivalence of time and mind. Results from experimental psychology as well as from psychoanalytic practice are used to support this hypothesis. If time and mind are equated, mental disorders are also disorders of time. A short case study of a schizophrenic patient illustrates that the very core of schizophrenic disorders is a disorder of time and of consciousness.

*   *   *

An effort to understand psychic reality is central to all psychoanalytic work and thought. This represents in no way a shift from the focus on conflict, since the construction of the fluid psychic realities is itself the result of conflicting forces and defensive operations against these forces. Many psychoanalytic authors, however, have tended to think of external reality as a relatively fixed, stable, and solid given. In the solid playing field that was reality, the psychology of conflict dealt with the macrodynamics of instinctual forces and defences activated against them. The psychoanalytic study of the microdynamics of perception, more precisely the study of conflictual and defensive operations in the perception of reality, has evolved more recently and represents a field in which psychoanalysis and cognitive science meet.

Attention to the microdynamics of perception can enrich psychoanalytic work with all patients, although many analysts have thought that such issues were of interest only when dealing with problems of the "reality testing" of more disturbed patients. My hypothesis is that each perceptual act recapitulates the ontogeny of perception, that it recapitulates the early development of the distinctions and discriminations that underlie the perceptual repertoire. Furthermore, rapid replays of the developmental history of conflicts occur in the perceptual processes that take place in a transferential frame during psychoanalytic treatment. The study of this temporal phenomenon, recapitulation, led to the recognition of the centrality of time in psychic activity and eventually to the notion of the equivalence of time and mind.

In this chapter, I will try to present a summary of the development of the ideas mentioned above, providing just enough detail so that this summary can serve as a platform for a sketch of currently evolving thoughts. They are:

The past that is being replayed is constantly being altered by newly available information. The retroactive attribution of meaning complicates recapitulative processes. Perhaps it would be more accurate to say that we repeat what we always remember in the same way than to remain with the formula that we repeat what we do not remember. The topic of memory, the very memory of continuity in time, is intimately connected to the topic of our consciousness of self, to consciousness itself, a concept more elusive perhaps than the concept of the unconscious.

The disconnection between schizophrenic patients' awareness of the existence of thought from the existence of its thinker, the examination of clinical findings and of experimental data suggest that a temporal double-take, a just long enough and not too long delay in mental and neuronal processing, offers an entry into our dawning understanding of consciousness.

In order to proceed with the explication of new ideas, I must first recapitulate the development of thoughts that has led to my current position. The term "recapitulation" occupies a central position for me. Whether or not it is true that the drowning man sees or experiences his entire life passing before him, the idea of such a panoramic experience condensed into perhaps fractions of a second can serve to introduce the notion of recapitulation. I believe that to the drowning man's hypothetical conscious panoramic experience corresponds to an actual ongoing *unconscious* equivalent phenomenon, recapitulations that occur in all of us under ordinary circumstances. I have amplified the notion that each perceptual act recapitulates the ontogeny of perception (Kafka 1977, 1989). The development of our perceptual capacities includes, but is not limited to, the development of our ability to discriminate the animate from the inanimate, the inner from the outer stimulus (and thus the size of ourselves as organisms), and the temporal from the spatial organization of psychic data. These three discriminatory abilities are of major importance in the development of the infant and of the young child, and they have a systemic interrelationship. An affinity exists between the animate, the inner, and the temporal on the one hand, and the outer, the spatial, and the inanimate on the other hand.

To the developmental progression of such major discriminatory functions correspond microdevelopments in each perceptual act. Clinical and experimental findings support this notion. Tachistoscopic experiments (studies involving very brief exposures of stimuli) are especially informative. They provide a kind of temporal dissection of perceptual processes that indicates the following: When the adult's perceptual act is interrupted by the disappearance of the stimulus after very brief exposure, the adult's perception resembles that of a young child (Stein 1949; Smith & Danielsson 1982; Westerlundh & Smith 1983). When stimuli are presented for extremely short periods, the responses which can be elicited from normal adults resemble the responses given by very young children to whom they are presented for an unlimited period of time. Slightly longer tachistoscopic exposure times elicit responses from adults that are similar to those given by somewhat older children. Still longer exposure times of stimuli to adults elicit responses similar to those given by still older children.

The most audacious formulation to which findings that support the notion of recapitulation have led me to the idea that mind and time are equivalent terms. In brief, the elements that have provided the steps to such a mind-time equation, include the following: Our psychologically constant objects are the result of subjective equivalences of different stimuli. The experimental work of Heinrich Klüver (1936) forms the background for this assertion. His basic paradigm is to train animals to distinguish between two stimuli and to then present them with a field in which *none* of the stimuli are identical to the stimuli presented originally. In this new situation the animal selects one new and unfamiliar stimulus as *subjectively equivalent* to the one that had been originally reinforced through a conditioning experiment.

I believe that this kind of subjective equivalence, as the term is used in general psychology, is also a necessary ingredient for the formation of constant objects in the psychoanalytic sense (Kafka 1964). In psychoanalysis, object constancy involves the notion that the gratifying and the frustrating object, the gratifying and the frustrating mother for instance, are not "split" from each other, but are one and the same.

Let us now expand the concept of subjective equivalence and consider that under different circumstances time passes more or less rapidly. An extensive literature deals with the factors that influence time judgments (Kafka 1989). Objectively different time intervals can be subjectively equivalent and objectively identical time intervals can be subjectively different. The circumstances that determine our subjective expansion or contraction of time experience have something to do with our drive states, our patience or impatience to have our hungers or other needs satisfied. The object that we are seeking, what we are scanning *for,* depends on the most unsatisfied need at the moment. The scanning speed depends on the intensity of the need, drive state or appetite and on the relative abundance or scarcity of the need-satisfying object in the available scanning field. To all this must be added that defensive operations enter these microdynamics of perception and contribute to the regulation of the expression of needs in our perceptual processes (Smith & Danielsson 1982). Neither our subjective "spatial" objects nor our subjective temporal units correspond to "external" and "linear" fixed reality, especially because the speed with which we scan our stimulus field is thus multiply determined by our drive state, our affective condition. While, until now, my thesis has seemed to focus on cognition in a narrow sense, let us note that *time*, through the consideration of drive state, expressing itself through scanning speed, introduces affect into my formulation. The field that is being scanned is itself an expanding and contracting one. It is being scanned for varying contents and at changing speeds. All these variations are related to complex interacting cognitive and affective elements. The very term *scanning* loses its somewhat narrow and mechanical features and takes on a broader meaning here. Perception in the narrow sense widens to the perception of meaning, and thus to thought and mental processes generally. The microselectivity of perceptual processes transforms them, as it were, into creators of what are ordinarily called stimuli. Perceptual acts include recapitulations of the development of our perceptions and of our perceptual capabilities. This means that there are ongoing recapitulations of the history of our subjective equivalences and of the history of our psychoanalytically understood defensive operations (for more details, see Kafka 1989).

The above condensed presentation of some ideas is sufficient to show how mental processes (mind) become more and more wedded to temporal processes, eventually so intertwined and indistinguishable from them that the terms become equivalent and lead to a mind-time equation. I believe that the initially startling notion of an *equation* of the concepts of mind and time, although it will perhaps remain unsettling, will be supported by further examination of mental processes.

Let us for a moment return to the somewhat less abstract level of the recapitulation in each perceptual act of the content of the ontogeny of perception. This recapitulation is understood as an ongoing and condensed repetition of past history in the face of new situations and stimu-li. This problem too becomes still more complicated if we consider the effects of new information on this process. Freud's use of the concept of *Nachträglichkeit*, inadequately translated into English in the Freud's works as *deferred action*, refers to a reworking of the past that is influ-enced by new information. At age of three and a half, Little Hans does not experience anxiety in the face of a direct castration threat made by his mother, but one and a half years later, after further intellectual and emotional development, with "retroactive attribution of meaning," he does become anxious.

The story of the rider over the lake of Constance (Der Reiter über dem Bodensee), who falls dead from his horse after learning of the danger he just survived by riding over the barely frozen deep lake, also illustrates the effects of *Nachträglichkeit*. As Freud used the term, he did refer to a rework-ing of the past in terms of the content of the psychic experience, with cognitive and emotional factors intimately fused. The implications for "re-construction", as this term is used in the literature on psychoanalytic technique, of such a notion of *Nachträglichkeit*, the retrospective attribution of meaning, can hardly be overemphasized. It has been greatly neglected and oversimplified in many discussions of the effects of "real" and fantasized events, real and fantasized trauma. Since we have learned that the microdynamics of perception involve the operation of complex defensive processes (Westerlundh & Smith, 1983), there are, psychologically, no raw and meaningless events. What then *can* be "reconstructed ?" If we take the example of "Little Hans," it should be theoretically and schematically possible, with sufficient regression and corresponding transferential developments, to "reconstruct" the castration threat that does *not* create anxiety. At age three and a half, Little Hans says calmly that if his mother cuts off his penis, he will simply sit down to urinate. Later the emotional and cognitive devel-opment of Little Hans, an "information" of sorts, has led to a reworking, in this case a traumatization, a retroactive attribution of traumatic meaning, to the threat. But apparently, for the neurotic patient, the reworking of the past, is strikingly unchanging and "ritualistic" in its apparently "mechani-cal" (inanimate?) "*stuck*" repetitiveness. Analysis, however, brings new information to the analysand and the past is reworked differently. Since we are always confronted with a *new* past, the psychoanalytic dictum that we repeat what we do not remember should perhaps be changed to the dictum that we repeat what we always remember the same way. In any case the fact that the psychoanalyst observes the restructuring of past experience in the present deserves our closest attention.

In our discussion of the reworking of the past, we have until now focused on the cognitive and emotional *content* of perceptions and memories. The *formal* aspects of the situation are perhaps of even greater interest and are, incidentally, pertinent to the idea of the time-mind equation. On closer examination the analyst is interested not only in the effects of restructuring the *content* of the experience of the past, but also in the effects of the restructuring of *formal* aspects of the experience of the passage of time and temporal perspective. A feeling of discontinuity of the course of their life is not a rare complaint of patients in analysis. I have likened this state of affairs to the situation of a rod traversing several layers of unmixed fluids that have different specific gravities and indexes of refraction. The straight rod seems to have angles at the interfaces of the fluids. Psychoanalysis may stir and mix the fluids, as if to straighten the rod, and lead to a feeling of integration, to a feeling of continuity between the previously discontinous ego states. Some experimental evidence bears on this subject of clinical interest.

Ornstein (1969) has demonstrated the retroactive effects of new information on judgment of past duration. Subjects in one experimental group learned a series of apparently random numbers and then were asked how long it took them to learn the series. Subjects in another group learned the same series, and then were given a code that transformed what was apparently a random series into an ordered one before being asked how long it took them to learn the series. The subjects who were given the code, whose actual learning period was the same, estimated the learning period as shorter than did the subjects who were not given the information that would have permitted them to reorganize—recode—their experience retrospectively. It is well established that ordered numbers are learned more rapidly than random ones. Subjects given the code which transformed the apparently random series into an ordered one after learning them, estimated their learning period as though they had known the ordering code at the time of learning.

New information does indeed have a retroactive effect on judgment of past duration. When we consider the formal aspects of retroactive restructuring, we may conclude that the "retroactive attribution of meaning" is perhaps also not an adequate translation of *Nachträglichkeit*. We are really dealing with a "retroactive attribution of meaning and of structure."

The following is a condensed description of a clinical situation in which the qualitative aspects of temporal experience played a part in psychoanalytic work. A patient who had been raised by adoptive parents, lived, during the course of his analysis, alternatingly with his mistress and his wife. In one analytic session, after he had again been living for a prolonged period with his wife, he spoke of his feeling of progress in his analysis, but he also spoke about his difficulty in "seeing himself" during his most recent prolonged period with his mistress, which had terminated almost two years previously. After the analyst commented that the analysand's state of mind and his mood had been less constant, had seemed more different from hour to hour during that period than now, the patient gradually began to describe his feeling that periods spent with his mistress had a different time texture from periods spent with his wife and children. Although his description of people, situations and feelings was complex, his focus was on the struggle to re-experience and reintegrate his "time out," his discontinuity of experience, his effort to "see" himself both in more constant times and in saccadic periods of rapid mood changes. He then talked about the eventual termination of the analysis, his anticipated joyful and nostalgic feelings. This was followed by talk of his plans to ask his adoptive parents about his biologic parents, whom he believed they knew. Historical details that he had never mentioned before about his adoptive parents began to emerge, and fantasies about his biologic parents as well. He then said that there might be a connection between characteristics of his mistress and of his fantasied parents. In the next session, in the context of expressing fears about what he might discover concerning his origins and how we would react to the discoveries—and in the context of talking about plans, wishes and fears for his future—he reported a dream of being in a corner room from which one could see in two directions.

The complex situation that faces us when we consider clinical and experimental data can be summarized as follows: We constantly recapitulate the past, but the past that we recapitulate is itself in constant flux because it is reshaped by new information in which the cognitive and emotional factors are inseparable. The affective, and therefore the transferential history, is also packaged in this recapitulation. The preconscious richness of our affectively informed contact with ourselves and with the world depend on and derive from the overtones of recapitulation and condensation, the constant rapid replay of *elements* of our cognitive and emotional histories. I emphasize that it is a replay of elements, not a repetition, because the past that is being replayed is constantly being altered by new information, by new "coding." In other words, we are gaining (new) insights.

Jacques Derrida, in a lecture a few years ago, spoke of the idea of publication of texts in which the discarded, the eliminated text elements would appear along with the final text. In this fashion the evolution of the author's thought could be followed by the reader in a fashion that would differ from the way he could follow it if the author were to simply describe the evolution of his thought. Even an author who would write that he had idea A, but then changed his mind and the idea evolved into B, would bring to this description a restructuring that is absent if the original idea, although crossed out, were preserved in the text. One way in which psychoanalysis differs from briefer therapeutic encounters is that the transferential text is written and crossed out many times. Sometimes the erased passages are looked at and examined in our psychoanalytic "reconstructions," and sometimes points of panoramic perspective are reached in which the sweeping *restructuring* ignores the detailed erasures in our insight guiding process.

Self-observation is a central concept in all our discussions of the work of the analyst and of the analysand. The patient's "observing ego" and the analyst's "working ego" examine the regressive transference and counter-transference developments, but despite the termporality of the concept of regression, we tend initially to have a spatial rater than a temporal metaphor in mind when speak of observing ego or of the therapeutic "split" in analysis. This spatial image, however, contains all the dangers of reification, whereas a focus on the bi-directional temporal movement of the recapitulation of an ever changing past may eventually facilitate our attempt to understand what is more mysterious than the unconscious, namely consciousness itself. There is a close affinity between "insight" and "consciousness" because they both involve a temporal split, moving positions on two temporal tracks.

If there is an equation of time and mind, one could comprehend mental disorders as disorders of time. I have come to believe that at the very core of schizophrenic disorders, there is a disorder of consciousness. A schizophrenic patient, after he had greatly improved, explained to me that previously C he now thinks he was much sicker then C he had sometimes sensed that there was some thinking around, but that he had not known that it was he who was doing the thinking. The Cartesian "I think, therefore I am" did not apply. I believe that such pathology can best be conceptualized as a failure, a disorder of the temporal "double-take", the time, so to speak, between "think" and "am" that is at the core of the Cartesian formula and of consciousness itself.

One of the advantages of a temporal focus in the study of mental phenomena is the possibility of an eventual bridge to the study of neuronal events, studies in which temporal approaches seem to be promising. If we now return to our discussion of the double-take of consciousness, it seems plausible that, for consciousness to emerge, the interval of the *double-/-take*, the interval between the schematic *think* and *am* of the Cartesian formula, should be within certain limits related to neuronal circuitry, ultimately to a kind of micro-memory. The time for this double-take of consciousness should be neither too short nor too long.

In this context it is interesting that at the dawn of "scientific" academic psychology, there were, among the very early psychological experiments, attempts to define a fundamental psychological temporal unit. The question was: How long is it "now?" Since very short intervals are overstimulated and longer intervals are underestimated, the meeting point, the intervals that tend to be estimated correctly, were thought to be such fundamental psychological units of time. Recently Jonathan Winson (1985) has suggested that consciousness may be related to the time it takes for specific feed-back circuits to process a stimulus. He cites the experiments carried out by Libby on neurosurgical patients. The interval between the sensation of having one's hand touched and the actual application of a stimulus, perhaps surprisingly, was *longer* when the cortex (cortical projection area of the hand) was stimulated directly than when the stimulus was applied to the hand, a condition in which the response was almost simultaneous. In Winston's view, the delay of awareness with direct cortical stimulation could correspond, could have some eventually definable relationship, to the neuronal circuitry underlying consciousness.

Again and again we have to use "spatial" words in our attempts to *describe* temporal experiences and phenomena. (Nonverbal music *communicates* it better.) Consciousness, as we have discussed it, is an *insight*, perhaps the fundamental insight, but we have to use the spatial seeing from the outside into, to describe this temporal double take. There are, however, some "spatial" expressions that we experience more "temporally" and that do not force us to work so hard to conceptualize in temporal terms. Although "surprise" (literally "take from above") is a spatial term, it provokes a temporal resonance, probably because it contains movement, therefore time. (Insight does not.) Actually, surprise deals with a double track of time, a kind of "two-timing", an expectation of one kind of timing and the occurrence of another kind of timing. Consciousness is a kind of overtaking of oneself, a temporal split, a *décalage*, a micro-jetlag, a catching up with one's shadow.

The schizophrenic patient who had not known that the thinking that was around was his own also believed that his improvement had started the moment one psychiatric aide told him that he had a choice, that he, the patient, could do what he wanted in a particular situation. I would say that his improvement *consisted* in his being *able* to hear this communication at that moment, to comprehend it, to conceptualize himself as a center of autonomous action, to be conscious of self, to be *conscious*. At this point we do not know what factors cause, or perhaps even consistently contribute to this emergence from the deepest psychotic states, which, as mentioned above, I believe to be disorders of consciousness. Perhaps a change of timing in the neuronal circuitry, a change in the rhythmic activities of neurotransmitter receptors, or a change in the patterns of circuitries involved brings the lag necessary for the double-take of consciousness within the acceptable limits for psychological "now." For our schizophrenic patient the intervention of the psychiatric aide was like the appearance of sunlight that permits a sundial to function. And—like in a sundial—it is the split between the object and its moving shadow that gives us consciousness and that gives us time.

References

Kafka, J. S. (1964). Technical application of a concept of multiple reality. *International Journal of Psycho-Analysis* 45:575-578.

Kafka, J. S. (1977). Zum Problem der Realität. *Psyche* 31:712-731.

Kafka, J. S. (1989). Multiple realities in clinical practice. New York: Yale University Press.

Klüver, H. (1936). The study of personality and the method of equivalent and non-equivalent stimuli. *Character and Personality* 5:91-112.

Loewald, H. W. (1962). The superego and the ego ideal. II. Superego and time. International Journal of Psycho-Analysis 43:264-268.

Ornstein, R. E. (1969). *On the experience of time.* Baltimore: Penguin Books.

Smith. G. J. W . & Danielsson, A. (1982). *Anxiety and defensive strategics in childhood and adolescence.* New York: International Universities Press. (*Psychological Issues*, Monograph 52.)

Stein, M. I. (1949). Personality factors involved in temporal development of Rorschach responses. *Rorschach Research Exchange and Journal of Projective Techniques* 13:355-414.

Westerlundh, B., & Smith, G. (1983). Percept-genesis and the psychodynamics of perception. *Psychoanalysis and Contemporary Thought* 6:597-640.

Winson, J. (1985). *Brain and psyche. The biology of the unconscious.* New York: Anchor Press.

Selected Writings

Society, Trauma, Holocaust

American Imago 65(4):547-565, 2008.

Chapter 19

Psychoanalysis and Democracy

This paper has been modified and expanded from the translated version of an invited lecture, given in German, in the Austrian Parliament, April 7, 2006, in celebration of Freud's 150th birthday.

This paper deals not only with Freud and his psychoanalytic legacy but also with the author's personal history as a refugee from Austria and its effects on his analytic thought and work. The difficulties of communication between those Austrians for whom the Nazi period represented an interruption of their usual existence and the victims whose lives were ruptured are discussed on a personal and a conceptual level. The meaning of the openness of the psychoanalytic process and of functioning democracy is explored. Although psychoanalysis and democracy must confront the denial of the past, both must function while recognizing the power of the irrational and the unconscious. Governments build monuments and organize memorial events. A focus on victims may not differentiate natural catastrophes from crimes committed by humans. By shifting attention away from the perpetrators, such memorials may be anti-memorials and serve organized amnesia.

Mrs. Prammer, Ladies and Gentlemen

In your invitation, you have asked me not only to deal with Freud and his legacy, with theoretical and technical matters, but also to speak about my personal history as a refugee from Austria, about the effects of this history on my life and work as well as on my ideological and political perspectives. I received this invitation on the basis of an earlier presentation I had made in a symposium, organized by the Vienna Psychoanalytic Association and the University of Vienna, focusing on the history of the expulsion of Freud and psychoanalysis from Austria. On that occasion, my lecture was entitled, *Zerbrechen und Unterbrechen: Die Gewalt der Nicht-Interpretation.* Although this can be translated as "Rupture and Interruption: The Violence of Non-Interpretation," the German word *unterbrechen* conveys, perhaps more strongly than does "interruption," that further development is only postponed, temporarily suspended, whereas *zerbrechen* conveys breakage beyond repair.

My contribution to this earlier symposium was also at once personal and theoretical. On both levels, I dealt with the topic of differences in memory among those who remained in Austria and those who had fled. I focused on the problems of communication between persons who were able to save themselves only through flight and others who remained in Austria without being in mortal danger. These problems of communication also exist for their children. In an interview with Peter Rudnytsky (2000), Jessica Benjamin has observed: "You may grow up as a contemporary Jewish person without experiencing cataclysmic breakdown in your personal life, yet your family is imbued with the culture of the Holocaust.... Breakdown experience is ... profoundly embodied in cultural forms and ... intergenerationally transmitted" (p. 265). Upon reading these remarks, any thoughts I might have had that my differentiation between *zerbrechen* and *unterbrechen* was too theoretical were soon dispelled. After I had proposed the title of my earlier presentation, I was surprised by an Austrian colleague's question: "Since the meaning of my title was not clear, did I mean perhaps that the time had come when we should stop, break (away from) this preoccupation with this (Nazi) past?"

*   *   *

Psychoanalytic research on memory has yielded many insights about remembering and externalization, repression and deferred action (*Nachträglichkeit*), the reworking of memories that enhances the feeling of continuity in one's life. I believe that psychoanalytic treatment, when successful, strengthens the feeling of having a non-interrupted self. Most analysts conceive of interpretation as playing an important role in this process of integration. Interpretation can build a bridge of comprehension between what happened before and after the interruption.

Interpretation, however, cannot heal what remains incomprehensible and has been *zerbrochen*. And it is in Austria (though not only here) that something incomprehensible, something seemingly impossible, occurred and became a fact of life. The difficulty of acknowledging that so many Austrians were actively involved in Nazi-era crimes often leads to spurious explanations and absurd rationalizations, which only further hamper communication between the "Interrupted" and the "Disrupted." I know, and can appreciate, how many people in Austria today are making the difficult attempt to grasp the truth of the matter in its entirety and to bring it to the attention of the public. The challenges are greatest for those who reveal the history of their own relatives' involvements because they are often shunned by family members.

When Professor Wilhelm Burian, M.D., a recent Director of the Vienna Psychoanalytic Institute, approached me about giving a lecture in the Parliament on the connection between psychoanalytic thought and politically responsible or irresponsible actions, I agreed because I believe that there indeed exists a deep connection between democratic and psychoanalytic thought. Both democracy and psychoanalysis are open systems in which it is always possible to gain new understanding—after a process has been *unterbrochen*. "Inter-ruption," however, implies that what went before continues to exist. Living memory is not killed. Continuity, the psychological coexistence of the new and the old, has to be preserved in the psychoanalytic and in the democratic process. In order to remain open, both must find ways to combat "memory killers," those who want the process to be *zerbrochen*.

*   *   *

In psychoanalysis, one distinguishes between intellectual understanding and emotionally processed insight. Analysts know that their choice of psychoanalysis as a profession and even their specific theoretical interests are deeply intertwined with their personal experiences and problems. I am going to speak about such experiences and my understanding of how they have influenced my psychoanalytic thinking.

I was born in Linz. My father died when I was six years old, before the *Anschluss* (i.e., the incorporation of Austria into the Third Reich). Dr. Eduard Bloch, the Jewish doctor of the Hitler family, was my uncle and became my legal guardian. After a period in France, my mother emigrated with me to America. The feeling of continuity in my life was severely damaged by my father's early death and my plight as a refugee from Austria and the Holocaust. Time itself was torn. This development spurred my abiding interest in how time is perceived and in the concept of time itself in psychoanalysis.

I believe that the reality of the Holocaust and its "madness," which cannot be comprehended rationally, contributed significantly to my interest in psychosis. The fact that I was bewildered by what psychotic people said triggered in me a "rage to understand." My research on psychotic language led me to the hypothesis (1989) that it is not that the logic of schizophrenic speech differs from "normal" logic, but rather that the objects addressed by this logic are different. A particular emotional-cognitive constellation, an atmosphere, can be "more real" and a safer "object" (p. 114) to someone with schizophrenia than to a differentiated person.

When I speak of the depersonalization in psychosis and of the dehumanization of "the other" by the Nazi ideology that was accepted by so many Austrians, I do not mean to imply that all Austrians, even all Austrian Nazis, were psychotic. Nor am I referring to mass psychology and mass psychosis, but rather to Joseph Gabel's (1962) idea that alienation, which provides the shared hallmark of ideology and schizophrenia, is grounded in an objectification, a spatialization of the temporal. According to Gabel, the "reification" found in both political ideology and schizophrenia is based on the following commonality: ideology is rigid and lifeless and does not respond to external and internal life. Gabel also develops the idea that every Utopia represents a frozen atemporal ideological concretization.

The openness of both psychoanalytic and democratic processes is in sharp contrast to the "New German Psycho therapy" (Gocks 1985) that, after the expulsion of Jews from the professional organizations, had the Utopian goal of transforming neurotics into "whole persons" whose psychic energy could be devoted to the state. Quite fitting here is the notice about the dissolution of the Vienna Psychoanalytic Association that appeared in the *Neue Freie Presse* (New Free Press)—the name of which takes on a bitter irony in this context—on July8, 1938: "The role of the leadership ideal is decisive and it is clear to all that the pure and healthy youth yearns for a leader. In leadership and the community the central issue is always the wholeness of personality and the people. The great task of psychology today is thus clearly defined" (quoted in Tichy and Zwettler-Otte 1999, 191).

Gabel's work (1962) was originally published under the title, *Lafausse conscience—Essai sur la réification* (False Consciousness: An Essay on Reification). The German translation, *Ideologie und Schizophrenie— Formen der Entfremdung* (Ideology and Schizophrenia: Forms of Alienation), appeared in 1967 with an introduction by the Austrian Igor A. Caruso. The different meanings of "ideology" are discussed by both Gabel and Caruso. Although it could be argued that "democracy" is itself an ideology, its emphasis on the "subjective" makes it non-ideological in Gabel's sense because it is the *abstract* that triumphs in ideology. Gabel (1962) quotes from Albert Beguin's book, *Faiblesse de l'Allemagne* (The Weakness of Germany), which argues that Germanic culture provided a particularly fertile ground for such a development: "More than the [other] supposedly rational [istic] people, the Germans are capable of such a complete suppression of the subject that only the intellectual] remains and the demon of the abstract celebrates unbelievable triumphs" (p. 152; my translation).

*   *   *

A central premise of my theoretical psychoanalytic work is that every perception, every present mental act, recapitulates its development. Just as some survivors of life-threatening situations—imminent death through suffocation or drowning, for example—describe how they consciously "relived" their entire lives in a matter of seconds, I believe that corresponding unconscious recapitulations occur continuously. Sometimes they take place only partly unconsciously. Analysis and self-analysis make it possible to gain access to naked, raw feelings. Those who have come close to annihilation, survivors of situations that spelled *zerbrechen*, are conscious of things that they do not share with those who have experienced merely an interruption. Can you imagine what kind of feelings, wishes, and impulses might be elicited in a person marked by such experiences if he were to see how a particularly affectionate Austrian mother treats her baby while he meanwhile cannot escape the image of a small child being slung against a wall and its skull shattering to pieces upon impact?

About ten years after the end of the war, I traveled by train from France to Germany and spoke with my fellow passengers in German. After I had shown my American passport to the customs officer at the border, the woman next to me got very excited. "How is it that you speak German so well?" she asked me. "I am a Jewish-Austrian survivor," I replied. She became noticeably more agitated and rather incoherent in her speech. "So why is it that you're coming back? My son reproaches me, but we didn't know anything back then. On the street with my husband one time, I noticed a group of people who had to clean the sidewalk. "Who are these people?' I asked my husband. 'Shhh,' he said. 'You didn't see anything. They're Jews.'" When I looked out the window of the train, I perceived the entire landscape as a huge burial ground, though by no means as a *Fried-hof* (the German word for cemetery that literally means "courtyard of peace").

*   *   *

The following are some personal variations on a pattern of scenarios that have been described by many "returnees." When I was in Tirol a few years ago, I vividly saw before my eyes the "illegal" Swastika bonfires high up in the mountains. Before the *Anschluss*, these fires greeted us at night whenever we were on vacation in Igls near Innsbruck. Also, before the *Anschluss*, the illegal Nazis had posted, on a certain street corner in Linz, a "transmitter" who passed on news to them. Even though different people would fulfill this function, they were all easy to recognize since they wore the same clothing.

In 1956, when I returned to Linz for a short visit, I saw a man in these clothes standing on the very same street corner. I could not believe my eyes. Morning and afternoon, there was always someone there wearing the same clothes. I asked our old family friend, Dr. Ernst Koref, the Mayor of Linz from 1945 to 1962 and later a member of Parliament, if these "transmitters" were actually still around. He confirmed that they were, adding that about a third of the population was in some way still Nazified, while another third did not care about anything, and the last third had "learned something."

Many personal stories, along with historical and cultural studies, show how fixating on the major crimes of the Holocaust can marginalize the manifold effects of the brazen and base behavior to which the disenfranchised were helplessly exposed. We know that such hurts often lead to severe lifelong inhibition of self-confidence and self-assertion; they can also be the source of defensively overcompensated aggressiveness. The need to make sense of some experiences and their impact can, however, also contribute to tenacity and great achievement. Eric Kandel (2006) has never forgotten the humiliating experience of the Nazis' robbing him of the blue toy car that he had just received as a birthday present. His curiosity about the intensity of another childhood memory that never faded, the banging on the door of the family's apartment in Vienna by two Nazi policemen, played a role in his interest first in the psychoanalytic and then the neuroscientific study of memory, a field in which he has made Nobel Prize-winning discoveries.

While many consequences of humiliating experiences are readily available in one's mind, psychoanalysis can expand and deepen one's understanding of their effects. My own analysis helped me to discover some of their unexpected repercussions. One personal experience of a humiliating event had a deep and lasting effect on me. I was the only Jew in my class. My best and dearest classmate, during a break, all of a sudden told me that he would not come to my house that afternoon. He was an Aryan and I was not. His father had forbidden him to play with me and come to our house. The effects of this humiliation were magnified because I was vaguely aware even then how much my mother, tall and blond herself, admired his "Aryan" good looks. Later, in my own analysis, I saw more clearly some implications of my mother's—and, incidentally, many Jews'—preference for "Aryan" characteristics.

Some years ago, I renewed contact with my former classmate. He did not remember this episode. After very long reflection, he told me that his father was not a convinced Nazi but that he was indeed an anti-Semite. My closest friend's past behavior remains a real sting in my heart. Even now, I can still feel the wound. AND HE DOESN'T REMEMBER A THING! He showed me how much he was not in touch with the history of Nazi Austria when he said, "But nothing could have happened to your [assimilated] family?" It is clear that his and my "realities" were strikingly different. In one's work as a psychoanalyst, it is not enough to recognize differences between one's own "reality" and those of one's patients. The analyst must attempt to comprehend, figuratively to wrap his arms around, multiple realities. Hence, the title of my book, *Multiple Realities in Clinical Practice* (1989).

In retrospect, the memory of one particular sudden shift is directly related to my departure from Austria and my subsequent interest in the temporal "forms" of multiple realities. I vividly recall the heavy oompah rhythm of a Tyrolean band that was playing at a railway station when I left Austria, and the almost frantic tempo of a quick-stepping band that marched past the railway station on my first stop in France. This was a radical change in "tempo" that foreshadowed many others to which I had to adapt: in cultures, environments, and languages.

In the 1970s, I participated in a conference of the Central European Psychoanalytic Association in Bad Ischl. The dialect of the *Salzkammergut* is very similar to that of Linz. Every night during the conference, I had a dream in which my father appeared. (This had not happened for many years.) In reality, my father had always spoken to me in the Linz dialect. Now, he did so in my dreams. When one is forced to become a refugee, the brutal necessity of struggling without any preparation to adapt to a different world, a different language, and a different economic situation almost

always severs the personal process of mourning. This has indelible consequences about which psychoanalysts know a great deal.

*   *   *

I heard about Freud and psychoanalysis for the first time before the *Anschluss* from an older friend, Kurt Sommer, who was also the only Jew in
his class. He told me how one of his teachers had said that Freud believed children have sexual interests and feelings. Only a degenerate Jew,
the teacher continued, could have come up with such an idea. My friend
Kurt proudly recounted how he had stood up and said that the teacher
had no right to demean and insult Jews.

*   *   *

Visiting one's homeland can be difficult for an emigrant. The sting in
the heart always tends to overshadow feelings of love. The point is not
only that those who remained behind have "forgotten"—that is, repressed—important events so vividly recalled by refugees, but also that
when events *are* remembered, the versions of the two groups are quite
different. Memories typically evolve. The memories of those who merely
experienced an "interruption" continue to develop in affectively and
cognitively shifting patterns. The childhood memories of emigrants, in
contrast, are isolated, more "stuck" in an earlier developmental phase.
They have been suddenly cut off, emotionally and cognitively severed.
Such memories often have a particularly vivid, "glowing" character, like
many "screen memories" (*Deckerin-nerungen*), in which the likelihood
that the story line is false is in sharp contrast with the pronounced and
accurate vividness of the sensory component.

   We were so Austrian! Even the sad jokes of emigrants are testaments
to this fact. An example: Some Jews are standing in line, waiting to be
deported to a concentration camp. Mr. Kohn smiles to himself. His
friend asks, "What's with you? How can you be laughing in a situation
like this?" "I just pictured," Kohn says, "how, after the war, I'll be sitting
in a cafe, reading the newspaper. Hitler is sitting at the table next to

mine and comes over to ask, 'Mr. Kohn, would you mind giving me the paper when you're done with it?'" (Kohn continues to smile to himself.) "No, Mr. Hitler, not to you. I will *not* give you this newspaper."

*   *   *

I have already pointed to the fact that psychoanalysis and democracy are open systems. This means that there always exists the possibility of understanding a situation differently, in a novel manner, and also that, in both systems, ways must be found to deal with "memory killers." What is meant by "openness" in the psychoanalytic process? Even the typical "Freudian slip" illustrates how something meaningful is concealed behind a seeming coincidence, but one may also discover that something apparently meaningful was accidental. A person may harbor an unconscious mistaken belief that she is the cause of an event for which she is not responsible. She may unconsciously believe, for instance, that a wish she had when she was four years old that her baby brother should disappear was responsible for his death that was actually caused by a kidney disease. Such unconscious guilt feelings may lead to many problems and difficulties in a person's life, the effects of which can be greatly mitigated by psychoanalytic treatment. It is this open sequence, the refusal to close the temporal series "coincidence-meaning-coincidence," the never-finished spiral of possibilities, that characterizes psychoanalysis as well as democracy.

Given the essential temporal unfinishedness of both the democratic and the psychoanalytic processes, the doors are always open to new information in its broadest sense, to newly learned facts, newly understood connections between external events and their internal cognitive and affective ramifications. Most psychoanalytic clinicians, as I have already mentioned, believe that achieving a greater feeling of continuity in one's life and experiences is an implicit goal of treatment. There are different layers of understanding, just as oil, water, and other liquids separate out and form layers when poured into a glass jar. A small stick dipped into this vessel no longer appears to be straight, but rather as if it were broken, until the mixture is stirred. Psychoanalysis, by providing such stirring and mixing up, facilitates an alternative understanding of the meaning of events. It prepares the ground and provides space for personal self-reflection that can lead to change. Democracy prepares the ground and provides space for debate and social self-reflection that can also lead to change. This debate is about what is possible, what can be actively influenced, and the ever-evolving limits of change that are determined by external and internal circumstances. It is appropriate to underline here, in the Austrian Parliament, that a healthy democracy requires this continuous stirring and mixing up. This is the hallmark of what a fellow Austrian, Karl Popper, called an "Open Society" (1945), which cannot tolerate intolerance without risking dictatorship *even if agents of intolerance are elected to political office.*

Debates are not always carried out in a calm and peaceful manner. At a certain point, one participant will usually assert that his own knowledge is superior to that of his opponent. The same is true for psychoanalysis. Piera Aulagnier, in her book *The Violence of Interpretation* (1975), writes that every interpretation is, in a sense, an act of violence since the analyst is thereby telling the patient that his previous understanding was wrong or at least insufficient. By bringing an outsider's view onto the scene, the foreigner attacks the analysand's narcissism. In a successful psychoanalysis, as in a successful democratic debate, however, the situation gradually changes. In both instances, the effort to feel one's way into the other's thoughts and feelings, the give-and-take between mutual identifications, plays a decisive role. An interpretation that, like the opinion of one's opponent in a debate, is initially perceived as violent because it *is foreign* can gradually be recognized as alleviating and liberating, sometimes only long after the fact, because what begins by being foreign does not remain completely and forever so. The world then grows larger and a different understanding becomes possible.

Neither psychoanalysis nor democracy could fulfill its functions if it worked as though there were no distinction between natural events and the consequences of human actions. In the printed program for the event on the expulsion of Freud and psychoanalysis, there appeared an image of a vortex of water or wind. Yet neither water nor wind forced Freud to leave Vienna. A radical break exists between those who see only a natural phenomenon beyond the influence of human actions and those who recognize the responsibility of perpetrators. I will develop this idea later when discussing memorials.

*   *   *

I want to return now to a more theoretical discussion of our central theme, "Psychoanalysis and Democracy." The essence of Jonathan Lear's (1999) view of the close relation between psychoanalysis and democracy is that both can function only if they recognize the existence and the power of the unconscious and the irrational. Lear writes:

> If we go back to the birth of democracy, in fifth-century Athens, we see that the flourishing of that democracy coincides precisely with the flowering of. . . Greek tragedy. This coincidence is not mere coincidence. The tragic theater gave citizens the opportunity to retreat momentarily from the responsibility of making rational decisions for themselves and their society. At the same time, tragedy confronted them emotionally with the fact that they had to make their decisions in a world which was not entirely rational, in which rationality was sometimes violently disrupted, in which rationality itself could be used for irrational ends. (29)

An example of an apparently rational argument that is dangerous for democracy is the insistence that a party advocating intolerance should be tolerated and represented in a democratic parliament.

As a clinician, I have found it useful to study the formal logic of paradoxes when considering the hypothesis that the so-called "double-bind" situation is the source of some severe psychopathology. Quoting from my book, *Multiple Realities in Clinical Practice*, "On the overpass is a sign saying, 'Ignore this sign'" (1989, 38). This sign, presumably a practical joke, is formally not contradictory, but it creates a true paradox through its self-reflexivity. In order to ignore it, one must notice it. But the very act of noticing it disobeys the injunction itself. Therefore, the sign can be obeyed only through disobedience.

The nature of such paradoxes was studied by Alfred North Whitehead and Bertrand Russell (1910). Russell's theory of types observes that paradoxes involve different levels of abstraction that are not immediately apparent. The "Ignore this sign" paradox, for instance, contains such a hidden shift since the *word* "sign" and the *material* sign on which the word is written involve different levels of abstraction. Whitehead and Russell would say that in the preceding sentence I have made explicit the hidden shift in "logical types." By communicating about the paradoxical communication, that is, I have "metacommunicated" and thus *escaped the paradox*. This examination of paradoxes is also pertinent to the democratic process. In order not to disrupt either the democratic or the psychoanalytic process, it is important that practitioners in both domains must avoid being paralyzed by those who misuse apparent rationality.

Jonathan Lear extends his argument:

What, after all, is Oedipus' complex? That he killed his father and married his mother misses the point. Patricide and maternal incest are *consequences* of Oedipus' failure, not its source. Oedipus' fundamental mistake lies in his assumption that meaning is transparent to human reason. In horrified response to the Delphic oracle, Oedipus flees the people he (mistakenly) takes to be his parents. En route, he kills his actual father and propels himself into the arms of his mother. It is the classic scene of fulfilling one's fate in the very act of trying to escape it. But this scenario is possible only because Oedipus assumes he understands his situation, that the meaning of the oracle is immediately available to his conscious understanding. That is why he thinks he can respond to the oracle with a straightforward application of practical reason. Oedipus' mistake, in essence, is to ignore unconscious meaning.... For Sophocles, this was a sacrilegious crime, for he took this obscure meaning to flow from a divine source. (1999, 29)

According to Lear, "in Sophocles' vision, Oedipus attacks the very idea of unconscious meaning" (1999, 29). That is the relevant point even if we now locate the source of this unconscious meaning in the human, not the divine, mind. Sophocles' message to the Athenians, Lear adds, is that "democratic citizens need to maintain a certain humility in the face of meanings which remain opaque to human reason. We need to be wary that what we take to be an exercise of reason will both hide and reveal an irrationality of which we remain unaware" (p. 30). Psychoanalysts must maintain a genuine humility for similar reasons.

For Lear, the bond between psychoanalysis and democracy is that both must recognize the importance of the unconscious. I would add that both must preserve an openness to *time*, and with this the awareness that the last word has never been spoken and no conclusion can ever be the "final solution." (We note here to what extent language can be poisoned since, for the Nazis, this phrase referred to the extermination of Jews.) According to Freud (1933, 74), the unconscious is not affected by time, yet it interacts with a world that knows change; and the solution to this paradox had to await further scientific and philosophical developments.

As already mentioned, the psychoanalytic study of time has been one of my major interests. The title of my paper, "Consciousness and the Shadow of Time" (1992), as well as of the German translation (1991) of my book, *Jenseits des Realitätsprinzips* (Beyond the Reality Principle), both point to the weightiness of the irrational and the unconscious and, thus, resonate with Lear's thesis. In the above-quoted passage, Lear writes that the Oedipus tragedy "is the classic scene of fulfilling one's fate in the very act of trying to escape it," that is, a self-fulfilling prophecy. But what is a prophecy? A prophecy brings the future into the present and, more broadly, it involves a de-differentiation of the past, present, and future. This de-differentiation also occurs in a dream, that royal road to the unconscious.

A brief reference to Matte Blanco's (1975) work is pertinent here. He distinguishes symmetrical from asymmetrical modes of thinking. "John is the brother of Paul" is symmetrical because "Paul is (also) the brother of John." "Mary is the sister of Paul," however, is asymmetrical because "Paul is not the sister of Mary." The phrase, "today is before tomorrow," is likewise asymmetrical because "tomorrow is not before today." The unconscious, according to Matte Blanco, does not recognize the difference between symmetrical and asymmetrical modes of thinking. This de-differentiation marks the so-called "timelessness of the unconscious." Lear (1999) makes clear that for him the prophet is the *bearer* of the unconscious. This is congruent with my conclusion that, because of their de-differentiation of before and after, which renders them timeless, prophecies *are* the unconscious.

Prophecies are usually intended to have a warning function. So do memorials. The conscious intention of both memorial events and monuments is to bring something of the past into the present, and, it is hoped, to preserve the same thing for the future. But sometimes "memorialists" who bring the past too vividly into the present, especially, if they do not focus only on the victims, suffer the fate of unwanted prophets. That a reference to Philipp Jenninger, the former President of the German *Bundestag* (Parliament), now seems obscure illustrates how effectively disturbing memories can be erased. Elisabeth Domansky's (1992) study of Jenninger and the end of his career may be of special interest here in the Austrian Parliament. Jenninger was the only speaker in the German *Bundestag* in 1988 on the occasion of the commemoration of the fiftieth anniversary of *Kristallnacht* (The Night of Broken Glass). This was supposed to be a high point in his career but it turned out to mark its end. During his speech, many members of Parliament left the assembly hall and only realized later that Jenninger had broken a taboo—he spoke of the perpetrators, not the victims. I cite from Domansky's study:

> When . . .Jenninger chose to deliver his speech from the persecutors' perspective, he actually, although *unintentionally*, recreated the Nazi *Volksgemeinschaft* [sense of national unity] among the perpetrators' successors in West Germany. ... [T] here were, however, many delegates who, by virtue of their party affiliation and age, felt unwilling to go along with this attempt and sought to resist Jenninger's *subconscious* strategy to lay claim to *their* membership in the community of the heirs and heiresses of the Nazis. (1992, 71; italics added to English words)

What is the purpose of memorials and commemorations? Who wants to remember and who wants to forget what? Domansky (1992, 63) has argued that commemorating victims allows the perpetrators to be forgotten. A memorial including perpetrators—one that portrays an SS officer standing behind a Jew and shooting him in the head, for example—has to my knowledge never been, and will most likely never be, built. Memorials to victims are especially blatant examples of organized amnesia, of how we can be distracted from dealing with the question of perpetrators.

Jan Phillip Reemtsma, the head of the *Hamburger Institut für Sozialforschung* (Hamburg Institute for Social Research), organized a traveling exhibit dealing with the crimes of the German Army during World War II to counteract the myth that only the SS, and not the Army, perpetrated crimes. He explicitly focused on the fact that ordinary soldiers were often the perpetrators. There is every reason to believe that this was the reason why Reemtsma's exhibit was not permitted to be shown in the Vorarlberg region of Austria.

To repeat, in Holocaust memorials, a focus on victims can serve to avoid dealing with the perpetrators. There also exist memorials for victims of natural disasters. But when Holocaust memorials resemble those for hurricanes and earthquakes, any reference to perpetrators is erased and, this, I believe, weakens their warning function. The complex function of memorials is discussed by Ellen Handler Spitz (2006), who observes how they can "relieve us, in fact, of our own responsibility to remember. . . . They give us license merely to feel . . . something. They even make it possible for us to feel, superficially, *good*" (p. 419; italics and second ellipses in original). She delineates how the personal history of the artist, Hors Hoheisel, played a role in his becoming an anti-memorialist. He, like other Germans who recognized the oblivion-inducing function of memorials, came to make anti-memorials. Spitz describes successful memorials that have in common the active participation of their "consumers," who write notes and attach these notes to stones, for example. On the other hand, Spitz acknowledges her negative reaction to the same artist when he projected the words, ARBEIT MACHT FREI, onto the Brandenburg Gate at night. (This phrase, which means "work makes [one] free," greeted the deportees at the entrance of Nazi concentration camps.) Spitz continues:

> This [memorial projection onto] "Gates of the Germans," therefore, I submit, while admittedly bold and passionate and obviously heartfelt by the artist who made it, has the power to affect positively principally those who, because they are already predisposed to his viewpoint, need not actually experience it, unsettling and disturbing as it is. Unlike the other more subtle works in his oeuvre that we have visited, it may fail to possess the psychological wherewithal to reach those viewers who, harboring within themselves a silent and unacknowledged melancholia (in Freud's terms) over the unmourned past of their country and of their own families, yearn, even without knowing it, for works that open up to them the possibility of grief. (429)

When Hoheisel's memorial is merely a counterattack, it does not, in Spitz's view, lead to true mourning. But she also considers the cathartic effect that this counterattack likely had for the artist himself. Previously, the massively *concrete* Brandenburg Gate had inspired fear in Hoheisel but, as he came into closer contact with the monument while working on his memorial, it gradually lost its fear-producing power. One of the unexpected functions of memorials that Spitz discovers is their therapeutic function for the artist. As her title, "Loss as Vanished Form," indicates, however, her emphasis remains on the connection of the *formal* with the working through that characterizes mourning. She would clearly object to the *concreteness* of any memorial showing the perpetrator in action.

I believe, however, that the demand of the victims and their descendants for any memorial, even the most abstract, always risks being perceived as an act of vengeance. Indeed, we cannot expect those who have been traumatized to be totally free of any trace of such a wish. This theme was palpable in debates about the placement of the Berlin memorial next to the *Reichstag*. The architect insisted on a location next to the center of power, and this memorial thus shares a feature with Hoheisel's projection of ARBEIT MACHT FREI onto the Brandenburg Gate.

I have emphasized the common ground of psychoanalysis and democracy but we must not forget one difference. Democracies have to act; they must have policies and laws. The acts of psychoanalysts are words. The back-and-forth flow of words in analysis proceeds faster than the formulation of new policies and laws in a democracy. These, too, can be changed but at a slower rate. The laws that protect democracy and thus also memorialize its loss must be built with careful deliberation.

Memorials have now been built that cannot be confused with those for victims of natural disasters. I have already mentioned the Holocaust Memorial in Berlin. It consists of huge stones that vary in size and are placed on uneven ground. Visitors disappear from sight as they walk on this uneven ground. An intimate participation, including elements of identification, with those who disappear is stimulated. Going into the grounds is also a feature of the Vietnam Memorial in Washington, mentioned by Spitz. And the fact that, in the Jewish Museum in Berlin, the floor is not horizontal and the inside walls are not vertical leads the visitor to experience the outside world as distorted. The inside and the outside are confused. Memorials are successful if the visitor is drawn into a world that doesn't make sense and thus identifies to some extent with the victims' experience.

During an interview on Austrian radio several years ago, I was asked how it felt to be in Austria. Among other things I said that it was quite difficult for me to travel to a country in which so many people had voted for a right-wing politician such as Jörg Haider. Afterwards, the interviewer told me that, even though he very much regretted it, this sentence would have to be cut because "you cannot say that on Austrian radio." Again, I believe that some laws *are* memorials. I gladly recognize the memorial function of a law against censorship, which is built on the memory of the death of freedom. I hope and trust that this memorial now exists in the form of a law against censorship that is being *enforced* in Austria.

I thank you for inviting me and for giving me the opportunity to regain a bit of continuity in a democratic Austria.

References

Aulagnier, Piera. (1975). *Violence of Interpretation: From Pictogram to Statement.* Trans. Alan

Sheridan. London: Routledge, 2001.

Cocks, Geoffrey. (1985). *Psychotherapy in the Third Reich: The Göring Institute.* New York:

Oxford University Press.

Domansky, Elisabeth. (1992). Kristallnacht: The Holocaust and German Unity. In Elisabeth Domansky and Harald Welzer, eds., *The Meaning of November 9 as an Anniversary in Germany.* Tubingen: Édition diskord, pp. 60-94.

Freud, Sigmund. (1933). New Introductory Lectures on Psychoanalysis. *Standard Edition* 22:5-182.

Gabel, Joseph. (1962). *La fausse conscience—Essai sur la réification* [False consciousness: An essay on reification]. Paris: Éditions de Minuit.

Gabel, Joseph. (1967). *Ideologic und Schizophrenie—Formen der Entfremdung* [Ideology and

schizophrenia: Forms of alienation]. Trans. Hans Naumann. Frankfurt am Main: Fischer.

Kafka, John S. (1989). *Multiple Realities in Clinical Practice.* New Haven: Yale University Press.

Kafka, John S. (1991). *Jenseits des Realitätsprinzips: Multiple Realitäten in Theorie und Praxis der Psychoanalyse.* Trans. H.-J. Grunzig. Berlin: Springer.

Kafka, John S. (1992). Consciousness and the Shadow of Time: Two Butterflies on My Head. In Marianne Leuzinger-Bohleber, H. Schneider, and R. Pfeiffer, eds., *Psychoanalysis in the Interdisciplinary Scientific Dialogue.* Berlin: Springer, pp. 87-95.

Kandel, Eric R. (2006). *In Search of Memory: The Emergence of a New Science of Mind.* New York: Norton.

Lear, Jonathan. (1999). *Open Minded: Working Out the Logic of the Soul.* Cambridge, Mass.: Harvard University Press.

Matte Blanco, Ignacio. (1975). *The Unconscious as Infinite Sets: An Essay in Bi-Logic.* London: Duckworth.

Popper, Karl. (1945). *The Open Society and Its Enemies.* London: Routledge.

Rudnytsky, Peter L. (2000). *Psychoanalytic Conversations: Interviews with Clinicians, Commentators, and Critics.* Hillsdale, NJ: Analytic Press.

Spitz. Ellen Handler. (2006). Loss as Vanished Form: On the Anti-Memorial Sculptures of Horst Hoheisel. *American Imago* 62:419-433.

Tichy, Marina and Sylvia Zwettler-Otte. (1999). *Freud in der Presse. Die Rezeption. Sigmund Freuds und der Psychoanalyse in Österreich 1895-1938* [Freud in the media: The reception of Sigmund Freud and psychoanalysis in Austria]. Vienna: Sonderzahl.

Whitehead, Alfred North, and Bertrand Russell. (1910). *Principia Mathematica.* Cambridge: Cambridge University Press.

"The Traumatized Individual in The Traumatized Society: Treatment, Memory, and Memorials." ("L'individu traumatise dans la societe traumatisee: traitement, memoire et monuments commenoratifs") In: *Revue Française de Psychanalyse 2000/1-Devoir de Memoire, Entre Passion et Oubli*: 81-96. And Presentation: *Symposium: Psychoanalysis in Times of Social and Political Upheaval*, September 2000, Washington, DC

Chapter 20

The Traumatized Individual in The Traumatized Society: Treatment, Memory, and Memorials

The contributors to this issue are asked to offer psychoanalytic perspectives on a clinical and on an "applied" psychoanalytic question. 1) The clinical question: Since psychoanalysis is much concerned with memory, with the memory of trauma and with the fate of memories, how as clinicians do we understand and treat those whose individual traumata were enmeshed in historical catastrophes? What do our psychoanalytic theories of memory, of individual and group experience and behavior contribute to understanding and treatment of victims, survivors and others who live under the lasting shadow of such cataclysms? What has our clinical experience taught us? 2) The "applied" question: Can psychoanalytic insights serve to lessen the chances of future social cataclysms? If so, how?

The emphatic superego injunction, the reference in the title to the "duty" to remember underlines the hope that we can go beyond the clinical tasks of understanding, helping, diminishing the suffering of victims and survivors. Complex as the clinical tasks may be, however, they are in principle more clear-cut, and analysts have a better track record with them than with "applying" psychoanalysis to understanding, and especially influencing social phenomena and policies. As analysts, can we really hope to influence societies to remember and therefore not to repeat genocides? Could it be that for analysts living under the lasting shadow of cataclysm, it is especially difficult to delineate clinical tasks from social "duties?" Be that as it may, theories about the individual and the group, and about memory, are pertinent both to clinical tasks and possible social applications. Since, however, most of psychoanalytic theory could be subsumed under the two topics "The individual and the group, the self and the other" and "memory and its vicissitudes" the theoretical part of our discussion must be focused, limited, selective and condensed.

Theoretical Considerations

We seem to take for granted the common sense definition of the "individual" as having a stable and unambiguous spatial and temporal "size." In modern biology the definition of "the individual" has become increasingly complex. Depending on the focus of a particular study, marine biologists may consider a certain organism to be either a distinct animal or a colony of unicellular animals. For sociobiologists, the "individual," i.e. the significant unit whose survival is crucial, is the gene.[1] Psychoanalytic hypotheses concerning the abdication of superego functions in group situations, the transgenerational transmission of "superego lacunae," of traumatic and conflictual experience,[2] as well as psychoanalytic speculations about a collective unconscious, all relativize the common sense notion of "the individual." Psychoanalysts also believe (despite questions raised by researchers studying infant behavior) that we do not have—from birth—a "psychic representation" of inner/outer discrimination, but rather that the development of this discrimination contributes to the formation of psychic structures. The synopsis of a further hypothesis[3] is that there is congruity, on the one hand, between "inner," "animate," "temporal" and "synesthetic" experience and, on the other hand, congruity between "outer," "inanimate," "spatial" and "sensorially compartmentalized" experience. Clinical and experimental findings support the idea that every perceptual act involves a micro-temporal recapitulation of the development of these discriminations and the repeated "reformations" of corresponding psychic structures.[4,5] Such a hypothesis implies that within extremely short periods of time we are—below awareness—in and out of touch with a world devoid of inner-outer, self-other, individual-group discrimination. One could say that we are individuals (in the narrow sense of the word) only some of the time. Using "individual" in a less narrow sense of the word, we can say that the person with a "normal" and not too severely traumatized psychic structure is capable of rapid pendulum swings between "isolating" and expanding psychic states in which dividing walls rise and fall. This is important in our context because trauma disrupts or, when it is extreme, abolishes these patterns.

The very existence of "meaning" depends on micro-memory bridges between moments, between different psychic states. Words lose their meaning for an individual under the influence of a drug, Sernyl for instance, that interferes with short term memory.[6] The assertion that time IS mind[7] is based on the elaboration of the notion that time-bridges of memory are essential for meaning. Without meaning there is no mind, no living mind, no life. Lewis Thomas[8] when contemplating a world in which nuclear explosions have destroyed all life, contrasts his somehow still bearable thoughts about his own death and the death of many in a world without nuclear bombs, with his no longer bearable thoughts about the death of all after a nuclear catastrophe, a world in which "nobody" will ever again listen to Mahler' Ninth Symphony, and when there will be no creature who can "remember" having listened to it. If we believe with Freud that death is not a psychological reality, an "experience," the destruction of memory, be it on a micro- or a macro- scale, is as close as we can come to envisage it. Our "passion" to remember is ultimately the passion to preserve some life-experiencing mind.

In the introduction, Jacques Angelergues and Eva Weil refer to Julien Rouart who *"a pu definir le souvenir comme 'amnesie organisee, traces reconstruites d'ou la dimension traumatique a ete expurgee."* There is, I believe, a defensive component in the formation of every memory, not only the particularly traumatic one, just as there is in every perception a defensive component directed, as it were, against what is not perceived. There is an ever-present point-counterpoint dynamic of remembering and forgetting but, in the absence of extreme trauma, there is a communality in our "patterns" of organizing our amnesias that permits us to communicate with each other. The individual who has survived extreme trauma has memories that result from "disorganized patterns" of amnesia. Let me first focus on these patterns in the individual, but later I will discuss how commemorations, rituals and memorials of traumatized societies reflect their "disorganized patterns" of amnesia.

The Treatment of the Individual

Dori Laub and Nanette C. Auerhahn have written about knowing and not knowing, about the forms of amnesia that make for the following "FORMS OF KNOWING (encountered in the analysis of traumatized individuals): Not knowing, Fugue states, Fragments, Transference Phenomena, Overpowering narratives, Life themes, Witnessed narratives, Metaphors."[9] Writing about "Not Knowing," Laub and Auerhahn explain that "In this form of traumatic memory, the centre of experience is no longer in the experiencing 'I'. Events happen somewhere, but are no longer connected with the conscious subject....This double state of knowing and not knowing leaves the survivor in grief not only for his dead loved ones but also for his lost memories. The lack of knowledge prevents the revival of despair that would accompany memory, but leaves the survivor alone and unknown to himself." Such aspects of a "sane" survivor's mind are reminiscent of features sometimes observed in psychosis. At the point of entry or exit from inaccessible psychotic states, states without any possibility of detecting or sharing "meaning," I have heard schizophrenic patients make statements such as "there is a thought somewhere, but I do not know whose it is." The disconnection of a memory or of a perception from self-experience is an extreme "pattern" disturbance that isolates the traumatized survivor as much as it isolates a psychotic individual. There are, however, less extreme pattern disturbances that also produce a sense of severe, but not total isolation. Ira Brenner[10] describes the vital importance to traumatized survivors of remembrances of touch and smell, although these are difficult to use as vehicles of communication. Trauma interferes with the formation of verbally organized memories that could facilitate later social contacts.

Survivors with whom I have worked clinically and others whom I have interviewed in the context of psychiatric evaluations for German compensation are characterized by a vague feeling that they are profoundly, somehow qualitatively "different", that they might as well not even try to establish a certain level of meaningful communication. They suffer not only from the memories of their traumata, their "reminiscences," but also from the very fact that the organization of their memories severely limits their communicability. Often they also suffer because others do not remember.

I have observed all and many combinations of the following patterns:

"I remember and you do not. I suffer from your forgetting."

"I suffer because you do not want to remember."

"I feel the duty to remember, and you feel free of this duty. I hate you for this. I envy you for this."

"I feel guilty because I contaminate you with my memory or with this duty to remember."

A not infrequent pattern is "I remember, but I feel ashamed because I still suffer from what I remember. I have 'symptoms.' If I were strong or normal, I should be 'over it by now.' As it is, I make my daughter, for instance, suffer because of my anxiety. When she comes home late from a date, I make her feel guilty if I am awake."

This last example raises the issue of the connection between trauma and repetitive behavior, the issue of the "stuckness" of the surviving victim. While Freud said that hysterics suffer from reminiscences, he also believed that patients repeat what they do not remember. I have arrived at still another formulation, namely that patients" repeat (even in action) what they always remember the same way." Behavioral changes, apart from those that are "conditioned" and mechanical, depend on evolving interpretations of the meaning of events. Behavior and experience becomes "stuck," repetitive if the trauma was such that it prevented the construction of meaning in the first place because the "center of experience (was not) ...in the experiencing I."[11]

A "center of experience" obviously refers to a spatially organized model of mind. In the framework of my model emphasizing temporal processes of mind, I have schematically spoken of the pendulum swings between contracting and expanding processes, those moving toward isolation and those moving toward connecting with the wider world and the experiences of others. The "I" that experiences itself connected to events and their meaning is one whose pendulum swings have not been radically disrupted. Trauma disrupts "time bridges" needed for the development of self-participating meaning. What happens to the experience of time during trauma underlines the usefulness of a temporal model of mind.

A history of trauma, in any case limits and, if severe enough abolishes the "reworking" of memories. Past trauma interferes with the interplay of mutual effects on current experience of new meanings attributed to past events and on interpretations of the past in the light of evolving experience of the present. The limitations of our therapeutic effectiveness with some survivors hinge on blockages of *Nachträglichkeit* in the hermeneutic sense of the term. (The "lingering" quality, the slowness of the word—carrying after—dragging—makes it more appropriate than the staccato quality of *après coup*.) Kettner[12] has recently spoken of two meanings of *Nachträglichkeit*, a hermeneutic and a "causal" meaning and of a *Spielraum*, an intermediary space in which both meanings can play (a role). The hermeneutic meaning involves changes of interpretation of memories and the "causal" meaning involves the causality of "actual" events, the *Nachwirkungen*, the after-effects as in the series of "après coups" of a series of billiard balls. One could say that the *Nachträglich* effect in the "causal" meaning of the word is the inability to interpret or re-interpret the past. The *Nachwirkung*, the after-effect of extreme trauma that has disconnected the "experiencing'" from the event, that has rendered impossible an "interpretation," a giving of personal meaning to the original event, also makes it impossible to "re-interpret" the event. The best hope for the analyst of the severely traumatized patient is to function in the *Spielraum* between the two meanings of *Nachträglichkeit* by not only recognizing the depth of the survivor's sense of isolation but also by experiencing at least traces of it in the countertransference.

Such countertransference identifications imply that the analyst has at least trace experiences of memory failures, of "not knowing," of the "disorganized amnesias" that I have described. The developmental consequences of many particular aspects of trauma, for instance witnessing of parents' reactions to humiliation, the effects of separation from them, early or later in childhood or adolescence, have been described by Kestenberg and Brenner[13] and others. The specific characteristics of individual traumatic histories find their echoes in the histories of the individual analytic treatments.

Memory and Society
Psychoanalytic Social Activism

Angelergues and Weil express the hope that the "devoir de memoire" ... "puisse avoir une valeur preventive contre le retour des figures de l'horreur."[14] It is important, if we wish to consider the possible "social" usefulness of our "duty to remember," to keep in mind the fate of earlier "applications" of psychoanalysis to broad social issues.

We know that Freud was skeptical about the possible effectiveness of a direct psychoanalytically inspired social activism. But psychoanalysis was born with, and as part of "modernity" and soon the hope of many— but not of Freud—was that psychoanalysis would play a major part in the formation of "the new man." Radical "psychoanalytic" educational experimentation was part of the project. One can contrast Freud's skepticism with the caricatured version of analysis that led Trotsky to believe that psychoanalysis could create the rational man freed from the irrational unconscious.[15] Caricatured as this may be, the caricature has its roots in the psychoanalytic hope of the slow gains, the slowly accumulating "victories" of the ego. Alexander Etkind, in his "Eros of the Impossible, the history of psychoanalysis in Russia," describes the rise and fall of "Freudism" in official and private Soviet culture and the peculiar vicissitudes of politicized so called "psychoanalysis."[16] Freud spoke of an "epidemic" of psychoanalysis in Russia.

A less radical and controversial psychoanalytically inspired effort to contribute to the development of a tolerant and peace-loving society was in the area of pedagogical and welfare applications of psychoanalytic thinking in Central and Western Europe. It is reflected in the *Zeitschrift fuer Psychoanalytische Paedagogik* (Journal of Psychoanalytic Pedagogy) published in the nineteen twenties and thirties. In Volume 4, number 8/9, 1930, for instance, the journal published an article *"Die Verwaisung als soziale Erscheinung"* (pages 317-328) by Siegfried Kraus, an official of the department of public welfare of the city of Vienna. The article deals with "orphanhood" as a societal development and is a social and statistical study of 95 school girls who were biological or "social" orphans, i.e., the children of parents who were not functioning as adequate parents. Paul Federn, the editor-in-chief, introduces the article and writes (p. 317), "The right of the child to normal conditions of upbringing can only penetrate the awareness of the people through a correct psychologic-analytically informed guidance."[17] (my translation) Today, psychoanalysts who consult in schools or who—for instance—offer a program of psychoanalytic ideas on infant and child development to nannies. (The Washington Psychoanalytic Foundation offers such a course) certainly hope to have an impact on individual and social development. But when reading the *Zeitschrift fuer Psychoanalytische Paedagogik* published in earlier in the century, it becomes clear that the authors' hopes and ambitions for a successful psychoanalytic social engineering of a better, more tolerant, less criminal, and more peace-loving world, far exceeds the expectations even of today's most socially active and optimistic analysts. The latter would include those who attempt to apply such understanding to international "conflict resolution," for instance, in organized face to face meetings of prominent individuals belonging to hostile ethnic groups. Psychoanalytically based insights, for example the necessity to recognize and acknowledge the "other's mourning, certainly play a role here.[18]

We must recognize, however, that psychoanalytically inspired efforts to influence the behavior of societies, and especially to serve a prophylactic function against social cataclysms, have been of very limited effectiveness. But let us examine, from a psychoanalytic perspective, what can happen to societies' institutionalized efforts to remember, efforts that are avowedly designed to serve such a preventive function. They can be, on closer examination, particularly salient illustrations of "organized amnesias."

Commemorations, Memorials, Souvenirs

Elisabeth Domansky[19] writes (p. 62) argues that "even the ways in which the remembrance of the Holocaust was used in West Germany represented strategies of forgetting rather than the desire to remember."

When the West German Bundestag commemorated the fiftieth anniversary of *Kristallnacht*, Philip Jenninger, president of the Bundestag, was the only speaker. His speech was supposed to be a highlight of his rapidly ascending career but, instead, resulted in the end of his career. Many of the delegates left the parliament during the speech. To quote Domansky: (ibid, p. 68) "....within a few days a consensus emerged between Jenninger's supporters and his critics that Jenninger had given a correct assessment of Germany's history in the Third Reich. The immediate reactions to the speech were entirely emotional and were triggered solely by Jenninger's performance. It was as if he had acted a part that belonged to a different play from the one in which he appeared. So powerful was the sense of witnessing something fundamentally wrong that most people were initially not even able to find explanations for their own reactions." Domansky's explanation for Jenninger's debacle is that he broke the tabu of speaking of the perpetrators rather than about the victims. Again Domansky (p. 71) "When...Jenninger chose to deliver his speech from the persecutors' perspective, he actually, although *unintentionally* (italics mine), recreated the Nazi *Volksgemeinschaft* (sense of national unity) among the perpetrators' successors in West Germany. ...there were, however, many delegates who, by virtue of their party affiliation and age, felt unwilling to go along with this attempt and sought to resist Jenninger's *subconscious* (italics mine) strategy to lay claim to their membership in the community of the heirs and heiresses of the Nazis." From a psychoanalytic perspective one might say that focus on the victims defends against elements of identification with the perpetrators. The listeners in the Bundestag, the memorialists enmeshed in the "organized amnesia" interpreted the fact that he spoke of the perpetrators and the world in which they lived as a commemorative "celebration" of the perpetrators. Ordinarily "doers" are celebrated and victims are memorialized. That is part of the "organized amnesia," or rather one of the different kinds of "organized amnesias," that are created by different kinds of psychoanalytically understood defensive constellations: identifications, defenses against them, projective identifications, and identifications with the aggressor.

It should also be mentioned in this context that the memorialization of the "heroic victim" can be a rallying point for the development of a "new sense of *entitlement for revenge.*"[20] On the 600th anniversary of the Serbian defeat by the Ottomans, for example, the mummified body of the Serb's defeated leader, Price Lazar, was returned to Kosovo and a huge monument to the battle of Kosovo was erected. At its inauguration, Milosevic gave a stirring speech fanning the flames of Serbian nationalism. His own career took off. We know the rest.

I have dwelt at length on the Jenninger story because it illustrates much about the vicissitudes of memorials, controversies about which we frequently read in our daily newspapers. Imagine a memorial monument showing an SS man shooting a concentration camp inmate in the back of the head! A memorial in Vienna showing Jews on their knees cleaning the sidewalk created problems related to the stimulation of identifications with the aggressors despite the fact that the perpetrators were only, as it were, "implied."

Let us pass from commemorations and memorials to "souvenirs." The opening of some Russian archives revealed to what extent many Germans in Eastern Europe behaved like tourists and collected souvenirs, although the snapshots they took might be of executions. (While I speak of the Germans in Eastern Europe, the topic of wartime souvenirs could be discussed in much more generic terms.) I believe that some of the soldiers who kept such souvenirs might today be genuinely in favor of the kinds of monuments that are usually erected, namely those that focus on the victims. I doubt, however, that they would accept monuments showing the perpetrators in action. "Organized amnesias" allow and even support memorial monuments. The point of all this is that we as analysts, if we insist on the "*devoir de memoire,*" owe it to ourselves to observe the complex defenses in public remembering, especially if we entertain hopes that they may have "preventive" effects against repetition.

Let us return for a moment to the Vienna holocaust memorial, sculptures of Jews on their knees forced to clean the sidewalk. Initially the memorial was unprotected by any fence, but eventually a fence had to be placed around it, because some passers-by occasionally sat on the figures, rested and smoked a cigarette. While the monument makers had clearly intended to intrude on the awareness of the citizens, to emotionally penetrate their daily activities, a monument not identified as a monument failed as a memorial. Without the clear metacommunication, "this is (only) a memorial," the intrusion into present "dailyness" was intolerable. Non-Jews protested against the memorial. Many Jews found it "undignified," and what is the implication of that? Does it mean that "I do not want to identify with those who have been deprived of their dignity? I do not want to remember that experience in my flesh? I do not want others to experience—re-experience—a vision of Jews deprived of their dignity? If so, why? Because, I believe, it is feared that their disdain, their aggression could be kindled—rekindled. The stimulation of a self-fulfilling prophecy must be avoided. The victim invites attack. In the chicken yard, when a hen that lays an egg and bleeds, it is usually hacked to pieces by the other chickens. Designers of memorials risk being criticized for serving "organized amnesias" too well or not well enough.

German psychoanalysts, and colleagues from other countries that have been under the yoke of tyrannical and cruel regimes, often deal in particularly interesting ways with the topic of identification with the aggressor. An example of a German colleague's discovery—through self-analysis—of an identification that surprised him was the following: when Israelis massacred Arabs in a refugee camp in Lebanon, he found himself thinking that he was glad that "they" could do it "too." And then he thought that "they" is opposed to "we." He had uncovered, he felt, a surprising element of identification within himself with Nazis. The ability acquired or enhanced through psychoanalysis to recognize one's own defensive operations, makes possible an awareness of elements of identification with the aggressor, a recognition that would be rigidly warded off by others.

Could there be some other ways of facilitating such insights? The visitor to Washington's Holocaust Memorial Museum gets an "identification" card of a victim. On his tour of the museum the visitor follows the fate of the victim with whom he is "identified." Imagine the visitor getting an identification card of a perpetrator. This card would have the same kind of information the victim's cards contain, information about birthplace of the perpetrator, information about the family, parents' work, siblings, the perpetrator's schooling, his/her spouse and children. It is important to note that nobody thought of issuing such cards. Because such "identifications" might be too dangerous? I will describe later how in Colonial Williamsburg, there are re-enactments of slavery in which identification cards "as slaves" and as slave-holders are issued to tourists.

Just as Jenninger suffered the consequences of focusing on the perpetrators, the exhibitions organized by Jan Philipp Reemtsma stirred up storms of protest. Reemtsma, the son of a wealthy German businessman who had been a friend of Goering, has devoted much energy and money to social research and activism. Reemtsma asked the heads of German corporations, that had used slave labor, to contribute to the cost of memorials to them. He then organized an exhibit that traveled throughout Germany, of the responses he received from the heads of these corporations. Many denied the history of the use of slave labor or the connection of the current corporation to the one that was implicated. Reemtsma's exhibit included also the evidence for what was being denied. A more recent exhibit organized by Reemtsma showed the evidence for the involvement of the German military, high officers and ordinary soldiers, in the holocaust and the slaughter of civilians on the Eastern front.[21] This evidence ran counter to the myth that had prevailed in Germany that only the SS and not the still idealized army had perpetrated such crimes. The "Crimes of the Wehrmacht" exhibit, circulated in German and Austria, provoked violent protests. In some cities politicians, responding to the appeals of their constituents, were successful in prohibiting the mounting of the exhibition.

Reemtsma's exhibits and publications are examples of social activism that indeed respond to the "duty to remember." Could they contribute in effect to the prevention of future cataclysms? As analysts, we are keenly aware of the mechanisms of defense against such remembering. It is not clear, I believe, how our specific psychoanalytic knowledge might best inform strategies to undo societies' defenses against such remembering.

What is clear, however, is that there is no substitute for civil courage, including the civil courage of analysts.

In their introduction, Angelergues and Weil also invite us to have a look at our own psychoanalytic organizations' history of demonstrating and failing to demonstrate civil courage. Such an obviously important self-examination must avoid some pitfalls and possible distortions. I have heard it said, for instance, that an injustice is done to the way a German psychoanalytic candidate, Rittmeister, might have wanted to be remembered, if we speak of him only as a German psychoanalyst who was executed by the Nazis and if we fail to mention his political convictions. As I understand it, he was executed because of these convictions—he was a communist—and not because he was a psychoanalyst.

Once again, the effectiveness of civil courage (and for some individuals their own experience as analysands may well enhance their civil courage) is a different issue from the socially prophylactic (against repetition of social catastrophes) effectiveness of memory. Earlier in my paper, I wondered if, for analysts living under the shadow of cataclysm, it is especially difficult to delineate clinical tasks from social "duties." In this context, I want to examine the analyst's motivations to stimulate affective intensity of memories.

For several decades now, there has been a concerted effort in the German school system to acquaint, even to confront, students with the history of the Holocaust. Recently, a German student in his mid-twenties was following a technical curriculum offered at an American university. While he was in the United States, some personal problems led him to seek psychoanalytic treatment. On one occasion, he mentioned to his analyst that he had met several Jews here and that he had not known any Jews in Germany. He reported having had a passing thought just then how much these Jews here were like him. In his classes in Germany, he had been exposed again and again to the history of the Nazi period and to pictures of piles of corpses in the concentration camps. They had lost their impact and he is not sure how much of an impact they ever really had since, as he now realizes, on some level he had thought of these corpses as belonging to a different species. The patient did not dwell on the topic and focused with much affect on the more immediate personal issues that had led him to seek analyses. Despite the analyst's thoughts about the persistence of "dehumanization" effects and other holocaust related issues, he followed the analysand's affective movement to other matters.

Let us reflect on this episode in the context of the question, if and how and, what kind of memory may help prevent repetition of cataclysms. This young German, despite the persistent "dehumanization" of these Jews and their copses, found the Holocaust incomprehensible and "absurd." He does not do "absurd" things. For him, it is the absurdity that militates against repetition. Would the possibility that he could be drawn into participating in a future holocaust be further diminished if his reaction to the corpses, and his reference to it in the analytic session, had been more emotionally charged? This is questionable at best, I think. In any case, our reaction to his lack of affect is probably not really fueled by an increased fear that he might be a future perpetrator. I think we have an impulse to impose a "duty" not just to remember but to remember with affect, to remember "passionately." I speculate that this has to do with the fact that those of us who identify more with the victims than the perpetrators, find it unjust that the "others" do not suffer. We do not want to be alone with our suffering and even want to extract some revenge. I recall a situation in which a Holocaust survivor who had lost almost all of his large family in the Shoah, happened to be the hospital roommate, many years after the war, with a German former bomber-pilot. The hospitalized survivor had a very painful physical condition. He confessed to me that his pain diminished when his telling of his family's story reduced his German roommate to tears. Perhaps this German veteran would now be a socially active "soldier for peace" but, all in all, we must recognize the limits of the prophylactic powers of memorialization.

Such a recognition leads to the question of the effectiveness of social legislation, the power of law. Reemtsma[22], in a study of the power of dictators, comes to the conclusion that the dictator's populist success does not so much depend on charisma as on permissiveness, the often only implied promise that some laws will not be enforced. Alix Strachy, (with thanks to the poster of R. de Clerck that called attention to the work of

Alix Strachy, at the IPA Congress, Santiago, 1999), (p.198) writes: "...there is no law to restrain a sovereign state from interfering with people outside it....a sovereign state cannot legitimately be interfered with by any person or group outside it....In these respects, then, the sovereign state seems eminently suited to function as a regressive group."[23]

Reemtsma's thesis and Alix Strachy's ideas support my belief that laws that are inspired by the history of cataclysms and that are enforced and have no statute of limitations for crimes against humanity are the most prophylactically effective "memorial" that can be achieved. This belief is bolstered precisely by psychoanalytic knowledge of the power of impulses and the power of the defenses against the kinds of remembering that might prevent repetition.

When the U.S. Supreme Court made the decision that ended legal racial discrimination, it abolished the doctrine of the "justice" of "separate but equal" facilities and schools. Basically the Supreme Court said that "separate is not equal," a statement strikingly congruent with psychoanalytic developmental theory that recognizes the early psychological equivalence of "inside" with good and "outside" with bad. Analysts know that separate is not equal. What analysts might call the court's "superego injunction against the persistence of splitting" has had a gradual effect on attitudes and behaviors, a kind of "working through" of identifications with victims and perpetrators.

In Colonial Williamsburg, a major tourist site in the southern state of Virginia where a vivid idealized memory of the Civil War persists, there have long been enactments of historical events in a restored setting and in period costumes. In an article in the *Washington Post* (July 7, 1999), the demise of a previous "rather bloodless version of history" is described. Visitors are now called upon to participate with professional actors in roles of slave holders as well as slaves. The "play" is so realistic that "new skits have inspired audience attacks on slave patrols." Black tourists previously had often avoided Colonial Williamsburg. Now there are many black visitors. They and their children participate in the enactments.

I think it is the effect of an enforced law against segregation that has made it possible finally to give play "identity" cards as victims and victimizers. Erik Erikson[24] has called ethnic groups "pseudo-species," but he believed that these pseudo-species would behave like different species for a long time to come. In the realistic enactments in Williamsburg, the play identity cards create a promising confusion between species and "pseudo-species."

Summary

The enforced law, monument of and memorial to racial and ethnic strife and its victims, provides the security in which memories "can play themselves out," in which borders, including borders of identification, can be crossed. The exploratory crossing and re-crossing of borders between different identifications and their plays of memory are an essential part of psychoanalytic treatment. Angelergue's and Weil's question can be rephrased as "What can be the role and the pertinence of psychoanalysis after traumatic destruction of the law?"

A study of the history of psychoanalysis reveals that it was born during a dissolution of "average expectable environment" and that the demands for analysis grew during and, especially, after major social shifts. But there are cataclysms that go beyond the quantitative shifts in social instability and reach qualitative mind—and—memory damaging proportions that demand modifications of psychoanalytic therapeutic approaches.

Moving from the clinical realm to that of the application of psychoanalytic ideas to social interventions designed to prevent future cataclysms, I have reviewed some of the history of psychoanalytic social activism and considered the ways in which societies "memorialize" trauma. Focus on the victim rather than the perpetrator can serve to make a memorial palatable, but diminish its effectiveness. In our current state of knowledge, the memorial with the greatest power against repetition of horrendous events is the law that is enforced.

References

1. Wilson, Edward. (1975). *Sociobiology*. Cambridge, MA: Harvard University Press.

2. Faimberg, Haydée. (1988). "The telescoping of generations: genealogy of certain identifications, *Contemporary Psychoanalysis* 24:99-117.

3. Kafka, John S. (1989). *Multiple Realities in Clinical Practice*. New Haven and London: Yale University Press.

4. Kafka, John S. (1989). *Multiple Realities in Clinical Practice*. New Haven and London: Yale University Press, pages 77 and 176.

5. Smith, G. J. W. and Danielsson, A. (1982). Anxiety and defensive strategies in childhood and adolescence. *Psychological Issues*, Monograph 52.

6. Kafka, John S. (1989). John S. (1989). *Multiple Realities in Clinical Practice*. New Haven and London: Yale University Press, page 65.

7. Kafka, John S. (1989). John S. (1989). *Multiple Realities in Clinical Practice*. New Haven and London: Yale University Press, page 78.

8. Thomas, Lewis (1983), Late Night Thoughts on Listening to Mahler's Ninth Symphony, pages 164 -168. In *Collection of Essays by Lewis Thomas*. New York: The Viking Press.

9. Laub, Dori and Auerhahn, Nanette C. (1993). Knowing and Not Knowing. Massive Psychic Trauma: Forms of Traumatic Memory, page 290. *International Journal of Psycho-Analysis* 74:287-302.

10. Kestenberg, Judith S. and Brenner, Ira. (1996). Multisensory Bridges in Response to Object Loss. Chapter 4:69-78. In *The Last Witness, The Child Survivor of the Holocaust*. Washington, DC: American Psychiatric Press, Inc.

11. Laub, Dori and Auerhahn, Nanette C. (1993). . Knowing and Not Knowing. Massive Psychic Trauma: Forms of Traumatic Memory, page 290. *International Journal of Psycho-Analysis* 74:291.

12. Matthias Kettner. (1999). Das Konzept der Nachtraeglichkeit in Freud's Erinnerungstheorie. *Psyche* 4 (53.Jahrgang April 1999).

13. Kestenberg, Judith S. and Brenner, Ira. (1996). Multisensory Bridges in Response to Object Loss. Chapter 4:69-78). In *The Last Witness, The Child Survivor of the Holocaust*. Washington, DC: American Psychiatric Press, Inc.

14. Angelergues and Weil. (2000/1). Introduction to this issue of *R.F.P. 2000/1-Devoir de Memoire, Entre Passion et Oubli.*

15. Etkind, Alexander. (1997). *Eros of the Impossible. The history of psychoanalysis in Russia.* Boulder, CO: Westview Press.

16. Etkind, Alexander. (1997). *Eros of the Impossible. The history of psychoanalysis in Russia.* Boulder, CO: Westview Press. Especially Chapter 7:225-258.

17. Kraus, Siegfried. (1930). Die Verwaisung als soziale Erscheinung. In *Zeitschrift fuer Psychoanalytische Paedagogik* (Journal of Psychoanalytic Pedagogy). (1930). Volume 4(8/9): 317-328, 1930.

18. Volkan, Vamik. (1999). Psychoanalysis and Diplomacy. Part I: Individual and large group identity. *Journal of Applied Psychoanalytic Studies,* Volume 1(#1):29-55 and Part II: Large Group Rituals. Journal of Applied Psychoanalytic Studies Volume 1(#3):223-247.

19. Domansky, Elisabeth. (1995). "Kristallnacht," the Holocaust and German Unity, pp.61-94. *Reader, Conference 'Interdisciplinary Research into Trauma and Violence'.* Breuninger Kolleg Stuttgart, Nov. 17-19 1995 in Bad Teinach.

20. Volkan, Vamik D.; Akhtar, Salman; Dorn, Robert M.; Kafka, John S.; Kernberg, Otto F.; Olsson, Peter A.; Rogers, Rita R.; Shanfield, Stephen B. (1999). Leaders and Decision-Making. *Mind and Human Interaction,* Volume 9(#3):168.

21. *Vernichtungskrieg. Verbrechen der Wehrmacht 1941 bis 1944. (1996).* Ausstellungskatalog. Hamburg.

22. Reemstsma, Jan Philipp. (1995). Institutions of violence and their potential dynamics. *Reader, Conference 'Interdisciplinary Research into Trauma and Violence'.* Breuninger Kolleg Stuttgart, Nov. 17-19, 1995 in Bad Teinach.

23. Strachy, Alix. (1957). *The Unconscious Motivations of War.* International Universities Press. page 198.

24. Erikson, Erik H. (1956). The problem of ego identification. *Journal of the American Psychoanalytic Association* 4:56-121; and *Toys and reasons: Stages in the ritualization of experience.* New York: W.W. Norton.

End Note

Freud thought that, when the patient says in an analysis "I have known this all along," the end of the analysis is near. (Freud 1913-14, p. 207) What is new, however, is the analysand's level and integration of knowledge—the deeper and affectively richer sense of continuity of the analysand's life and self experience. I believe that the explicit statement about there being "nothing new" hides the analysand's deeper understanding of the continuing—not ending nature of the psychoanalytic process and that is this understanding that signifies that the end of the analysis is near.

For myself, as I write these end notes, I continue to discover new feelings and thoughts about myself and about psychoanalysis itself. The theme of *not ending*, of an infinite process runs sometimes explicitly and always implicitly through my work and my writings.

I will close this book with a talk I gave to the Belgrade Psychoanalytic Society at its conference on psychoanalysis and modernity in September 2004. This paper, *Resonance Between Psychoanalysis and Other Modern Perspectives*, addresses recent developments in science and philosophy but is newly relevant to the resurging threats of authoritarian popularism. It is time to re-read Freud's *Civilization and Its Discontents*. (Freud, 1930)

*   *   *

Resonance Between Psychoanalysis and Other Modern Perspectives
John S. Kafka (September 2004)

Thank you for inviting me. I extend my heartiest congratulations on your achievement in becoming a provisional society under the conditions that you faced. When I first came to Belgrade and Tamara told me that there would be a civil war, I had serious doubts about her judgment because I was convinced that this could not happen in *modern* post World War II Europe. We all, but especially you were soon plunged into new dark ages.

In this conference on "Psychoanalysis in the Modern World," I will not attempt to describe and discuss the impact of psychoanalytic ideas on modern education, the justice system, advertising, and public relations. A British Broadcasting Series on "Freud's Century" is particularly successful in describing how a relative of Freud, Bernays, the father of American public relations and marketing, applied psychoanalytic ideas in stimulating and manipulating consumer demands and shaping public opinion. I will also not deal here with the attempts to use psychoanalysis for social or political "engineering." In retrospect, many of these efforts did not fare well. Freud was very skeptical about such attempts and I remind you of his remark that there was an "epidemic" of psychoanalysis in Russia at the beginning of the Soviet regime. (Freud, 1912, pp. 494-495)

But what could better illustrate the importance of psychoanalysis today then your use of it in extricating yourselves from the hold of these new dark ages. This has become clear to me in my contacts with many of you and with others in so-called "Eastern Europe." In the recent New Orleans panel on Eastern Europe, Aleksandar Vuko, for example, described how psychoanalytic thinking served him personally in undoing the knots that held together the web of insanity.

And yet there is in the minds of many a perception that currently psychoanalysis is *in crisis*. In many locations, some manifestations of this crisis are a smaller number of patients and candidates, fewer academic appointments of psychoanalysts and a lowering of the prestige of analysts. There are also some public perceptions that analysis is out of step with modern cultural, political and scientific perspectives. Even those who praise the humanistic and literary value of psychoanalysis, when they emphasize its connection to a rich past, sometimes imply that psychoanalysis may be less pertinent to some new developments and modern clinical, philosophical and scientific perspectives. I believe that a more profound examination of the situation reveals a very different picture. Psychoanalysis is not in crisis because it cannot keep up with modern developments. My central point is that, on the contrary, to the extent that psychoanalysis *is* in crisis, this is because so much of the public cannot keep pace with modern developments, modern paradigms with which psychoanalytic thinking clearly resonates.

Psychoanalysis was already attacked and *in crisis* in Vienna as soon as Freud had *invented* it. This was clearly not because it was out of step with *modernity*, but because it was in its forefront. Where and when does analysis flourish in our modern world? Hartmann (1939) spoke of an *average expectable environment* in which analysis supposedly functions best, but neither clinical psychoanalysis, nor psychoanalytic training, nor psychoanalytic theory building ever existed in such an *average expectable environment*. Let us return to Vienna where psychoanalysis was born during the stormy beginnings of *modernity* near the beginning of the twentieth century. Freud's Vienna was also the Vienna of Hitler, who lived there from 1907 until 1913. Brigitte Hamann (1999) in her book "Hitler's Vienna" is one of the authors who portray the Austrian capital as anything but "an average expectable environment." The brewing storms of political, social and ethnic conflicts were barely contained and antisemitism was profound. New artistic and literary movements and new scientific paradigms emerged, but a "conservative" or "reactionary" majority labeled this mix that included psychoanalysis, "degenerate" and attacked it viciously.

Our subsequent history also shows that interest in psychoanalysis and the growth of analytic movements are connected to rapid social and political change. During such times individual needs for psychoanalysis and some degree of flexibility in social and political structures coincide. Such favorable conditions often exist when autocratic regimes crumble. Germany after Hitler, the situation in some Latin American countries and—for us of special interest here—situations in Eastern Europe that you have examined and studied, can serve as examples.

The term "reactionary" usually has a heavy political loading, but it can be understood more broadly and can include scientific reactionary attitudes. In any case reactionary forces come in different versions, but in the past and at present those who attack analysis and wish to see it in, or provoke its *crisis*, come from reactionary quarters. The attacks come from *conservative* directions, conservative in the sense that their representatives are not ready or not able to move in the required new directions, that they hold onto outmoded social, political, but especially philosophical and scientific paradigms. My central point: psychoanalysis faces difficulties precisely because it is in the vanguard of modern perspectives and resonates with other modern developments that arouse resistance. The resistance is directed at the essential personal, social and scientific openness of psychoanalysis. To elaborate: The recognition of unconscious motivation is at the core of psychoanalytic thinking. The apparently *accidental* Freudian slip turns out to be meaningful. *Vice versa* an analysand is freed of unconscious guilt feelings when he discovers that his wish to harm his brother was not the cause of brother's illness. But the new insights are always open to revision. The possibility that what was considered accidental may again turn out to be meaningful remains open. This essential *openness* of psychoanalytic thought makes it receptive to ever new scientific paradigms. But this formal characteristic of the psychoanalytic process also underlies its political openness that is in such sharp contrast with the closed ideology imposed by authoritarian systems of government. This openness, or open-ended-ness, of psychoanalysis is the underlying magnet attracting individuals and societies when authoritarian regimes weaken or collapse.

If we want to assess the place of psychoanalysis in the modern world, exploring if and how psychoanalysis resonates with other modern scientific and philosophical perspectives, is worth while in its own right. But is this pertinent to clinical psychoanalysis? In subtle ways, I believe it is. Of course the essential quality of the analyst is his capacity to tune in on the unconscious. I am aware that there are colleagues who consider all else pretty much irrelevant. But the analyst's capacity to tune in on the unconscious is not impaired if he is also aware that in every session we implicitly explore individual epistemology, how the individual *knows.*

And how the analysand and the analyst *know,* can never be disconnected from the current knowledge that surrounds us.

We can select a few modern areas of knowledge, a few modern perspectives and explore if and how psychoanalysis resonates with them. Freud used the science, the apparatuses and the engineering of his day to construct his models of the mind, for instance, the hydraulic model (Freud, 1901, pp. 169-174) and the magic writing pad but warned against the premature and simplistic use of these developments in analytic theory building. Since Freud's time, for instance, Einstein's relativity theory has been *translated, transformed* from an abstraction into *tangible* effects, nuclear energy and nuclear weapons. I wonder if the *material* effects of scientific abstractions have stimulated some beginning changes in the "thinking" of the broader public. Is *information* and *process* perhaps less removed from the tangible concrete, material and *common sense* "object." In any case, the struggle against *reification* in our psychoanalytic theory building has a long history. David Rapaport (1960), for instance, recognizing the absurd consequences of reification in our theories, stressed that in psychoanalysis *structure* is simply slower function, *slower process.* Laplanche and Pontalis (1967) also point to Freud's avoidance of the reification of *the self* (*Das Selbst* is a neologism in German) by his reflexive ambiguous use of terms that emphasize the reflexive process, a point to which I will return later. Speaking in very broad terms, there is a congruity between psychoanalytically understood *process* and *psychic reality* on the one hand, and the study of *processes* in the basic physical and biological sciences on the other. Both are far removed from common sense material objects. The experienced *dissolution* into *process* of matter, mater, mother, creates resistance, a discomfort produced by science and psychoanalysis.

"Uncertain" is an inaccurate translation of *unbestimmt.* The German word means "indeterminate," but also refers to what does not have a *Stimme, a voice.* It is not so much that *we* are uncertain, but that we are faced with an indeterminate reality. This resonates with the psychoanalytic work of giving voice to what is *unbestimmt,* to what is indeterminate until it has been given linguistic structure.

There are many domains in which the resonance between psychoanalysis and modern science could be demonstrated. They include the work of Stanley Palombo (1999) who believes that complexity theory, chaos theory is the basic science of psychoanalysis. Gil and Boroditsky (2004), as summarized in *The Economist*, "Indonesan Linguistics"), may have discovered a spoken language that has a *primary process* structure. Tachistoscopic perceptual experiments confirm psychoanalytic hypotheses of the hierarchy of defenses. In general, cognitive scientists and psychoanalysts converge more and more in their studies of unconscious processes. It is the search for an understanding of *consciousness* that has now moved into the foreground.

I have already touched on the question of the relevance for psychoanalysis of developments in other disciplines. One inescapable fact is that psychoanalysis exists in a world in which psychoactive medications are and will be used and where other "biological" treatment methods, such as magnetic stimulation of different areas of the brain, are on the near horizon. We also know that psychological interventions, talk therapy, can have "biologically" detectable effects. For us, the so called "mind-body" problem is neither irrelevant nor distant and esoteric at this time.

A focus on *process* (remember Rapaport's (1960) statement that in psychoanalysis structure is only a slower process), a refusal of reification, and is at the basis of a resonance between psychoanalytic thinking and the work of some biologists who, by focusing on *process*, avoid simplistic reductionism. This is especially true of Gerald Edelman who won a Nobel prize in immunology before turning to neuroscience. Prior to focusing on the study of consciousness, he wrote on *Neural Darwinism* or "The Theory of Neuronal Group Selection" where he emphasizes the plasticity of individual development. "A key idea (of Darwin is that) ...functioning structures and whole organisms emerge as a result of selection among the diverse variant individuals in a population..." For Edelman (2004), the brain is such a "population" and the "neuronal group selection" of each *individual's* brain depends on "...different genetic influences, different epigenetic sequences, different bodily responses, and different histories in varying environments. The result is enormous variation at the levels of neuronal chemistry, network structure, synaptic strengths, temporal properties, memories and motivational patterns governed by value systems. In the end, there are obvious differences from person to person in the contents and styles of their streams of consciousness." (Edelman, 2004, pp. 32-34) The *openness, the open-endedness* of development that Edelman (2004) postulates is the characteristic that makes it so compatible with psychoanalytic thinking. He bases his study of consciousness on his theory of neuronal group selection and therefore maintains this openness. He presents us with a complex picture of neuronal networks that take into account current knowledge of brain anatomy, functional visualizations, the interactions of feedback systems, the functioning of "affect" connected brain areas with those that function at other levels of organization. He combines what is known with some speculations about other neuronal network complexities. Edelman's engagement with psychoanalytic hypotheses is illustrated by the following quote, "During highly focal attention...it is as if the attending subject is unconscious of all but the attended task. The inhibitory loops of basal ganglion circuits and the ability to modulate inhibition by balance between the direct and indirect pathways would seem to be well adapted to this mechanism. The hypotheses put forth here are based on the notion that the complex reentrant dynamics of the thalamocortical core can be influenced by nonconscious brain activity." (Edelman, 2004, p. 95) I have not dealt with the Freudian unconscious and the notion of repression, which remains to some extent a vexed subject. But it is conceivable the modulation of value systems, (in Edelman's work 'value systems' have a specific meaning of ascending neural pathways influencing many areas of the brain), could provide a basis for the selective inhibition of pathways related to particular memories..." We could say, *if* we do not accept his notion that the process he describes IS consciousness, that he presents us with a machine model of the mind greatly more complex than the models that Freud used, such as the magic writing pad, but a machine model nevertheless.

Edelman (2004) does deal with this question --and I cannot do full justice to his discussion here-- but my understanding of his essential point is that the complexity of *processes*, particularly processes that involve re-entrant circuits, is all that we can hope to study and understand. For him, process is experience, but he tells the reader who insists that experience is outside of process that he is asking a question on the level of "why is there something instead of nothing?"—a philosophical question beyond scientific reach.

The resistance to Edelman's (2004) proposition is enormous. To the original narcissistic blow of psychoanalysis that, since the discovery of the unconscious, we are not always in charge is added this new injury that even the "I" is a process. Martin Buber understood "the unconscious" as a process, for him the unconscious was something like a process of "falling." But now, when consciousness is *only* a process, there is no longer a little homunculus in the brain or anywhere else that represents a solid "central I." Edelman (2004) does deal with various levels of consciousness. His description of "higher order consciousness" is based on his understanding of neuronal processes involving, "... multidimensional and situated discriminations. What they lack in absolute precision, they make up for by enhancing our ability to generalize, to imagine and to communicate in a rich environment." (Edelman, 2004, p. 35) In Edelman's chapter, "Identity, The Self, Mortality and Value, he introduces a neuronal understanding of ambiguity, an ambiguity that resonates with some ambiguities that are cultivated in psychoanalytic theory, Freud's reflexive ambiguity between "I and Self," for instance.

In Conclusion:

The resistance we experience in abandoning the fixity of the common sense object, the material, and the resistance to recognizing that *process*, with its inherent openness and open-ended-ness, *is* the basis of the malaise induced by psychoanalysis and other modern paradigms with which psychoanalysis resonates. Reactionary responses include the rejection of psychoanalysis and the embrace of cults of what is closed: dogma, nationalism, and ideology.

References

Edelman, G. (2004). *Wider Than The Sky: The Phenomenal Gift of Consciousness*. New Haven: Yale University Press.

Freud, S. (1901). The Psychopathology of Everyday Life: Forgetting, Slips of the Tongue, Bungled Actions, Superstitions and Errors (1901). *The Standard Edition of the Complete Psychological Works of Sigmund Freud.* Volume VI (1901): 169-174. Also: Introductory Lectures on Psycho-Analysis. *The Standard Edition of the Complete Psychological Works of Sigmund Freud.* Volume XV (1915-1916): Introductory Lectures on Psycho-Analysis (Parts I and II): 1-240.

Freud, S. (1912). Letter from Sigmund Freud to C.G. Jung, March 21, 1912. *The Freud/June Letters: The Correspondence Between Sigmund Freud and C. G. Jung,* pp. 494-495.

Freud, S. (1913-1914). "Fausse Reconnaissance (*'Déjà Raconteé'*) in Psycho-Analytic Treatment." In Freud 1953-1974, vol. XIII: *Totem and Taboo and Other Works* (1913-1914), 199-207.

Freud, S. (1923-1925). "A Note Upon the 'Mystic Writing Pad.'" *The Standard Edition of the Complete Psychological Works of Sigmund Freud.* Volume XIX (1923-1925): 225-232.

Freud, S. (1930). "Civilization and Its Discontents." *The Standard Edition of the Complete Psychological Works of Sigmund Freud.* Volume XXI (1927-1931): 57-146.

Freud, S. (1927). "Letter from Sigmund Freud to Sandor Ferenczi, January 2, 1927." The Correspondences of Sigmund Freud and Sandor Ferenczi Volume 3 (1920-1933): 292-293. Also: Freud, S. (1936). Letter from Sigmund Freud to Albert Einstein, May 3, 1936." Letters of Sigmund Freud 1873-1939: 428.

Gil and Boroditsky, (2004). *The Economist,* Jan 10, 2004, pp. 69-70.

Hamann, B. (1999). *Hitler's Vienna: A Dictator's Apprenticeship.* Translator: T. Thornton. Oxford University Press.

Hartmann, H. (1939). *Ego Psychology and the Problem of Adaptation.* New York: International Universities Press, 1958.

Kafka, J.S. (2004). "Resonance Between Psychoanalysis and Other Modern Perspectives." *Belgrade Psychoanalytic Society Conference.* Belgrade. September 2004.

Laplanche, J., Pontalis, J. B. (1967). *The Language of Psycho-Analysis.* Translator: D. Nicholson-Smith. New York: Norton, 1973.

Palombo, S. R. (1999). *The Emergent Ego: Complexity and Co-evolution in the Psychoanalytic Process.* New York: International Universities Press.

Rapaport, D. (1960). *The Structure of Psychoanalytic Theory.* New York: International Universities Press.

Bibliography

Publications

"Notes on the clinical use of future autobiographies." Kafka, J. S. and Bolgar, H. *Rorschach Research Exchange & Journal of Projective Techniques* 13:341 346, 1949

"Diagnostic implications of a study in time perception." Eson, M. E. and Kafka, J. S. *Journal of General Psychology* 46:169 183, 1952

"A note on the therapeutic and teaching use of projective techniques with groups." *American Journal of Psychotherapy* 11:839 840, 1957

"A method for studying the organization of time experience." *American Journal of Psychiatry* 114:546 553, 1957

"Art therapy and psychotherapy." *Bulletin of Art Therapy* 1:21, 1961

"Technical applications of a concept of multiple reality," *International Journal of Psychoanalysis* 45:575 578, 1964

"The latent family in the intensive treatment of the hospitalized schizophrenic patient." Kafka, J. S. and McDonald, J. W. In: *Current Psychiatric Therapy*, Masserman, J.S., editor, pp.172-177. New York, Grune & Stratton, Inc., 1964

"Some effects of the therapist's LSD experience on his therapeutic work." Kafka, J. S. and Gaarder, K. *American Journal of Psychotherapy* 18:126 243, 1964

"The body as transitional object: A psychoanalytic study of a self mutilating patient.@ *British Journal of Medical Psychology*, 42:107 211, 1969. Also presented at a meeting of the American Psychoanalytic Association, 1968

"Not to substitute doing for living." *Voices: the Art and Science of Psychotherapy* 5:40 41, 1969

"Separating and joining influences in courtship and early marriage." Ryder, R. G.; Kafka, J. S.; and Olsen, D. H. *American Journal of Orthopsychiatry* 41:450-464, 1971

"Separating and joining influences in courtship and early marriage." Ryder, R. G.; Kafka, J. S.; and Olsen, D. H. *Medical Aspects of Human Sexuality* VI(#5) 13-35, 1972

"Ambiguity for individuation A critique and reformulation of double bind theory." *Archives of General Psychiatry* 25: 232 239, 1971

Report on Panel on "The Experience of Time: A psychoanalytic perspective on the organization and integration of time experience." *Journal of the American Psychoanalytic Association,* 20:650 667, 1972

"Notes on marriages in the counter culture." Kafka, J. S. and Ryder, R. G. *Journal of Applied Behavioral Science* 9:321-330, 1973. Also, as a chapter in *Renovating Marriage.* Editors: Libby, R. and Whitehurst, R. Danville, CA: Consensus Publishers, 1973

"On Reality: An examination of object constancy, ambiguity, paradox, and time." *Psychiatry and the Humanities* 2:133-158, 1977. New Haven, CT: Yale University Press

"Psychic effort, drift and reality structures: observations from psychoanalytic work with neurotic, borderline and schizophrenic patients." *Excerpta Medica* 121 132, 1979. Editor: C. Muller. Amsterdam Oxford. Also a presentation at: *6th International Symposium on Psychotherapy of Schizophrenia,* Amsterdam, 1979.

"The dream in schizophrenia." Chapter in *The Dream in Clinical Practice,* pp 99-110. Editor: J. Natterson. New York-London: Jason Aronson, 1980

"Challenge and confirmation in ritual action." *Psychiatry* 46:31-39, 1983

"Timing process and mental illness." Kafka, John and Kafka, Marian. Abstracts (F 193): *VII World Congress of Psychiatry*, page 302, 1983. Austria: Vienna. Also: a presentation: *VII World Congress of Psychiatry*, Vienna, 1983.

"Biographical sketch—Ping-Nie Pao." *Psychoanalytic Inquiry* 3:173-175, 1983

"Thoughts on meeting in Germany." *Journal of American Psychoanalytic Assn* 33:972-974, 1985

"Gedanken zur Begegnung in Deutschland." *Forum der Psycho-analyse* 1(1), 1985 (German) Also, published in *PsA-Info* Nr. 24, Sonderheft zum 8, IPSO-Vorkongress, Juli 1985

"Reaktionen auf den Hamburger Kongress." *Psyche* 40:10:874-877, 1986

"The schizophrenic's objects: Implication for treatment strategies." In: *Towards a Comprehensive Model for Schizophrenic Disorders. Psychoanalytic Essays in Memory of Ping-Nie Pao, M.D.*, pp. 289-297. Editor: D. B. Feinsilver. Hillsdale, N.J.: Analytic Press, 1986

"On re-establishing contact." *Psychoanalysis and Contemporary Thought*: 11:299-308, 1988. Also a presentation at the Hamburg Congress of Division of Psychoanalysis, American Psychology Association, 1987.

"On the question of insight in psychosis." *The Journal of the American Academy of Psychoanalysis* 18:18-28, 1990

"Long term psychotherapy of a schizophrenic patient." Chapter in: *Schizophrenia and Aging*, pp. 299-307. Editors: N. Miller & G. Cohen. New York: Guilford Press, 1987

"Us and them: The psychology of ethno-nationalism." *Committee on International Relations of the Group for Advancement of Psychiatry*, Report 123. New York: Brunner/Mazel, 1987

"On re establishing contact." *Psychoanalysis and Contemporary Thought* 11:299 308, 1988

Multiple Realities In Clinical Practice. New Haven, CT: Yale Univ Press, (Also published in German (1991 --*Jenseits des Realitätsprinzips: Multiple Realitäten in Theorie und Prexis der Psychoanalyse,* Springer); Italian (1992—*Le Nuove Realtà, Percezione e psycoanalisi,* Bollati Boringhieri, Torino); Russian (2007), Romanian (2000); Some chapters were also published in Romanian journal: *Psihanalyiza,* annul VI 2, 1999.) French (2009): *Réalités Multiples en Psychiatrie et Psychanalyse,* translated and adapted by Michel Vincent and Nathalie Gluck, (Editions Doin, marque de Wolters Kluwer France, 1, rue Eugene et Armand Peugeot 92856 Rueil-Malmaison Cedex)

"On the question of insight in psychosis." *Journal of the American Academy of Psychoanalysis* 18: 18 28, 1990

"A Critique of pertinent published material by Helm Stierlin." *Journal of Preventive Psychiatry and Allied Disciplines,* Vol 5(1), 1990. Also, a presentation at *Conference on Childhood and Trauma, San Francisco,* April 1990

"How do We Change?" *Psychoanalysis and Psychosis.* Editor: Ann-Louise Silver. New York: International University Press, pp. 319-337, 1989

"Consciousness and the Shadow of Time." *Two Butterflies on My Head. Psychoanalysis in the Interdisciplinary Scientific Dialogue.* Editors: M. Leuzinger-Bohleber; H. Schneider: R. Pfeiffer. Berlin: Springer—Verlag, pp. 87-95, 1992. Also, published in *IPSO Newsletter* Anniversary Edition, Summer 1991

"Anmerkungen zur Emigrantensprache." *Gift, das du unbewusst eintrinkst..., Der Nationalsozialismus und die deutsche Sprache.* Editors: Werner Bohleber und Jörg Drews. Germany: Asthesis Verlag, Beilefeld, 1991. Title translation: Poison that One Drinks Unaware.

"Recognition of Events." *The Learning Process in Psychotherapy, Supervision and in Psychotherapy: Theories and Applications.* Editors: Imre Szecsödy and Karin Gyllensköld. 1st Nordic Symposium for Supervisors, Karolinska Institute, Stockholm, pp. 52-67, November 1991. Also a lecture at *1st Nordic Symposium for Supervisors,* Karolinska Institute, Stockholm, November 1991

"Körperphantasien." *Prax Psychothery Psychosomatic.* Heidelberg, 37:81-91, 1992

"Einsicht in Psychosen." *Psyche*, Stuttgart, 7:613-625, 1992

"Einleitende Bemerkungen.@ *Antisemitismus*. Editors: W. Bohleber & J. Kafka, J.(Hgg.) Germany: Aisthesis Verlag, Bielefeld, pp. 18-19, 1992

"The schizophrenic object, insight and consciousness." *The Psychotherapy of Schizophrenia*. Editors: G. Benedetti & P. Furlani. Switzerland: Hogrefe & Huber, Bern, 1993.

"Selbstdarstellung." *Psychoanalyse in Selbstdarstellungen* III (relating life events to development of psychoanalytic ideas). Editor: L. Hermanns. Germany: Sonderdruck, Tübingen, pp. 141-187, 1995

"Consciousness and the shadow of time." (Russian translation). *Moscow Journal of Psychotherapy*, pp 156-165, 1996

"Resistance, regression and change." (Russian translation). *Bulletin of Russian Psychoanalytic Federation*, 1996. Also, a Romanian translation, *Psihanaliza, Bulletin of Romanian Psychoanalytic Society*, Annual IV 1-2:8-14, 1997

"Le temps en psychothérapie et en psychanalyse." *Revue Française de Psychanalyse*, pp 1821-1828, May 1997

"The romantic and classic visions in the therapy of psychosis: a personal perspective and an evolving theory of schizophrenia." *Psychiatry* 60:209-221, Fall 1997

"The Analyst's Autonomy: Individuation and Flexibility of Technique." (Dutch translation). Published in: *Festschrift for Han Groen-Prakken*, Chapter 7, Hanfest, Amsterdam, January 1998

"Psychodynamics of Leaders and Decision-Making." *Mind and Human Interaction* 9(#3)129-181, 1999. Committee on International Relations (members: Vamik D. Volkan, M.D., Chair; Salman Akhtar, M.D.; Robert M. Dorn, M.D.; John S. Kafka, M.D.; Otto F. Kernberg, M.D.; Peter A. Olsson, M.D.; Rita R. Rogers, M.D.; Stephen B. Shanfield, M.D.)

"The Traumatized Individual in The Traumatized Society: Treatment, Memory, and Memorials." ("L'individu traumatise dans la societe traumatisee: traitement, memoire et monuments commenoratifs") In:

Revue Française de Psychanalyse 2000/1-Devoir de Memoire, Entre Passion et Oubli: 81-96. Also, a presentation at the *Symposium: Psychoanalysis in Times of Social and Political Upheaval*, September 2000, Washington, DC

"Some Lessons Learned From the History of Psychoanalysis: Implications for Psychoanalytic Education, Clinical Practice, and Wider Applications." (Russian translation. Published in: *Psychoanalytic Herald*, Volume 1(7):151-153, 1999

"Personalitati ale psihanalizei americane." (published in Romanian), *Review of Psychoanalysis*, Volume VI(2):15-22, 1999

"Zeit: Rahmen und Inhalt; und die Zeithaftigkeit der psychoanalytischen Erfahrung." *Forum der Psychoanalyse* 17(#4):299-311, December 2001. Also, a presentation in Regensberg, Germany, April 2000.

"Time: the uncertainty of frame or content.@ Chapter 6: *Time: the Uncertainty of Frame or Content*, pp. 79-84, 2001. Editors: Paul Harris & Michael Crawford. Boston, MA: Brill.

"Terrorizing and Being Terrorized." *International Psychoanalytical Association Newsletter,* Spring 2002

"Unterbrechen and Zerbrechen (The Violence of Non-Interpretation)." *Schriftenreihe Bulletin der Wiener Psychoanalytischen Vereinigung,* Austria: Picus Verlag, Wien, 2003. Also a presentation at the Vienna Psychoanalytic Society, October 2003

"Psychoanalysis in Eastern Europe: A Laboratory for Developments in Psychoanalysis and Psychoanalytic Education." Newsletter, *American Psychoanalytic Association*, pp. 11-13, 2003

"The International Perspective: Differences and Commonalities in Psychoanalytic Theory and Practice." *Freud at 150: 21st Century Essays on a Man of Genius.* Editors: Merlino, Jacobs, Kaplan, Moritz. New York: Rowman & Littlefield Publishers, pp. 85-87, 2007

"Zerbrechen und Unterbrechen." *Psyche—Zeitschrift Fur Psychoanalyse* 61:368-374, April 2007

Drawing of a Rat. Cover drawing for: *Mental Zoo* and *Cultural Zoo: Animals in the Human Mind and Its Subliminations.* Editors: Salman Akhtar & Vamik Volkan. New York:International Universities Press, 2005

"Time: The Uncertainty of Frame or Content." Abstract in : *KronoScope, Journal for the Study of Time* 7(#1-2):106, 2007. Publisher: Koninklijke Brill NV, Leiden, The Netherlands

"Psychoanalysis and Democracy." *American Imago* 65(#4):547-565, 2008

"On Schizophreniform Crisis and on Schizophrenia." Commentary on ARestitutional Functions of Symbol and Myth in Strindberg's *Inferno.* The Sixteenth Annual Freida Fromm-Reichmann Memorial Lecture," by Donald L. Burnham, published in *Psychiatry* 36:229-243, August 1973. Commentary published in *Psychiatry* 72(2):139-142, Summer 2009

"Chestnut Lodge and the Psychoanalytic Approach to Psychosis." *Journal of the American Psychoanalytic Association* 59:27-48, 2011. AResponses to Commentaries." *Journal of the American Psychoanalytic Association* 59:81-84, 2011. Also, published in Hungarian Journal: *Pszichoterapia*, Vol 25:5-16, February 2016 B www.pszichoterapia.hu. Also published in Italian: *Psychoanalysis of Psychosis. Present point of view*, pp. 33-53. (2016) Editors: R. Lombardi, L. Rinaldi, S. Thanopulos. Authors: M. J. Blechner, S. Calamandrei, G. Civitarese, F. De Masi, D. Houzel, J. Kafka, R. Lombardi, G. Martini, M. Robbins, L. Rinaldi, I. Steinman, S. Thanopulos, P. Williams. Milano: Raffaello Cortina.

"From Despair to Poignancy." *American Imago* 72(3):283-291, 2015

"Psychoanalysis and the Temporal Trace." *Time and Trace,* Volume 15: 197-214, 2016. International Society for the Study of Time. Publisher: Koninklijke Brill NV, Leiden, The Netherlands. pp. 197-214

Presentations, Lectures, Seminars

"On the experience of duration in psychotherapy." Presentation. *Symposium at Chestnut Lodge*, Rockville, Maryland, 1957

"An experimental case study of the effects of Sernyl." K. Gaarder & J. S. Kafka. Presentation. *Symposium, Chestnut Lodge,* Rockville, Maryland, 1963

"LSD in psychotherapy and alcoholism." Discussion of a paper by Dr. Harold Abramson. *Association for Advancement of Psychotherapy,* Gutheil Memorial Conference, 1965

"Déjà vu phenomena—Observations and a theory." Presentation. *American Psychoanalytic Association,* 1966

"Different version of ambiguity tolerance and individualization (Mathematico-logical emphasis)." Presentation. *Child Research Branch of Chestnut Lodge,* Rockville, Maryland, 1966

"Parameters in psychoanalysis." Presentation. Panel member. Panel on "Parameters." *Washington Psychoanalytic Society,* 1967

Discussant. Philip Weissman's paper "Psychological concomitants of ego functioning in creativity." *Washington Psychoanalytic Society,* 1967

"The body as transitional object: a psychoanalytic study of a self-mutilating patient." Presentation. Meeting. American Psychoanalytic Association, 1968. Also, published in *British Journal of Medical Psychology* 42:207-212, 1969, Great Britain

"The patient's and the therapist's responsibility." Panel presentation: Symposium on *Clinical and Experimental Research in Behavior Therapy,* National Institute of Mental Health, 1968

"Marriage and Psychoanalysis." Presentation. *Child Research Branch,* National Institute of Mental Health, Spring 1968

"The body as transitional object: A psychoanalytic study of a self-mutilating patient." Presentation. Meeting. American Psychoanalytic Association, 1968. Also, published in *British Journal of Medical Psychology,* 42:107-211, 1969

"Déjà phenomena, transitional ambiguous states and the double bind." Presentation. *Adult Psychiatry Branch,* National Institutes of Mental Health, 1969. Also, presentation at *Double Bind Symposium,* American Psychological Association, Washington, D.C., 1969

"Adolescence and the Consolidation of Values." Discussion. *American Psychoanalytic Association,* 1970

"Paradox, time and object constancy." Presentation: *British Psycho-Analytical Society,* 1972. Also, published in *Scientific Bulletin of British Psychoanalytical Society* 5:23-29, 1972

"Some observations on constancies and temporal fragmentation in psychoanalysis." Presentation. *Western Regional Psychoanalytic Society,* San Diego, CA, 1972

"Some problems and potentialities of present day psychoanalysis." Discussant of paper by Leo Stone, 1973

Discussant. P. Hartocollis' paper "Time and Affect in Psychopathology." *American Psychoanalytic Association,* 1973

Discussant. Paul Ricoeur's paper "Psychoanalysis and the work of art." *Washington Psychoanalytic Society,* 1974

"Technische Implikationen eines multideminsionalen Realitätsbergriffs." [Discussant of paper: Depersonalization: A Self-Relations Model by Allen Frances, Michael Sacks, and Michael Aronoff]. *German Psychoanalytic Society,* Stuttgart, 1974

"Ambiguität und Psycho-analytische Technik." Presentation. *Zurich Psychoanalytisches Seminar,* 1975

Discussant. Allen Frances, Michael Saks, and Michael Aranoff's paper "Depersonalization: a self-relations perspective." *American Psychoanalytic Association,* 1975

Discussant with Marian Kafka. S. Feder's paper "Gustav Mahler um Mitternacht." *American Psychoanalytic Association,* 1977

"Zum Problem der Realität." Presentation: *South German Psychoanalytic Group,* Ulm, 1977

"On reality: an examination of object constancy, ambiguity, paradox and time." Presentation. *New York Psychoanalytic Society,* 1978

"The patient's and therapist's responsibility." Panel Presentation: *Laboratory of Psychology Symposium,* National Institute of Mental Health 1978

"The Interpretation of Dreams in the Treatment of Schizophrenia." Presentation. *Dept of Psychiatry,* Walter Reed Army Medical Center, 1979

"Psychic effort, drift and reality structures: observations from psychoanalytic work with neurotic, borderline and schizophrenic patients." Presentation: *6th International Symposium on Psychotherapy of Schizophrenia,* Amsterdam, 1979. Also, published in *Excerpta Medica* 121-132. Editor: C. Muller. Amsterdam-Oxford, 1979

Discussant. Martin Wangh's paper "Boredom." *Washington Psychoanalytic Society,* 1981

"Ritual as the need to ask." Presentation. *Washington Psychoanalytic Society,* 1981

"25 Years of therapy of a schizophrenic patient: perspectives and lessons." Presentation. 7th *International Symposium on Psychotherapy of Schizophrenics,* Heidelberg, 1981

"Long-term psychotherapy of a schizophrenic patient." Presentation. *Schizophrenia, Paranoia, and Schizophreniform Disorders in Later Life Conference.* National Institute of Mental Health, 1982

"The borderline: effort, drift and disorganization." Symposium: *American Psychological Association,* 1982

"Aspects of self-analysis while working with difficult patients." Symposium: *American Psychological Association,* 1982

"How do we change?" Presentation. *Frieda Fromm-Reichmann Memorial Lecture,* Washington School of Psychiatry, National Institute of Mental Health, 1982

"Timing process and mental illness." Kafka, John and Kafka, Marian. Presentation: *VII World Congress of Psychiatry,* Vienna, 1983.

Discussant. Ernst Ticho's presentation "The influence of the German language culture on Freud's thought." *Washington Psychoanalytic Society,* 1985

"A comparison of object formation in schizophrenic and neurotic patients: Implications for treatment strategies." Presentation. *British Psychoanalytical Society,* 1986

Discussant. Theodore Jacobs' paper "Transference relationships, the relationship between transference and reconstruction." *Washington Psychoanalytic Society*, 1986

"On re-establishing contact." Presentation. Division of Psychoanalysis, *American Psychology Association*, 1987. Published in *Psychoanalysis and Contemporary Thought*: 11(#2)299-308. Hamburg Congress, 1988

"Insight in psychosis." Presentation. *Dept of Psychiatry*, University of Michigan, 1987

"Structural change and the executive ego." Presentation. *35th Congress, International Psychoanalytical Assn*, 1987

Letter in response to J. Kihlstrom's "The Cognitive Unconscious." *Science* 238:1638, 1987

"The schizophrenic object. Insight and consciousness." Presentation. *IX International Symposium on Psychotherapy of Schizophrenia*, Turin, Italy, 1988

"Le temps dans l'épistomologie psychoanalytique et sa perception dans la cure." Presentation. *Paris Psychoanalytic Society*, 1988

"Die Zeit als Kern psychischer Wirklichkeit; Implikationen für die psychoanalytische Theorie und Praxis." Presentation. Symposium on "Zeiterleben und psychoanalytischer Prozess." *Zurich Psychoanalytic Society*, 1988

"Clinical and cognitive perspectives on time." Presentation. *Department of Military Psychiatry*, Walter Reed Army Institute of Research, 1988

Discussant. Eric Marcus' paper "Dreams, psychoanalysis and social science research: medical students dream about medical school." *American Psychoanalytic Association*, 1988

"Evolution of the personal past." Presentation. *Washington Psychoanalytic Institute*, 1989

"Psychosis or psychotic aspects of the personality." Presentation and Co-chair of special discussion panel: *International Psychoanalytical Association*, Rome, 1989

"A Critique of pertinent published material by Helm Stierlin." Presentatio.: *Conference on Childhood and Trauma*, San Francisco, April 1990. Also, published in *Journal of Preventive Psychiatry and Allied Disciplines*, Vol 5(1), 1990

Discussant. David Rosenfeld's paper "Psychosis and psychotic part of the personality: a clinical approach." *American Psychoanalytic Association*, 1990

"Körperphantasien." Presentation. Lindau, Switzerland, Summer 1990

Letter to the Editor. Response to H. Sno and D. Linszen: "Déjà Phenomena." *American Journal of Psychiatry*, p. 951, 1991

"Psychotherapy in Psychiatry." Lecture. *International Congress of Psychotherapy*. Hanover, Germany. September 1991

"Recognition of Events." Lecture. *1st Nordic Symposium for Supervisors*, Karolinska Institute, Stockholm, November 1991. Published in: The Learning Process in Psychotherapy, Supervision and in Psychotherapy: Theories and Applications. Editors: Imre Szecsödy and Karin Gyllensköld. 1st Nordic Symposium for Supervisors, Karolinska Institute, Stockholm, November 1991, pp. 52-67

"Passivity and timing in psychoanalytic technique. The interpretive function of process or "The analyst's selective 'passivity', Determinants and interpretive functions of formal aspects of technique." Lecture: *Swedish Psychoanalytic Society*, Stockholm, November 1991

Lecture on "Psychoanalytic Technique." *Gelderland Klinik*, Geldern, Germany, 1991

"Le Temps en psychothérapie." Presentation. *Policlinique Psychiatrique Universitaire*, Lausanne, 1993

"Psychose et psychothérapie." Presentation. *Hôpital psychiatrique de Marsens*, Fribourg, January 1993

"Psychoanalytic approach to the study of prejudice." Presentation. Panel on "Psychoanalytic Perspectives of Prejudice and Beyond." *American Psychoanalytic Association*, New York, December 1993

"The analyst's prejudice and countertransference." Presentation. Panel on "Psychoanalytic Perspectives of Prejudice and Beyond," *American Psychoanalytic Association*, San Francisco, May 1994

"Special characteristics of antisemitic prejudice." Presentation and Chair of panel on "The Treatment of Schizophrenia and Severe Psychopathology: Its History and Current Practice in the Washington Psychoanalytic Community." *International Symposium for Psychotherapy of Schizophrenia*, Washington D.C., June 1994

"Narcissism." Presentation. *3rd Clinical Conference between European and American Analysts*, Antibes, July 1994

"Prejudice and the Family Romance." Presentation. Panel on Psychoanalytic Perspectives of Prejudice and Beyond, *American Psychoanalytic Association*, New York, December 1994

"Problems in supervision." Presentation. Congress of Training and Supervising Analysts, 39th Congress *International Psychoanalytical Association*, San Francisco, July 1995

"Consciousness in psychosis and characteristics of the psychotic object." Presentation. Panel on "Psychic reality in psychotic states," 39th Congress *International Psychoanalytical Association*, San Francisco, July 1995

"Resistance, regression and change." Presentation. *International Psychoanalytical Association-European Psychoanalytic Federation Joint Summer School and Seminar.* Constanza, Romania, September 1995

"Transference, countertransference and the process of change." Presentation. *American Society of Psychiatric Physicians*, Washington DC, September 1995

"Psychoanalysis in Eastern Europe." Presentation. Panel on "The Self and the Other." Third Annual World Bank Conference on Environmentally Sustainable Development, Washington D.C., October 1995, pp.16-18.

"Object formation in psychosis: implications for the treatment of nonpsychotic patients." Presentation. *Sociedad Psicoanalitica de Caracas*, February 1997

"On the nature of psychoanalytic interventions." Presentation. *40th Congress of International Psychoanalytical Association.* Spain: Barcelona, August 1997

"Psychoanalytic Perspectives of Prejudice and Beyond." Panel Presentation. *American Psychoanalytic Association,* New York, December 1997

"Psychotische Realitäten und die Handhabung Psychotischer Übertragungs-phänomene." Presentation. *Ort: Studienzentrum Bregenz,* Austria, January 1998

"Radical Social Change and the Structure and Functions of Psychoanalysis: The 'Rebirth' of Psychoanalysis in Russia and Elsewhere." Presentation. *Austen Riggs Center,* March 1998

"Freud and Austrian Culture." Presentation. *Chancery of Embassy of Austria,* Washington, DC, April 1998

"Memory of the Holocaust." Presentation. *Washington Psychoanalytic Foundation* (New Directions Program), Washington, DC, February 1999

"Affect and Psychosis." Presentation. 41st *International Psychoanalytical Association* Congress, Santiago de Chile, July 1999

"Assessing the Patient: The Analyst's and the Patient's Motivations and the Question of 'Ego Strength'." Presentation. Latvia: Riga. August 1999

"Consciousness and Object Formation in Psychosis: Bridging Psychoanalytic and Neurobiological Perspectives." Presentation. *Freud at the Threshold of the 21th Century Conference,* Sigmund Freud Center, The Hebrew University of Jerusalem. Israel: Jerusalem. December 1999

"Conviction and Self-Doubt After Freud: The Autonomous Development of the Analyst." Presentation. *5th Delphi International Psychoanalytic Symposium.* Greece: Delphi. July 2000

"The Development of an Analyst's Clinical Listening: A Close Look at Some Analytic Interventions." Presentation. Romania: Bucharest. September 2000

"The Traumatized Individual in The Traumatized Society: Treatment, Memory, and Memorials." Presentation. *Symposium: Psychoanalysis in Times of Social and Political Upheaval,* September 2000, Washington, DC

"On the Nature of Psychoanalytic Interventions, Clarification and Interpretations and Psychotherapy." Presentation. *Virginia Psychoanalytic Society*, November 2000

"Time: the uncertainty of frame or content." Presentation. *International Society for the Study of Time Conference*: July 8-14, 2001; Castello di Gargonza, Italy.

"History of psychoanalysis: Freud and dream. Contributing to and Celebrating the Centenary of 'The Interpretation of Dreams' As the Origin of the Psychoanalytic Method. Panel, *42nd Congress, International Psychoanalytical Association*. Nice, France. 24 July 2001

Reporter. Panel Report: "History of Psychoanalysis: Freud and Dream. Contributing to and Celebrating the Centenary Of **'The Interpretation of Dreams'** As the Origin of the Psychoanalytic Method." 42nd Congress of the *International Psychoanalytical Association*, Nice, France, 24 July 2001.

"Thinking about Transference and Interpreting It." Presentation. *2nd European Seminar For Candidates in Psychoanalytic Training*. Hungary: Dobogokö. October 1, 2001

"Immer übertragung denken, manchmal übertragung deuten. Theorie und Praxis—Beispiele von Zweifeln und Entscheiden." Presentation. *Vienna Psychoanalytic Society*. Austria: Vienna. December 2001

"A Psychoanalytic View of the Traumatized Individual in the Traumatized Society." Presentation. *George Washington University Human Sciences Conference*, 13-14 April 2002, Washington, DC

"Narcissism and the Psychoanalytic Process." Presentation. Panel on German Psychoanalysis After the Holocaust *International Psychoanalytical Association European Psychoanalytic Federation*. Summer School (Oct 26-Nov 2), 2002. Serbia: Palic

"Psychanalyse et changements sociaux Radicaux: l'individu traumatisé dans la société traumatisée." Presentation. *Société Suisse De Psychanalyse*. Switzerland: Geneva. March 2003

"Resistance." Presentation. Panel on "The Resistance in Psychoanalysis." *International Psychoanalytical Association, European Psychoanalytical Federation.* Estonia: Haapsalu. July 2003

"Unterbrechen and Zerbrechen (The Violence of Non-Interpretation)." Presentation. Vienna Psychoanalytic Society, October 2003. Published in *Schriftenreihe Bulletin der Wiener Psychoanalytischen Vereinigung,* Picus Verlag, Wien, 2003

Discussion. Play: "God's Donkey (A Play on Moses)." Theatre J, Washington, DC. November 2003

"Resistance." Presentation. Panel on "The Resistance in Psychoanalysis." *International Psychoanalytical Association, European Psychoanalytical Federation.* Estonia: Haapsalu. July 2003

"Psychoanalysis in Eastern Europe: A Laboratory for Developments in Psychoanalysis and Psychoanalytic Education." Presentation. *International Psychoanalytical Association,* New Orleans, March 2004

"Psychoanalytic Micro-Process." Presentation. *International Psychoanalytical Association, European Psychoanalytical Federation.* PIEE Candidates' Seminar. Russia: St. Petersburg. March 2004

"Psychoanalysis Never Developed in an 'Average Expectable Environment.'" Presentation. Conference on Psychoanalyst at Work. *International Psychoanalytical Association European Psychoanalytical Federation.* Russia: Moscow. May 2004

"Resonance Between Psychoanalysis and Other Modern Perspectives." Presentation. *Belgrade Psychoanalytic Society Conference.* Belgrade. September 2004

Interview. Advanced Candidates Seminar. Latvia: Riga. February 2005. Published in *Latvian Psychoanalytic Journal, No. 5,* May 2005

"Time, History, and Psychoanalysis." Presentation. Panel on Time and History in Psychoanalysis. *44th International Psychoanalytical Association.* Brazil: Rio de Janerio. July 2005. Review of the Panel: Time and History in Psychoanalysis. *International Psychoanalytical Association E-Newsletter,* No. 1, February 2006. Harold P. Blum, Moderator; Sandra Pine, Reporter.

"The Traumatized Individual In the Traumatized Society." Presentation. *44th International Psychoanalytical Association*. Brazil: Rio de Janerio. July 2005

"The Wider Context: Maternal Pathology and Freud As a Consultant." Presentation. Panel on Little Hans. *American Psychoanalytic Association*, New York, January 2006

"On the Occasion of Freud's 150th Birthday." Presentation. *Parliament*, Vienna, Austria, 7 April 2006. Topic for Special Meeting of Parliament: "Psychoanalyse Und Demokratie."

"On the Occasion of Freud's 150th Birthday. On Different 'False Memories' From Screen Memories to *Deja-Vu*." Presentation. Conference on Freud's Screen Memories In the Light of Contemporary Psychoanalysis and Neurosciences. *Czech Psychoanalytical Society*. Czech Republic: Prague. 5 May 2006

"Dreams: Privileged or Under-Privileged in Psychoanalysis." Presentation. Panel members: Marshall Alcorn, Edwig Plotnick, Linda Geurkink, Scott Twentyman, John S. Kafka. *Washington Center for Psychoanalysis*, Washington, DC, January 2007

"Have You Even Been Bored In a Dream? Dreams and Psychoanalytic Technique." Plenary Lecture. *International Psychoanalytical Association* PIEE Summer School. Ukraine: Odessa. June 2007

"Twenty Years in East Europe." Presentation. *International Psychoanalytical Association*. Germany: Berlin. July 2007

"Harvesting Today the Fruits of Chestnut Lodge." Presentation as the Keynote Speaker at 10th Annual *International Society for the Psychological Treatments of the Schizophrenias and Other Psychoses*, US Chapter. Oct 2-4, 2009, Rockville, MD. Conference Topic: Interpersonal Approaches to Treating Psychosis: The Living Legacy of Chestnut Lodge.

"The Subculture of Psychoanalysts in Societies under Threat." Presentation. *International Psychoanalytical Association* Meeting, Chicago, Illinois, July 2009

"When You Die, You Will Miss Me. Some Thoughts and Questions on Narcissism." Presentation. *International Psychoanalytical Association*, *PIEE Summer School*. Ukraine: Odessa, Aug 29—Sep 4, 2009

"Life and Treatment Goals." Presentation. *Moscow Psychoanalytic Society 20th Anniversary Celebration.* Russia: Moscow, May 2009

"The Trauma Victim in the 'Average Expectable Environment' and in the Gravely Traumatized Society. Presentation. Conference Title: *Trauma: Intersections among Narrative, Neuroscience, and Psychoanalysis.* Washington, DC, March 2010

Discussant. Werner Bohleber's paper "Implicit theories in the psychoanalytic treatment of traumatized patients." Oct 14, 2010, *Washington Center for Psychoanalysis,* Washington, DC

Discussant.: Marilia Aisenstein's paper "A Contemporary Approach To Psychosomatic Theory and Clinical Practice." May 18, 2012, *Washington Center for Psychoanalysis,* Washington, DC

"Psychoanalysis and the Temporal Trace." Presentation. Conference Title: Time and Trace. *International Society for the Study of Time.* The Orthodox Academy of Crete. July 2013.

"From Despair to Poignancy." Presentation. "Time and Pain" Panel. (Also, Chair of Panel). *48th International Psychoanalytical Association.* Czech Republic: Prague.. 2 August 2013. Also, given as a lecture at the PIEE Summer School, Budva, Montenegro, Sep 22-25, 2014.

"Psychosis." Lecture. December 2013. *Washington Psychoanalytic Institute*

"Cultures in Psychoanalysis and Psychoanalytic Cultures." Presentation. Conference: Culture and Aggression. *Washington Center for Psychoanalysis.* Washington, DC. November 9, 2014

"What's New About Time in Psychoanalytic Theory and Practice." Presentation. *International Psychoanalytical Association.* MA: Boston. July 2015

Book Reviews

Book review. *The Psychiatric Hospital as a Small Society.* Author: William Caudill. *Journal of Social Therapy* 5:106-108, 1959

Book review. *The Psychology of Time.* Author: P. Fraisse. *Psychiatry* 27:182-184, 1964

Book Review. *Sanity, Madness and the Family: Vol. l—Families of Schizophrenics.* Authors: R. D. Laing and A. Esterson. *Contemporary Psychology* 1:472-473, 1966

Book review. *Analytical Psychology, Its Theory and Practice.* Author: C. J. Jung. *Human Inquiries* 10:205-208, 1970

Book Review. *The Courage to Love.* Author: Edith Weigert. *Psychiatry and Social Science Review* 5:18-21, 1971

Book Review. *The Origin and Treatment of Schizophrenic Disorders.* Author: Theodore Lidz. *Journal of the American Psychoanalytic Association,* 24(3):706-714, 1976

Book Review. *Adolf Hitler: A family perspective.* Author: Helm Stierlin. *Psychiatry* 41:221-225, 1978

Book review. *Borderline Personality Disorders: the Concept, the Syndrome, the Patient.* Editor: P. Hartocollis. *Journal of the American Psychoanalytic Association* 29:236-247, 1981

Book review. *Das Borderline Syndrom.* Author: C. Rhode-Dachser. *Journal of American Psychoanalytic Association* 31(1):348-351, 1983

Book review. *Hitler's Psychopathology.* Author: N. Bromberg & Small Volz. *Journal of Nervous and Mental Disease* 173(7):441-442, 1985

Book Review. *Freud, Race and Gender.* Author: Sandor Gilman. *International Journal of Psychoanalysis,* 76(#2):411-414, April 1995

Book review. *The Last Witness--The Child Survivor of the Holocaust.* Editors: Judith Kestenberg & Ira Brenner. *Journal of Applied Psychoanalytic Studies* 1(#3):277-279, 1999

References

Abramson, H. A., ed. (1959). *The Use of LSD in Psychotherapy.* New York: Josiah Macy, Jr., Foundation.

Ackerman, N. W. (1963). Family diagnosis and therapy. In *Current Psychiatric Therapies*, vol. 3. J. H. Masserman, editor. New York: Grune & Stratton.

American Psychiatric Association. (1980). *Diagnostic and Statistical Manual of Mental Disorders (DSM-III).* 3d ed. Washington, D.C.: American Psychiatric Association.

Anderson, C. M. (1983). A psychoeducational model of family treatment for schizophrenia. In *Psychosocial Intervention in Schizophrenia*, edited by H. Stierlin, L. C. Wynne, and M. Wirsching. Berlin: Springer-Verlag.

Angelergues and Weil. Introduction to this issue of *R.F.P. 2000/1-Devoir de Memoire, Entre Passion et Oubli.*

Aulagnier, Piera. (1975). *Violence of Interpretation: From Pictogram to Statement.* Translator: Alan Sheridan. London: Routledge, 2001.

Arieti, S. (1963). Studies of thought processes in contemporary psychiatry. *American Journal of Psychiatry* 120:58-64.

Arlow, J. (1959). The Structure of the *Déjà Vu* experience. *Journal of the American Psychoanalytic Association* 7: 611-631.

Arlow, J.A. (1989). Delusion and metaphor. In *Psychoanalysis and Psychosis*, ed. A.-L. S. Silver. Madison, CT: International Universities Press, pp. 173-182.

Artiss, K. L. (1962). *Milieu Therapy and Schizophrenia*. New York: Grune & Stratton.

Bakker, C. B., and Amini, F. B. (1961). Observations on the psychotomimetic effects of Sernyl. *Comprehensive Psychiatry* 2:269-80.

Barnes, D. (1987). Biological issues in schizophrenia. *Science* 235:430-433.

Bateson, G., Jackson, D.D., Haley, J., and Weakland, J.H. (1956). Toward a theory of schizophrenia. *Behavorial Sciences* 1:251-264.

Bavelas, A. (1970). Description of experiment on persistence of erroneous convictions regarding "causality." In *Problem Solving and Search Behavior Under Non-Contingent Rewards*, edited by J. C. Wright. Ann Arbor, Michigan: University Microfilms.

Bechgaard, D. (2003). Lessons in how to ruin a study in psychotherapy effectiveness: A critical review of the follow-up study from Chestnut Lodge. *Journal of the American Academy of Psychoanalysis and Dynamic Psychiatry* 31:119-139.

Berlyne, D.E. (1966). Conflict and arousal. *Science American* 215:82-87.

Bonaparte, M. (1940). Time and the unconscious. *International Journal of PsychoAnalysis* 21:427-68.

Borges, J. L. (1964). A new refutation of time. In *Labyrinths*, edited by D. A. Yates and J. E. Irby. New York: New Directions.

Boring, E. G. (1933). *The Physical Dimensions of Consciousness*. New York: Century.

Bowen, M. (1961). The family as the unit of study and treatment. *American Journal of Orthopsychiatry* 31:40-60.

Brody, W., and Hayden, M. (1957). Intra-team reactions: Their relation to the conflicts of the family in treatment. *American Journal of Orthopsychiatry* 27:349-55.

Bullard, D., Jr. (1973). Foreword. In *Psychoanalysis and Psychosis*, ed A.-L. S. Silver. Madison, CT: International Universities Press, pp. xix-xxi.

Bullard, D., Jr. (1994). *History and current practice of treatment of schizophrenia at Chestnut Lodge.* Paper presented at the International Symposium for Psychotherapy of Schizophrenia. Washington, DC.

Burnham, D. L. (1966). The special-problem patient: Victim or agent of splitting? *Psychiatry* 29:105-22.

Burnham, D.L. (1973). Restitutional functions of symbol and myth in Strindberg's *Inferno. Psychiatry: Interpersonal and Biological Processes* 36:229-243.

Burnham, D.L., Gladstone, A.I., & Gibson, R.W. (1969). *Schizophrenia and the Need-Fear Dilemma.* New York: International Universities Press.

Caruso, I. A. (1967). Zu Joseph Gabels Theorie des falsehen Bewufsteins. In: J. Gabel, *Ideologie und Schizophrenic: Formen der Entfremdung (Ideology and Schizophrenia: Forms of Estrangement).* Frankfurt am Main: S. Fischer Verlag.

Cocks, Geoffrey. (1985). *Psychotherapy in the Third Reich: The Göring Institute.* New York: Oxford University Press.

Cohen, R. (1969). Foreword. In: D.L. Burnham, A.I. Gladstone, & R.W. Gibson, *Schizophrenia and the Need-Fear Dilemma.* New York: International Universities Press, pp. xv-xvi.

Cohen, R. (1982). Notes on the life and work of Frieda Fromm-Reichmann. *Psychiatry* 45(#2): 90-98.

Cohen, R. (1994). *History and current practice of treatment of schizophrenia at Chestnut Lodge.* Paper presented at the International Symposium for Psychotherapy of Schizophrenia. Washington, DC.

Conci, M. (1994). *History and current practice of treatment of schizophrenia at Chestnut Lodge.* Formal discussion of panel at the

International Symposium for Psychotherapy of Schizophrenia. Washington, DC.

Cytowic, R. (1996). *Neurology Side of Neuropsychology.* Massachusetts Institute of Technology Press.

Domansky, Elisabeth. (1992). "Kristallnacht," The Holocaust and German Unity. In Elisabeth

Domansky and Harald Welzer, eds., *The Meaning of November 9 as an Anniversary in Germany.* Tubingen: Édition diskord, pp. 60-94.

Domansky, Elisabeth. (1995). "Kristallnacht," the Holocaust and German Unity. *Reader, Conference 'Interdisciplinary Research into Trauma and Violence'*, pp. 61-94. Breuninger Kolleg Stuttgart, Nov. 17-19, 1995 in Bad Teinach.

Dyrud, J. E. (1989). The early Frieda, and traces of her in her later writings. In *Psychoanalysis and Psychosis*, ed. A. L. S. Silver. Madison, CT: International Universities Press, pp. 483-494.

Eissler, K. R. (1953). The effect of the structure of the ego on psychoanalytic technique. *Journal of the American Psychoanalytic Association* 1:104-143.

Eissler, K. R. (1955). *The Psychiatrist and the Dying Patient.* New York: International Universities Press, Inc.

Eissler, K.R. (1978). Tod und Zeit. In: *Der sterbende Patient.* Zur Psychologie des Todes. Stuttgart, Germany.

Eissler, K.R. (1993). On the Possible Effects of Aging on the Practice of Psychoanalysis. *Psychoanalytic Inquiry* 13: 316-332.

Erikson, Erik H. (1956). The problem of ego identification. *Journal of the American Psychoanalytic Association* 4:56-121.

Erikson, Erik H. (1956). *Toys and Reasons: Stages in the Ritualization of Experience.* New York: W.W. Norton.

Erikson, E. H. (1966). Ontogeny of ritualization. In: R. M. Loewenstein et al., eds., *Psychoanalysis—A General Psychology: Essays in Honor of Heinz Hartmann.* International Universities Press.

Etkind, Alexander. (1997). *Eros of the Impossible. The History of Psycho-analysis in Russia.* Boulder, CO: Westview Press.

Faimberg, Haydée. (1988). The telescoping of generations: genealogy of certain identifications. *Contemporaty Psychoanalysis* 24:99-117.

Federn, P. (1952). *Ego Psychology and the Psychoses.* New York: Basic Books.

Fonagy, P., & Target, M. (2007). Playing with reality: IV. A theory of external reality rooted in intersubjectivity. *International Journal of Psychoanalysis* 88:917-937.

Fraser, J.T. 1981. Temporal Levels and Reality Testing. *The International Journal of Psychoanalysis* 62: 3-26.

Freud, A. (1971). Address to the International Psycho-Analytic Congress, Vienna.

Freud, S. (1893-1899). Screen Memories. In Freud (1953-1974), vol. III: *Early Psycho-Analytic Publications (1893-1899)*, pp. 299-322.

Freud, S. (1909). Analysis of a Phobia in a Five-Year-Old Boy. In Freud (1953-1974), vol. X: *Two Case Histories (Little Hans and the Rat Man) (1909)*, pp. 1-150.

Freud, S. (1913). Totem and taboo. In *Standard Edition of the Complete Psychological Works*, vol. 13. London: Hogarth, 1955.

Freud, S. (1913-1914). Fausse reconnaissance (*Déjà Raconté*) in psycho-analytic treatment. In Freud (1953-1974), vol. XIII: *Totem and Taboo and Other Works (1913-1914)*, pp. 199-207.

Freud, S. (1915). The unconscious. *Standard Edition of the Complete Psychological Works of Sigmund Freud* 14:166-215.

Freud, S. (1917). A metapsychological supplement to the theory of dreams. *Standard Edition of the Complete Psychological Works of Sigmund Freud* 14:222-235.

Freud, S. (1919). The "uncanny." In *Standard Edition of the Complete Psychological Works*, vol. 17. London: Hogarth, 1955.

Freud, S. (1923-1925). A Note Upon the Mystic Writing Pad. In Freud 1953-1974, vol. XIX: *The Ego and the Id and Other Works (1923-1925)*, pp. 225-232.

Freud, S. (1932-1936). New Introductory Lectures on Psycho-Analysis. In Freud 1953-1974, vol. XXII: *New Introductory Lectures on Psycho-Analysis and Other Works (1932-1936)*, pp. 7-182.

Freud, S. (1942). *Standard Edition of the Complete Psychological Works of Sigmund Freud*. Volume 7:305. London: Hogarth Press.

Freud, S. (1942). *Standard Edition of the Complete Psychological Works of Sigmund Freud*. Volume 9. London: Hogarth Press.

Freud, S.(1953-1974). *The Standard Edition of the Complete Psychological Works of Sigmund Freud*. Translated from the German under the general editorship of James Strachey, in collaboration with Anna Freud, assisted by Alix Strachey and Alan Tyson. 24 vols. London: Hogarth Press and the Institute of Psycho-Analysis.

Freud, S. (1971). Screen Memories. In *Abstracts of the Standard Edition of the Complete Psychological Works of Sigmund Freud*, edited by Carrie Lee Rothgeb. Rockville, MD, National Institute of Mental Health (Philadelphia, PA: Scientific Literature Corporation, Philadelphia).

Freud, S. (1985). *The Complete Letters of Sigmund Freud to Wilhelm Fliess 1887-B1904*, edited by J.M. Masson. Cambridge, Mass. and London: Harvard University Press.

Freud, S. The uncanny. In: *The Complete Psychological Works of Sigmund Freud*, Volume 17. London: Hogarth Press.

Fry, W. F., Jr. (1968). *Sweet madness: A study of humor*. Palo Alto, Calif.: Pacific Books.

Gaarder, K. (1963). A conceptual model of schizophrenia. *AMA Archives of General Psychiatry* 8:590-598.

Gaarder, K., and Kafka, J. S. (1963). An experimental case study of the effects of Semyl. Presented at *Chestnut Lodge Symposium*, Rockville, Maryland.

Gabel, J. (1962). *La fausse conscience—Essai sur la réification*. (False consciousness: an essay on reification). Paris: Les Éditions de Minuit.

Gabel, Joseph. (1967). *Ideologic und Schizophrenic—Formen der Entfremdung* [Ideology and

schizophrenia: Forms of alienation]. Translator: Hans Naumann. Frankfurt am Main: S. Fischer Verlag.

Gödel, K. (1931). Über formal unentscheidbare Sätze der Principia Mathematica und verwandter Systeme: I. *Monatschrifte für Mathematik Physik* 38:173-198.

Goodrich, D.W., Boomer, D.S. (1963). Experimental assessment of modes of conflict resolution. *Family Process* 2:15-24.

Graetz, H. (1873). *Geschichte der Juden*. Leipzig: Leiner & Lowit.

Green, A. (1977). The borderline concept. In *Borderline Personality Disorders*, P. Hartocollis, editor. New York: International Universities Press.

Green, H. (1964). *I Never Promised You a Rose Garden*. New York: Holt, Rinehart & Winston.

Green, J. (1964). *I Never Promised You a Rose Garden*. New York: Holt, Rinehart & Winston.

Greenspan, S. I. (1982). Three levels of learning: A developmental approach to "awareness" and mind-body relations. *Psychoanalytic Inquiry* I:659-94.

Grotstein, J.S. (1977). The psychoanalytic concept of schizophrenia: I. The dilemma. II. Reconciliation. *International Journal of Psycho-Analysis* 58:403-452.

Group for the Advancement of Psychiatry. (1989). Us and Them: The Psychology of Ethno-Nationalism. New York: Brunner/Mazel.

Gunderson, J. G., and Carroll, A. (1983). Clinical considerations from empirical research. In *Psychosocial Intervention in Schizophrenia*, edited by H. Stierlin, L. C. Wynne, and M. Wirsching. Berlin: Springer-Verlag.

Gunderson, J. (1993). Commentary: schizophrenic patients. *Psychiatry* 56(3):308.

Hacking, I. (2009). Humans, aliens and autism. *Daedalus: Journal of the American Academy of Arts & Sciences* 138(Summer):44-59.

Handke, P. (1969). *Die Innenwelt der Aussenwelt der Innenwelt.* Frankfurt am Main: Suhrkamp. Eng. trans, by Michael Roloff. New York: Continuum, 1974.

Hartmann, H. (1939). *Ego Psychology and the Problem of Adaptation.* New York: International Universities Press, 1958.

Hartocollis, P., ed. (1977). *Borderline Personality Disorders: The Concept, The Syndrome, The Patient.* New York: International Universities Press.

Hayman, A. (1969). What do we mean by "id"? *Journal of American Psychoanalytic Association* 17:353-80.

Hoch, R. H., Pennes. H. H., and Cattell, J. P. (1958). Psychoses reduced by the administration of drugs. In *Chemical Concepts of Psychosis,* edited by M. Rinkel. New York: McDowell, Oblensky.

Hoff, S. (1982). Frieda Fromm-Reichmann, The Early Years. *Psychiatry* 45(#2): 115-121.

Hofstadter, D. R. (1979). *Gödel, Escher, Bach.* New York: Basic Books.

Hohage, R. and Kuebler, J. C. (1985). *The Emotional Insight Rating Scale.* Paper presented at Ülmer Werkstatt, University of Ülm.

Holden, C. (1987). A top priority at NIMH. *Science* 235, 431.

Hollos, S. and Ferenczi, S. (1922). *Zur Psychoanalyse der paralytischen Geistesstörung.* Vienna: Internationaler Psychoanalytischer Verlag.

Holzman, P. (1987). Recent studies of psychophysiology in schizophrenia. *Schizophrenia Bulletin* 13:49-75.

Israeli, N. (1936). *Abnormal personality and time.* New York: Science Press.

Jaffe, D. S. (1971). The role of ego modification and the task of structural change in the analysis of a case of hysteria. *International Journal of Psychoanalysis* 52:375-93.

Kafka, J. S. and Bolgar, H. (1949). Notes on the clinical use of future autobiographies. *Rorschach Research Exchange and Journal of Projective Techniques* 13:341-46.

Kafka, J. S. (1957). A Method for studying the organization of time experience. *American Journal of Psychiatry* 114:546-553.

Kafka, J.S. (1957). *On the Experience of Duration in Psychotherapy.* Read before the Chestnut Lodge Symposium, Rockville, MD.

Kafka, J. S. (1964). Technical applications of a concept of multiple reality. *International Journal of Psycho-Analysis* 45:575-578.

Kafka, J. S., and Gaarder, K. R. (1964). Some effects of the therapist's LSD experience on his therapeutic work. *American Journal of Psychotherapy* 18:236-243.

Kafka, J.S., & McDonald, J.W. (1965). The latent family in the intensive treatment of the hospitalized schizophrenic patient. In *Current Psychiatric Therapy*, ed. J.S. Masserman. New York: Grune & Stratton, pp. 172-177.

Kafka, J.S. (1966). *Déjà vu phenomena: Observations and a theory.* Read before the 119th annual meeting of American Psychiatric Association. Atlantic City, NJ.

Kafka, J.S. (1966). *Practical and conceptual developments concerning work with families.* Read before the Southern Divisional Meeting of American Psychiatric Association. Florida: Hollywood.

Kafka, J. (1969). The Body as transitional object: a study of a self-mutilating patient. *British Journal of Medical Psychology* 42: 207-212.

Kafka, J. S. (1971). Ambiguity for individuation: a critique and reformulation of double-bind theory. *Archives of General Psychiatry* 25:232-239.

Kafka, J. S. (1971). *A Psychoanalytic Perspective on the Organization and Integration of Time Experience.* Paper presented at panel on the Experience of Time, American Psychoanalytic Association, December 1971.

Kafka, J. S. (1972). The Experience of time. (panel report). *Journal of the American Psychoanalytic Association* 20:650-667.

Kafka, J. S. (1977). On reality: an examination of object constancy, ambiguity, paradox, and time. In J. H. Smith, ed., *Thought, Consciousness, and Reality*, Vol. 2 of *Psychiatry and the Humanities*. New Haven: Yale University Press.

Kafka, J. S. (1977). Zum Problem der Realität. *Psyche* 31:712-731.

Kafka, J. S. (1979). Psychic effort, drift and reality structures: observations from psychoanalytic work with neurotic, borderline and schizophrenic patients. In: C. Muller, ed., *Psychotherapy of Schizophrenia. Proceedings, 6th International Symposium on the Psychotherapy of Schizophrenia.* Lausanne. Amsterdam-Oxford: *Excerpta Medica.*

Kafka, J. S. (1981). Review of *Borderline personality disorders*, edited by P. Hartocollis. *Journal of the American Psychoanalytic Association* 29:236-47.

Kafka, J. S. (1983). Challenge and confirmation in ritual action. Psychiatry 46:31-39.

Kafka, J. S. and Kafka, M.S. (1983). Timing process and mental illness. *Abstracts, VII World Congress of Psychiatry*, Vienna, p. 302.

Kafka, J. S. (1986). The schizophrenic's objects. In: D. Feinsilver (ed.), *Towards a Comprehensive Model for Schizophrenic Disorders: Psychoanalytic Essays in Memory of Ping-Nie Pao, M.D.* Analytic Press, Hillsdale, N.J.

Kafka, J.S. (1989). *Multiple Realities in Clinical Practice.* New Haven: Yale University Press.

Kafka, J.S. (1989). Déjà Vu, Drugs, Synesthesia. In Kafka (1989), *Multiple Realities in Clinical Practice*, pp. 51-78.

Kafka, J.S. (1989). Time, Timing, and Temporal Perspective. In Kafka (1989), *Multiple Realities in Clinical Practice*, pp. 18-25.

Kafka, J.S. (1990). On the question of insight in psychosis. *Journal of the American Academy of Psychoanalysis & Dynamic Psychiatry* 18:18-28.

Kafka, John S. (1991). *Jenseits des Realitätsprinzips: Multiple Realitäten in Theorie und Praxis der Psychoanalyse.* Translator: H.-J. Grunzig. Berlin: Springer.

Kafka, J.S. (1992). Consciousness and the shadow of time. In *Two Butterflies on My Head: Psychoanalysis in the Interdisciplinary Scientific Dialogue*, ed. M. Leuzinger-Bohleber, H. Schneider, & R. Pfeiffer. Berlin: Springer, pp. 87-95.

Kafka, J.S. (1997). The romantic and classic visions in the therapy of psychosis: A personal perspective and an evolving theory of schizophrenia. *Psychiatry: Interpersonal & Biological Processes* 60:209-221.

Kafka, J.S. (2009). Commentary on "restitutional" functions of symbol and myth in Strindberg's Inferno: On schizophrenifom crisis and on schizophrenia. *Psychiatry: Interpersonal & Biological Processes* 72:139-142.

Kafka, J.S. (2011). Chestnut Lodge and the Psychoanalytic Approach to Psychosis. *Journal of the American Psychoanalytic Association* 59:27-47.

Kafka, R. (1897). Weltanschauung und Perspektive. In: *Die Gesellschaft, Monatschrift für Litteratur, Kunst U Sozialpolitik.* Conrad, M. And Merian, H., editors. Leipzig, Hermann Haache. pp. 15-26.

Kafka, M. S., Benedito, M. A., Blendy, J. A., and Tokola, N. A. (1986). Circadian rhythms in neurotransmitter receptors in discrete rat brain regions. *Chronobiology International* 3:91-100.

Kafka, M. S., Benedito, M. A., and Roth, R. H. (1986). Circadian rhythms in catecholamine metabolites and cyclic nucleotide production. *Chronobiology International* 3:101-15.

Kafka, M. S., Benedito, M. A., Steele, L. K., et al. (1986). Relationships between behavioral rhythms, plasma corticosterone and hypothalamic circadian rhythms. *Chronobiology International* 3:117-22.

Kafka, M. S., van Kammen, D. P., Kleinman, J. E., Nurnberger, J. I., Siever, L. J., Uhde, T. W., and Polinsky, R. J. (1980). Alpha-adrenergic receptor function in schizophrenia, affective disorders and some neurological diseases. *Communications in Psychopharmacology* 4:477-86.

Kafka, M. S., Wirz-Justice, A. and Naber, D. (1983). Circadian rhythms in rat brain neurotransmitter receptors. *Federation Proceedings* 42:2796-2801.

Kafka, R. (1897). Weltanschauung und Perspektive. In: *Die Gesellschaft, Monatschrift für Litteratur, Kunst U Sozialpolitik.* Conrad, M. And Merian, H., editors. Leipzig, Hermann Haache. pp. 15-26.

Kandell, E. R. (1983). From metapsychology to molecular biology: Explorations into the nature of anxiety. *American Journal of Psychiatry* 140:1277-93.

Kandel, Eric R. (2006). *In Search of Memory: The Emergence of a New Science of Mind.* New York: Norton.

Kestenberg, Judith S. & Brenner, Ira. (1996). Multisensory bridges in response to object loss. *The Last Witness, The Child Survivor of the Holocaust,* pp. 69-78. Washington, DC: American Psychiatric Press, Inc.

Kettner, M. (1999). Das Konzept der Nachträglichkeit in Freud's Erinnerungstheorie. *Psyche* 4: 309-342.

Klüver, H. (1933). *Behavior Mechanisms in Monkeys.* Chicago: University of Chicago Press.

Klüver, H. (1936). The study of personality and the method of equivalent and non-equivalent stimuli. *Character Personality* 5:91-112.

Kohut, H. (1971). *The Analysis of the Self.* International Universities Press.

Kraus, Siegfried. (1930). Die Verwaisung als soziale Erscheinung. *Zeitschrift fuer Psychoanalytische Paedagogik (Journal of Psychoanalytic Pedagogy)* 4(# 8/9): 317-328.

Kris, E. (1952). *Psychoanalytic Explorations in Art.* International Universities Press.

Laplanche, J., and Pontalis, J.-B. (1967). *The Language of Psychoanalysis* (1967). Translated by D. Nicholson-Smith. Norton, 1973.

Laub, Dori & Auerhahn, Nanette C. (1993). Knowing and not knowing. Massive psychic trauma: forms of traumatic memory. *International Journal of Psycho-Analysis* 74:287-302.

Lear, Jonathan. (1999). *Open Minded: Working Out the Logic of the Soul.* Cambridge, Mass.: Harvard University Press.

LeFever, H. (1961). *To Antipodes and Back: Some Observations on the LSD Experience.* Paper presented at Chestnut Lodge Symposium, Rockville, Maryland.

Lestienne, Rémy. (2013). On the limits of time in the brain. *KronoScope* 13: 2:228-239.

Levander, S. & Cullberg, J. (1993). Successful psychotherapeutic work with a schizophrenic woman. *Psychiatry* 56 (3):284-293.

Libet, B. (2004). *Mind Time: The Temporal Factor in Consciousness.* Cambridge: Harvard University Press.

Liberman, R. & Corrigan, P. (1993). Designing new psychosocial treatments for schizophrenia. *Psychiatry* 56(3):238-249.

Lichtenstein, H. (1974). The effect of reality perception on psychic structure: A psychoanalytic contribution to the problem of the "generation gap." *In Annual of Psychoanalysis,* vol. 2. New York: International Universities Press.

Lidz, T., and Fleck, S. (1960). Schizophrenia, human integration, and the role of the family. In *The Etiology of Schizophrenia,* edited by D. D. Jackson. New York: Basic Books.

Loewald, H. W. (1960). On the therapeutic action of psychoanalysis. *International Journal of Psychoanalysis* 41:16-33.

Loewald, H. W. (1962). The superego and the ego ideal. II. Superego and time. *International Journal of Psychoanalysis* 43:264-268.

Loewald, H. W. (1979). The waning of the oedipus complex. In *Papers on Psychoanalysis.* New Haven: Yale University Press, 1980.

Loewald, H. W. (1980). Some considerations on repetition and repetition compulsion (1971). The Waning of the oedipus complex (1979). In H. W. Loewald, *Papers on Psychoanalysis.* New Haven: Yale University Press.

London, N. (1973). An essay on psychoanalytic theory: Two theories of schizophrenia: Part I. Review and critical assessment of the development of the two theories. Part II. Discussion and restatement of the specific theory of schizophrenia. *International Journal of Psychoanalysis* 54: 169-193.

Longuet-Higgins, H. C. (1968). The Non-local storage of temporal information. *Proceedings of Royal Society, London* 171:327-334.

Longuet-Higgins, H. C., Willshaw, D., & Buneman, O.R. (1969). Non-holographic associative memory. *Nature* 222:960-962.

Longuet-Higgins, H. C. (1970). Theories of associative recall. *Quarterly Review of Biophysics* 3:223-44.

Luby, E. D., Cohen, B. D., Rosenbaum, G., Gottlieb, J. S., and Kelley, R. (1959). Study of a new schizophrenomimetic drug—Sernyl. *AMA Archives of Neurology and Psychiatry* 81:363-69.

Malcolm, J. (1987). Reflections: J'appelle un chat un chat. New Yorker, April 20, pp. 84-102.

Mandell, A., Knapp, S., Ehlers, C. and Russo, P. (1982). The stability of constrained randomness: Lithium prophylaxis at several neurobiological levels. In *The Neurobiology of the Mood Disorders*, edited by R. M. Post and J. C. Ballenger. Baltimore: Williams & Wilkins.

Matthias Kettner. (1999). Das Konzept der Nachtraeglichkeit in Freud's Erinnerungstheorie. *Psyche* 4 (53. Jahrgang April 1999).

Matte-Blanco, Ignacio. (1959). Expression in Symbolic Logic of the Characteristics of the System Ucs or the Logic of the System Ucs. *The International Journal of Psychoanalysis* 40: 1-5.

Matte Blanco, Ignacio. (1975). *The Unconscious as Infinite Sets: An Essay in Bi-Logic*. London: Duckworth.

Matte-Blanco, Ignacio. (1988). *Thinking, Feeling, and Being: Clinical Reflections on the Fundamental Autonomy of Human Beings and World*. New Library of Psychoanalysis 5. London and New York: Tavistock/Routledge.

McAfee, L.I. (1989). Interview with Joanne Greenberg. In *Psychoanalysis and Psychosis*, ed. A.-L. S. Silver. Madison, CT: International Universities Press, pp. 513-533.

McCarley, R., Shenton, M., O'Donnell, B., & Nestor, P. (1993). Uniting Kraeplin and Bleuler: The psychology of schizophrenia and the biology of temporal lobe abnormalities. *Harvard Review of Psychiatry* 1:36-56.

McGlashan, T. (1984a). The Chestnut Lodge follow-up study: I. Follow-up methodology and study sample. *Archives of General Psychiatry* 41:573-585.

McGlashan, T. (1984b). The Chestnut Lodge folow-up study: II. Long-term outcome of schizophrenia and the affective disorders. *Archives of General Psychiatry* 41:586-601.

McGlashan, T. (1986). The Chestnut Lodge follow-up study: III. Long-term outcome of borderline personalities. *Archives of General Psychiatry* 43:20-30.

McGlashan, T. (2009). Psychosis as a disorder of reduced cathectic capacity: Freud's analysis of the Schreber case revisited. *Schizophrenia Bulletin* 35:476-481.

Meyer, J. S., Greifenstein, F., and Devault, M. (1959). A new drug causing symptoms of sensory deprivation. *Journal of Nervous and Mental Disease* 129:54-61.

Modell, A. (1968). *Object Love and Reality*. New York: International Universities Press.

Monod, J. (1972). *Chance and Necessity*. New York: Random House.

Mueser, K. (1993). Commentary on Liberman and Corrigan. *Psychiatry* 56(3):250-253.

Murray, H. A. (1938). *Explorations in Personality*. New York: Oxford University Press.

Murrough, James W.; Iosifescu, Dan V.; Chang, Lee C.; Al Jurdi, Rayan K.; Green, Charles E.; Perez, Andrew M.; Iqbal, Syed; Pillemer, Sarah; Foulkes, Alexandra; Shah, Asim; Charney, Dennis S.; Mathew, Sanjay J. (2013). Antidepressant efficacy of ketamine in treatment-resistant major depression: a two-site randomized controlled trial. *American Journal of Psychiatry* 170: 1134-1142.

Nagel, E., Newman, J.R. (1958). *Gödel's Proof*. New York: New York University Press.

Nielsen, Tore A. & Stenstrom, Philippe. (2005). What are the memory sources of dreaming? *Nature* 4/7 (27 October): 1286-1289.

Noble, D. (1951). A study of dreams in schizophrenia and allied states. *American Journal of Psychiatry* 107:612-616.

Noble, D. (1963). Early days at the "The Lodge." *The Ninth Annual Chestnut Lodge Symposium*, Friday, October 25, 1963, Rockville, MD. Privately published, pp. 93-103.

Novey, S. (1955). Some philosophical speculations about the concept of the genital character. *International Journal of Psychonalysis* 36:88-94.

Olson, D.H. (1969). *Empirically unbinding the double-bind.* Read before the 119th annual meeting of the American Psychological Association, Washington, DC.

Ornstein, R. E. (1969). *On the experience of time.* Baltimore: Penquin Books.

Palmquist, D. A. (1996). *A study of critical variables in the anxiety of schizophrenics by means of structured clinical interview and percept-genetic experiment.* University of Lund, Department of Psychology.

Pao, P.N. (1973). Notes on Freud's theory of schizophrenia. *International Journal of Psychoanalysis* 54:469-476.

Pao, P.N. (1983). Therapeutic empathy and the treatment of schizophrenia. *Psychoanalytic Inquiry* 3:145-167.

Pestalozzi, J., Frisch, S., Hinshelwood, R.D., & Houzel, D., eds. (1998). *Psychoanalytic Psychotherapy in Institutional Settings.* London: Karnac Books.

Pollard, J. C., Bakker, C., Uhr, L., and Feuertile, D. F. (1960). Controlled sensory input: A note on the technique of drug evaluation with a preliminary report on a comparative study of Sernyl, psilocybin and LSD-25. *Comprehensive Psychiatry* 1:377-80.

Popper, Karl. (1945). *The Open Society and Its Enemies.* London: Routledge.

Pribram, K. H. (1986). The cognitive revolution and mind/brain issues. *American Psychologist* 41:507-20.

Prigogine, I. (1976). Order through fluctuation: Self-organization and social system. In *Evolution and Consciousness: Human Systems in Transition,* edited by E. Jantsch and C. H. Waddington. Reading, Mass.: Addison-Wesley.

Psychoanalyse in Selbstdarstellungen (1992, 1994, 1995). L. Hermanns, editor. Tuebingen: Edition Diskord. Volume I (1992). Volume II (1994). Volume III (1995).

Psychoanalyse in Selbstdarstellungen (1995). L. Hermanns, editor. Tuebingen: Edition Diskord. Volume III:141-187.

Rabin, M. (1977). *Handbook of Mathematical Logic, Part C.* Amsterdam: North Holland.

Rabin, M. and Halpern, J. (1987). Logic to reason about likelihood. *Artificial Intelligence* 32: 3:379-405.

Rangell, L. (1981). From insight to change. *Journal of American Psychoanalytic Association* 29:119-41.

Rapaport, D. (1960). *The Structure of Psychoanalytic Theory.* New York: International Universities Press.

Reiser, M. F. (1984). *Mind, Brain, Body: Toward a Convergence of Psychoanalysis and Neurobiology.* New York: Basic Books.

Reiss, D. (1995). Editorial: Families and schizophrenia redux. *Psychiatry* 58(1):1-5.

Reiss, D., Plomin, R., & Hetherington, E.M. (1991). Genetics and psychiatry: an unheralded window on the environment. *American Journal of Psychiatry* 148(3): 283-291.

Reemstsma, Jan Philipp. (1995). Institutions of violence and their potential dynamics. *Reader, Conference 'Interdisciplinary Research into Trauma and Violence'.* Breuninger Kolleg Stuttgart, Nov. 17-19, 1995 in Bad Teinach.

Ringuette, E.L., Kennedy, T. (1966). An experimental study of the double-bind hypothesis. *Journal of Abnormal Psychology* 71:136-141.

Rose, G. J. (1980). *The Power of Form: A Psychoanalytic Approach to Aesthetic Form.* New York: International Universities Press.

Rose, S. R. (1980). Can the neurosciences explain the mind? *Trends in Neurosciences* 23:2-4.

Rudnytsky, Peter L. (2000). *Psychoanalytic Conversations: Interviews with Clinicians, Commentators, and Critics.* Hillsdale, NJ: Analytic Press.

Ryder, G., Kafka, J.S., Olson, D.H. (1971). Separating and joining influences in courtship and early marriage. *American Journal of Orthopsychiatry* 41:450-464.

Ryder, R.G., Goodrich, D.W. (1966). Married couples' responses to disagreement. *Family Process* 5:30-42.

Ryder, R.G. (1966). Two replications of color matching factors. *Family Process* 5:43-48.

Ryder, R.G. (1968). Husband-wife dyads versus married strangers. *Family Process* 7:233-238.

Ryder, R.G. (1969). *Three myths: Brief ruminations on interaction procedures while contemplating the color matching tests.* Read before the annual meeting of National Council on Family Relations. Washington, DC. (Unpublished)

Ryder, R.G. (1970). Dimensions of early marriage. *Family Process* 9:51-68.

Ryder, R. G., Kafka, J. S., and Olson, D. H. (1971). Separating and joining influences in courtship and early marriage. *American Journal of Orthopsychiatry* 41:450-64.

Sandler, J. and Joffe, W. (1967). The tendency to persistence in psychological function and development, with special reference to fixation and regression. *Bulletin of the Menninger Clinic* 31:257-71.

Sandler, J. and Rosenblatt, B. (1962). The concept of the representational world. *Psychoanalytic Study of the Child* 17:128-45.

Sartre, J. P. (1960). *Search for a Method.* Translated by H. E. Barnes. New York: Knopf, 1967.

Savage, C. (1955). Variations in ego feeling induced by d-lysergic acid diethylamide (LSD-25). *Psychoanalytic Review* 42:1-16.

Schachtel, E.G. (1947). On memory and childhood amnesia. *Psychiatry* 10:1-26.

Schechter, S. (1996). How the brain gets rhythm. *Science* 274:339-340.

Schilder, P. (1935). *The Image and Appearance of the Human Body.* New York: International Universities Press, 1950.

Schizophrenia costs U.S. billions; more research, better care needed. (December 19, 1986). *Psychiatric News,* p. 8.

Schulz, C.G. (1994). *Evolution of current treatment of schizophrenia.* Paper presented at the International Symposium for the Psychotherapy of Schizophrenia. Washington, DC.

Schulz, C. G., and Kilgalen, R. K. (1969). The treatment course of a disturbed patient. In *Case Studies in Schizophrenia.* New York: Basic Books.

Searles, H. F. (1960). *The Nonhuman Environment in Normal Development and in Schizophrenia.* New York: International Universities Press.

Searles, H.F. (1963). Transference psychosis in the psychotherapy of chronic schizophrenia. *International Journal of Psychoanalysis* 44:249-281.

Searles, H.F. (1965). *Collected Papers on Schizophrenia and Related Subjects.* New York: International University Press.

Searles, H.F. (1965). On driving the other person crazy. In: *Collected Papers on Schizophrenia and Related Subjects.* New York: International University Press.

Silver, A.-L. S., ed. (1989). *Psychoanalysis and Psychosis.* Madison, CT: International Universities Press.

Silver, A.-L. S. (1993). Countertransference, Ferenczi and Washington, DC. *Journal of the American Academy of Psychoanalysis* 21(4):637-654.

Smith, David L. (2000). The Mirror image of the present: Freud's Theory of Retrogressive Screen Memories. *Psychoanalytische Perspectieven* 39:7-29.

Smith, G. J. W. and Danielsson, A. (1982). Anxiety and defensive strategies in childhood adolescence. *Psychological Issues,* Monograph 52.

Smith, J. H. (1976). The psychoanalytic understanding of human freedom: Freedom from and freedom for. *Journal of the American Psychoanalytic Association* 26:87-107.

Smith, J. H. (1983). Rite, ritual and defense. *Psychiatry* 46:16-30.

Spitz. Ellen Handler. (2006). Loss as Vanished Form: On the Anti-Memorial Sculptures of Horst Hoheisel. *American Imago* 62:419-433.

Squire, L. R. (1986: June 27). Mechanisms of memory. *Science* 232:1612-19.

Stern, D.N., Sander, L.W., Nahum, LP., Harrison, A.M., Lyons-Ruth, K., Morgan, A.C., Bruschweiler-Stern, N., & Tronick, E.Z. (1998). Non-interpretive mechanisms in psychoanalytic therapy: The "something more" than interpretation. *International Journal of Psychoanalysis* 79:903-921.

Stein, M.I. (1949). Personality factors involved in temporal development of Rorschach responses. *Rorschach Research Exchange & Journal of Projective Techniques* 13:355-414.

Stierlin, H., Wynne, L. C. and Wirsching, M., eds. (1983). Psychosocial Intervention in Schizophrenia. Berlin: Springer-Verlag.

Stirnimann, F. (1947). Das Kind und seine früheste Umwelt. *Psychologische Praxis*, vol. 6. Basel: Karger.

Stoerig, P. (2006). The impact of invisible stimuli. *Science* 314:1694-1695.

Stone, L. (1986). Psychoanalytic observations on the pathology of depressive illness: Selected spheres of ambiguity or disagreement. *Journal of the American Psychoanalytic Association* 34:329-62.

Strachey, J. (1934). The nature of the therapeutic action of psychoanalysis. *International Journal of Psychoanalysis* 15:127-59.

Strachy, Alix. (1957). *The Unconscious Motivations of War*. International Universities Press. page 198.

Strenger, S. (1989). The classic and the romantic vision in psychoanalysis. *International Journal of Psychoanalysis* 70(4):563-610.

Symposium (1961). *Chestnut Lodge Symposium*: Papers Presented on the Fiftieth Anniversary, 1910-1960. Washington, DC: William Alanson White Psychiatric Foundation.

Thomä, H. and Kächele, H. (1987). *Principles.* Vol. 1 of *Psychoanalytic Practice.* Translated by M. Wilson and D. Roseveare. New York: Springer-Verlag.

Thomas, Lewis. (1983). Late night thoughts on lListening to Mahler's Ninth Symphony. In: Lewis Thomas: *Collection of Essays*, pp. 164-168. New York: The Viking Press.

Ticho, E. (1972). Termination of psychoanalysis: treatment goals, life goals. *Psychoanalytic Quarterly* 41:315-333.

Tichy, Marina & Sylvia Zwettler-Otte. (1999). *Freud in der Presse. Die Rezeption Sigmund Freuds und der Psychoanalyse in Österreich 1895-1938* [Freud in the media: The reception of Sigmund Freud and psychoanalysis in Austria]. Vienna: Sonderzahl.

Tienari, P., Lahtri, I., Sorri, A., Naarla, M., Moring, J., Whalberg, K.-E., & Wynne, L. C. (1987). The Finnish adoptive family study of schizophrenia. *Journal of Psychiatric Research* 21(4):437-445.

The Psychoanalytical Society and the Analyst. With special reference to the history of the Dutch Psychoanalytical Society. (1933). Editors: H. Groen-Prakken & A. Ladan. Dutch Annual of Psychoanalysis. Volume I:13-37. Amsterdam: Lisse.

Treuerniet, N. (1991). Introduction to "On Narcissism"—Introduction to an Introduction. In: *Freud, S., "On Narcissism: An Introduction.* Editors: Sandler, J., Person, E., Fonagy, P. International Psychoanalytical Association. London: Hogarth Press. Page 82.

Tsushima, Y., Sasaki, Y., & Watanabe, T. (2006). Greater disruption due to failure of inhibitory control on an ambiguous distractor. *Science* 314:1736-1788.

Turner, V. (1977). Process, system, and symbol: a new anthropological synthesis. *Daedalus* 106(no. 3):61-80.

Turner, Frederick (2006). Interdisciplinary Research Opportunities: Limits and Constraints. In: *Time's News*, No. 37, February 2006.

Unger, S. M. (1963). Mescaline, LSD, psilocybin, and personality change: A review. *Psychiatry* 26:111-25.

Vernichtungskrieg. Verbrechen der Wehrmacht 1941 bis 1944. (1996). Ausstellungskatalog. Hamburg.

Volkan, Vamik. (1999). Psychoanalysis and Diplomacy. Part I: Individual and large group identity. *Journal of Applied Psychoanalytic Studies* 1(#1):29-55 & Part II: Large Group Rituals. *Journal of Applied Psychoanalytic Studies* 1(#3):223-247.

Volkan, Vamik,; Akhtar, Salman; Dorn, Robert M; Kafka, John S.; Kernberg, Otto F; Olsson, Peter A; Rogers, Rita R.; Shanfield, Stephen B. (1999). Leaders and Decision-Making. *Mind and Human Interaction* 9(#3).

Vonnegut, K., Jr. (1969). *Slaughterhouse-Five.* New York: Delta.

Waddell, J. (1964). The evolution of nursing at Chestnut Lodge. *The Tenth Annual Chestnut Lodge Symposium,* Friday, November 6, 1964, Rockville, MD. Privately published.

Wallerstein, R. S. (1973). Psychoanalytic perspectives on the problem of reality. *Journal of the American Psychoanalytic Association* 21:5-33.

Watts, Vabren. (2013). A Ketamine shows rapid action in treatment-resistant depression. *Psychiatric News* September 10: 1, 23.

Watzlawick, P., Beavin, J.H., Jackson, D.C. (1967). *Pragmatics of Human Communication.* New York: W.W. Norton & Co, Inc.

Wegner, D.M. (2002). *The Illusion of Conscious Will.* Cambridge: MIT Press.

Westerlundh, B. & Smith, G. (1983). Percept-genesis and the psychodynamics of perception. *Psychoanalysis and Contemporary Thought* 6:597-640.

Whitehead, A.N., Russell, B. (1910). *Principa Mathematica.* Mass.: Cambridge University Press.

Willick, M.S. (2001). Psychoanalysis and schizophrenia: A cautionary tale. *Journal of the American Psychoanalytic Association* 49:27-56.

Wilson, Edward. (1975). *Sociobiology.* Cambridge, MA: Harvard University Press.

Winson, J. (1985). *Brain and Psyche. The Biology of the Unconscious.* Anchor Press, Doubleday, New York.

Winnicott, D.W. (1958). Transitional objects and transitional phenomena. In: *Collected Papers.* New York: Basic Books, Inc.

Winnicott, D. W. (1958). Hate in the countertransference. In *Collected Papers.* New York: Basic Books.

Wynne, L. C, Ryckoff, I. M., Day, J. and Hirsch, S. I. (1958). Pseudomutuality in the family relations of schizophrenics

Yourgrau, Palle. (2005). *A World Without Time. The Forgotten Legacy of Gödel and Einstein.* New York: Basic Books.

CPSIA information can be obtained
at www.ICGtesting.com
Printed in the USA
FFOW02n1621180917
40062FF

9 780998 083315